The Trial in American Life

The Trial in American Life

ROBERT A. FERGUSON

The University of Chicago Press   *Chicago & London*

ROBERT A. FERGUSON is the George Edward Woodberry Professor of
Law, Literature, and Criticism at Columbia University. He is the
author of *Law and Letters in American Culture*; *The American
Enlightenment, 1750–1820*; and *Reading the Early Republic*.

The University of Chicago Press, Chicago 60637
The University of Chicago Press, Ltd., London
© 2007 by The University of Chicago
All rights reserved. Published 2007
Printed in the United States of America

16 15 14 13 12 11 10 09 08 07   1 2 3 4 5

ISBN-13: 978-0-226-24325-2 (cloth)
ISBN-10: 0-226-24325-7 (cloth)

Library of Congress Cataloging-in-Publication Data
Ferguson, Robert A., 1942–
The trial in American life / Robert A. Ferguson.
p. cm.
Includes bibliographical references and index.
ISBN-13: 978-0-226-24325-2 (cloth: alk. paper)
ISBN-10: 0-226-24325-7 (cloth: alk. paper)
1. Trials—United States. 2. Trials—United States—History. I. Title.
KF220.F37 2007
345.73'07—dc22
2006022239

The University of Chicago Press gratefully acknowledges the generous
support of the John Simon Guggenheim Memorial Foundation
toward the publication of this book.

For Priscilla Parkhurst Ferguson

and in memory of
James Vorenberg (1928–2000) and
Walter Harp (1942–2005)

Touchstones for Life

Contents

Acknowledgments

The inspiration that the law allows is grudging but firm; that of literature, more compelling but often imprecise; that of history, impossibly complex. A number of institutions have helped me puzzle over the combinations. An Andrew W. Mellon Professorship at the University of Chicago gave original impetus. The Newberry Library, the John Simon Guggenheim Memorial Foundation, and the National Humanities Center provided fellowships. Other resident scholars at the Newberry and the National Humanities Center, particularly the historians and the anthropologists, offered valuable insights. A full generation of research assistants, too many to name, gave their aid and enthusiasm to the project. An earlier version of chapter 4, entitled "Story and Transcription in the Trial of John Brown," appeared in the *Yale Journal of Law and the Humanities* 6 (Winter 1994): 37–73.

I owe a special level of gratitude to my colleagues at Columbia Law School. The faculty of the Law School meet twice a week over food and drink to discuss ideas in the same spirit as the classical symposium. The questions and answers raised there are invariably more important than the original presentation, and I have learned from all three. To have steady intellectual companions who truly believe in ideas, who conduct themselves in the belief that arguments matter, and who value each other enough to disagree constructively and fairly is a great privilege as well as a rare occurrence. If I do not single them out, it is because the collectivity in common endeavor has mattered the most to me.

Some individuals from other venues have given of themselves in a detailed way. The readers of the manuscript for the press, Karen Halttunen and Richard Posner, saw things that I did not, saved me from errors, and helped with the overall organization and balance of the book. I am grateful for their care and encouragement. My editor, Alan Thomas, supplied important advice on the final shape of the book. He and his assistant, Randolph Petilos, gave of themselves in many ways. Erin DeWitt was the ideal copy editor, catching mistakes and improving the manuscript with many careful positive suggestions. My own assistant, Gabriel Soto, has the virtue without which the others do not matter: accuracy. His computer expertise, goodwill, and friendship beyond the requirements of mere duty made the sequent toil of draft after draft much easier than they otherwise would have been.

Walter Harp, in the last months of his life, even as he was losing strength and knew it, left his own work to comment on a penultimate draft. He had an eagle eye for the right word as well as the wrong word and helped to sustain the courage of my convictions over controversial aspects of the book. I would have been utterly lost without two others. John Paul Russo read the manuscript several times, pushing, cajoling, and blotting when necessary. He was ruthless, kind, and amusing all at the same time. Priscilla Parkhurst Ferguson and I share a study, all of our writing, and our lives; bound together, they are the fundamental source of happiness and achievement.

Introduction

This book has been written for every person who has fallen under the spell of a courtroom trial or worried about its verdict. Most Americans have lived through such an experience. Famous trials appear with regularity in the history of the United States, and they tend to generate intense communal interest. *The Trial in American Life* does not offer another version of this history; it seeks instead to explain the impact, the significance of such events. Heat as well as light go with a controversial trial, and excitement over the outcome divides those who identify too strongly with one side or the other. When many are attracted to what takes place in a courtroom, previous inclinations apply, and the ensuing debate reshapes and occasionally warps thought at the deepest levels of ideological formation.

High-profile trials resemble presidential elections or even wars in this regard. They formalize conflict and make victory the focus of meaning for everything that takes place around them. Some trials become bywords, and when that happens, the marks they have left on history trigger instant recall as occasion warrants. Happenstance in origin, they become permanent in effect. Courtrooms and their communities normally cooperate with each other by definition in a rule of law, but they compete for articulation in a high-profile trial, and the tension between them opens the field of commentary beyond the legal issues involved. Memorable trials thus become barometers of social thought and, as such, deserve more careful study than they have received.

The Trial in American Life responds by combining distinct modes of analysis in a three-part structure. Part 1 turns to cultural studies, anthropology, and legal analysis to examine the relation of courtrooms to their communities. These chapters, 1 and 2, address the confusions that swirl around high-profile trials, the stereotypes that inhibit understanding, and the allure in the performative elements of a courtroom. Chapters 3 through 7 (part 2) provide a case-study sequence, using literary tools of criticism and history to gauge the price that is paid when a community becomes overly alarmed by a trial in its midst. Part 3 (chapters 8 and 9) applies media studies and constitutional law to gauge the parameters of the high-profile trial of today.

Properly used, interdisciplinary tools balance time present against time past. To understand what happens and why it happens in a high-profile trial, the aggressive presentism or synchronic impulses of legal advocacy must be balanced against the diachronic or chronological commitments of later interpretation. Advocacy is functional; it plunders the past to win in the moment. The contrasting history of such a moment searches the past to explain it and learn from it. Separating the priorities of those who conduct a trial from those who study it is the beginning of wisdom in appreciating any trial that is simultaneously a legal decision and an exclamation point in history. By keeping both frames of reference aloft, we gain a check on the passions in controversy while underscoring the investments in court.

The Trial in American Life also documents the rise of a crucial third party. Media sources have exercised ever-greater control over what takes place in a courtroom, and the result is a growing paradox. Heightened excitement through the evolution of communication technologies leaves courtrooms vulnerable to publicity, and yet the same tendency goes hand in hand with the definition of a public trial. At issue is increasing conflict between the right to a fair trial and the equally fundamental rights of free speech and freedom of the press. Moreover, current legal thought deals with these growing tensions only in clumsy, indirect ways. It is time for new answers, and these pages will carry the inquiry into uncharted constitutional territory. The solutions offered are unavoidably controversial, but even those who disagree will gain by seeing the problem itself more clearly than before.

There is just one other preliminary to settle with a willing reader. The ambiguity in the title chosen for this volume, *The Trial in American Life*, is deliberate. A trial is an indictment of individual behavior, but it is also a challenge from and to those who accuse; it is a gauntlet thrown down by the law and taken up by the watching public. The state must always justify its actions. Those who conduct a trial are always on trial themselves. However, this ambiguity must also be understood carefully and not in the way that many think. Blame is the natural coin of the legal process as it proceeds, not of the critic who would understand what happens there.

The saving balances in a fair trial are always fragile, and this fragility explains why some trials go awry and others fail altogether. Many observers respond to these perceived failures by criticizing one party or another. Did counsel err? Was the judge too strict? Too lenient? Did the jury do its duty? Critics are fond of insisting on hidden skeletons in the legal closet and asking, "Who hid the body?" But there is only one honest answer to these questions by anyone who would understand the explosive possibilities in a high-profile trial. The bodies hidden in legal closets are invariably put there by the American people who built the closets in the first place. Blame gets in the way of analysis. It fails, among other things, to explain why so many presumed villains or fools could be so successful in their own time.

The truth of this proposition appears in one of the starker facts of American legal history. A presumed injustice in a courtroom almost always enjoys the support of the community that watched that injustice unfold. The bystanders of history who believe they might have made a difference delude themselves and ignore the tyranny of circumstance. Why did communities act in ways that we can now deplore from a distance? The truth requires an insight not easily sustained in a country that likes to think of itself as progressive. We resemble our forebears in their strengths, their weaknesses, their anxieties, and their beliefs, and because of that, we must understand the tendencies in communal behavior through existing frames of thought rather than against them. There is neither credence nor common sense in feeling superior to the past. No intelligent observer turns to history to discard it. The next trial of the century is capable of awakening the same overriding emotionalism and misguided voyeurism at any moment. One goal of this book is to strengthen the present against a permanent danger. We learn from the past in order to guard us from ourselves.

PART ONE

The High-Profile Trial

Courtroom trials are central ceremonies in the American republic of laws, even though over 90 percent of all legal actions never reach that stage. Preliminary devices—settlements, nonsuits, dismissals, dispute resolutions, plea bargains, mediations, and prior admissions of guilt—drive the legal process from behind the scenes, but only formal hearings and trials take place in public. Courtrooms thus become the face of the law, the place where outside observation operates as a check on authority. Habeas corpus ("have the body in court") signifies the right of an accused person to appear *in public* before a judge, where judgment itself can be judged. When a trial proceeds inappropriately—when even a minority of observing citizens believe it to be unjust or unfair or arbitrary or merely imbalanced—the law and its officials face public criticism. Debate then extends beyond the courtroom, leading to controversy of a different order and magnitude.

These tendencies are natural enough. The adversarial nature of the trial in the American system gives public voice to division. It pits one side against another, and the greater the division, the more outside controversy a trial is likely to produce. But neither formal division nor the fact of heightened controversy fully explains courtroom extravaganzas that become focal points in the rule of law. High-profile trials are a distinct phenomenon at the nexus of the legal system and public life. Episodic as they are powerful, they surprise by attracting massive attention beyond the locality in which they take place and by influencing social thought generally, and although they come in many different forms and situations, they share qualities that aid the interpretation of history and culture.

When an official dispute in court generates intense coverage and public concern, three separate but interlocking catalysts can be found at work
somewhere in the mix. First, there is a *spread of conflict*, though the concept is more complicated than the descriptive phrase conveys. Second, an
element of shock or sudden reversal of circumstance or a startling twist
in recognition is present. Again the concept is greater than any single
expression of it, but the ancients captured the power in the idea with the
word *peripeteia*, literally "to fall away" or undergo a stunning or swift
change in direction. Third, in an extension of the performative element
in every trial, there must be an inviting *iconography* at work, a visceral
appeal that carries from the concrete to the imagination of the onlooker.
These catalysts illustrate why certain trials become enduring events and
why other trials that would seem to qualify do not.

A *spread of conflict* sets the pattern of thought in a high-profile trial.
All trials begin in a formal dispute. They expand into a memorable event
when the calibrated legal basis of complaint in an official indictment
spawns less restrained quarrels all around it. Conflict in such a case is
never singular. It reaches beyond the disputants in court, and its proliferation in communal debate insures appeal of the event. The critic Kenneth
Burke suggests how to study this manifestation. He argues that dramatic
allure depends on recognition of the range in complication. "We should
watch for the dramatic alignment," writes Burke; by this, he means that
an interpreter should look beyond obvious disagreement in determin-
ing exactly "What is versus what."[1] To extrapolate from Burke to a legal
context, the interpreter of a high-profile trial must determine how many
"whats" are engaged in conflict with each other in and around a trial.
Once all of the "whats" have been identified as the range of complication, obvious questions follow. *Which* impulses play in media coverage
as major contributions to communal narratives of the event and *why*?
Which ones do not and *why not*?

Surprise or *peripeteia* supplies the second or unsettling element that
every major trial has somewhere in its makeup. Often enough, this uneasiness involves a minority grouping that feels endangered or alarmed
by majoritarian assumptions at play. The threatening factor can also be
more general: an entire community can be forced to reflect on behavior
that is unprecedented, particularly horrifying, or invasive. Then again, a
trial can raise a suppressed issue or development that a community has

tried to avoid. Courts do not ask for the problems that come to them out of the intricacies and ingenuity of human deviance. They must take what comes, and occasionally they must evaluate an action that social norms have not yet fathomed or coped with out of uncertainty, fear, insecurity, or lack of imagination. To be caught unawares becomes an especially exciting element when settled premises and procedures at trial are thrown off balance. Notably, the threat in surprise to some invariably gives a thrill of hope to others, and this contributes to the spread of conflict.

The third catalyst, *iconography*, involves the symbolism and imagery of personality. Many problems are more easily grasped through example, and courts abet the inclination. The law examines individuals and their motivations, not ideas. It assigns responsibility for specific conduct, and its ceremonial aspects magnify character, appearance, and deportment. Given anything to work with, these personality issues grow more intense in a high-profile trial. Participants turn into celebrities through prolonged exposure and speculation about their integrity in conflict. As captive figures in the fixed setting of the courtroom, their smallest mannerisms become sources of fascination when on display day after day. Observers like to assume that demeanor counts for much in reaching their own determinations, and it is the rare onlooker indeed who ignores visual clues or fails to identify with one performer or another. The public eye of a high-profile trial invariably magnifies as it judges. No figure of importance emerges from the experience with the same status and identity as before.

These three characteristics do not turn an ordinary trial into an extraordinary one by themselves, but they control patterns of perception, and because each of them welcomes exaggeration, they distort awareness of the balances in courtroom decorum and leave contention and misdirection in their wake. They are, in sum, primary causes of confusion in following a high-profile trial and therefore become pivotal sources of analysis. Lord Hardwicke, the founder of modern equity law, raised the legal answer to this predicament long ago. "Certainty is the Mother of repose," he declared in 1753; "therefore the Law aims at Certainty."[2] But if this aspiration still holds, certainty and repose are hard to find in the confusion and turmoil that regularly invade a high-profile trial today.

We can, however, identify the misperceptions and misrepresentations in controversy. Part 1 of *The Trial in American Life* reacts to the confusions that make high-profile trials so problematic in American history and takes up problems that can best be expressed in interrogative form. Can communities be expected to approach controversial trials in a better way? What degree of awareness and accuracy can one realistically expect to achieve in public opinion? If so many of the confusions seem to be intrinsic to a high-profile trial, what more can be done to clarify them? Why, for that matter, is heightened public awareness necessary? Why not leave the meaning of controversial trials to the trained perceptions of the professionals who run them? The modern nation-state delegates many elements of current public discourse to the authority of experts and professional elites. Why should trial performance be different than so many other areas requiring licensed knowledge?

The Trial in American Life, as the very title suggests, rejects the negative thrust in such questions. A public trial is public only if there is sufficient communal vigilance to observe and understand it. To be worthy of the name, a rule of law requires that the governed know how to observe and sometimes answer those who govern. Nor is that all. Never before has there been as much coverage of trials or as many different avenues for understanding them as there are at this moment. The opportunity for awareness is real, and the tragedies of previous misperceptions litter the history of the country. Solutions lie not in deference to those who are supposed to know but in the tools for all to understand the nature and gravity of legal conflict as part of a democratic society.

CHAPTER ONE

Where Courtrooms and Communities Meet

THE MONKEY TRIAL

The most famous confrontation in an American courtroom took place in 1925. Clarençe Darrow, the renowned lawyer of his day, and William Jennings Bryan, the leading orator and three times the Democratic Party's candidate for president, squared off as opposing counsel over the teaching of evolution in the public schools of Tennessee. For the defense, Darrow declared: "I am going to argue [the case] as if it were serious, and as if it were a death struggle between two civilizations. . . . [B]igotry and ignorance are ever active. Here we find today as brazen and as bold an attempt to destroy learning as was ever made in the Middle Ages." Bryan responded in kind. "Talk about putting Daniel in the lion's den!" he complained for the state of Tennessee. "How dared those scientists put man in a little ring like that with lions and tigers and everything that is bad?" The impudence of science had patriotic implications for Bryan. Evolution wanted to teach Tennesseans that they had come "not even from American monkeys, but from Old World monkeys."[1]

The audiences attracted to a high-profile trial encourage this kind of rhetorical excess. Playing to the gallery is standard entertainment in such an event, but the clashes between Darrow and Bryan, both outside counsel brought in to spike interest in the trial, would turn most bitter in the moment that everyone remembers. Darrow surprised everyone by convincing Bryan to appear as an expert witness on the Bible and then using Bryan's literal interpretation of Scripture to make him look foolish on the stand. If the serpent of Genesis was actually "compelled to crawl upon its belly" for tempting Eve, ran a typical question to the nodding

Figure 1. Clarence Darrow and William Jennings Bryan at Dayton (1925). Photograph © Bettmann/CORBIS. Well beyond its notoriety as the "monkey trial" of 1925, *Tennessee v. Scopes* symbolizes the way courtrooms mold public opinion. Darrow and Bryan look like the political allies they long had been in this photograph, but their bitter and increasingly personal exchanges over the theory of evolution, as prominent outside counsel placed on opposite sides of the case, helped to polarize thought about science and religion into the twenty-first century.

Bryan, "[h]ave you any idea how the snake went before that time?" "Do you know whether he walked on his tail or not?" "Up to 4,143 years ago, every human being on earth spoke the same language?" Darrow asked, referring Bryan to the Tower of Babel. "Yes, sir," Bryan had to respond. These are the comments that everyone recalls, and yet none of the exchanges between the two leading players had anything to do with the trial as a legal matter.

In its misdirection, hyperbole, and fascination, *State of Tennessee v. John T. Scopes* epitomizes problems that arise in a high-profile trial. Fought out across eleven days, *Scopes* familiarized Americans with "the never-ending story," the media's need for "new news" and fresh excitement every day. The trial produced more words in print than any comparable event to that point in the country's history, and yet all of the attention led mostly to confusion and turmoil. Both sides would misconstrue the effect of their actions and come to regret what happened in Dayton. John Washington Butler, the sponsor of the anti-evolution act, committed the first mistake, one Americans make with some frequency. He assumed that law would eliminate the problem. "When the bill passed," he observed, "I naturally thought we wouldn't hear any more about evolution in Tennessee." Instead *Scopes* would put the subject on every tongue and in a particular way. The extremes of advocacy and news coverage transformed an inchoate discrepancy between science and theology into a raging national debate and a permanent standoff fueled by anger, self-righteousness, and humor.

Everyone miscalculated in *Scopes*. The Butler Act made it unlawful for anyone in an institution funded by the state "to teach any theory that denies the story of the Divine Creation of Man as taught in the Bible, and to teach that man has descended from a lower order of animals." Lawyers for the American Civil Liberties Union decided that this language violated freedom of speech and arranged for a test case to prove it through town leaders in Dayton, who cooperated to make money and put their town on the map. John T. Scopes, a twenty-four-year-old high school biology teacher in Dayton, agreed to become the nominal defendant because he shared the view of the ACLU. "Restrictive legislation on academic freedom is forever a thing of the past," he would claim long after his trial. *Inherit the Wind*, a play written about the trial thirty years later, would do much to solidify this line of interpretation. When asked today, most people will tell you how Darrow confused his opponent Bryan on the witness stand over interpretations of the Bible and routed the opponents of evolution in the process. Nothing, however, could be further from the truth.[2]

The anti-evolutionists *won* their case in Dayton. After days of strenuous debate, the jury took all of eight minutes to *agree* with Bryan and find Scopes guilty of breaking the law. Darrow's famous confrontation with Bryan was expunged from the court record as soon as it was completed. His supposedly withering examination of Bryan had no legal significance, and the Butler Act that convicted Scopes would prevail in Tennessee for another forty years, spawning a whole series of additional anti-evolution laws in other states. Publishers still skirt the subject of evolution in biology textbooks to "avoid offense to a scientifically illiterate segment of the adult population."[3] What the ACLU "won" from *Scopes* was a virulent division between science and religion. Even Dayton achieved far less than it wanted. Its place on the map of public opinion would be secured but as one of ridicule. H. L. Mencken, the pundit of his era, ended his own coverage of the trial by describing Dayton as once an obscure but happy town but now "a universal joke."

Tennessee suffered from both ends. Its citizens felt threatened but ashamed of the image the "monkey trial" gave the world. State senator Butler conveyed the threat when he wrote, "Darwin dope shall not rob our children of future hope." Embarrassed, the Tennessee Supreme Court countered by suppressing the whole affair on appeal through a false technicality and the claim that "nothing is to be gained by prolonging the life of this bizarre case." The court confirmed the constitutionality of the Butler Act but rejected the verdict because the jury, not the judge, should have assessed the fine of $100. It then induced Tennessee's attorney general to enter a *nolle prosequi* ("no longer prosecuting") to prevent further appeal from Scopes. Effective politically by checkmating all sides, this decision made no legal sense. The Butler Act *mandated* a fine of "not less than One Hundred ($100.00) Dollars," and everyone had agreed not to raise on appeal the question of who should impose the fine. Judge John T. Raulston did only what the law demanded of him at trial. His superiors, the justices of the Tennessee Supreme Court, turned against him to end the case as quickly and quietly as possible.[4]

Tennessee v. Scopes supplies a cautionary tale about all high-profile trials. Controversy in such a case tends to be dangerously open-ended. Legal consequences had nothing to do with the tumult aroused in *Scopes*; the defendant faced a misdemeanor charge with a $100 fine that others would pay. Neither the law nor punishment but ways of life were on trial in Dayton, and it is usually a mistake to try to solve this kind of problem in a courtroom. Advocacy inflames nonlegal issues, as the defining expressions of *Scopes*, "a circus in the courtroom" and "monkey trial," indicated at the time. The references of Bryan to lions and tigers in a ring, one of many allusions at trial to circus and animal imagery, enabled a voracious press to sell copy and make "circus" the pejorative term of reference for any trial where officialdom is overwhelmed and made to look foolish by outside influence. *Scopes* demonstrates how legal language can explode into "monkey business" just beyond the court's control. An arresting phrase in a high-profile trial can give language an unforeseen life of its own.

Dayton also reveals the dynamic nature of conflict. Permanent controversies have a way of changing while staying the same. Even Mencken would prove to be half wrong about *Scopes* in the end. The monkey trial survives today not as a source of shame and scorn but as an important tourist attraction in Dayton, fulfilling the financial hopes that the town leaders of 1925 sought. The legal profession of Tennessee, which tried to make *Scopes* go away, now learns its trade under representations of the event. Two huge murals of scenes from the trial hang in the Vanderbilt University Law School in downtown Dayton. Even so, and well beyond threat or shame, "the controversy over evolutionary teaching is as lively today as ever." Eighty years after *Scopes*, in the summer of 2005, both the Roman Catholic Church and the president of the United States would call for modern creationism, "intelligent design," to be taught against scientific theories of evolution in high school biology classes.[5]

When ideas tear a community apart, the pattern of controversy can return with astounding speed and force. The issues here—religion against science, rejection of change, fear over biological self-examination, divergent definitions of humanity itself—can reappear at any moment. A widely reported and vigorous legal rejection of the teaching of "intelligent design" in the high school biology classes of Dover, Pennsylvania, in 2005 has not stopped continuing challenges to the teaching of evolution in forty-one of the fifty states. The next major *Scopes* trial may even now be on the way over evolution or, in a new wrinkle, over the availability of genetic manipulation.[6]

High-profile trials like *Scopes* teach that the law is not a linear progression toward explanation anywhere near as much as it is a circulating mode of consensus on a variety of levels. Yes, the legal process in a courtroom moves from uncertainty toward decision, from simple description to expert procedure, from conflict to a solution articulated by a professional elite, and, often enough, from politics to the courtroom, but the requirements of understanding and acceptance extend in many directions at once, and they neither begin nor end in judgment. Most controversial trials furnish a simple proof of the reciprocities involved.

Anyone who studies courtroom events learns that it is almost impossible to secure a verdict at trial against the settled convictions of a surrounding community.[7]

The pressure on courtrooms grows especially serious when the legal stakes are higher and the defendants unpopular as they were in the trial of Nicola Sacco and Bartolomeo Vanzetti for felony murder in 1921. Whatever regrets Americans have today over the conviction and execution of Sacco and Vanzetti in Massachusetts in 1927 on flimsy evidence, questionable procedures, and a flawed appeal process, these inclinations were not in vogue when it counted. Most Americans and an overwhelming percentage of the legal profession were heavily in favor of conviction and execution in the 1920s. The names of Sacco and Vanzetti would be cleared of "stigma and disgrace," and alternative blame would be assigned to "prejudice against foreigners" and general communal "intolerance, fear, and hatred" only when Massachusetts governor Michael Dukakis signed a special statement to that effect in 1977. Half a century too late, the Dukakis proclamation acknowledged tacit truths: the cost of apparent injustice is high, and it has a long half-life in a republic of laws.[8]

We must come to a better comprehension of how misunderstandings, false excitement, and confusion arise out of such trials. Clarification of the problems may not solve them, but it can at least keep the issues that alarm a community in proper focus. It can reduce the spread of conflict, keep peripheral anxieties in check, and reduce the distorting power of celebrityhood. Even more ambitiously, clarification can allow the law to grow through a trial instead of fixing it to a moment through communal lines of force that threaten to overwhelm an answer in court. Courtrooms are supposed to educate communities as well as decide for them, but for that to happen effectively the legal profession as well as citizens and the media that inform them must grasp the nature of dynamic interaction in a high-profile trial. Language of importance comes from both directions in such moments, and the larger task must be to bring those languages closer together.

TELLING THE TRUTH IN COURT

The first source of misunderstanding emanating from courtrooms is also the most shocking. The greatest experts on trial performance, those officially involved or informed, can be the worst guides in explaining the communal context of a trial, even though their authority gives them a platform for such commentary. It is an old truth but worth repeating: "The members of the bar are peculiarly unrepresentative of the public."[9] Professionalism gets in the way of larger communication. Lawyers have the task of informing and protecting their clients, and judges certify that these tasks are performed precisely. Both are sworn to uphold procedures that guarantee fairness and protect the process from bias, but they acknowledge fewer obligations where the desires of citizens to be informed are concerned.

All professions endorse a degree of separate knowledge with credentialism, special terminology, and protective autonomy, but nowhere have these tendencies been more rampant than in the law, and nowhere is a countervailing understanding more important. The authority of experts does not suffice in the explanation of a high-profile trial. As one critic writes, "Specialized knowledge can give neither structure nor direction to the conception of a general culture."[10] Lawyers also compound the problem by sliding between professional and general commentary without noting the difference, and that temptation is greatest in a high-profile trial. When Clarence Darrow finds conflict over the teaching of evolution "a death struggle between two civilizations" in *Scopes*, he thrills a huge appreciative audience beyond the courtroom, but the same words distort the legal issue, insult the locality that will decide the case, and forget the client that Darrow is supposed to serve.

The internal legal standards that protect in court are not meant to inform the public, and often enough they do not. Procedural precision, formal language, and the control of precedent are all tenets for insuring justice in court, and no one would want to be without them, but these tenets are also stratagems for restricting debate and were never designed as engines of general explanation. Consider only the most prominent principle just noted, stare decisis, the control of precedent. *Stare decisis et non quieta movere*, to give the complete expression, conveys more than the rule of precedent. The full phrase means "to adhere to precedent and not unsettle things that are established." Legal thought depends on what will *not* be discussed in court as much as it does on the words that control decision, a spirit of efficiency that takes much for granted. Just as "not unsettling things that are established" brings certainty to the decision-making process, so it can miss the more general concerns of a community. There are losses as well as gains in this manner of proceeding, "another way of saying that law has flourished on the corpse of philosophy in America."[11]

Although the aspirations of the law in court are easily conveyed, actual litigation is much harder to comprehend and easily misunderstood. Here is the American Bar Association's summary of what should take place in a courtroom:

> The best way to get to the truth is to allow all the competing parties to present their views to an impartial third party as adversaries, or opponents, under rules that permit the evidence to be presented fairly and in an orderly fashion.[12]

Left unsaid are the illusive nature of truth and barriers to the desire for it. At least one of "the competing parties" at trial will not welcome the answer that is found, and the search for truth is always a self-interested enterprise in court.

Courtroom performers must answer to a well-known rubric. They are to "tell the truth, the whole truth, and nothing but the truth." But "what is truth?" The question can be asked with the offhand cynicism of a Roman procurator, Pontius Pilate, in the trial of Jesus, or it can be raised with the precision, relativism, and penetration of a modern philosopher.[13] Either way, truth is a variable in advocacy, and it must be fashioned to be believed. In one of the leading tactics at trial, "the best way to get to the truth" is through the most believable story told in court. "Despite the maze of legal jargon, lawyers' mysterious tactics, and obscure court procedures, any criminal case can be reduced to the simple form of story."[14] This modern adage is accurate as far as it goes, but how much truth is lost in the reduction?

The form of story in court must be simple because common people must believe it. The law demands belief in the telling. A trial recounts a past event to reach a decision about the future. It moves between "remembered life" (the past dispute or crime under investigation) and "real life" (what should happen to the accused). Every good story uses remembered life to reveal the meaning of real life, but at trial this dynamic follows the narrow concern that attorneys bring to real life.[15] A litigator does not seek knowledge except as it regards the fate of the accused. Storytelling thus becomes a uniquely cutthroat business in court. Conflicting versions of the "remembered life" (the imputed crime) fight to control the decision to be reached. In fiction and even in history, different versions of a story can coexist, each creating a unique space for itself, but an advocate's story claims a *definitive* truth and must compete with rival narratives for the same discursive space. A courtroom account flattens the "narrative desire" or search for meaning in a story.[16] It reduces everything said to one overwhelming concern: guilty or not guilty as charged. Nothing else really matters at trial.

This all-or-nothing approach leads to a devastating conclusion. Most stories told in a courtroom are true only in an instrumental sense. The priorities on truth telling notwithstanding, a story succeeds only when it is well told, and the best story requires imagination as well as the truth. Lawyers look for a version of the truth that jurors will accept, and they learn that a credible story will be one familiar to the listener through convention or experience. This compulsive search for familiar ground leads away from the intricacy of the law and, often enough, away from the problem at hand.

Textbooks on advocacy put the matter this way: "Focus on the people, not the problem"; "your storytelling must emphasize the parties and witnesses and the events they were part of, not the legal issues involved." In the $253.5 million award against the drug company Merck in 2005 over the painkiller Vioxx, which may or may not have killed the patient, the plaintiff lawyer's "folksy" story, channeled through the bereaved widow and her daughter, shaped jury preferences in an otherwise uncertain case. The treatment of mere facts through the cold and insensitive expertise of Merck's lawyers alienated at least some jury members.[17]

The construct of guilt against innocence rewards corresponding simplifications in court, even though the more complicated truth may fall somewhere in between or in another dimension of understanding altogether. In the 1976 trial of Patricia Hearst for bank robbery as a member of the Symbionese Liberation Army, two months after she had been kidnapped by the SLA, the contrast offered to the jury was "common criminal" and "spoiled brat" by the prosecution versus "brainwashed heiress" and "prisoner of war" by the defense.[18] Rape trials afford similarly harsh alternatives. The imputed victim becomes a "virgin" destroyed by the experience or a "vamp" who provoked the accused, depending on whether the prosecution or the defense is to be believed. These stereotypes flourish even though a victim's sexual experience should have no bearing on whether or not a crime has taken place. Advocacy rewards narrative pre-dispositions over the facts in a case. Even a judicial opinion will manipulate the facts in the record to craft a better story for a given result.[19]

The presumed balance in descriptions of advocacy can also be misleading. If the law thinks that "the best way to get to the truth is to allow all the competing parties to present their views to an impartial third party," the neutrality of the claim misses a fundamental disparity in the *manner* that stories must be told in court. The separate functions of prosecuting attorney and defense counsel require different tactics in storytelling. The prosecution's indictment or initial story must contain every permutation of the relevant offense to guard against a nonsuit or declaratory judgment in favor of the defense, and this need explains the numbing repetition found in a formal complaint. The prosecution must cover every technicality even as it overcomes them with a story that will convince "beyond a reasonable doubt."[20]

Telling such a story requires art. The indictment must carry "a moral certainty" of the charge, a handicap for any storyteller. A prima facie case must be effective enough for a court to believe that it will prevail against all others unless contradicted by evidence not noted by the prosecution. This initial burden of proof is qualified, but it grows as a trial proceeds. In narrative terms, the chain in the prosecution's story line— the integrity and connection of a beginning, middle, and end—must be strong enough to survive interruption, contradiction, alternative explanation, and every irregularity. Two legal maxims control the asymmetrical challenge in prosecutorial storytelling: *lex appetit perfectum* and *omnis indemnatus pro innoxis legibus habetur*. The first, "the law covets perfection," warns that mistakes in an accusation will not be tolerated. The second, "innocent until proven guilty," protects the accused from anything less than ironclad proof. The prosecution must adjust every narrative inclination to this imbalance. It labors against an in-built favoritism for the defense. As the second maxim is sometimes put, "The law is tender of the accused."

The first strategy of the defense in response is naturally one of evasion. The defense tells no story until it has to. Its follow-up, the defense's second strategy, relies on the most bizarre trait in the entire adversarial system. To break down the prosecution's story, the defense foists a proliferation of story lines to create "a reasonable doubt." If credible to a willing jury, almost any alternative explanation of events can succeed. Did the police tamper with the evidence, as claimed in the trial of O.J. Simpson? Law students used to imbibe this lesson through the example of an early legal hero. Theophilus Parsons, "first giant of the law in Massachusetts," put the premise this way:

> A plaintiff brings an action against a neighbor for borrowing and breaking the iron pot in which he cooked his dinner. The defendant says he never borrowed any pot; and that he used it carefully; also, that the pot was broken and useless when he borrowed it; also, that he borrowed the pot of somebody not the plaintiff; also, that the pot in question was the defendant's own pot; also that the plaintiff never owned any pot, iron or other; also that the defendant never had any pot whatever.[21]

An admission of pettifoggery to outsiders, this anecdote never fails to rouse cynical pride when quoted within the profession. Here, in cameo form, is the lawyer's instinctive appreciation of the power in storytelling. If any combination of stories from the defense's arsenal succeeds in creating a reasonable doubt, the defendant must be found not guilty. This prospect makes "counternarratives" standard fare in a courtroom. The classical adage of Archílochus explains the situation nicely: "The fox knows many tricks, the hedgehog one—a good one." Defense attorneys are foxes in the system; they have many tricks or stories to tell. Prosecutors have to be hedgehogs, and their one account had better be a good one.[22] For if the multiplication in story lines by defense counsel strains probabilities, juries are receptive to alternatives that make sense to them.

Boredom presents yet another hurdle in communal understanding of accounts in a courtroom. Stories at trial appear hopelessly repetitious to a nonprofessional observer and are more monotonous than an audience would tolerate in any other setting. A trial develops through endless retellings. The indictment gives the story as an assertion (more than conjecture but less than proven fact). Factual renditions supporting the assertion, or denying it, come next in the opening statements of opposing counsel. These statements are supposed to be non-argumentative and confined to the facts to be proven. Nonetheless, they reiterate opposing versions of what happened in excruciating detail. Then, in another telling, true argument over the facts unfolds in the presentation of evidence, objections, examinations, and cross-examinations. Procedural compulsions make each side retell the incidents not once but many times. The need to prove events through the oral testimony of witnesses—witnesses who can describe only what they did and saw themselves—brings each storyteller back and forth over the same ground more than once. Closing arguments and the judicial opinion repeat what has gone before, though mercifully in more concise form.[23]

One of the many difficulties for a community is the relevance of such redundancy, and in their impatience, observers extrapolate beyond what has been said in court. Lawyers are given great license to repeat themselves because the law assumes that reiteration contributes to a truth beyond rhetoric. By granting maximum leeway, a courtroom encourages acquiescence in judgment. It creates a zone where procedural correctness and final decision making meet and protect each other. Accuracy on both levels provides a double check, a second chance to rectify error.[24] Repetition in this sense is not just time spent. By thoroughly considering "all possible descriptions to which one might plausibly conform one's judgments," a court achieves what John Rawls has termed "reflective equilibrium," the stance required for changing a held point of view when change is desirable. In more dramatic terms, "the perfect narrative" emerges "through the layers of a variety of retellings." Repetition encourages "getting it right" for "getting it behind us."[25]

Obviously, "the best way to get to the truth" in court is highly specialized. The illusive and instrumental nature of truth in advocacy, the oversimplifications and melodrama in argument, and the imbalances, repetitions, and proliferations in storytelling distract and annoy the nonprofessional observer. Properly understood, however, and taken together, these legal devices are tools of communal explanation. If the accounts at trial amount to self-serving constructions in competition with each other, the final story, the one that "wins" at trial, says something about the community that is willing to receive it.

The thoroughness of storytelling at trial also means that trials are interesting for what is *not* said in them. When a lawyer *fails* to make use of an available story, we have another sign of the times. In the *Scopes* trial of 1925, no one on either side bothered to raise the overtly racist explanation of evolution in the high school textbook at issue, George William Hunter's *A Civic Biology*. Hunter's "scientific text" describes an elaborate "evolution" in "The Races of Man" through five ascending categories from "the Ethiopian or negro type," up to "the highest type of all, the

Caucasians, represented by the civilized white inhabitants of Europe and America."[26] Presented as science, can anyone imagine such a comment going unnoticed in an American courtroom today?

These criticisms of "legal truth" and the failures of a community to appreciate them must be understood in context. The arcane nature of trial performance does not undercut the importance of law as a central mode of explanation, but it does suggest the need for stronger connections between legal explanation and communal reception when trials and particularly high-profile trials are so readily subject to public misconception. Misunderstandings when people are already angry are dangerous, and the sensationalism in legal argument can give error a lasting imprint. In *Scopes* we have seen that a high-profile trial can cause more harm than good. To summarize the problem in a sentence, the rule of law is too important to be left to lawyers and their explanations.

For while the law endures in its own right and has its own purposes and spheres, a communal rule of law survives only where the structure of regulations (the law) exists in relation to the disposition of cultural forces (social norms).[27] A public trial is the place where regulations and norms visibly meet, and the more attention a trial draws, the greater the need for a meaningful connection. At the same time, we have seen that many sources of misunderstanding seem intrinsic to a given situation. What is to be done with a community, or a prominent section of it, that willfully misunderstands with its own purposes in mind?

HEARING THE TRUTH IN COURT

An inbred suspicion of law itself informs the first level of communal dissociation at trial. "Law is born from despair of human nature," explains José Ortega y Gasset. "Out of mutual distrust of their own humanity people are careful to interpose between each other for the purposes of commerce and intercourse something deliberately inhuman: the law."[28]

Although most people do not articulate this thought in its pessimism, they intuit it. Law provides the neutral restraints that are necessary for individuals in coping with each other. Only utopian communities based on wish fulfillment are without this drab umbrella of restriction, and although those who study the law sometimes call it beautiful, the subject is distasteful to those who merely obey or pay the consequences of disobedience. The related fear of what the law might do to a person in its presumed indifference to individuality encourages many observers to instinctively question what happens when someone steps into the dock.

This inherent, even healthy, skepticism deepens into something more intense when people differ passionately over the stakes involved, as they often do in a high-profile trial. One of the sadder comments on human nature would seem to be that "nothing can be proved untrue to everyone's satisfaction."[29] No amount of evidence will convince some people that the Holocaust took place or that Lee Harvey Oswald acted alone in killing John F. Kennedy. There are always individuals who identify strongly with the other side of an issue. Belief trumps reason and explanation when people invest heavily in one side of a conflict. A high-profile trial is peculiarly susceptible to these kinds of narrow investment. The lines of force are so clear and the arguments made on both sides are so ingrained that they stimulate opposite trains of thought in habitual reaction to each other. Continuing debate over the teaching of evolution proves the point, but so do many other trials of note.

A last basic trait in human nature may be more important than all of the rest in clouding perception of a high-profile trial. Although we would like to believe otherwise, a courtroom appeals at once to the best and the worst in us. A painful recognition is at stake in this realization. The virtuous citizen who extols legal remedies is also the voyeur who enjoys the tragedy, the guilt, and the pain of others as a casual observer at trial. The poet William Blake spoke the truth when he claimed, "Cruelty has a human heart."[30] There is something in our makeup that enjoys the sight of others in trouble, that causes us to speculate about our superiority to those who have been targeted, that relishes in the punishment of someone else, and that gives low pleasure while others twist under the threat of sanction.

Voyeurism is not just a factor; it is a central motivation in the way people regard a controversial trial. Moreover, this unpleasant but very natural propensity gets in the way of comprehension. Self-righteousness, vicarious excitement, sentimental identification, and intrusive curiosity are besetting flaws in courtroom observation. To appreciate the point, one need only think of a few relatively harmless parallels: sports fans watch an automobile race in anticipation of a crash (always included on highlight films), and the first expectation in an observed ski race or skating exhibition is the possibility of a spill.

Against malice, willful misconstruction, and emotional fixation, there is no defense except for the law to disagree with each manifestation in clear and measured tones. The legal process does so by insisting on our better selves, an aspiration that is essential to achieve even a modicum of justice. "The wickedness of men," notes Montesquieu in *The Spirit of the Laws*, "makes it necessary to suppose them better than they are."[31] To measure the unacceptable deviance of others honestly and fairly is one of the most trying tasks in human endeavor. Trial procedures appeal to the sense of duty in performers, and they succeed most of the time, but the law has no comparable hold over the mere observer of a trial beyond the requirement of minimal decorum when in court.

Even attentive people can be confused by the variety of purposes at work in a courtroom. We tend to forget that trials perform many different functions at once. Most conspicuously, they resolve conflict, protect the innocent, punish the guilty, compensate for injury, and declare the law. But they also satisfy revenge, purge communal resentments, assign limits to deviance, identify acceptable otherness, give victims a say, rationalize change, place controls on the unknown, and publicize power. At still another level, they publicize the available answers to a problem and guard the status quo ante by seeking to return a community to its place before the disruption of crime.

These many functions compete with each other and complicate perception. Caught within them, though without an explicit role to play, is the *participant observer*, symbol of the public in a public trial. This freely involved figure enters a courtroom as a passive witness (present and watching) but also as a secret sharer (through personal identification and projection). The mere observer must abide by courtroom etiquette at all times under the threat of sanctions that apply to any other person in the presence of a presiding judge, but the participant within the observer remains otherwise free of constraints and can identify with any number of objectives and roles. The result is an inverse relationship. Participant observers exemplify and strengthen public decorum through the passivity of their presence, but their interest in a case carries them beyond what is being said and done in court.

The sharp restrictions on courtroom officers, consigned to carefully defined roles, unleashes speculation in the participant observer over what is happening. Eager for what has been repressed in official behavior, the typical interested person enters a compensatory zone of alternative

explanation. The restraint, regularity, gravity, measured pace, and tedium of courtroom procedures inspire hyperbole, spontaneity, humor,
speculation, and transgressive behavior just beyond its boundaries. Rare
in 1925 is the outside commentator who does not joke about monkeys
and exaggerate misbehavior in coverage of the *Scopes* trial.[32]

High-profile trials like *Scopes* fluctuate between acceptance of hier-
archical impositions and a very different leveling spirit of speculation
(what anthropologists call "*communitas*"). An official differentiation of
forms exists side by side with a spontaneous communion of individuals
in unstructured exchange. The natural tension in these positions is part
of the pleasure in observing a trial, but when the differentiation itself
collapses, as it did in Dayton, you have "a circus in the courtroom."[33]

High-profile trials are exciting by definition. Few who follow a trial remain indifferent to its appeal or the free-ranging commentary around it,
and the patterns that control that appeal are yet another source of confusion. Courtroom procedures are deliberately rote in their hope of avoiding unfair surprise, but they possess a peculiar allure in the familiarity
of their forms. "Many purely formal patterns," the critic Kenneth Burke
observes, "can readily awaken an attitude of collaborative expectancy
in us."[34]

The patterns in trial procedures offer a regularity, a rhythm, and a
progression that guarantee shared reception. But the collaborative expectancy encouraged by the familiar march of procedures also invites
loose prognostication as part of the appeal in observation. The procedures of the moment turn into the cultural capital of outside commentary. Accepting the tiresomeness of courtroom decorum is the price paid
for a delicious anticipation beyond its confines. It is the ticket of admission to a collective excitement, a dynamic that shapes communal involvement in powerful ways.

The most effective way to grasp the dangers in these affinities is to
think of a trial as a communal ritual.[35] To be more precise, trials operate
as contests that become rituals with the major technical distinction that
these terms imply. In Claude Lévi-Strauss's formulation, contests have "a
disjunctive effect; they end in the establishment of a difference between
individual players or teams." The essence of difference in contest is the
separation of winners from losers, an inescapable by-product of every
courtroom decision. "Ritual, on the other hand, is the exact inverse; it
conjoins, for it brings about a union (one might even say communion

in this context) or in any case an organic relation between two initially separated groups."[36] Where contest divides observers in the excitement it produces, ritual mollifies and placates through mutual acceptance of the result that follows from contest.

The contest in a trial decides punishment and exoneration. It satisfies the search for revenge, exculpation, expiation, and compensation—all dear to the adversarial process through direct advocacy. The natural analogue in contemporary society is to the athletic contest. The question asked with greatest frequency in the ongoing coverage of a noteworthy trial is an automatic one: "Who is winning?" Ritual, on the other hand, invokes a less dramatic stance with a more subtle ideal of participation in mind. The concepts of judgment, closure, publication, and the status quo ante play themselves out in the consensual procedures of a trial. Contest is the time-bound special event reaching toward a result; ritual is the resolution and recognition of a decision reached. The ideal trial moves from contest toward ritual in communal acceptance of the result achieved in court.

Unfortunately, trials that capture the imagination tend to divide sharply along the axes of contest and ritual and often remain at the level of contest. When a group overly identifies with a defendant, victim, or the behavior under examination, it views a trial as a contest in which its own fortunes are engaged. This level of identification runs counter to the holistic pattern natural to the rest of a community, and the discrepancy between citizens sets off waves of social tension that lack easy resolution.

Tennessee v. Scopes became a permanent contest when fundamentalist Christians felt threatened by the scientific rationalism behind the teaching of evolution in schoolrooms, and they could not bear the presumed superiority of other segments of the population in their condescending assumption that scientific advance would automatically win out. The trial of O.J. Simpson, a celebrated black man accused of murdering his white ex-wife in 1994, had similar dimensions when minorities in America thought of Simpson as a scapegoat and themselves as victims of the limits that the dominant culture had assigned them against the ideals of equality and integration.[37] When prolonged, the tensions in contest lead to permanent disjuncture. Those who care passionately denounce less committed observers; those denounced charge their accusers with bias.[38] Mutual accusation in this situation grows dangerous; it rekindles the threat to community that a trial is supposed to subsume.

Extremes in courtroom contest and ritual can help us to understand why the two elements must balance in a successful trial. Contest yields to ritual through acceptance of the decorum in procedural fairness, but if a community is genuinely and deeply divided over a trial, the rhythms of contest prevent the more subtle and less absorbing elements of consensus from working themselves out. The sharp regional conflicts that emerged during the trials of Aaron Burr and John Brown, pitting East against West in 1807 and North against South in 1859, provide cases in point in chapters 3 and 4. Burr's not guilty verdict and Brown's contrasting guilt at trial represented unacceptable solutions for conspicuous sections of the country and kept a consensus in law from emerging.

Notably, a trial can also devolve into empty ritual when a community feels so vulnerable that it is willing to eliminate the element of contest in a rush to judgment. The murder of a leading farmer in Kansas and his family, Herbert Clutter with his wife and two of their children, became an overnight sensation in 1959 and a national bestseller when Truman Capote's account, *In Cold Blood*, appeared in 1965. The murders—without warning, at night, of a family, in their own home, by men who had never met their victims and who traveled hundreds of miles to their destination, all with the specific design of committing murder with burglary in mind—touched off a permanent nightmare of invasion and death in middle-class America. "The next time they go slaughtering it may be *your* family," the prosecutor at trial warned the Clutter jury. So addressed, the jury took barely forty minutes to convict *and* recommend the death penalty for the two accused killers.[39]

Courtroom ritual that lacks contest loses sight of the individuals at trial and becomes a communal quest for its own meaning. The decision in a matter of minutes to execute the Clutter killers extracted revenge. In the words of an observer counting the two killers against their four victims, "an eye for an eye. And even so we're two pair short." Trial rituals operate as a response to broken meaning. By formalizing an upsetting event and measuring it, they bring an insecure community back together again, but the price of renewed security can be high if the element of contest is not given its due. In chapter 6, we will examine the Haymarket Riot trial, where lack of regard for the elements in conflict led to failures in explanation of the crime and to faulty identification of its presumed perpetrators.

If the relation between contest and ritual in a courtroom can be hard to gauge, the desired momentum is not. Contest in the courtroom fastens on oral advocacy as its logical symbol, the conflict between lawyers. As the modality that resolves conflict, ritual benefits from a crucial shift in trial procedure. Oral exchange, the scene of argument, gradually accedes to the binding power of conclusive written statements. The speaking witness is replaced by the printed record. Fact-finding (the jury debating with itself) submits to the more elevated certainty of a judicial decision drafted in the separate sanctity of a judicial chamber, read from the bench, and then printed. Through transference, the successive stages of courtroom performance become textual confirmations of what has been done.[40]

Few observers of a trial hold out for long against procedures that press so relentlessly toward an answer. From arrest warrant to indictment to arraignment to pleadings, on to jury selection, the listing of witnesses, opening statements, presentation of evidence, examinations, cross-examinations, rebuttals, final motions, closing arguments, charges to the jury, jury deliberations, verdict, and judgment—the protracted form of decision making is connected and predictable. The observer need not agree with every stage, strategy, or direction in order to share in "collaborative expectancy." Everyone in the end wants a decision. To borrow Shakespeare's evocation of process from Sonnet 60, "In sequent toil all forwards do contend." Contention in the courtroom feeds an ideal of sequence, a forward motion in which participation curbs anger, redundancy establishes pattern, order answers conflict, and advocacy succumbs to decision. Through procedure, the messiness of fact and disagreement give way to the accommodations that ritual is designed to encourage.

The problem in a high-profile trial is to get from contest to ritual. Ritual can be a synchronization of disparate forms, a complementarity of rules and persons, an answer to indeterminacy, a celebration of regulation and explanation, and each possibility brings its own impetus to consensual decision making.[41] Less apparent are the earned congruities that come from trial decorum. Ritual permits the hopeless bustle of officialdom to appear solemn rather than ridiculous in the attention that it lavishes on a relatively silent and often dysfunctional or petty defendant. Ritual harmonizes. It brings the complexities of the law into line with the simpler stories told to juries. It provides a calming influence, allaying the anger that accompanies every probe of serious crime.

Ritual is especially useful in diagnosing the mixed emotions that a community directs toward an accused person. In theories of ritual, "liminality" supplies a zone for gauging deviance; it is the rhetorical space where questionable behavior awaits examination and where fascination and abhorrence meet. Ritual at trial works to aid the deviant individual by holding the gaze of the community to the liminal state and by allowing the arrangement of both a positive and a negative "legal mask" to serve either end result.[42] Innocent citizen or guilty criminal: these categories are states of mind to be held in suspension by procedure until a decision can be reached in court, and as binaries, they prepare a community to work through conflict in collaborative expectancy. Placed together, they furnish indicators of what a community will allow itself to think.

Many of the distortions in the *Scopes* trial came down to a failure in liminality. The defendant was a cipher rather than a focal point for the resolution of the deviance addressed. So attention fixed instead on the warring attorneys, and "war" was indeed the metaphor of choice in media coverage. Newspapers gave front-page coverage to "battle" and "bombardment" themes with continuous reference to "attacks," "fortifications," "salvos," and "the long-range guns of science and theology." Nothing was held in suspension while combat imagery sparked communal discord. "Free thinkers" were arrested in Dayton, threats filled the air, and a pro-evolutionist pastor was forced to resign.[43]

Neither side in Dayton or the country at large could free itself from the corrosion of mere contest. Fundamentalists believed that ridicule of their position was blasphemy; progressive intellectuals believed just as strongly that "the simple case for light against darkness" made everyone on the other side a moron. As H. L. Mencken would exclaim for the defenders of light, "Tennessee needs only fifteen minutes of free speech to become civilized."[44] Claims of free speech and its absence are really about unending argument. Where contest refuses to yield to the pull of ritual, there is the measure of such an event.

THE CONTINUUM OF PUBLICATION AT TRIAL

As the *Scopes* trial reveals, misplaced communal agitation owes much to the vehicles of information. We attend trials and we listen to them, but more often than not we read about them. The most difficult meaning of "public" in public trial comes through *publication* and the *publicity* that attends it, with all of the tangled implications that these related terms imply. The two hundred reporters who descended on Dayton in 1925, each straining for an original story, made the *Scopes* trial the event it became, but their capacity to have such influence depended on words first written down in court.

Courtrooms are compulsive generators of texts. Everything said is part of an official transcript, and when a trial begins to become controversial, a host of additional writings and media presentations exploit the available record for their own quickly published versions of the event. So much is written that actual reading becomes a selective process fraught with conscious and unconscious choices. In effect, the presentations around a high-profile trial form a *continuum of publication*, and the synergy between texts is an ignored resource in understanding what happened.

This continuum of publication is where legal and nonlegal narratives meet and compete over a trial, and it extends from the original indictment, to the trial transcript, to the judicial decision, to the court report, and then on to such unofficial texts as newspaper reports, television and Internet coverage, journal articles, historical accounts, and fictional projections. This overabundance naturally favors the nonlegal narrative. No one questions the primacies of a legal transcript and judicial decision in describing the legal import of a case, but how many citizens read judicial decisions or a trial transcript? Nonlegal narratives accordingly flourish in ways that control communal perceptions, and much depends on how closely those narratives adhere to the official one in a high-profile trial.

Three recent concepts in literary criticism help to make the continuum of publication a useful analytical tool. First, law is now recognized as a *form of literature* subject to the same kind of critical inquiry as other writings. The standard building blocks in close reading—theme, form, style, tone, symbol, rhetoric, narrative, and point of view—apply as easily to a legal work as to an essay or novel. As long as the separate authority of the legal text is acknowledged, use of these critical tools reveals the power of legal language in new ways.[45] Second, current *genre theory* allows better analysis of the conformities and goals in writing. Genre pinpoints the receiving audience. It identifies "the schematic imprint" and "the conceptual promise" that attracts a willing reader.[46] Third, the relatively new concept of *intertextuality* allows the relation of texts to be more than a comparison. Intertextuality argues that distinct texts share the same discursive space in a culture through the sum of knowledge available to them, an idea that opens into the interactive nature of writings around a trial.[47]

These ideas help us to approach a dangerous anomaly in a high-profile trial. Legal texts in a courtroom are always vulnerable to refraction and displacement by more transparent nonlegal narratives of the same trial, and they are especially vulnerable through the intrusions of modern technology. Consider the plea of Los Angeles County Superior Court Judge Lance A. Ito in 1994. "Please, please, please," Judge Ito begged his jurors in the trial of O.J. Simpson, "I know it's against human nature, but don't let yourselves be polluted by the information in the media."[48] Alas, it *is* against human nature to resist the nonlegal narratives in a case, and those narratives contribute willy-nilly to conceptions of the rule of law by reaching more readers than their legal counterparts.

Legal and nonlegal narratives inevitably compete in the different aims they fulfill even as they respond to equally compelling social needs. In generic terms, legal decisions are authoritative with all of the in-built strategies that command requires: they are monologic in voice, declarative in tone, attentive to "the logic" of a situation, interested in a pre-arranged conclusion, emphatic in their reading of the world, and steeped in a language of affirmation.[49] In contrast, nonlegal narratives on the same subject are loosely discursive, multivoiced, inquisitive productions. As judicial language satisfies a craving for order and demonstrates competency in a final decision, so nonlegal narratives open a trial to every implication in search of the largest audience. A legal narrative declares itself; nonlegal narratives question those declarations. The contrasts are striking but also necessary. People will always require more than official writings to understand what they want to know about a trial.

Of course, the need for nonlegal narratives only begins to explain why those narratives intrude so readily on legal understandings. Why is the legal text so vulnerable to qualification and manipulation by an outside text about it? In part, nonlegal narratives respond transgressively to the propriety, restraint, expertise, and self-sufficiency found in legal narratives. Generic impulses in writing are always subject to challenge, and legal forms are interesting when this happens to them precisely because the law is so attached to pattern. To a writer who makes transgressive use of another text, the form of it is a leading mark, and the forms of the law are readily apparent and vulnerable.[50]

The most vulnerable legal text of all lies at the very center of the continuum of publication, and it is the court transcript. Seemingly formless, controlling but also controlled, the transcript is literally "a helpless narrative." It slavishly records verbatim what has been said at trial to duplicate as closely as possible the official experience in court. It is discursive space completely filled. The total record of language used under extraordinary pressure, a transcript holds the thought of all legal performers as they challenge each other, but because it is virtually unreadable in its aggregate massive nature, it is mined and excerpted by everyone with ulterior motives. Transcripts welcome intrusion by courtroom performer and reporter alike; they function thereby as the perfect intertext.

The cannibalism of a legal transcript for other uses is made easier by the fact that nonlegal narratives are invariably embedded in it. Trials, particularly high-profile trials, unfold through narratives that strain for heightened effect. Lawyers will try any combination of themes in their need to win. Innocent and guilty, yes; but these categories are rarely sufficient for the enmeshed advocate who quickly converts them into right and wrong, good and evil, harmless and dangerous, saved and damned, chaste and polluted, admired and ignored, loved and hated, worthy and unworthy.

These additional binaries in adversarial rhetoric conjure up whole streams of nonlegal narratives within advocacy, whether as sermon, sentimental fable, cautionary tale, mystery story, melodrama, gothic legend, romance, or adventure yarn.[51] The winning story in a controversial trial almost always has an extralegal dimension familiar to a community, and the greater the familiarity, the more its form attracts nonlegal narrators into the continuum of publication in search of new variations on its success. Indeed, nonlegal narratives can occasionally challenge legal texts successfully. Restless under the restrictions that the law demands, the nonlegal narrator writes in revision and as a medium of social change.

The first instance of this phenomenon in America is among the best. On October 8, 1692, a Boston merchant named Thomas Brattle wrote in alarm over the execution of witches in Salem, Massachusetts. Two hundred people had been accused of witchcraft over a matter of months, twenty-nine had been found guilty by the Salem Court of Oyer and Terminer, and nineteen had been executed. When Brattle decided to reject demonology as a reliable source of evidence, it pushed him to interpret disaster in terms other than the presiding convention of divine retribution, and the effort made him the first pious New Englander to think that way in public. His "free-and-easy" letter began as a loose satire on the false solemnities of his day, but writing against the law made it more. Brattle's protest turned belief into scrutiny, cosmic design into human mistake, sin into legal error.[52]

A discrepancy of this kind between legal and nonlegal narratives is symptomatic. It indicates that a completed trial is still "at work" in social understanding. Thus, where a community decides to focus within a continuum of publication around a controversial trial is an important variable in interpretation of the culture. Despite its inaccuracies and its claim to be fiction, *Inherit the Wind* became the text that controls much of contemporary thought about *Tennessee v. John T. Scopes*, and it could do so because it dramatizes the way that many Americans, though by no means all, would prefer to solve that controversy. The story that survives after trial, the story with the longest half-life in cultural memory, marks the boundary between conflict and consensus.

The permeable nature of this boundary leaves us, however, with a vast problem to solve. If misunderstandings are endemic between courtrooms and their communities—if the gaps between contest and ritual, between speaker and listener, between truth and advocacy, between one legal purpose and another, and between legal and nonlegal narratives are so wide—what can be done about them? How can one expect general understanding to emerge from a courtroom filled with legal intricacies and conflict? To answer, we must take these difficulties inside the courtroom and ask the questions in a more pointed way. What, realistically speaking, can people hope to know about what happens in the parts of the legal process that are available to them?

CHAPTER TWO

Inside the Courtroom

THE STEREOTYPES

Public attitudes regarding legal performance are deep-rooted but superficial in content, and they arise out of stereotypical thinking more than personal experience. Clichéd opposites dominate in the polar battles of innocence against guilt. Indeed, the favorite designations are almost always popular rather than professional in origin. Is the lawyer a hero or a trickster? A helper or an ambulance chaser? A public servant or a mouthpiece for hire?[1]

Modern psychology teaches that oversimplifications of this kind are unavoidable. Stereotypes represent "a requisite component of ordinary cognitive functioning." As mental shortcuts, they are also tenacious no matter how naive in original conception, and their intrinsic power makes them natural tools of argument in a high-profile trial. It follows that stereotyping cannot be avoided or even minimized in the adversarial process. The more practical approach, accordingly, must be to understand them better than we currently do instead of just deploring the phenomenon. The real concerns are how stereotypes in law have developed, how they operate, how they dictate perception, and how a more exact knowledge of them can improve communal comprehension.[2]

Stereotypes invariably feed rather than settle arguments, but by cataloging them at work against the formal requirements in legal performance, we can address some basic confusions that muddle and aggravate disagreements in a high-profile trial. Performers at trial are first greeted through role recognition. Each speaker stands where parallel speakers have stood before, even though they are simultaneously caught in a web

of professional constraints not immediately apparent to a courtroom audience. This discrepancy generates its own tensions. As a community falls
back on its fund of stereotypes, friction between popular recognition and
professional obligation creates an "interactive reality" in public opinion
regarding court behavior. In language that every law student reads at the
beginning of a career, "[The legal] words change to receive the content
which the community gives to them."[3]

The catalog of performers affected by these tensions must begin with
the official most responsible for balance and coordination at trial, the
presiding judge. Judges in an American courtroom enjoy authority unprecedented in any other aspect of democratic life, and they receive a
mixture of unbounded respect and suspicion because of it. Next in line
is the *prosecuting attorney,* servant of the people but also the arm of the
state with all of the power that institutional authority and organization
bring. Standing in the way is the *defense counsel,* presumed protector and
champion of the rights of the accused. The contesting advocates then
present the *witness,* who as observer or expert can determine a trial outcome when credibly informed. Next are the *jury,* symbol of representative democracy and official listener until the moment of decision; the
defendant, more controlled than controlling; and last, in a final category
not considered a performer until recent times, the *victim.* The rapid rise
of the victim is one of the great curiosities in contemporary American
law. No consideration of trials would be complete without an analysis of
this new priority in the legal system.

Another often forgotten element must also be reckoned with: namely,
the *courtroom itself.* Courtrooms routinize expected behavior in a further stereotyping of performance. They set the scene of performance.
Demeanor, movement, delivery, and display mean everything in convincing anyone of anything, and trials are all about the need to convince.
The ironic tone or sneer in a cross-examination, the raised eyebrow of
a judge, the querulous tone or posture of an attorney or witness—these
and other moments of personality bend the decorum of trial procedures,
and although they never appear in a transcript, they influence understanding. A courtroom is thus much more than a backdrop or occupied
space; it is the controlling presence that codes all effort and recognition
at trial.

THE JUDICIAL FIGURE

A linguistic gap signals the preeminence of the judge, "Your Honor" in American parlance. Pejorative terms for other professionals abound. Ministers are "Bible thumpers"; lawyers are "ambulance chasers"; doctors are "sawbones"; psychiatrists are "shrinks"; accountants are "number crunchers"; and journalists turn into subhuman predators who indulge in "feeding frenzies"; but judges are always and only judges.

No regular term of colloquial opprobrium attaches to the judicial function. Even the epithets for a severe or false magistrate, "hanging judge" and "corrupt judge," retain the title. Judges perform above us, and they are supposed to remain staunchly aloof. They are described in the most hyperbolic terms. "The ultimate guardians of our freedoms," they form "a secular priesthood" above vulgar reproach. "The courts are the capitals of law's empire, and judges are its princes." Judges enjoy a prestige unmatched elsewhere in the culture, and a good one can expect descriptions in the encomiastic mode. Service on the bench evokes testimonials that would embarrass the listener in any other context.[4]

We set judges apart. No other civil servant in American society can serve a life term, operates from a raised platform, cuts off debate without explanation, silences protest with peremptory gestures, punishes summarily for disobedience, commands elaborate ceremonial deference at all times, wears a distinctive uniform, or retreats so pointedly to private chambers to make a public decision. These prerogatives are further enhanced by the unique position of the highest judges in the land. The nine justices of the Supreme Court of the United States possess enormous powers of social interpretation through the doctrine of judicial review, and these powers have made them "the nation's most influential practical political philosophers" as well as the guardians of "liberty and justice for all," paramount values in American thought so designated by the pledge of allegiance.[5] By extension, all other judges share in these missions at their own levels in the system.

Judges must be better than the lawyers they once were—or at least very different. Voracious caterpillars as lawyers in the adversarial process, they turn into butterflies above it all when "elevated" to the bench. They must rise beyond the highly competitive appetites of the courtroom— appetites that made them successful in the first place. On the bench instead of arguing before it, they are to appear patient, detached, and disinterested. Unlike lawyers, they must also work in studied and lonely isolation.[6]

The failure of Abe Fortas to become chief justice of the United States, often interpreted as a vital turning point in American constitutional history, and his subsequent resignation as associate justice of the Court in May 1969 are often traced to just such a failure to distinguish between the roles of lawyer and judge. No matter how brilliant, a judge who remains overly invested in the adversarial process invites a telling criticism. "The robe," it is said of one who crosses that line, "is just too much for him."[7] Yet strangely, American society gives no extended instruction in the way that many other cultures do to the legal person who would become a judge. We expect the metamorphosis, for it is nothing less, to take place through personal realization of a new and exalted status.

Communal expectations of a judge extend in opposite directions. Strong judges are congratulated for imposing their personalities over a controversial case.[8] Not always, however. A judge who renders an unpopular decision can anticipate harsh criticism, removal petitions, talk of impeachment, even death threats.[9] Accusations of "judicial activism" tap an anti-judicial strain in the culture, and recent curbs on judges through tighter and sometimes mandatory sentencing guidelines suggest that suspicion of the figure may be growing.[10] So strong are these negative feelings that a presiding judge will often receive the blame for an unpopular outcome at trial. Even the highest court suffers in this way. Held above all others in esteem, the U.S. Supreme Court serves as "a sort of public whipping boy."[11]

Negativity regarding the judiciary is most often explained as part of "the counter-majoritarian difficulty." As independent officials, judges can anticipate criticism for remaining less accountable to democratic culture than others in authority.[12] But this argument only begins to plumb a deeper ambivalence in American attitudes. An independent judiciary is at once the signature of a free society and a form of expression alien to its underlying impulses. Both of the extremes—inflated hopes regarding the judicial role and acute suspicion of every exercise of judicial power—are available for stereotypical use, but they exist together in any explanation of the function. "A judge has to walk a tightrope," explains one from the ranks. "Some decisions must be made by the letter of the law and some decisions must take into account community sentiment."[13] Here is the connection of courtroom and community at work, and the leeway claimed by a judge to move in either direction represents the license that critics of the judicial function want to resist.

We demand too much of judges even as we distrust them, and some of it is their fault. When Felix Frankfurter writes that the ideal judge "should be compounded of the faculties that are demanded of the historian and the philosopher and the prophet," it should be remembered that a judge is neither a historian nor a philosopher nor a prophet. No human being, no matter how capable, can fulfill all of those roles at once.[14] The aggrandizing mode that judges, lawyers, and their subalterns reserve for the bench compounds the problem and should not be encouraged, as it is now in legal circles. Already dehumanized by the restraint and detachment demanded of them, judges appear superhuman when wrapped in the rhetorical excess of professional acclaim. It is one thing to applaud Alabama Judge Frank Minis Johnson Jr. for his "unflagging moral courage and legal brilliance" while enforcing school integration decrees against the depredations of segregationist governor George Wallace in the 1960s; quite another to extol him as "the real governor of Alabama."[15]

But if the hagiographical tendencies in praise of judicial worthiness do more harm than good in thinking about what takes place in a courtroom, the tradition is too firmly entrenched to be punctured, much less done away with. Nor is there much point in rehearsing recent debates over the capacity of a judge to be objective. The need, rather, is to separate mythology from mechanics while recognizing that assigning punishment demands more than authority. As Judge Learned Hand once wrote, "The degree to which [a judge] will secure compliance with his commands depends in large measure upon how far the community believes him to be the mouthpiece of a public will."[16] The phrase "mouthpiece of a public will" identifies a mystical element always present but difficult to articulate.

The American Bar Association offers a more grounded description of the judicial function. A trial judge is "the umpire in disputes under the American system of 'adversary' justice," one who "keep[s] the case in proper legal bounds by ruling on points of law and procedure."[17] Judges also issue arrest and search warrants, set and revoke bail, and hold preliminary hearings. They rule on pretrial procedural motions, decide on the evidence that will be allowed, and set the trial docket and agenda. Each of these lesser duties contains power. Even a seemingly innocuous task, setting the docket, becomes a tool of discipline and a weapon in the hands of an active judge. U.S. District Judge Edward W. Nottingham, in Denver, held hearings at dawn (6:15 A.M.) to discourage lawyers from raising what he called frivolous issues. There is no real limit to such power. "The guy has a lifetime appointment," noted a litigant in "Nottingham's breakfast club." "He could make us dress up in bunny suits if he wanted."[18]

Even so, "umpire" is a well-chosen noun of limitation. Umpires do not play the game; they enforce its rules and watch over its activity. A passivity marks the overseer in the adversarial process, especially when compared with magistrates elsewhere. American judges do not conduct their own investigations of the evidence, as do judges in many continental European regimes. They do not select legal issues, and, in their dependency on oral advocacy, they do not normally possess a prior written record of the investigations of a case—both of which are alternatives in many European courtrooms. In the United States, litigation flows from nominally equal parties in conflict. Prosecution and defense devise and act out their separate strategies while the judge insures a neutral arena. Only in America can a defendant avoid a judicial determination altogether by requesting that a jury decide guilt or innocence.

How much power a judge wields is impossible to answer, another reason for anxiety about the function. For every judge who complains over lack of authority, there is another who claims great influence, and yet both sides regularly stress the effort that it takes to *appear* powerful—to get others "to see Olympian perfection in a black robe."[19] The struggle to appear powerful depends on a personality that must remain veiled. All judges accept the need to curb personal traits as officials. The judge who draws a happy face next to his signature on a death warrant can expect to be criticized heavily for it, even though the drawing is a regular part of his signature and a symbol of born-again faith. A judge who urges gun control on jurors as they convict in a murder case has overstepped proper bounds, and it will be no justification to claim he was "so upset by the waste of human life due to one handgun that I just had to urge them to push for reform." A judge who asks an aggressive lawyer if he is Jewish or who decries sending children to a Catholic school can expect censure or worse.[20]

But judicial power in any given moment is absolute. No lawyer can expect to win a case when the judge exhibits even guarded hostility within the accepted boundaries of decorum, and this level of hostility occurs with some frequency. The only real control on judicial behavior lies in adverse publicity and subsequent complaint. Declaratory policies of "judicial restraint" certainly pertain, but it is difficult to know how to apply them. There is a conundrum in the discipline expected. As a federal judge in New York puts the problem, "Our commission is to keep our personal predispositions under control," but "it can cut both ways—if you control what you personally feel, then there's not much room for mercy."[21]

Many observers, including whole critical movements in legal thought, find an easy solution to this apparent dilemma: judges, they say, hide their true feelings but act upon them when it counts.[22] The notion of a veiled personality, one objectified by the robe, invites skepticism, suspicion, or outright disbelief, and there are deeply rooted theoretical premises in American culture to support all three attitudes. In a political system based on checks and balances, why should anyone expect judges to police themselves in a unique act of self-control? Yet the system expects just this kind of inner discipline. "Judicial restraint" assumes that judges will define the limits of their power strictly and independently of all pressures placed upon them. Thus, and without being contradicted, Justice John Paul Stevens could answer a recent dispute on the subject by claiming that his sense of duty had overcome even the strongest personal views that he held of the law.[23]

Searches for the hidden human factor in a judge can reach ludicrous proportions. A leading article on Justice David Souter as a "surprising" figure on a divided Supreme Court tried to penetrate the private reserves of the man by devoting whole paragraphs to the question of whether or not Justice Souter eats his apples whole, core and all, the aim being to distinguish rash from restrained behavior in a very quiet life. When in 1996 Federal District Judge Harold Baer Jr. threw a major drug case out of his courtroom in lower Manhattan on the grounds of an unreasonable police search, the *New York Times* began its article on the controversy by examining the dozen or so stuffed bears in Judge Baer's chambers. Was their near namesake and owner fierce or merely cuddly?[24] Accounts of a controversial judge rarely deviate from this established pattern: the mystery of restraint implies a concealed personality that can be revealed through individual idiosyncrasies that have nothing at all to do with the process of decision making.

The desire to know more about judges is a reasonable impulse. In an

age of sentimental exposure, judges lead comparatively reclusive lives to
honor the restraint expected of them in their official capacities. By the
same token, obsession with the veiled personality diverts attention from
an underlying truth that is more elemental than personality. Judges do
not always decide, but they always sentence. They alone *punish*, and in
imposing sentences, they possess one more element of power: discretion.
Without discretion or prudence, one of the four cardinal virtues from
antiquity, a judge would no longer be a judge but a rubber stamp. Judicial
discretion is the corollary to judicial restraint. We hear so much about
restraint because it guards discretion.

No other figure possesses this kind of control, and the basis is again so
elemental as to be overlooked. When the law punishes an individual who
has been found guilty of a crime, we require flexibility, however small, in
the determination. We ask that everything be taken into account when
judgment is made. The legal adage for this desire—"justice should be
tempered by mercy"[25]—contains a paradox. To temper means to harden,
strengthen, or toughen through the refining process of heat. Mitigating *and* aggravating factors enter into the consideration, and the person
who brings both to bear is the presiding judge. No other trial performer
is equipped to think for everyone. No other possesses the comparative
frame of reference on which mercy must be based. No other can hope
to gauge the ultimate merit of conflicting arguments over the question
that a court must ask and then quantify. Guilty or not guilty? That is the
question, but punishment goes further; it is about *how* guilty.

If the need for discretion is quickly arrived at and easily assigned to
the judicial figure, the exercise of mercy that follows therefrom is more
mysterious. When a federal judge warns that "if you control what you
personally feel, then there's not much room for mercy," we are left with
several questions. What is the role of personal feeling in mercy? "We are
meant to squirm when issues of life and liberty are at stake," writes another well-known judge, but does this discomfort apply on an intellectual
or an emotional level?[26]

When should judicial prerogative deviate from a normal sentence?
How are presumably consistent judges to explain the variation that mercy
allows them? At bottom, what Americans seem to fear most in their
judges is the presence of mercy coded as leniency. A notable and at times
unpleasant characteristic of American thought lies in its fixation with retribution. When questioned in the abstract, most Americans prefer severe

punishment after a conviction rather than leniency. "Soft on crime" is a charge that no public official wants to hear, and it is one that has made for much longer prison sentences than elsewhere in the Western world. The incarceration rate in American prisons is seven and a half times the rates in France, Italy, and Germany, and eighteen times the rate in Japan. Sentences also tend to be longer in the belief that "soft on crime" increases crime rates. No other society hands out as many life sentences as the United States of America.[27]

The current battleground over judicial power has revolved around mandatory sentencing guidelines. Judges of every persuasion, from very conservative to liberal, have fought this new limitation on their discretionary power because it "has taken the judging out of judging and replaced it with an oppressively mechanistic regime, one with the abstruseness of the Internal Revenue Code and overtones of Franz Kafka, George Orwell, and Rube Goldberg." Jose Cabranes, a leading federal appeals judge, has outlined the contradiction in the limitation: "The basic premise of the guidelines—that the human element should be wiped away from the sentencing process and replaced by the clean, sharp edges of a sentencing slide rule—is itself highly questionable."[28]

Early in 2005 the Supreme Court, in a divided opinion that showed how vexed the issue of mandatory sentencing has become, implicitly threw the issue back to Congress by making legislatively mandated guidelines merely advisory. Rote punishment puts pressure on the system that it cannot bear. Associate Justice Stephen Breyer, in noting the great variety in crime and explaining why certain guidelines had to be advisory, protected "judicial efforts to determine, and to base punishment upon the *real conduct* that underlies the crime of conviction."[29] An automatic sentence implies lack of respect for both circumstance and investigation, important reasons for holding a public trial in the first place.

This controversy, like so many others, flows from a general failure in understanding. Opponents of judicial discretion assume that mercy in sentencing injects arbitrary or unpredictable ingredients into the legal process. Mercy, in this hypothesis, draws upon Christian understandings of the term: "forbearance and compassion shown by one person to another who is in his power and *who has no claim to receive kindness*," a definition in keeping with the belief that God forgives a sinner even though the sinner has no right to such a reward. There is, however, an older, less arbitrary conception, and it is the one that a knowing judge should employ in the moment of sentencing. The Latin term for mercy, still used in French, is *misericordia*. The term signifies *heartfeltness* for actual misery and situation as part of an innate human sympathy for wretchedness where it is found.[30] Here, at the very center of the controversy, is the mystery and least understood aspect of judicial performance.

The pursuit of happiness may be an inalienable right, but it leaves many individuals by the wayside, and when their unhappiness becomes unbearable, they often end up in court. Every trial is about an unhappiness that someone has been unable to stand, and every courtroom decision contains a mountain of misery for someone, either the victim or the defendant or the losing side; sometimes all three. The listening judge performs a poignant service in this regard—a service that becomes difficult to meet over time, or rather difficult to meet time after time. In the final moment of sentencing, the judge must encompass the collective misery brought into a courtroom and then, against all odds, find a way to articulate its meaning in a useful way for the participants and the culture at large.

Although the mercy of heartfeltness belongs to everyone, its official reach depends on the capacity to deliver a sentence that is true to facts while remaining recognizably fair to all. The immediate facts of the case have just been in dispute at trial. The judge's sentence responds to them and clarifies the significance and priority to be assigned to them. In this moment, the composure and ascendancy of the presiding judge makes sense of the whole process. No judge can afford to be overcome by the torment revealed in a courtroom, and yet every judge must convey some knowledge of that torment to embody communal satisfaction over the sentence delivered.

A sentence with the proper amount of punishment is no easy calculation to make. To prove the point, a federal district judge recently asked his community to quantify in real-life terms a "short" sentence of seventy-eight months. "Imagine," he wrote, "being sent away from your family when your daughter was eleven, and returning on her eighteenth birthday."[31] When a sentence is pronounced, we listen because the speaker who addresses the convicted defendant and still horrified victims has digested the trouble not only in this case but in others like it. We expect to be informed and relieved by the words that are offered. Distress, suffering, dysfunction, and loss must give way to a clarification that contains protest, censure, reason, knowledge, clarity, compassion, and forbearance. The judge at this moment—no matter how aloof or detached—is the "human factor" in the system. We cannot do without the personal authority of this speaker and the discretion that makes it possible.

THE PROSECUTOR

If judges direct the courtroom, prosecutors exercise most control over the legal system. They are the power brokers in criminal justice, and power in a situation of conflict means success. Ninety percent of all convictions come through a guilty plea gained by the prosecution's use of plea-bargaining agreements. When the decision is to press felony charges, the conviction rate is over 95 percent by plea bargain or verdict. Of all defendants that go to trial in criminal court, 75 percent are convicted. A limited number of those who appeal, fewer than 10 percent in most courts, have convictions reversed, and most are reconvicted at a later point in the process.[32]

Defendants come into criminal court on the state's terms. Prosecutors decide whether to prosecute, whom to prosecute at which level, and what charges to stress in shaping the case. High conviction rates also mean that a decision *not* to prosecute (in exchange for cooperation in another case or for policy reasons) gives a prosecutor enormous leverage over the rest of the system. In New York City, 40 percent of the cases typically disposed of in criminal courts end in a dismissal orchestrated by the prosecution.

The numbers are important because they provide definition. Prosecutors are measured to an alarming degree by their success rate. Convictions must be high to meet professional and communal expectations, and while the legitimacy and prestige of the state are on the line in court, the expectation of success gives credibility to the accusations it brings. As the voice of the people, an identity frequently claimed, prosecutors enjoy unusual freedom in court. They receive leeway in presenting their cases, and, unlike defense counsel, they are almost never found in contempt of court if they step over the line. A prosecutor who stretches the limits of a court's patience will be given every benefit of the doubt, and there is a hidden explanation for such indulgence.[33] If courts tend to be flexible during the accusations at trial, it may be because many of them are run by judges who are themselves former prosecutors with the same training and mentality in presenting a case and thinking about crime.[34]

Justice Souter, a former prosecutor himself but speaking for a majority of the Supreme Court in 1997, epitomizes the helping hand that a prosecutor can expect to receive in court. In *Old Chief v. United States*, Souter grants special latitude to a prosecutorial charge that "not only satisfies the formal definition of an offense, but tells a colorful story with descriptive richness." "The persuasive power" allowed the state extends beyond an objective presentation of evidence. A prosecutor is free "as much to tell a story of guiltiness as to support an inference of guilt, to convince the jurors that a guilty verdict would be morally reasonable as much as to point to the discrete elements of a defendant's legal fault."[35] This is latitude indeed, and with it comes the advantage of superior resources and what rhetoricians call the principle of primacy. Prosecutors get to go first at trial, a significant benefit. Eighty percent of jury verdicts follow the impression formed during opening statements.[36]

These empowerments confirm a classic observation from 1940 by Robert H. Jackson, then attorney general of the United States and soon to be associate justice of the Supreme Court. Jackson warned that "the prosecutor has more control over life, liberty, and reputation than any other person in America," and the negative possibilities led him to add a dramatic admonition. "While the prosecutor at his best is one of the most beneficent forces in our society, when he acts from malice or other base motives, he is one of the worst." Jackson realized that the worst as well as the best could thrive in the system and that prosecutorial discretion was as "tremendous" as any given to a judge and in need of a comparable restraint in basic functions.[37] Although one rarely sees the connection made, the warnings against activism so often voiced against judges apply with greater force to prosecutors.

Discretion is a loose variable where prosecutors are concerned. While judges act individually, they must justify their decisions in public and often in writing. There is no such opportunity for review of a prosecutor in preliminary negotiations, team-oriented investigations, plea-bargaining arrangements, and venue shopping. Oversight is especially lacking early in the legal process when many of the important decisions are made. Even the fairest-minded district attorneys must also cope with a special temptation: the demand that high conviction rates must be met. District attorneys cannot afford to lose often, and studies show that the pressure to win grows with time in their offices. A "conviction psychology" motivates many decisions in the experienced prosecutor.[38]

Robert Jackson chose to acknowledge these temptations when he emphasized the need for voluntary restraint. Prosecutors, he insisted, must do more than convict criminals or protect the innocent. As accusers, they had higher duties to perform in maintaining "the spirit as well as the letter of our civil liberties" and "sensitiveness to fair play." Prosecutors had to commit themselves to "truth and not victims," "the law and not factional purposes." Similar to judges, they were supposed to operate somewhere above the proceedings as well as in them, but how far above? Jackson set the bar high. "Although the government technically loses its case," he claimed, "it has really won if justice has been done."[39]

Jackson's aspirations demand a great deal of prosecutors; perhaps too much. An objective "arbiter of truth and justice," a prosecutor must nonetheless drop down and be a vigorous "advocate in a dialectic system." But when, in the tension between roles, does the hardworking prosecutor rely *less* rather than *more* on the dialectic of the system to decide a case? How delicate must the balance between high-minded official and embroiled advocate be in the quest for a high conviction rate? Self-restraint appears as the prosecutor's operative control because there is so much room for "freedom of choice." A prosecutor must "temper zeal with integrity" and remember the "upright presence in his mantle of office." Important in themselves, such phrases are also the whistles of the legal profession as it skips past the darkest graveyard in its neighborhood. The prescribed limits on prosecutors are more declaratory in tone than supervisory in nature, and they are easily ignored.[40]

It is also true that prosecutors have never been more dominant in the legal process than they are today and that expansions in their role have come at the expense of safeguards previously enjoyed by defendants. More authority and statutory control have created unprecedented levels of influence and intervention both before and during the formal legal process. "Over the past thirty-five years, police and prosecutors have become far more powerful agents in choosing whom to arrest, whom to criminally charge and with what offenses, and what sentencing ranges will bind the judge's sentencing process after a conviction."[41] One upshot has been a dramatic increase in the percentage of guilty pleas in federal courts, up from 62 percent in the 1970s to 85 percent of all defendants in 2001. "Most sentencing rests in the prosecutor's hands," explains one district judge of the current situation, "and it is seldom that the defendant wants to take a risk on sentencing [at trial]."[42]

If the public remains unaware of the prosecutor as very large over-dog, it is because a trial that attracts communal attention changes the dynamic at work in startling ways. Just as a judge in a high-profile case experiences an added sense of restriction through public surveillance, so prosecutors encounter more questions as well as better, more aggressive defense counsel and a more uncertain result. When these things happen, the stakes go up for all concerned, but they go up most for the prosecution. The state is expected to win when it forces an issue into court, and the public gaze in a high-profile trial increases the pressure on an office that must answer at some point to the people.

Psychological burdens also fall on the prosecution when publicity is an issue. Aroused communal sympathy may lie with a defendant through special qualities or celebrity status. From Jonathan Wild, a notorious criminal in the eighteenth century, to John Gotti, "the Teflon Don" of modern gangster fame, human nature reserves a measure of admiration for the exotic person who escapes the law; it heaps a corresponding degree of ridicule on the officials who have allowed the imputed criminal to get away.[43]

If instead a trial is sensational through heinous events or a loathsome defendant, the prosecution faces a different problem. People at trial who agree on everything else often disagree violently over the terms of judgment. The nature of punishment can embarrass a prosecutor almost as much as failure to punish at all. Consider, for example, the public outrage in 2003 when a prosecuting attorney in Seattle announced a "plea deal" sparing the life of Gary L. Ridgway, the Green River murderer who admitted strangling forty-eight women, a total that made him "the deadliest convicted serial killer in the nation's history."[44]

Although a district attorney's office represents one of the most honorable services in the legal profession, a high-profile trial awakens atavistic instincts against the exercise of its power. There is no more potent symbol of authority than the government in the act of accusation, and distrust of that authority in contemporary society approaches a reflex reaction. Criticisms of the accusing arm of the state may include everything from the charges made, to the strategies employed, to the motives behind each move, to the nature of the law itself.[45] If doubt relapses into suspicion, it may be because of expanding claims of secrecy in government generally and because open court supplies an increasingly rare opportunity to test the state's policies in criminal justice. The number of federal criminal prosecutions resolved by trial dropped to less than 5 percent in 2002, down from 15 percent in 1962, and there have been comparable trends in state courts.[46]

People regard the people's lawyer, *their* lawyer, with an intensity that is unfair but understandable. The invisible elements of the criminal justice system (plea bargaining, negotiation, dismissal, and settlement—all driven by an increasingly draconian sentencing structure) make vigilance in a public trial important as a check on all prosecutorial tactics. The result is an instability in how Americans regard their own enforcement mechanisms. Most citizens expect serious punishment as a result of an indictment, but many rightly worry about the means to that end. The hidden factors in the punishment of most offenders in an overburdened system are legitimate causes of concern. "Every thing secret degenerates, even the administration of justice," wrote Lord Acton; "nothing is safe that does not show how it can bear discussion and publicity."[47]

COUNSEL FOR THE DEFENSE

Defense attorneys are the designated losers in criminal justice. Private counsel as well as public defenders regularly admit the guilt of their clients in exchange for shorter sentences through preliminary negotiations. "A lawyer's function," explains an attorney steeped in plea bargaining, "is simply to minimize the painful consequences of criminal proceedings for his client." A defendant who loses at trial draws a much stiffer sentence than an accused client who pleads guilty, and lawyers who take their clients to trial know they will lose at least 75 percent of the time. As claimed, the calculation is a simple one. Going to trial exercises a constitutional right, but it gambles against heavy odds with years of a client's life.[48] Meanwhile, a decision to minimize pain never translates into *absence* of pain. Convicted clients rarely appreciate a reduced sentence engineered by an attorney who works as "a double agent" in cooperation with the prosecution and the court.[49]

Much of the negativity about lawyers comes from contradictions in the role that defense counsel play. Lawyers protect rights, but they live by manipulating the financial possibilities in the process. The private defense lawyer is a hired gun making money off of someone's misery. The available alternative is an overworked but free public defender in a system where you generally get what you pay for.[50] In moments of candor, defense counsel admit that their clients are guilty of something. They fight back furtively with delay, obstruction, obfuscation, avoidance, and forum shopping. When pushed, they seek relief by convincing a client to exchange information for a lighter sentence or dismissal, an exchange that can materialize only when the information offered will help prosecute another person connected to the client. No matter how you slice these dealings, there is unpleasantness all around.[51]

The public deplores plea-bargaining tactics and responds by questioning the presumption of innocence as a premise of the system. "Try as we might," writes a critic, "we really have a great deal of trouble accepting that those who are accused might not be guilty." When taken to this level, suspicion of the accused recasts the understanding of a trial. The right of "innocent until proven guilty" is seen as a tool for extracting criminals from crimes committed, and the lawyers who wield the tool become facilitators who are "soft on crime" and manipulate the system for their own gain.[52] By defending a "guilty" client in a cynical battle of wits instead of admitting the truth, they sink in the popular imagination. "Our relatively low regard for truth-seeking is perhaps the chief reason for the dubious esteem in which the legal profession is held," Marvin E. Frankel, U.S. District Judge for the Southern District of New York, explains. Angered by these slights, defense attorneys counter with a standard jibe: resentment evaporates the moment "someone near and dear to them is arrested."[53]

Tarred with the same brush, prominent defense attorneys enjoy a radically different image. For the celebrity attorney, the so-called "megalawyer," the admission that "almost all criminal defendants are, in fact, guilty" becomes a boast of prowess, and the willingness to brag about it underlines a major difference. Prominent attorneys become that way by winning against the odds and by trumpeting their success. They are sought by the press and the public for their ability to mix legal victory with lucrative enterprise. Their stardom in court overshadows any disparagement about personal gain, and their desire to win at all costs turns a trial into a high-stakes "game" geared to communal entertainment.[54]

Rhetorical self-promotion separates big-name trial lawyers from their run-of-the-mill counterparts. In the words of Thomas Puccio, "the quintessential combative New York lawyer" who won acquittal for Claus von Bulow (the socialite accused of trying to murder his wife), "You hire Tom Puccio and Tom Puccio wants to win for you and Tom Puccio wants to win for himself," and this same Tom Puccio will use "every possible legal angle that can be exploited." Combative to the nth degree, "megalawyers" talk about their work as "white collar warfare." They "go for the jugular" and command the resources and ability that can level the table or tilt it toward them in a high-profile case.[55]

The valuable thing that money can buy for a defendant who faces a serious charge is quality time in a court; those without it have almost no chance to reverse the momentum of accusation.[56] For the client who can reach this stage with top counsel, the situation changes, often dramatically. A good defense lawyer can manipulate the facts in a way that the prosecution cannot, and freedom to exploit the possibility of doubt grows with the gravity of the offense. Very few judges will curb the strategies of defense counsel when punishment might be extreme. "I don't really have to get into fine distinctions of guilt or innocence," explains an attorney who deals with such cases. "Most of it is gray." Resisting black-and-white in the name of the gray area in between creates the reasonable doubt that the defense needs. The harvest in uncertainty comes when attorneys "isolate the key facts that provide the foundation for the state's case" and "wreak havoc" with them.[57]

The unique imaginative range given to defense counsel is a major weapon and a catalyst in the creation of high-profile trials. Megalawyers for the accused turn into divas with arias against the indictment, while prosecutors are forced to plod in the lower registers of melody and rhythm in mundane proof of it. They seek and often gain publicity for themselves and their clients in the knowledge that entertainment attracts media coverage.[58] What obligation does a lawyer have to control building excitement between courtroom and community? None, according to experts: it is "totally cricket" to use "hardball tactics" and "play to the court of public opinion." Ironically, prosecutors use the same conceit in complaint: high-profile trials, they protest, leave the state "playing cricket in an alley fight."[59]

The defense wields four basic modes of argument: refutation, alternative explanation, suppression (either by objection or by a stipulation that eliminates or minimizes evidence or testimony thought to be prejudicial), and finally, when all else fails, pleas for mercy.[60] The defiant tones that these modes of presentation require can be seen even in appeals for clemency. End-game requests for mercy invariably conflate legal demand with moral entreaty. The argument begins in obfuscation (the defendant

has been charged either falsely or too severely by a callous or manipulative government) before shading into qualifications of agency (the defendant is less responsible for what has happened because of the behavior
of others or an unfortunate background). These elements then bolster
the ultimate demand for leniency (the defendant's punishment does not
fit the accusation so unfeelingly pressed upon a misunderstood and now
forlorn and penitent figure).

It takes courage, bumptiousness, and a degree of insolence to defend
an unpopular cause. "In representing criminal defendants—especially
guilty ones," explains leading defense lawyer Alan Dershowitz, "it is often necessary to take the offensive against the government: to put the
government on trial for *its* misconduct." "Overzealousness," all-out confrontation, motivates the megalawyer. By taking vilification to the limits
of what the court will allow, defense counsel turn themselves into attack
dogs against the system. They act with their client exclusively in mind,
and they ignore the conventional "models of integrity" set before them.
In Dershowitz's view, "It is the job of the defense attorney—especially
when representing the guilty—to prevent, by all lawful means, the 'whole
truth' from coming out." Nor do the relevant codes of professional conduct apply with exactitude. "The question of how far a defense attorney
can go in challenging the government without going over the undefined
edge [of professional conduct] is still very much unresolved."[61]

Claims of this sort must be understood in a certain way. Defense
lawyers who would challenge the system need more than the system to
win. They must argue as aggressively as possible and out of a resource-
fulness that will answer the law from a separate platform of merit and
assurance. The challenge has to be antagonistic to have even a chance
of succeeding. A flaw in common human behavior, self-righteousness, is
the calling card of defense counsel, and no one else in court gets to show
it half as often. Where does the audacity to stand so loudly against come
from? Courage is the fourth of the cardinal virtues from antiquity—
the first three being justice, moderation, and wisdom—but the ancients
knew that the others didn't matter without courage to drive them.

Real courage cannot be taught, and it is rarely even discussed in law
school, but prominent defense counsel refer to it all of the time in celebrations of their cases. There is no patented way to develop courage; it is
the virtue that must be experienced to be learned. The ability to oppose
in a constructive way, to argue against the grain, to represent an unpop-

ular position, to say "no" when all around are arguing for "yes"—this kind of fortitude is rare in any setting. Defense counsel admittedly have the principles of free government and the code of professional conduct to protect them when they mount their challenges, but something more intrinsic to the person is required for success.

A signal component in leading defense attorneys involves their assumed prowess in combat. Metaphors of battle figure heavily in self-portraits. They are rebels *with* a cause, and they relish a fight. Figures such as Clarence Darrow, Joe Jamail, Dershowitz, and Michael Tigar celebrate their ability to defy the system. F. Lee Bailey speaks for them all when he says, "Our system requires that mavericks stand for the defense."[62] But while this image of heroic defiance taps into an attractive strain of American individualism, it also raises a sobering truth. Defense counsel who win regularly are rare, and their actions, whether just or unjust, are based on marked differences in behavior from the rest of their profession. Do successful defense lawyers break down the system to beat it unfairly, or is the system itself so unfair as to require such action? There are no good answers to these questions, and recognition of the ambiguity breeds public distaste for all lawyers.

THE WITNESS

A witness who speaks a vital truth in court with sincerity can determine a trial outcome single-handedly, but this degree of influence depends on the qualifications just noted. The truth, its relevance, its delivery, the perception of it, and the worth of its impact are all variables in search of coherence. When these elements do harmonize, the witness is such an overwhelming force that the law distrusts the claim of coherence at every step of the way. Witnesses, and only witnesses, endure elaborate ceremonies of warning and reservation as they perform in court. Only they swear in court to tell the truth and find themselves minutely challenged over what they have sworn, and the challenge has a stick behind it. Witnesses face imprisonment for perjury if they can be shown to have sworn falsely.

Truth telling is not the witness's only hurdle. Even witnesses known to be telling the truth can expect to have their veracity, their character, their intelligence, their consistency, and their motives impugned during cross-examination.[63] There is no other form of public statement that compares in difficulty, frustration, and potential humiliation to testimony in court. No matter how well prepared or how carefully coached beforehand, a person who takes the stand is terribly alone in front of others.

Speaking only in direct reply and under intense scrutiny, the witness must answer without protest or qualification or prevarication while enduring questions that mislead, misconstrue, undercut, bully, dismiss, and attack everything that has been said. Witnessing represents "a radically unique, non-interchangeable and solitary burden." Unpleasantness is its certainty; emotional devastation, a distinct possibility. The tension at trial between truth seeking and partisanship comes perilously close to an absolute contradiction when a witness undergoes cross-examination.[64]

Many of the constraints on witnesses have been with us since antiquity. The Greek word for oath, *horkos*, meant to enclose, or confine, literally to be fenced in, and the original fencing came from above. Truth told in court was protected and enforced by divine will. Francis Bacon justified placing "Of Truth" first in *The Essays or Counsels, Civil and Moral* by claiming that "a lie faces God, and shrinks from man." The prayerful incantation required of the witness at English common law is very similar: "I will present the truth, the whole truth, and nothing but the truth to the best of my skill and understanding, so help me God." This oath was a plea for providential assistance—literally, Help me, God!—in the presence of a guide to universal truth. Delivered before God as well as the law, it also signified divine punishment, quite possibly through all eternity, if the witness lied in court. The practice of kissing the Bible while taking the oath was not abolished in England until the twentieth century.[65]

Definitions of truth have changed for the modern witness. In the nineteenth century, a leading lawyer could still convince an American jury through the unseen world. "Murder will out!" thundered Daniel Webster in imitation of Shakespeare. Webster warned that Providence "glances through all disguises." God had so made the world that "secrets of guilt are never safe from detection, even from men." Today belief in the control of a higher truth figures less or not at all in litigation. A more contextual truth applies to contemporary human practice, and "the whole truth" in the oath has lost some of its significance.[66] If the solemnity of the oath remains, the makeup of truth has changed and with it a witness's role.

Postmodernity assumes that truth will be hard to find, that many will ignore or reject it once found, that it can be permanently lost, that it

must be fought for every step of the way, and that identification of it requires tactical measures. *Sincerity* and *accuracy* are its touchstones, with
emphasis placed on the variables in presentation.[67] Lawyers therefore
assume that a witness can be sincere but inaccurate, accurate without
appearing sincere, insincere while remaining accurate, knowledgeable
without being able to convey either, or, worst of all, clever enough to
fabricate sincerity and authenticity without fear of a serious penalty. The
idea of a preestablished harmony between truth telling and well-being
has lapsed, allowing greater flexibility and comfort in a witness who ignores the truth or deceives altogether.

The requirement that one "cling everlastingly to the truth" is now, especially in law, "an instruction to question every assertion that purports
to be '*the* truth.'" Truth has become "value-truth (which is always a basic
lie)," and it has been recast into subdivisions of "factual truth, higher (or
'legal') truth, and symbolic truth."[68] Contemporary scholars and writers
even claim falsehood as a special value. Aspects of philosophy, psychology, and art equate the capacity to lie with sophistication and successful
adulthood—tendencies with pernicious implications for truth telling in
court.[69] Few witnesses are punished today for perjury, even though experts assume that witnesses lie or actively mistake the truth. "Everybody,"
observes a leading authority on cross-examination, "is willing to lie for
some reason that to them is sufficiently grave."[70]

The law answers by underlining *sincerity* with the oath and challenging *accuracy* through stringent investigations that question the truth
in a witness on both levels. Predictably, the impact in court has been
increased rancor in cross-examinations and a nasty time for most witnesses. As one analyst describes the inquisitorial side of this relationship,
"The most decisive weapons of the cross examiner are: repetition of question, ridicule of the witness, and the tactical maneuvering of a witness
so as to ensnare him in an admission favorable to the cross-examiner's
client." Or, from a manual for lawyers, "battering and legal-style 'kicking
the witness around' not only humiliates but subdues him."[71]

Witnesses testify in two basic categories: those who have something
to say from what they have seen or learned by participation (occurrence
witnesses), and those who provide outside information and opinions on
what has taken place (expert witnesses). Each type faces special difficulties. Occurrence witnesses are often upset or angered or embarrassed by
the firsthand knowledge that brings them into court, where they must

relive a disagreeable experience. Examination on the stand opens old wounds. At the very least it re-creates "not just what the witness saw, heard, and did, but also the atmosphere and intensity of feelings that existed during the event."[72]

Simple recall is also a problem for the occurrence witness. Most witnesses with firsthand knowledge will be reluctant or unable to describe some part of the problem before the court, and the examination itself will disrupt the previous basis of that knowledge by requiring the witness to cope with a foreign mode of explanation. For whatever a witness originally knows about what happened, it will not be couched in legal understanding.

At issue are two elements in conflict: first, clarity in describing events geared to court determination; and, second, the credibility or spontaneity of the describer, who must explain those events in a way artificial to actual memory. Without clarity, credibility, and some spontaneity, the witness is worthless, but neither clarity nor credibility can be accomplished without prearrangement, and prearrangement comes at the cost of spontaneity. Only in movies does the attorney ask a witness to describe matters "in your own words." The overall result is an oddly stilted colloquy on the stand—the prescribed question-and-answer format of counsel leading the witness. These factors join in a larger goal. The sincerity of experience in the witness must overcome the artificiality in legal exchange.

The expert witness presents a different story. Occurrence witnesses are forced through legal subpoena to testify in public about upsetting personal or controversial experiences. The detached expert tries instead to dazzle the courtroom with special knowledge garnered away from the problem at hand. Experts testify voluntarily and for pay, and although the other professional performers in court receive money to be present, criticism falls on experts for "prostituting" their knowledge to satisfy one litigant or another as a customer.[73] The intensity and frequency of these vilifications are a puzzle in advocacy. Why, in a system already driven by money, is the expert singled out as an acquisitive hireling? Admittedly, no one would expect an occasional witness to be paid for telling the truth, but the accusations of venality against experts reflect a deeper hostility, and it is growing.

Experts are expensive, add-on components. Not everyone can afford them. Unlike an occurrence witness, experts have no direct knowledge of *there*; they bring an imputed wisdom to bear from *elsewhere* with an *opinion* based on extraneous data or training, a facet of thought alien to other aspects of the legal process. Expert testimony as knowledgeable opinion is much more difficult for opposing counsel to answer, and its influence is further increased by offers of immunity from the penalty of perjury over false or misleading testimony—an immunity that removes the main sanction for keeping a witness in line. Experts thus become unusually powerful and flexible instruments of persuasion in court. Lawyers seek them, fear them, and attack them with abnormally aggressive tactics. "A good expert presentation," they realize, "is like an extra summation [of the case]."[74]

Acrimony over the role of the expert witness also mirrors changing expectations about knowledge itself. The rise of the expert in contemporary life is displacing common sense in many forms of thought, including legal thought.[75] Nevertheless, courts have to assume that a general understanding will suffice at trial to reach and support a jury decision. The ensuing tensions between commonsensical and expert levels of discourse breed resentments on all sides. The legal process allows increasing kinds of expertise into its deliberations, but it stubbornly clings to common truths; it also resists any acknowledgment that its own procedural bridge from argument in advocacy to truth in judgment might fail when cluttered with special know-how and technical testimony.

Adversarial tendencies further complicate the issue. An expert's perspective, presumably formed along more objective or technological or scientific lines, is not inherently partisan, yet it is used that way at trial, and it has a tremendous advantage when presented with a credible sincerity that prevents common understandings from testing its merits. "The true role of the expert witness is to offer the court the best assistance he can by getting at the *truth*," notes one aggravated judge.[76] But whose truth and at what level of control? How should the special credentials or authenticity supporting expert truth be regarded? When should deference be paid and to what kind of expertise?

The problems in answering these questions explain much of the animosity in litigation today. An increase in the number and kinds of expert witnessing has produced parallel intensities in the frequency, significance, and antagonism of cross-examinations. Just as an expert's certainty is hard to challenge on the merits, so lawyers respond by attacking in more brutal and circuitous ways. Tactics include deliberately confusing experts on the stand, impugning their reputations unfairly, and denigrating expertise as either foolishly irrelevant or easily contested at the level of common sense.

Litigators are rarely at a loss, and they control the questions. They know how to create vulnerabilities, turning strengths into seeming weaknesses. Arrogance is presumed to be "the expert's disease," and a good lawyer can make it appear even when it is not present. "Spouting off the biography from memory or from notes makes almost any expert look arrogant," writes one litigator. The lawyer who unearths or manufactures pomposity in an expert witness empowers a resentful jury to disregard that testimony.[77]

The differences in the two categories of witnessing, occasional and expert, raise a more general social issue. Pitfalls in the occasional witness flow from ignorance or incoherence. Failings in the expert are the reverse, coming most often out of false erudition and arcane explanation. These same stumbling blocks vex public discourse in contemporary culture. The limited awareness and inarticulateness of the one and the overconfidence and prolixity of the other reflect troubling patterns in both courtroom and community. The endless loquacity, opaque technicalities, and intrusions of the expert up against the uncertain thought, inarticulateness, and resentments of the common citizen may be robbing each of the wisdom that might otherwise be found in the combinations of both.

THE JURY

Nowhere are the contrasting stereotypes of the legal process more seriously debated than over the American jury. Juries provide the most potent symbol of self-rule ever invented and represent the high-water mark of democratic understanding and republican principle. On the other hand, and at almost every stage of its existence, the institution has been found wanting or suspect in practical application. Disturbing examples of poor decisions made by juries can be found in every era, and systematic research into the workings of the modern jury system have exposed alarming instances of delay, inconsistency, misunderstanding, and outright nullification of the law.[78]

The legal stipulation that a jury of twelve previously uninvolved and arbitrarily selected citizens ought to be able to decide the fate of a defendant in court depends on many ideals. It implies that the ultimate authority in government belongs to ordinary people, that common sense can decide even complex matters, that a diverse group of decision makers will be wiser than any one individual, that decisions about liberty should be made as democratically as possible, that jury deliberation gives justice a human face, and that a decision reached in this manner protects the culture from special interests while legitimating state authority in its need to punish unacceptable deviance effectively.

Much of the original idealism for what is now quintessentially an American institution came from an Englishman and a Frenchman. William Blackstone made trial by jury "the grand bulwark" of eighteenth-century common law, the primary means of righting communal wrongs, and a fundamental source of national definition. Liberty in England was secure "so long as this *palladium* remains sacred and inviolate." Visiting the United States in 1831, Alexis de Tocqueville praised the American version in similar terms. The country's jury system insured "the sovereignty of the people." It invested "each citizen with a kind of magistracy." It was "a gratuitous public school, ever open." Tocqueville concluded that "the practical intelligence and good political sense of the Americans" could be traced to their regular involvement in the enterprise of jury service.[79]

Modern critics tell a different story. "No attorney ever thinks a jury will be objective," they argue. Instead, "all jurors are predisposed to certain choices that have nothing to do with the evidence in the case"; panels typically contain "a cross section of global-village idiots"; the average juror is "Rip Van Winkle, someone who has been snoozing in the hills for the past twenty years." Judges as well as lawyers protest in this vein. "Erratic and irrational jury behavior makes verdicts a crapshoot," complains a respected member of the New York bench based on twenty-five years of experience.[80]

More analytical accounts support these criticisms. American Bar Association studies have shown that many jurors "are stymied by the least bit of complexity" and "succumb all too easily to emotional appeals."[81] Juries "decide cases according to emotion, prejudice, and sympathy"; cases are being won and lost not on the law or the facts but "on the basis of who the jurors are"; "justice depends on the race, gender, religion, or even national origin of jurors." "Ideal jurors," warns a judge, "are uncommon."[82]

Yet the institution continues to thrive, "attracting at once the most extravagant praise and the most harsh criticism." It thrives because the ideal remains central to national belief, because it is constitutionally guaranteed, and because from its inception it has been "an exciting experiment in the conduct of serious human affairs."[83] More than 160,000 jury trials take place in the United States every year, and no amount of criticism will change that arrangement, even though the American system is now a fairly isolated phenomenon, with 80 percent of all jury trials taking place in the United States. Most countries have dropped the institution, if they ever had it. Even England, the creator of the jury system, has deserted the use of it in most cases.[84] In short, both the ambivalence regarding it and the singularity of dependence on it make the jury a source of sharp encounter in the American system.

Some of the controversy regarding juries has to do with radical changes in the institution over time. The precursors to juries in the emerging common law tradition in England took the form of neighbors who were summoned to answer questions and swear an oath from their own knowledge. These oath takers or "compurgators," as they were called, evolved into groups that would recognize and swear to land titles, and they became "recognition panels" for deciding property disputes. Somewhere between the role of witness and juror, the first jurors brought specific knowledge to their deliberations. Only gradually did the juror develop into a trier of fact who could use that basis to resist abuses of authority at trial. Knowledgeable in communal affairs, an eighteenth-century juror in England or America brought relevant information about the dispute or the disputants into court.[85]

Modern juries proceed under a different conception. The legal process has moved "from the jury as an intimate institution of small-town justice, where members were expected to bring their own local knowledge of the facts to bear on their deliberations, to the jury as a distant institution of impartial justice, where jurors are expected to know as little as possible about the matters and persons on trial." A jury whose members held outside knowledge of a case today would risk a mistrial.[86]

The shift, a dramatic one, can be traced to the psychological insight of tabula rasa in British empiricism, the theory of the mind as a blank slate that receives everything it knows through the senses. John Locke and others argued that all knowledge comes through direct experience with accurate understanding best achieved through the *absence* of preconception. In time, this fundamental idea led American law to the belief that an individual with prior knowledge of a case could not sit objectively as a juror on it.[87] But is it possible to find a competent juror who knows nothing about events leading to a high-profile trial in an age of telecommunications and saturation coverage?

It is *not* possible, and the predicament receives less attention than it might because lawyers do not look for informed jurors in the first place. Attuned individuals get rejected during selection or find ways to take themselves out of the pool. Every study of jury selection makes these points. Lawyers, enamored of the malleable possibilities in the theory of tabula rasa, want jurors who can be molded to their arguments. They look for those who are "ill-informed about public affairs and uninterested in the topic." "Jurors may be getting dumber," reports one judge, "but it's because attorneys (especially defense attorneys) want them that way."[88]

The presumed ignorance of jurors—always the easiest stereotype to apply since jurors, by definition, are supposed to work from no special knowledge—receives greatest play in instances of jury nullification, the term used when a jury appears to run roughshod over the law. Communal and legal anger are also greatest, or reinforce each other, when a runaway jury reaches a lenient verdict. Such a jury is said to apply "reasonable doubt" more assiduously than judges require and to "hunt for doubt" in their deliberations.

Even so, most juries follow the law, agree with the judge more than 75 percent of the time, and hand in guilty verdicts more frequently than judges in bench trials. When a jury does find against the law, studies show that "it is not fundamentally defendant-prone, rather it is non-rule minded; it will move where the equities are." In consequence, and to the extent that a jury decides to differ from the law, it plays a part in "a uniquely subtle distribution of power." Not always, but at its best, the jury fulfills the goal of building discretion and flexibility into the legal system.[89]

Most anger against juries comes from a procedural impact beyond anyone's control. A jury operates as the most passive of all instruments in court until given the ultimate power of deciding a case. It has no control until the moment it assumes absolute control. Jurors listen patiently, waiting in silence for their moment to arrive. They remain collectively inscrutable and, therefore, the subject of speculation. Their companion in decision making, the judge, will often have indicated the direction a trial seems to be going through preliminary rulings and objections sustained or overruled. Not so with the jury. A jury is the mythic symbol of mystery in judgment. It remains an officially unknown quantity until its verdict, and the potential for surprise when it emerges is enormous.

Outrage over a decision naturally falls on the decision maker. As the last and suddenly visible decision maker at trial, a jury absorbs whatever animus follows from its verdict of guilty or not guilty. "Conscientious" and "incompetent" are the conventional poles of reference used to describe its completed work, and the positive stereotype is noticeably less generous than the negative alternative is critical. A jury's deliberations are the only major part of a trial that have not taken place in public, and so a restless uncertainty resides there. Even judges exclaim, "Heaven knows what the jury had in mind" or "God only knows."[90] Here, as well, is a growing source of "juror dread." The escalation in public animus and in media demands for information about jury deliberations have led to an increased reluctance to appear on juries and to requests that greater protective anonymity be given to service.[91]

At their most powerful as they are about to return to ordinary life, jurors stand both for and against the community when they speak in open court for the first and final time. They represent citizenship but apart. Lawyers, defendants, the public, and even judges hold their breath at this moment. If a jury cannot decide, everyone's time has been wasted; if it can, it holds an ephemeral authority beyond its powers of realization. Most jurors hew closely to the legal expectations assigned them.[92] Still, they do not have to obey a court's stipulations no matter how stringently a judge has instructed them.

Anxiety about juries has a lot to do with this unacknowledged level of power within the unpredictability of their decision-making moment. The defendant's fate is in the hands of twelve presumably normal people who have little or no experience in dealing with such matters. They are told that they have no authority beyond the facts, but this is not literally true. Jurors possess all of the hidden capacity they will ever need to decide on the spirit rather than the letter of the law. The question that no one likes to answer is whether or not the legal system is better off for the possibility. So here is an answer: it *is* better off. Not for nothing has the U.S. Supreme Court decided in recent years to allow juries more discretionary power when certain kinds of harsher sentences are in view.[93]

THE DEFENDANT

The criminal defendant resists definition more than any other courtroom performer. To be sure, an appropriate legal designation is easily found: the defendant is the person accused of crime by indictment in the courtroom. But much more than law is involved in the courtroom's scrutiny. Everyone present is there for one reason: to pass judgment on the behavior and reach an understanding of the person in the dock. A defendant is peculiarly helpless and splintered under this gaze. An unfortunate event has taken place. Sometime in the past something has gone badly wrong, and the defendant is accused of causing that trouble to a degree that has led to the charge of culpable and shameful responsibility.

Defendants are "threshold people" thrust betwixt and between.[94] They enter court somewhere in the undefined middle of freedom and constraint, rights and vulnerabilities, success and failure, sympathy and blame, awe and ridicule, innocence and guilt; each polarity complicates identity and the communal consideration that will be given. Why are so many individuals attracted to trials? People come *to see,* and no one who enters a courtroom ever refuses to look for the defendant. Craving for a view is about how the defendant might be "different," and it includes a boundless appetite for descriptions, character sketches, drawings, photographs, the recent phenomenon of the "perp walk" (display of the presumed "perpetrator" in handcuffs), and television coverage.

Innocent until proven guilty but on the cusp, defendants can never remain where they are. Their suspended status in court is an irritation to be dealt with. Communities in this situation demand a level of certainty about matters that individuals don't expect of each other in daily life. A free citizen holds on to inherent mysteries of personality and circumstance. These privileges, as well as many others, are lost in court, and the person accused is subject to every probing question. What has the defendant *done* to have been placed in this situation? *Why* was it done? What does it *say* about the defendant's character? What will be done *to* the defendant in response? The interrogative mode dominates in what always remains an inquiry, and it never stops at the facts in dispute as it strips the person in the dock of every privacy.

The nature of the legal accusation and the personality of the defendant will dictate the amount of curiosity and annoyance driving these questions. Is the defendant charged as a mother who has killed her own child? As a serial killer of many women? As a CEO who has cheated pensioners of their life savings? Or is the defendant simply a shoplifter or the thief of a stop sign? Excitement over the more innocuous categories just noted requires more than crime. A special person (a Hollywood actress charged with shoplifting) or a horrible consequence (fatalities as a result of the missing stop sign) can stimulate the same expansive desire for larger answers when a community has been aroused.[95] Trials are exercises in redress. Once attracted, communities want to know if conventional standards of accountability will apply or be discarded. They want to grasp the righteousness of the decision made in their midst, and to do that they feel they must know the defendant.

Defendants also represent endless ingenuity in human behavior. Deviance is an exploding variable with unique elements in its composition, and when it crosses the line into presumable crime, a court can proceed fairly only by knowing "Why?" such behavior has taken place as well as "What?" and "How?"[96] Without answers to all three questions, the legal process falls into mere derogation. It is never enough to convict just the act. The minuet of request and response in the adversarial process works toward a deeper result, and no one welcomes evasion of this lower stratum. A trial implicitly asks several larger questions of the person charged: "Who *are* you?" and "Who are *you*?" There is no greater moment of exposure in communal life, and all of this is done with a publicity and display that is its own form of humiliation. Neither the court nor the media can stop themselves in a high-profile trial. There must be "a revelation of what one is" to determine what one has done.[97]

An unfathomed defendant unleashes another level of communal anxiety. Failure to explain leaves the deviance in question unchecked and open to the fear that other nominally law-abiding citizens might break out in similar fashion. In recognition of the problem, trials "mark off the ways the guilty defendant is different from the law-abiding public audience."[98] Everyone wants to know what drove a defendant over the edge of something that all recognize. The expression "I could kill you" is frequently used and does not mean crime, but articulation of the saving distances between expression, thought, and act reminds every speaker of the progression for what it is.[99]

Lack of explanation also enlarges a transgressor, one reason the legal process tries to break down a defendant's actions into mundane terms

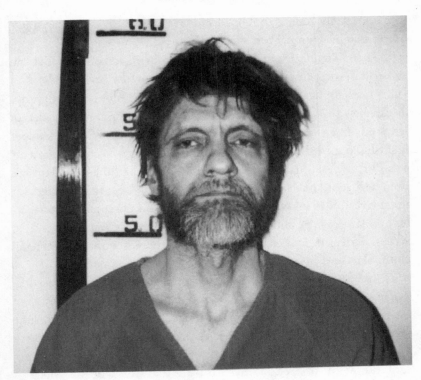

Figure 2. The Unabomber caught (1996). Photograph: AP Photo/ho (APA904419). Behavior at trial can either magnify or diminish a participant. The Unabomber of the 1980s and 1990s grew into a mythical figure as an elusive rebel delivering social protests through the newspapers while mailing bombs that killed or maimed random victims in a seventeen-year reign of terror. Brought into a California courthouse in 1997, Ted Kaczynski seemed uncertain and copped a plea to save his own life. Media would use the plea bargain to make him a coward, a reclusive fool, "a sickie," and a source of humor on late-night television.

and safe classifications. The Unabomber, who conducted a hidden seventeen-year reign of terror by sending packaged bombs through the mail in the 1980s and 1990s, took on colossal dimensions while at large as a mystery. Accounts described "an intriguing hybrid of Robin Hood, the Green Hornet, and Mick Jagger" rolled into one, but only until his day in court. Revealed instead as Theodore Kaczynski accepting a plea bargain in federal court to save his own life, he became "pathetic" rather than legendary in scope and a source of consoling humor on late-night television as "a nut" and "a coward." The explanations in court, while more measured, served the same purposes. The trivialization of Kaczynski in courtroom appearances contained and then extinguished the magnitude of fear that his criminal behavior had aroused.[100]

Stigma attaches to every defendant in court. Even an acquittal can ruin a life, especially in a high-profile case known to many people.[101] Not guilty does not signify innocence; it means that the state could not prove its case beyond a reasonable doubt. There are, of course, higher levels of ignominy in a conviction, and distinct echelons apply to the defendant in civil as opposed to criminal court. To lose in a civil action represents a misfortune that many will sympathize with even if the defendant has been negligent, foolish, or grasping. Many people fear this prospect for themselves and identify with the defendant. A fine or settlement, no matter how large, is a penalty rather than a punishment.[102] The person fined accepts a price tag in social readjustment and has lost ground in material culture but remains free to try again.

To face prison or to serve time plunges a defendant into a very different and alien territory. This is punishment, an absolute expression of communal resentment and outrage. Even to have been accused of a crime "brands" a defendant, and conviction brings disgrace. The criminal with a prison sentence takes the name of "con" or "jailbird" and will always carry the stigma of "ex-con." Experts teach that "the 'labeling' effects of conviction and sentence" are permanently harmful; something is being destroyed when a defendant is found guilty in court, and no one should forget that 75 percent of all defendants in court are indeed found guilty.[103] Stigma begins with indictment as "the situation of the individual who is disqualified from full social acceptance"; the accused begins to enter a "half-world" on the other side of normality.[104] If the court proceeds to punishment, it puts the defendant at final remove, and its demeanor in the act takes on the technical definition of "moral cruelty."[105]

The instigator of moral cruelty extracts satisfaction and sometimes outright pleasure in subjecting a recipient to loss of previous identity through deliberate and persistent humiliation. In receiving sentence, defendants are stripped of personal autonomy and of every explanation they may have made. Few observers face up to how this moment translates into diminished worth. The court tells the convicted that they are as bad as their accusers have said they have been, and that, unfit for society, they must be thrust away in glaring isolation. The verb "to convict" changes into the personal noun "convict." Prisoners endure guards who watch, correct, and confine their every moment. Equal human relations are limited to other convicts who have lost the same communal trust and who may try to drive the new inmate toward further depravity. To be under surveillance and under orders at every moment while in fear of others is the very symbol of degradation in an adult. "Prison," explains one longtime convict, "is wanting to breathe with someone's fingers up your nose."[106]

Critics argue that "we believe the person with a stigma is not quite human," and the definition is a useful one.[107] Observers in a trial contemplate a defendant from a safe but available distance. They are just close enough to glimpse the volatility of the accused without the bother of that object's subjectivity. Watching a trial is like a foxhunt with the defendant as the object of chase. The observer in this scenario never sees the accused clearly unless caught. Until then, the viewer or hunter's satisfaction comes through the flashing glimpses of an alien reality. Distance is the necessary factor in this form of pleasure because a fox up close, a fox in your own chicken coop or a criminal in your house, represents catastrophe. Still, the main aim is always to get more than a glimpse. The goal of the observer, like that of the hunter, is to see the fox a great deal during the chase or somehow to catch it.

Two things of interest can happen: the fox can escape or be killed. The fox who eludes the hunters (the defendant who is found not guilty) receives praise for its cunning in flight, and to it the observer brings the added zest of blaming others. Clumsy chasers have allowed their prey to get away![108] In the other possibility, the fox who is killed (the defendant who is convicted) suffers exposure as something less than everyone saw during the chase. All mystery has been removed. Punishment is a communal sedative, and it answers to the excitement in court in another way. The fox when caught appears a trivial thing. A varmint has been dealt with; a pest has been eradicated.[109]

If the resolution of a court case into a foxhunt seems gratuitously unpleasant, consider the reality. American prisons function only nominally as "houses of correction." The citizens who favor incarceration with stiffer sentences far outnumber those who believe in rehabilitation. Longer prison terms are really about catching the fox. They are about stereotyping crime with the pretense of eliminating it, and the satisfaction this brings. Imprisoning others is about putting our fears behind us.

THE VICTIM

Heightened concern for the role of the victim in trial performance says as much about the culture as it does about the practice of law, because in many ways it has been forced on the law by outside interests. No one disputes that "victims' rights" in official procedures are new and powerful phenomena.

Victims are now "important claimants in lawmaking and litigation, pressing for statutory provisions targeting certain crimes, greater victims' services in police departments, and prosecutors' offices, and increased victim input into charging, bargaining, prosecution, and sentencing decisions." The last twenty years have brought "*enhanced recognition at every stage of the crime response process of the rights and interests of crime victims.*" Scholars trace these developments to the presumed failure of liberal policies to cope with crime in the 1960s and to the way crime has become a major campaign issue in elections since then, but the factors that have led the nation toward an emphasis on victimization are broader and more philosophical than politics might suggest.[110]

Three legal events, two legislative and one judicial, enhanced victims' rights at the end of the twentieth century. First, Congress passed legislation that granted victims access to trial proceedings. The federal Victims' Bill of Rights in 1990 required that victims "be notified of court proceedings" with the right "to be present at all public court proceedings related to the offense, unless the court determines testimony by the victim would be materially affected if the victim heard other testimony at trial," along with the added right "to confer with [the] attorney for the Government in the case." The same statute demanded that all available government officials were to help the process along. Courts had to "make their best efforts to see that victims of the crime are accorded the rights" so conferred.[111]

Second, when Federal District Judge Richard Matsch restricted the courtroom access of victims who planned to testify in the penalty phase of the Oklahoma City bombing trial of Timothy McVeigh in 1997, Congress answered the outcry from victims by passing the Victims' Rights Clarification Act, which allowed victims of federal crimes to view the guilt phases of a trial even if they were to testify later in the sentencing phase. The emotional needs of victims outweighed the danger of partiality.

Third, victim impact statements became legal in 1991 when the Supreme Court reversed a five-to-four decision in *Booth v. Maryland* from just four years before. Speaking for the six-to-three majority in *Payne v. Tennessee*, Chief Justice William Rehnquist adjusted the adversarial equilibrium of the penalty phase in capital cases. The Court allowed statements of "the human cost of the crime" to be balanced against "relevant mitigating evidence" for the defendant. Henceforth, the chief justice declared, "a state may legitimately conclude that evidence about the victim and about the impact of the murder on the victim's family is relevant to the jury's decision as to whether or not the death penalty should be imposed."[112]

The sharp divisions on the Supreme Court in these cases, coming so close together and by narrow margins, reveal less than the trajectory of them. Justice Antonin Scalia came closest to the communal mark when he complained as a dissenter in *Booth* that "recent years have seen an outpouring of popular concern for what has come to be known as 'victims' rights.' " He then exalted with the majority in *Payne* over "a public sense of justice keen enough that it has found voice in a nationwide 'victims' rights' movement." His words would prove prophetic. Forty-nine states now have introduced victim impact statements of some kind into their official courtroom processes.[113]

Movement everywhere in American law has been toward further recognition of the victim. Both presidential candidates in 1996 urged the passage of a victims' rights amendment. The 1994 rape and murder of first-grader Megan Kanka in New Jersey and the 1993 murder of twelve-year-old Polly Klaas in California (both victims seized close by or in their homes) brought prolonged national media coverage to the plight of the surviving families. When New Jersey, lagging behind other states, finally allowed victim impact statements to be made in court in 1996, Megan's grieving mother spoke with the authority of experience and to the widest audience. "That is going to go a long way for victims' families," she announced. "It gives the victims a chance to let the jury know what life has been like and how devastating it is." She also clarified what had been previously lacking in the legal process. "Often the court system," Maureen Kanka explained, "is so impersonal."[114]

The comments of Justice Scalia and Maureen Kanka imply what some have warned against. Victims now operate as "proxies" for the general public, with the difference between observation and participation beginning to blur as categories.[115] "When someone is a victim, he or she should be at the center of the criminal justice process, not on the outside looking in," insisted President Bill Clinton while signing relevant legislation in 1997. At the center of the process? But to what end? The law protects a victim's dignity and privacy whenever possible, but therapy is not an assigned function even in a therapeutic age.[116]

To think otherwise is to adjust the meaning of impersonal and personal as values in a process dedicated to categorical decision making over individual investments. "Victim-impact evidence has no place in a rationally conducted sentencing proceeding," cautioned Chief Justice Robert Wilentz of New Jersey even as his court admitted such statements. Some victims themselves have questioned the new tendencies. Writes one, "The solemn activity of mourning has become a raucous and public blood sport. . . . [F]amily members leave the court room with high fives and fists in the air, as though sentencing someone to death were no more serious than a football game."[117]

Media sources bear heavy responsibility for the focus on victims. If thirty people emerge stone-faced from a courtroom and the thirty-first dissolves in tears, reporters cover the person who sobs before the cameras. "In the television age," explains one commentator, "anguish only seems real when broadcast over the airwaves." Media coverage invariably concentrates on the emotive element in a trial. Suffering sells, and it is easier to describe than the arid complexities of legal procedure.[118]

Thus, in the trial of Colin Ferguson, the Long Island Rail Road gunman who killed six passengers and wounded nineteen others during a shooting spree in 1993, newspapers focused on the victims watching the trial, and the court conducted "a virtual memorial service," giving a day and a half of testimony to victim survivors, each of whom addressed the defendant directly. With the courtroom a stage in a *three-day* sentencing hearing, the survivors made themselves active players by orchestrating a mass exit from the courtroom but returning opportunely for delivery of the sentence and the media wrap-up.[119]

A turning point in the validation of victim testimony came in the summer of 1997 with reportage of the Oklahoma City bombing case in Denver. In the Federal Building blown up by Timothy McVeigh and Terry Nichols, 168 people died and 500 others were seriously injured. The scope and horror of the crime led the presiding judge to curtail sensationalism by restricting electronic coverage to closed-circuit television. He also put

a gag order on all attorneys in the case and resisted inflammatory testimony during the two days of impact statements from 38 victim survivors.

Commendable in themselves, these tactics achieved very limited success. Frustrated media sources circumvented the lockout by giving most
of their coverage to victim survivors, who were not so constrained. Survivors from the explosion and the families of the dead became daily commentators. Reporters regularly asked for their feelings on the proceedings
of each session and made victims the "real story" of the trial. Faced with
a virtually autistic defendant and a reserved judge, even legal scholars
trumpeted the rights of victims. "Should such pain and passion be part of
the legal proceedings?" volunteered constitutional expert Laurence Tribe
in the *New York Times*. "Of course." [120]

Anyone victimized by crime has a claim on the system today, but the
added features are not without problems in a balanced system. The reality
that "victims and defense lawyers are natural enemies within the adversary system of criminal justice" has led to claims that victims lack a voice
in court and that prosecutors, less trusted than before, do not provide
one. Victims' rights establish that the legal process owes injured parties
more than before: more support, greater visibility, better information,
and something of a say. [121] But where should the new fulcrum for balance
be placed? For what purposes should a victim have the right to be heard
in the penalty phase of a trial? Actual pain *inflicted* by a defendant indicates something about the nature of a crime, but mental suffering and the
collateral loss of survivors are unquantifiable and amorphous elements
after the fact.

Although the phrase "pain and suffering" from tort law is frequently
used to answer these worries, the appropriation glosses a significant distinction. In technical terms, *pain* implies physical distress while *suffering*
refers to mental or emotional trauma. The second word, *suffer*, comes
from the Latin *su[b]* (under) and *ferre* (to bear). Hence, "to suffer" is to
bear up under a plight with relevance to the spirit more than the body.
If we then carry the term into less spiritual spheres without losing its
emotional force, we begin to see the form that victim impact statements
have taken in postmodern America. [122]

Chief Justice Rehnquist's desire to strike a better balance for victims
against defendants by legalizing impact statements is instructive. The
killer who might be executed for a crime today is no longer a damned

soul and retains, in secular terms, the possibility of rehabilitation. The
initiation of mitigating evidence for the defendant at the penalty phase
addressed this possibility. "You just want the jury to appreciate that each
of us is more than the worst thing we've ever done," writes Bryan Stevenson, director of the Equal Justice Initiative representing death penalty
defendants in Alabama. [123] Defense counsel in the penalty phase of a trial
unearth every possible smidgeon of goodness in the defendant in search
of that spark of humanity that might keep a jury from seeing a monster
who should be put to death. Victim impact statements gain their legitimacy from the widespread fear that defense counsel are too successful
in these endeavors. But what kind of balance are the victims and their
surrogates seeking to restore, and how is their newfound fear to be measured?

Two contingencies, one psychological and the other theological, join
in the rise of the victim. In the first, a society dedicated to happiness has
made suffering anathema instead of an unfortunate facet of experience.
Given to material satisfactions and festooned with remedies and balms
of all kinds, a postmodern inhabitant can assume that suffering and pain
are not just undesirable; they should be avoidable. The huge impact of
painkilling and anxiety-reducing remedies allows us to resent both conditions more than previous civilizations did. No writer today would join
William Wordsworth with anything but bitterness of heart in the final
movements of "Intimations of Immortality from Recollections of Early
Childhood" and "The Old Cumberland Beggar." When the poet writes
that "the soothing thoughts that spring out of human suffering" are the
truest source of "the philosophic mind" and then extols "vital anxious-
ness" as a value, we no longer know what he means. Those who suffer
today receive mostly pity for what should not be: that is, a substitution
of sentimentality for discernment. [124]

Americans now live in a blame culture or "culture of complaint," and
it fuels collective interest in the latest sufferer's right to be heard. One
of the strangest constants in a society of such unprecedented prosperity
and security comes in the number of people who share a feeling of being
deeply wronged by life and are given national platforms to talk about it.
In the race for riches and in befuddlement over the rapid pace of change
that divides each generation from every other in the United States, even
quite successful citizens think that they have been left behind, betrayed
by forces beyond their control. The assumption that something has gone

wrong in American civilization is part of an "all-pervasive claim to vic-timhood" and "personal grievance." Empathy for the victim feeds on this latent self-pity, and in nourishing itself, it yearns to hear whatever the victim wants to say.[125]

The second contingency in the rise of the victim has to do with what punishment now means in modern life. A previous understanding would have thought very differently about the matter. When, for example, the ghost of his dead father instructs Hamlet to "revenge his foul and most unnatural murder," Shakespeare's spirit specifies that no action be taken against the faithless wife who has married his killer. Hamlet, the quintes-sential victim in literature, receives this instruction: "taint not thy mind, nor let thy soul contrive against thy mother: leave her to heaven," which will presumably consign her to hell. Then, as he actually has an opportu-nity to kill Claudius in prayer, Hamlet rightly resists, for to kill Claudius in the act of confession would "this same villain send to heaven."[126]

Victim statements have become fashionable at a time when many have lost faith in the certainty of eternal punishment and no longer trust Prov-idence to correct human affairs. A victim today fears the lack of a fi-nal reckoning and the absence of an ultimate plan. Even if final judg-ment lends a hand, the oblivious defendant may live out a life without any dread of that moment or any thought of repentance for the horri-ble acts that have made capital punishment a possible sentence. Merely convicted, the killer who tormented a loved one may only endure an un-reflective prison term of undisclosed length and possible reprieve.

Without the certainty of ultimate punishment, victims want to speak in court because they find it difficult to believe their situation will be addressed if they remain silent. The procedure adopted to meet this fear is called an *impact* statement. The announced goal is fuller realization of what the crime has done to others, and most manifestations of it empha-size the lack of remorse or failure of comprehension in the defendant. Nevertheless, the poignancy of the impact statement, the element that causes courtrooms to weep and a whole nation to read, lies elsewhere and at a more chilling level of concern. The surviving victim who rises in the penalty phase of a capital trial has a more terrible thing to relate than anyone else has said in court. "There is nothing anywhere in this world or in any other," the victim tells the defendant, "that can make you as miserable as you have made me and mine."

THE COURTROOM

It may seem perverse to raise the element of a mere room to the level of
character, but anyone who enters a courtroom notices an immediate difference: this is the sanctuary of the law. All seven performers just analyzed
take on a dignity beyond themselves from their place and participation
in the legal process. Even the most objectionable share in public recognition of a meaningful form, and the guarantee of that form is indeed
place. Not exactly a performer, the courtroom dictates and shapes the
ceremony of performance. Think of the courtroom as knowable space
striving to reach for a still unknown answer; it is the aesthetic element of
control in legal procedure.

Courtrooms have depended since antiquity on elaborations of form to
provide decorum. They require obvious arrangement and setting if they
are to encourage recalcitrant participants to bury their differences long
enough to enter into consensual roles and acceptance of judgment. The
locus of judgment is already a site of ritualized restraint in the earliest
Greek descriptions. The divine shield of Achilles, in all of its concentric-
ity, depicts a courtroom at the center of the city of peace and is the definition of it. Heralds in *The Iliad* "keep the people in hand," while elders
sitting within the confines of the *hieros kuklios,* "the sacred circle," deliver
their judgments from special benches of polished stone after disputants
present their sides of the case to the court, with each speaking in proper
order. [127]

The modern courtroom answers to the same needs with similar devices enlarged and refined. Much thought has gone into the array of the
modern courtroom as a forum that must reduce conflict to reason, anger
to cooperation, and argument to decision making. The space, the align-
ments, the furnishings, the equipage, and even the minor trappings of
this site are arranged with these needs in mind, and practitioners quickly
learn that the size, shape, style, and provision of the actual arena will influence the decisions that are made there. Courtrooms require "an aura,"
a mystique of authenticity and legitimacy that will aid the angered, the
resentful, and the injured to accept an impersonal, institutional solution. [128]

Critics conventionally compare the courtroom to a theater or stage,
but the analogy is misleading even if many theoretical terms of dra-
maturgy are useful concepts in thinking about courtroom performance.

Staged appearance in drama "suppresses the practical function of phenomena in favour of a symbolic or signifying role." Theatricality works through a suspension of disbelief. It creates a separate world for the sake of a vicarious enjoyment that is distinct from mundane levels of reality.[129]

At trial, by way of contrast, the import of actual events and the utilitarian functions that help to explain them (evidence methodically presented) are everything. Facts and the import of proffered objects reach *toward* rather than *away* from the mundane reality that will clarify and justify decision making. Then, too, enjoyment is not a value in court as it is in a play. The law can be dramatic, but it privileges a "voice of banality (to say what everyone sees and knows)." It aims for the practical solution that is possible and fair in a setting that reflects restriction and control rather than imagination.[130]

The easy parallels of courtroom to theater occur because trials lend themselves to the techniques of staged performance: both consciously use blocking (placement), proxemics (the use of spatial relations and orientations), kinesics (body movements), and paralanguage (variations in speech tones and patterns). As the differences between how characters move and talk onstage distinguish the amateur from the professional actor, so similar manifestations separate effective litigators from a poor substitute. But even here there are major differences. "It is a mistake to think of a setting as a copy of a real place," writes a renowned director of drama while urging improvisation in his actors. By making the terrain of the stage symbolic, the director wants an actor to accept that "the *doing* is more indelibly memorable than what the actor said."[131] Courtrooms cannot afford to be anything other than real places in formulaic control of their participants. The performers who take part in a trial must never forget that what they *do* must always serve what they *say*.

Since everything that is said will be challenged repeatedly in unsettling and acrimonious ways, courtrooms project calm through the solemnities of ceremony and setting. It is the rare courtroom that fails to make graphic use in some way of the constitutive metaphor of balance, symbol of justice, to convey harmony in visual terms. The central, raised position of the judicial bench, the equilibrium formed in the triangularity of the bench in balance with opposing counsels' tables, the arrangement of flags, mottoes, portraits, and gallery seating—all seek to confirm what everyone has in mind, the scales of justice. The same devices temper authority with the promise of access through strategic doorways and other symbols of democratic identity. Courtrooms are elaborate but highly routinized and conventional places of business.[132]

Setting and performance reinforce each other through the forms of blocking, proxemics, kinesics, and paralanguage. Reflect for a moment on the nature of movement in a courtroom. Every physical position taken and relinquished is based on a restriction that extracts collaboration in the act. When a judge enters a courtroom from private chambers, moving through the room in flowing robes, everyone present must rise silently in place until the judge assumes utter command by occupying the seat of justice. Justice, it seems, is delivered sitting down—perhaps in order to convey the time and reflection that such deliberation deserves. In the act of presiding, the sitting judge never moves but controls all other movement as long as the court remains in session. When the judge rises, it indicates either a recess or the end of a court session, and all present must rise as well and remain in place until the judge has left the courtroom. Bailiffs patrol the aisles of most courtrooms to ensure compliance.

Movement supports decorum everywhere in a courtroom. The only performers allowed relative freedom during a trial are the attorneys of record, but they must gain permission from the motionless judge to do anything, and some judges maintain sharp restrictions, holding attorneys to what is known as "the well" of the courtroom (between counsels' tables, the bench, and the witness stand). Counsel must ask to approach the bench and abide by whatever other restrictions a judge places on their movements.

In the kinesics of the courtroom, witnesses can approach only when summoned, and they are confined to a chair appropriately named the box while examined. Defendants never move unless they voluntarily assume the comparable restraint of the witness box. Juries remain similarly stationary except to enter and leave a courtroom. This stress on overall immobility carries the legal process toward the quiescence of tableau. Everyone in court is instantly recognized in a particular role by the place they have been assigned, and anyone entering in the middle of a trial can fix the moment by where each performer is standing or sitting at the time. The tiniest of movements take on significance in a choreography of proximities that is part observance and part gamesmanship.

Manipulation of the arena of the courtroom can be clever, picayune, and sometimes hilarious, but every movement has three goals in mind: to be seen clearly, to be heard distinctly, and to fill as much of the arena as the court will allow. Professional advice manuals differ, but most experts advise attorneys to allow nothing between themselves and judge, jury, witness, or defendant during a moment of address; no notepad, not even a lectern should intrude. If a judge requires an attorney to use a lectern before a jury, frequent in federal courts, the attorney should stand beside it so as not to obscure the view of the jury. (Jurors who have to turn their heads even slightly to follow an argument are thought to listen less carefully.) Attorneys lean toward a judge to denote cooperation and move away from an adverse witness to indicate insignificance in the testimony given. Turning away, though, can be dangerous; a partial view "communicates timidity." All parts of the body belong to an instrument controlling attitudes in court. To ask a question with rising inflection conveys earnestness; a drop in tone implies that no one cares about the answer. Crossing the arms separates listener from speaker. A hand in a pocket conveys that an attorney has something to hide.[133]

These obsessions with detail in movement illustrate the importance of the courtroom as performative space. Advocacy manuals rely heavily on proxemics, which identify four basic zones or spheres of comfort in human relations: intimate distance (six to eighteen inches—and under!), personal distance (from one and a half to two and a half feet), social distance (four feet to twelve feet), and public distance (between twelve and twenty-five feet).[134] Consultants focus on when an attorney should invade the space of another trial performer and the distance to assign for various moments of address. These experts all agree that the location of personnel affects the outcome of a trial. Most disputes begin over *where* lawyers should try to position themselves at given moments and *when* freedom of movement should be used to invade "the body buffer zones" of others in seizing courtroom territory. This advice can reach body-snatching proportions. Urged to "climb into the jury box" as a figurative thirteenth member, lawyers learn to approach slowly, otherwise "you can actually see the jurors recoil."[135]

The same creative manipulation applies to display or *ostension*. Legal arguments require evidence, evidence must be *exhibited*, and *exhibition* encourages *exhibitionism*, depending on what a court will allow. How acceptable is it for prosecutors to brandish a murder weapon repeatedly in the face of a witness or to display an angel pin in sympathy with the lost victim in a case? Is it reasonable for an attorney to sit in the witness box to bemoan absent testimony? Can defendant and counsel claim public

Figure 3. Thomas Hart Benton, *Trial by Jury* (1964). Oil on canvas, 30 x 40 in. Art ©
T. H. Benton and R. P. Benton Testamentary Trusts / UMB Bank Trustee / Licensed by
VAGA, New York, New York. Photograph: The Nelson-Atkins Museum of Art, Kansas
City, Missouri. Bequest of the artist, F75–21/11. Photograph by Mel McLean. Trials are
scenes of performance in which movement, display, demeanor, and countenance are
important. This oil painting, by Thomas Hart Benton from 1964, displays many of
the strategies that lawyers learn to use in court. The attorney knows to allow nothing
between himself and the jury and to get as close to them as possible as "the thirteenth
juror." He conveys with his pointing finger and forward thrust a certitude, sense of
direction, and confidence that he might not actually feel. The trick of holding a paper
that he does not consult demonstrates prior preparation but also mastery of his case.

solidarity by wearing string bracelets from Jerusalem's Western Wall or
symbolic neckties that they say ward off injustice?[136]

    Should an attorney in an injury case be able to dump the artificial limb
of his client in the laps of jury members to let them feel "the warmth of life
in the soft tissues"? Are there limits beyond good taste in "the wifely art
of standing by," a favorite tactic in dealing with the high rollers in white-
collar crime cases? Here consultants call for subtle displays of affection
in court. There is a "playbook for wifely comportment—what to wear,

when to touch, how to cry."[137] Everyone assumes such details are important. Performers in court tailor their behavior to their understanding of the stereotypes favorable to them in the belief that demeanor and display will affect how arguments will be received.

It follows that anyone really interested in a trial must *see* and not just *hear* or *hear of* the event in question to understand what happens in court. In the most famous trial of the last half century, it was not enough to read about how Johnnie Cochran asked a jury with nine black members to take a stand against racism in the Los Angeles Police Department by acquitting O.J. Simpson. "Police the police," he told them. The language was clear enough, but you had to see the leading black lawyer of his day hugging his client, holding his hand, and pleading, "Do the right thing," to grasp the full impact of his appeal—an impact that led to the swiftest not guilty verdict on record in a recent major murder trial. The Simpson jury would reach its decision in less than four hours without checking any of the 1,105 pieces of evidence and 45,000 pages of testimony made available to it in a trial that had lasted nine months. "I know the downtown jury pool," Cochran boasted in gratitude. He also knew the stereotype of police corruption that he could call up and count on. "When it came to the issue of race," he observed early in the case, "it was not gonna be any patty-cake."[138]

One understands the ultimate power in the connection of courtroom and community by recognizing the stereotypes that work at trial. As we have seen, the stereotypes available are ones of contrast pitted against each other for selective use. Superficial in themselves, they can lead or mislead, but they are always present, and they invariably simplify a complicated matter. Public comprehension depends on the battle of these mental shortcuts as much as it does on argument, and the implications for the impact of a high-profile trial are vast. If a citizenry decides to measure the integrity of the law through a high-profile trial (as many did in *California v. Simpson*), if the bombardment of information contains many inaccuracies (as happened in *Simpson*), if the stereotypes afloat have serious consequences (as was true of *Simpson*), and if that trial continues to shape public opinion (as critics on all sides have claimed of *Simpson*), then the goal of accurate perception takes on quadruple importance.

That said, accurate perception is more easily wished for than found, and only so many observers in a community actually get *to see* what happens in a courtroom. The misgivings that follow from that are again fourfold. How significant is it when information sources fail to provide, or misconstrue, or distort, or overly magnify what is taking place in a high-profile trial? What can be done to correct these inaccuracies? How many people should be present to observe such a trial to encourage reliable public understanding of it? What should be the circumstances under which those who observe do observe? These four questions are not easily answered, and their ramifications will dominate the rest of this book. We turn to the next section not in digression but in deeper confirmation. Only history can tell us why the questions themselves are so important.

PART TWO

A Case-Study Sequence

The five chapters in this section offer case studies, starting with the trials of Aaron Burr in 1807 and John Brown in 1859 and continuing through those of Mary Surratt, one of the accused assassins of Abraham Lincoln, in 1865; the anarchists accused of leading the Haymarket Riot in 1886; and Ethel and Julius Rosenberg in 1951. These trials have been selected for a number of reasons. Each involved a perceived threat to its community, each received extensive coverage, each disturbed the nation enough to shape ideological formations for years to come, and through those ideological formations, each is still with us in some significant way. Taken together, they confirm the importance of courtroom events as barometers of American thought and sources of cultural analysis.

The case method is used by every law school in the country and by every lawyer preparing to argue in court. Note, however, an important difference from the norm of legal analysis in what follows. Each chapter in this part of *The Trial in American Life* presents the official record of a court decision in interactive tension with nonlegal narratives that have dealt with the same event. Instead of the customary reach for legal holdings, chapters 3 through 7 study the way legal choices and communal reactions cohere and diverge.

Aaron Burr, to take just the first case offered, was found not guilty when tried for treason in 1807, but treatment of Burr in nineteenth-century America made him the universal scoundrel of national lore. Why? The question has redoubled significance in the light of twentieth-century accounts that try to rehabilitate Burr. More is obviously at stake in a high-profile trial than the determination of guilt.

The pairing of legal narratives with nonlegal narratives of the same event reveals the long "half-life" of certain trials in American culture. Warnings against "witch-hunts" are voiced today, three hundred years after the Salem witchcraft trials, even though few Americans now believe in witches or could give an accurate account of what happened in 1692. We should be interested in the way communal memory changes the original meaning of an event for later ideological use. The trials examined here are offered not for one more revisionist reading but to recognize the nature of obsessions that keep trials alive in either practical or imaginative terms. Why is the trial of Aaron Burr still cited frequently in law today? Answers reveal as much about the contemporary United States as they do about condemned witches or Aaron Burr or the courtrooms that dealt with them.

The profusion of competing narratives around a notorious trial presents evidentiary problems. How do we gauge explanatory worth? Narratives that either clarify contemporary behavior around a trial or continue to be read long after the event would seem to be of particular interest. These chapters respond by using such accounts in relation to the official language in court, and they have another purpose in mind. They seek to identify and demonstrate the integrity of interdisciplinary tools of criticism as windows into trial performance—tools that should help to clarify any trial in progress. Chapter 3 explains the role of *storytelling* at trial; chapter 4, that of *genre theory*; chapter 5, *gender studies* and *intertextuality*; chapter 6, *point of view* and *ethnic studies*; chapter 7 completes this exercise with a discussion of *narrativity* as a device in control of courtroom rhetoric.

No one should feel intimidated by these critical terms. They are instruments of frequent if unconscious use, and when their power is explained, every thinking citizen should be interested in the way they influence thought and writing in courtrooms and beyond. Lawyers are wordsmiths as well as mouthpieces. The language employed by them to protect unpopular defendants or to put them at risk speaks to a general community in surprising ways. How that actually happens is worth knowing because it will happen again. The extraordinary power of courtroom conflict as an ideological stimulus resides in the language used at trial in relation to communal interpretation of its larger implications.

What a writer in the public domain takes or rejects from the official transcript of a trial is always interesting. Can we approach the meaning of language in the law through the idiosyncratic exploitation of the same medium in literature? The question is a difficult one to answer in the abstract, another reason for case-study demonstrations. Concreteness is important because current use of a facile alliteration, "law and literature," can mislead effective investigation through loose connections. Interdisciplinary in intent, such terminology hides another and vital link. The missing element in declarations of law *and* literature is, of course, history: law, literature, *and* history. Legal action relies on history as on no other discipline for a record of what has been done, grounding itself for that purpose in the study of precedent. Meaningful analysis of any trial has to respect the moment of writing. Accordingly, historical context will be the interpretative control in these chapters.

History figures in another analytical dimension. A recounted series of trials often suffers from an episodic quality, and readers of it move, more or less randomly, from one celebrated event to another. The five high-profile trials examined here have been selected instead for a common problem that all raise. Together they form a *case-study sequence* on a subject of long-standing and troubling interest. A consensual culture, the United States rarely appears at its best when that consensus is even minimally threatened. The defendants in these trials were all accused, formally or not, of treason, and each suffered inordinately under the accusation even though other charges usually pertained and were easier to articulate in court.

Americans have been haunted by the crime of treason, a natural obsession in a republic that defined itself in revolution with the cry of "traitor" heard on every side. Treason is the one crime set off by separate article in the U.S. Constitution. The framers all heard those cries in 1776. They knew the dangers in the accusation and defined the crime with care when they had the chance in 1787. In effect, they defined treason so carefully that the state has experienced difficulty in sustaining its charges and has fallen back on the more flexible and vaguer crime of conspiracy to sustain its accusations. Understandable in reaction, the nature of this legal convenience is one that deserves to be watched. Nothing in our legal system is more suspect than the alarms and artifices that have been used to forge a link between the idea of treason and looser forms of accusation and condemnation.

If the title of this study, *The Trial in American Life*, has yet another meaning, it comes in acknowledgment of this peril. The angers in the American polity have never been small or limited in range when aroused against a foe. The country has always reserved a special rage for "the enemy within," and it has been quick to find those enemies in its history. Each of the defendants at trial in these five chapters was treated by the accusing culture as an enemy. Their trials resonate anew and take on extra meaning in a nation that currently thinks of itself as under attack. Americans are not the only people to react excessively when they feel threatened, but no other nation has been as historically secure as this one, and whole communities quickly lost their heads over the trials taken up here. It should be instructive for the citizen of today to reflect on how and why that happened.

The loosely federated society of the United States fears and resents those who fall just outside of its artificially established but now traditional borders and conventions. Moreover, the energy in these anxieties has occasionally led the nation astray. Some difficulties over acceptance and membership have been inevitable. The ideal of citizenship has changed considerably across two centuries and counting, and few of these changes have come easily. A landowning, white, male citizenry that found and then defined itself in the originating anger of revolt has been forced to adjust to ever-more intricate tests of order, addition, heterogeneity, regulation, materialism, institutionalism, and loyalty.

National identities thrive on exclusions as much as inclusions. This makes new categories difficult to accept, especially if they must be welcomed on terms of equality. But what does exclusion entail in a multicultural, technologically expansive, overwhelmingly prosperous, and diverse state with unprecedented influence and economic ties that bind it securely to the rest of the world—a state that officially supports and has tried to defend democracy, international peace, and human rights for all? The binaries of loyalty and betrayal, connection and severance, acceptance and dismissal cannot be the same in the altered circumstances of global dependence and responsibility. The difficulties that previous Americans faced on a different scale in the trials investigated here can be instructive in this regard. For like then, and however difficult the new answers to difficulties will be, they are likely to come in court.

CHAPTER THREE

The Punishing of Aaron Burr

A PERSONAGE IN THE DOCK

Unresolved communal anxieties magnify courtroom events, and no trial illustrates this phenomenon better than the first one to capture the national imagination, the trial of Aaron Burr for high misdemeanor and treason in 1807. Held in the Circuit Court of the United States in the District of Virginia, the trial would have been notorious anyway given the personality at the center of it. Aaron Burr, fifty-one years old, had been a Revolutionary War hero, the leader of a political party, a New York lawyer of note, a senator of the United States, and, three years before, the country's third vice president.

There were other notables involved. Presiding was none other than John Marshall, Chief Justice of the United States, an embattled figure in 1807. Around him, arguing the case, were the principal lawyers of the Virginia bar, men with national reputations and connections that allowed Virginia to dominate the executive branch of the federal government for a quarter of a century, an unprecedented span of control in U.S. history. An even greater personality loomed just beyond the courtroom. Burr's prime accuser and the man who orchestrated the prosecution was the president of the United States, Thomas Jefferson.

Magnified personalities count for much in a controversial trial, but they become locked in conflict for reasons beyond their control. No one wants to be in court, and the underlying reasons for being there in 1807 were so many, so vexed, and so complicated that the trial remains a subject of controversy today. The specific question—Was Aaron Burr guilty of treason against the United States?—raised a series of problems that the country was not ready to cope with, and the extraordinary range of those problems pitted region against region. All of this uncertainty and spread in conflict created a new phenomenon, the first high-profile trial to capture national attention.

The politics of the time were controlling elements. Burr used his leadership role in the new Republic to further his own agenda and wealth, and his naked ambition defied existing norms. A governing elite wanted to believe that civic virtue could maintain a disinterested mien at the highest levels of the republican experiment.[1] It was a losing battle, but those who fought it took the goal seriously. Burr, who didn't, already had stepped over the line in 1804 when he killed Alexander Hamilton in a duel over political differences. Dueling remained a practice in a society where concepts of honor still dominated behavior, but it was against unspoken rules, as well as a crime, for one political leader to kill another on the dueling ground.[2]

Burr had called Hamilton out with single-minded ruthlessness. As he would boast later, "[I] was sure of being able to kill him," an admission that made the duel "little better than murder" in the eyes of many others.[3]

Burr was also a known sexual predator. In a question still asked in American politics, what was the proper relation between private and public virtue in an official elected to guide the people? Other transgressions turned on questions of status. Burr fought in the Revolutionary army and could legitimately call himself a founder of the Republic. The extravagant welcomes he received during travels in the communities of the West in 1805 and 1806 were based on that reputation, but what restraints were expected of a founder in the pursuit of personal business? No one knew exactly, but Burr flouted voluntary restrictions that others accepted.

Imperiously aristocratic in bearing, Burr owed his original standing to an exalted birthright; for unlike other founders, he was the grandson and son of celebrated men. His immediate forebears, Jonathan Edwards and Aaron Burr Sr., were famous religious figures in colonial America, and both had been presidents of Princeton (the College of New Jersey). So significant were these credentials that John Adams complained that Jefferson won the presidency from him in 1800 because Burr had been Jefferson's running mate, bringing "100,000 Votes from the single Circumstance of his descent."[4]

Filled with entitlements, Burr pushed the limits of acceptable behavior in early republican society even as he embodied its conflicting understandings. The Bible culture of early America and the emerging secular enlightenment were both in him, and they clashed in the wake of those 100,000 votes from 1800. No one knew the appropriate answers when religious and secular spheres met in one person, nor where aristocratic place ended and republican worth began. Living imperiously on the edge, Burr always knew that trouble would follow him. "The Fates never decreed that I should go anywhere but that someone should be the worse for it," he wrote early in life.[5]

The events for which Burr was on trial aggravated uncertainties of another kind. Between 1805 and 1807, Burr schemed as a private citizen to gain power in the western territories, and each scheme tweaked a growing pain in the new nation. His plans included vague alternatives: secret expeditions of armed men into the western territories to appropriate land, the expansion of American holdings at the expense of Spanish claims, the outright conquest of Mexico for the United States, and even the conceivable creation of a separate western empire to be financed by England or Spain.

The anxieties that these plans touched off cannot be fully appreciated today because the circumstances no longer apply. No one in 1807 could more than begin to guess at the ultimate dimensions of the United States, and those who did guess divided sharply over what the inclusion of additional territory would mean for the existing arrangement. These debates over the extent of the experiment grew fierce, and they pitted region against region depending on where annexation would take place. Local identifications and disputed borders dominated the new states in their still loose idea of union.[6]

The questions raised by Burr's behavior thus extended well beyond him. Numbers of Americans, some with only peripheral identifications to the nation, were venturing westward in search of new lives on independent terms. Few knew or cared when actions taken to improve one's lot within uncharted and disputed territories might constitute treason against the United States. What was treason, anyway, in a country where every American had faced the charge in embellished rhetorical terms during the Revolution? Western adventurers eagerly contested Spanish and French claims to territory with little concern for the crisis in international relations that an aggressive pursuit of new territory might bring.

Jefferson himself had absorbed criticism when he unilaterally purchased huge tracts in the Louisiana Territory from the French as president in 1803. What were the limits of executive authority in adding new regions beyond the official Union, and how were such lands to be distributed? These questions had no immediate answer, but they led to another. Foreign claims over large western tracts were facts as well as threats in 1807. How dangerous was it for a recognized founder of the Republic to involve foreign powers in his own design for advancement in those claimed territories?

These uncertainties, together with Burr's notorious behavior, meant that arguments in court over the defendant's guilt or innocence spilled into the public domain, where they took on a life of their own. In effect, unbridled use of collateral arguments would undo Aaron Burr in a way that the trial itself could not sanction. Most Americans ignored the not guilty verdict reached in court, choosing a prosecutorial narrative instead to decide what had happened. Their selective interest had little to do with the law, and everything to do with ideological needs, and this was true even though Marshall's controlling opinion the other way held great national import. Indeed, the extent of the discrepancy between legal result and communal effect encourages a larger premise: when the public emphasizes aspects at trial that either ignore or reject the court's decision, it is safe to assume that something more than crime and punishment are at work.

Countless newspaper articles, thirty-three plays, twice as many works of fiction, and numerous poems take up the life of Aaron Burr, and they all rely on a curious juxtaposition. The feckless adventurer and ineffective traitor emerges in popular lore as a capacious figure, a master of disguise, and the seducer of every woman in sight. Edmund Stedman's poem "Aaron Burr's Wooing" catches the essence of this trend: "Where's the widow or maid with a mouth to be kist, / When Burr comes a wooing, that long would resist?"[7] These refashionings of Burr make seduction his primary attribute with special attention given to the most vulnerable elements in society. In most accounts the historical figure's political opportunism melts into a sinister capacity to commit any despicable act; unaided virtue is particularly susceptible to the traitor's charms unless communal vigilance responds. In victory, this fictional Burr plays on American fears; in defeat, he purges doubt.[8]

The puzzle in these representations deepens in the twentieth century.

Starting with Gore Vidal's novel *Burr* in 1973, revisionist accounts have wanted "to restore Aaron Burr to the Pantheon of the Founders." Not treason but circumstance and party politics explain this new protagonist. The myth of history rather than patriotism is the modern novelist's theme, and recent biographers have followed suit. Burr is the victim of events and a proto-abolitionist who resists slaveholding Virginians on principle. A "jackal pack" of politicians engineers Burr's "fall from power," and Jefferson deteriorates as "the first President to make to the people assertions he later admitted were not true."[9]

The basis for this shift in narrative trajectories is not hard to trace. Nineteenth-century citizens who feared foreign encroachment and other uncertainties in the western territories have given way to those who have forgotten the country's formative difficulties. Modern Americans worry instead about executive power, malfeasance in office, and the manipulation of truth by those in authority. There is, nonetheless, a significant similarity across the generations. Whether for or against the historical figure, all accounts make Aaron Burr the linchpin of communal anxieties.

THE POWER OF STORY

Advocacy embraces hyperbolic use of prevalent norms, one reason why controversial trials are good barometers of ideological concerns. The example of Burr is of interest in this regard because it demonstrates how debate in the adversarial process marks a path in communal explanation. A trial presents contrasting stories of guilt and innocence for legal determination, and when the community accepts a story *against* legal resolution, it is an indicator of something more generally at work; it tells us how a community thinks about its problems and even more about how it identifies and regards its enemies.

The argument that controlled communal perceptions in *United States v. Aaron Burr* was given by William Wirt, a protégé of Thomas Jefferson and junior counsel for the prosecution in 1807. Every later account of the trial agrees that Wirt's vivid speech in condemnation of Burr on August 25 "dazzled his audience—and posterity."[10] What made Wirt so memorable? Most explanations allude to the speaker's towering eloquence and leave it at that. Wirt used the familiar tools of the early republican lawyer:

Figures 4 & 5. (*Left*) John Vanderlyn, *Aaron Burr* (1802). Profile portrait. Oil on canvas, 22¼ x 16½ in., negative number 6227, accession number 1931.58. Collection of the New-York Historical Society. (*Right*) Jacques Jouvenal, *Aaron Burr* (#22.00003). Photograph: U.S. Senate Collection. Portraits of Aaron Burr convey little of the man's acknowledged magnetism and ascendancy over others. Jacques Jouevenal's sculpture of the third vice president of the United States in the Senate Gallery of the Capitol does a better job of conveying the power noted by both sides in 1807. The bust of Burr is significant for another reason. It represents the one identification with country that could not be taken away from the accused after his trial for treason.

oratorical profusion, literary reference, and a balance of secular and religious explanation.[11]

The biographer of Patrick Henry and the longest sitting attorney general in the country's history, Wirt would solidify his reputation for eloquence across subsequent decades, but other lawyers, especially Luther Martin for the defense, were at least as eloquent at the time, and John Wickham, Burr's main defense counsel, gave an address five days earlier that professional observers called "the greatest forensic performance of the American bar." It was Wickham's argument, not Wirt's, that Chief Justice Marshall would accept when instructing the jury as a matter of law (Burr could not be found guilty of treason on the evidence presented), and it was Wickham's argument that was admired in court.[12]

Wirt's capacity to control perceptions belongs to another level of understanding altogether. He turned the concerns about Burr into a familiar story that presented and then alleviated those concerns. The charge of treason depended on whether Burr could be shown to have been "levying War" against the United States or to have been "adhering" to the enemies of the United States, "giving them aid or comfort," and it required the sworn testimony of two witnesses to the same overt act.[13]

In practical terms, the prosecution had to prove an overt act had been committed on Blennerhassett Island, the part of Virginia in the middle of the Ohio River that gave the federal court in Richmond control of the case. Jurisdiction in the East was crucial. Burr had been acquitted of all wrongdoing by three sympathetic grand juries in the West, two in the state of Kentucky, and a third held in the Mississippi Territory. The West had been generous to Burr because it, too, wanted war with Spain. It cared little about Burr's schemes of personal advancement except to acknowledge that he was a war hero who would adopt more heroic measures in opening western lands to further settlement.

The government's fourth attempt to prosecute Burr—in the East, where the defendant and war with Spain were viewed with suspicion and alarm—depended on whether or not a given fact could be tied to two controversial premises. Thirty to forty armed men had gathered on Blennerhassett Island at Aaron Burr's behest to sail down the Ohio River into the Mississippi Territory to Louisiana and Spanish territory. But had an overt act of rebellion taken place on the island on December 10, 1806, and had Aaron Burr conducted it? The main flaw in the charge lay in an undisputed detail. Burr had been two hundred miles away in Kentucky on December 10. Everything hinged on the prosecution's ability to prove that Burr and one of his financial backers on the island, Harman Blennerhassett, had conspired together to commit treason and then acted upon that plan *on* the island.

Blennerhassett had emigrated with his wife from Ireland in 1796 and had spent a fortune carving a plantation out of the wilderness. He turned what had been called Backus Island (near what is now Marietta, Ohio) into a·personal haven dignified by his own name. Burr had been attracted by the refined setting, Blennerhassett's money, and some said by Blennerhassett's wife, and he had used his expertise and wiles on all three. His high social status and political fame allowed him to play upon his Irish backer's dreams of even greater possessions. Burr had convinced Blennerhassett that unlimited opportunities would materialize when the

United States declared war on Spain, which seemed likely in 1806, but he carefully left the rest of his plans in vague terms.

When William Wirt attacked for the prosecution on August 25, he had to counter difficulties in both aspects of the proof against Burr. John Marshall for the court had indicated clear reluctance to accept the available evidence as proof that an overt act of treason had taken place before two reliable witnesses on Blennerhassett Island, and he had openly questioned whether Aaron Burr's *constructive* presence on the island could be established as a matter of law. One long paragraph will be sufficient to demonstrate Wirt's rhetorical acumen in response to these difficulties:

> Who is Blannerhassett? A native of Ireland, a man of letters, who fled from the storms of his own country to find quiet in ours. His history shows that war is not the natural element of his mind. If it had, he never would have exchanged Ireland for America. So far is an army from furnishing the society natural and proper to Mr. Blannerhassett's character, that on his arrival in America, he retired even from the population of the Atlantic States and sought quiet and solitude in the bosom of our western forests. But he carried with him taste and science and wealth; and lo, the desert smiled! Possessing himself of a beautiful island in the Ohio, he rears upon it a place and decorates it with every romantic embellishment of fancy. A shrubbery, that Shenstone might have envied, blooms around him. Music, that might have charmed Calypso and her nymphs, is his. An extensive library spreads its treasures before him. A philosophical apparatus offers him all the secrets and mysteries of nature. Peace, tranquillity, and innocence shed their mingled delights around him. And to crown the enchantment of the scene, a wife, who is said to be lovely even beyond her sex and graced with every accomplishment that can render it irresistible, had blessed him with her love and made him the father of several children. The evidence would convince you, that this is but a faint picture of the real life.[14]

If the attractions in the passage are obvious, they worked on the nineteenth-century imagination in a particular way. Blennerhassett appears as every romantic adventurer's wish fulfilled. He has managed to start life over, transforming a new world, one entirely of his own choosing, into paradise by retreating from a noxious world and by rendering nature mediate to his every need. His wealth, his taste, his technical knowledge ("philosophical apparatus"), and the ideal wife ("lovely even beyond her sex and graced with every accomplishment") provide the "mingled delights" of the virtuous man. Family values and a nation dedicated to "peace" and "quiet" guarantee continuing "tranquillity." Brief references to antiquity ("Calypso and her nymphs") and to English pastoral traditions (William Shenstone) cap the Horatian ideal of retreat born again as the American dream.

Hardly a "picture of the real life," Wirt's scene of wish fulfillment illustrated a well-known Johnsonian adage: "The natural flights of the human mind are not from pleasure to pleasure, but from hope to hope."[15] Wirt gave the dream such scope because he wanted to shatter it with power for every auditor with similar aspirations. The paragraph turns even as it lingers on what can be hoped for:

In the midst of all this peace, this innocent simplicity and this tranquillity, this feast of the mind, this pure banquet of the heart, the destroyer comes; he comes to change this paradise into a hell. No monitory shuddering through the bosom of their unfortunate possessor warns him of the ruin that is coming upon him. A stranger presents himself. Introduced to their civilization by the high rank which he had lately held in his country, he soon finds his way to their hearts, by the dignity and elegance of his demeanor, the light and beauty of his conversation, and the seductive and fascinating power of his address. The conquest was not difficult. Innocence is very simple and credulous. Conscious of no design itself, it suspects none in others. It wears no guard before its breast. Every door and portal and avenue of the heart is thrown open, and all who choose enter it. Such was the state of Eden when the serpent entered its bowers. . . . In a short time the whole man [the unfortunate Blennerhassett] is changed, and every object of his former delight is relinquished. No more he enjoys the tranquil scene; it has become flat and insipid to his taste. His books are abandoned. His retort and crucible are thrown aside. His shrubbery blooms and breathes its fragrance upon the air in vain; he likes it not. . . . His enchanted island is destined soon to relapse into a wilderness; and in a few months we find the beautiful and tender partner of his bosom, whom he lately "permitted not the winds of" summer "to visit too roughly," we find her shivering at midnight, on the winter banks of

the Ohio and mingling her tears with the torrents, that froze as they
fell. (2:96–97)

The intertext in this passage is *Paradise Lost,* a familiar work in this
Richmond courtroom and the model for epic poetry in America at the
beginning of the nineteenth century. Wirt held to the theme of loss,
though in his version the biblical story had secular dimensions. He emphasized what Blennerhassett gave up materially to Burr as Satan rather
than what Adam lost spiritually in the sight of God. The modern ac-
cents left Wirt's auditors with a very different set of questions. How had
Blennerhassett managed to lose the material happiness that he had pur-
sued so eagerly and gained so completely through his own labor and
intellectual planning? Was Blennerhassett typical in his vulnerability?
Was everyone as susceptible to destruction?

Wirt answered by playing upon the anxieties that made the trial so
sensational. In his attack on Burr, the shift from paradise to wilderness
comes in the blink of an eye. The great promise of the West gives way
to fearful possibilities: the materiality of an unyielding and inhospitable
wasteland. Wirt incorporated yet another threat to explain matters. The
welcome solitude gained in bucolic retreat left every possessor vulnerable to the sudden appearance of a stranger ("every door and portal and
avenue . . . is thrown open"), and the "unfortunate possessor" is easily
dispossessed. Wirt turns the ideal of prosperous possession into the uncertainty that it actually was. The country's first major novelist, Charles
Brockden Brown, had written just such a story as gothic horror a decade
before in *Wieland; or, The Transformation.*

Wirt's Blennerhassett qualified as an intelligent and educated man,
but it didn't matter in his case, and it might not in another. The ap-
parition of the stranger in Burr was particularly frightening. The Revolutionary hero gone amok possessed insidious powers that could not
be matched. Burr had taken unfair advantage through the sources of
seduction at his disposal. He had exploited the exalted role of founder,
misusing "high rank" to undermine the patriotism and civic balance of
"the unfortunate Blannerhassett." What is the role of a founder, Wirt
asked, when the act of founding is complete? The biblical serpent lurk-
ing elsewhere in the paragraph represented "the poison of [Burr's] own
ambition," and it had been loosed upon the newly created Republic.
Thinly veiled allusions to class also applied. The self-made man in the

Irish immigrant naturally fell to the born aristocrat in Aaron Burr, who possessed a more innate elegance of demeanor and address.

The questions raised by Wirt do not end there. How had the obvious man of peace turned so completely and suddenly into a man of war? (In the same paragraph, we learn that Blennerhassett "no longer drinks the rich melody of music" but "longs for the trumpet's clangor and the cannon's roar.") Thirst for territory, a besetting vice in the rampant land speculation of the early Republic, supplied one answer, and the imperialism in this mentality challenged the complacent image of a quiet, peace-loving nation. Wirt led his auditors to the edge of even deeper waters. Long before Satan engineers the fall in the Garden of Eden in book 9 of *Paradise Lost,* we know in book 1 that "The mind is its own place and in its self / Can make a Heav'n of Hell, a Hell of Heav'n."[16]

Prosperity becomes its own trap in Wirt's fable of the fall. Blennerhassett's wealth draws Burr inexorably to him. The charm in the victim's innocence and ease robs him of vigilance. As the leading moralist of the age put the matter in *The Vanity of Human Wishes,* "Wealth heap'd on Wealth, nor Truth nor Safety buys / The Dangers gather as the Treasures rise." What kept Blennerhassett from being satisfied with his ideal lot? "With listless Eyes the Dotard views the store / He views, and wonders that they please no more."[17] Easily threatened, the reality of possession soon grows insipid to the holder of it. Wirt toys here with a massive cultural predicament. In a country dedicated to the pursuit of happiness, what if mere wealth failed to satisfy?

Another and more obscure intertext compounds these issues but with a psychological escape route in mind. Virtue, it seems, is even more difficult to maintain than satisfaction in wealth. The buried quotation at the end of Wirt's passage—"whom he lately 'permitted not the winds of' summer 'to visit too roughly' "—comes from Hamlet's speech "frailty, thy name is woman!" Hamlet's mother, the symbol of happiness in Denmark as Queen Gertrude, has remarried within two months of the king's death to the king's own brother, Claudius, soon to be exposed as a regicide. In the most famous speech in all of Shakespeare, Hamlet's realization of this fallen state has caused him to lose all interest in his surroundings in much the same way as Blennerhassett. "How weary, stale, flat and unprofitable, / Seem to me all the uses of this world!" Hamlet complains as he gazes on "an unweeded garden that grows to seed." The parallels carry a further message. By implication, Blennerhassett's wife succumbs to "the seductive and fascinating power" of Aaron Burr much as Gertrude falls into the "incestuous sheets" of Claudius.[18] As Wirt put the matter in context, "*Every* door and portal and avenue of the heart is thrown open." The real problem, it turns out, is not the psychological state of Blennerhassett but the triggering depredations of Aaron Burr. It is the seducer who has destroyed the fabric of happiness.

The spice of sexual connotation heightens the passage and gives the full answer that Wirt wanted. Through such innuendo, his speech frees his contemporaries from too much self-examination. Every problem could be explained through the untoward presence and actions of Aaron Burr. Could Burr be made to carry the weight of so many contradictions within the American dream, and could he be stretched even further to cover the intrinsic maladies of the human condition? Yes, he could. As long as the expanded frame of reference that Wirt sought to create in the courtroom could be taken for granted, Burr symbolized "the destroyer" on multiple levels of reference. By inverting the spiritual associations that adhered to Burr's name from high to low, Wirt made his subject the obverse of his famous forebears. Politics and religion together confirmed the negative agency in Burr.

What had Aaron Burr ultimately been guilty of? In Wirt's pivotal description, Burr went to Blennerhassett Island "to change this paradise into hell." Crime and sin, seduction and evil, human endeavor and cosmic design merge in Wirt's account, allowing his audience to fall back on familiar typologies. These conflations between the human and spiritual worlds proved that Burr was condemned even if his guilt remained mysterious. Could anyone plumb the ultimate depths of Burr's intentions? No, but it didn't matter as long as one knew that the intentions were there. "They can be known only to the man himself," Wirt intoned, while calling on a higher authority, "and to that Being whose eye can pierce the gloom of midnight and the still deeper gloom that shrouds the traitor's heart" (2:104).

A modern reader finds only wretched excess in such posturing, but the legal mores of the time willingly gave Wirt the "picture of life" that he painted in such lurid tones. Language used in court is always subject to manipulation. Wirt looked around him and found ready material. The formal indictment read that Burr acted "not having the fear of God before his eyes"; that instead he had been "moved and seduced by the instigation of the devil" to commit treason against the United States (1:430,

431). It was a short step to find the devil *in* Aaron Burr. Nor was Wirt the first to invoke the fall in the garden or *Paradise Lost* at trial. Luther Martin for the defense gathered that honor early on, castigating Thomas Jefferson for not divulging papers under court subpoena. Trials like this one usually turn on the cooperation of a co-conspirator who turns state's evidence. Martin, seeking to impugn the informers against Burr, argued that they had "instilled as much poison into the ear of the president, as Satan himself breathed into the ear of Eve" (1:129).

What did it mean that both sides of the case drew on spiritual categories and patterns of Miltonic reference for expressing them? Pretty language? Certainly, but it also showed that a religious stamp of approval would convince early republicans that they were hearing the whole story.[19] The age embraced Wirt's account at trial through reigning verisimilitudes, the means of making the story told at trial believable. The legal designation of crimes of a certain dimension in early America followed English Common Law procedures in assigning theological terms to explain the level of depravity understood to have been reached. Since treason constituted "the highest civil crime which (considered as a member of a community) any man can possibly commit," it bespoke the gravest depravity, the hardest crime to explain. Wirt conveyed immeasurable evil as measured crime when he claimed only God could pierce the gloom of the traitor's heart.[20]

A conception of country was also at work in the Miltonic references employed by Martin and Wirt, as ready acceptance of it in later accounts of Aaron Burr would confirm. John Adams, a very interested observer in 1807, put the matter this way to Benjamin Rush: "I think something must come out on the trial, which will strengthen or weaken our confidence in the general union." The significance that both men attached to the trial as a national test appeared in a detail that would prove to be at odds with history. Adams and Rush were among the most perceptive observers of their age; yet both believed if Burr gained an acquittal in 1807 that his popularity would soar, that his escape could redefine the unfolding republican experiment, and that he might still become president of the United States.[21]

The conception of the country itself was on display in this trial of a national figure for treason, and conflicting versions of the defendant's reputation spoke to elements of it. For those who were afraid, it was absolutely necessary to demonize Burr.

"A MAN HERETOFORE DISTINGUISHED"

Stabilizing the new nation required celebrations of its achievements, and the earliest celebrations turned on the "transcendent meaning" of its leaders. The apotheosis of figures like George Washington and Benjamin Franklin contributed to an emerging civil religion.[22] Even today, chronicles of the early Republic foreground the stories of founders and the respective roles of each. While they lived, the founders jockeyed for position as part of their quest for the one selfish object that most of them were willing to publicly condone, "the love of fame, the ruling passion of the noblest minds." Who belonged and in what place in the pantheon of the founders? Who was overrated? Who did *not* belong at all? These questions were food for thought among the survivors of the Revolution. "You rank Colonel Hamilton among the Revolutionary characters," ran a typical letter from John Adams to Benjamin Rush. "But why? The Revolution had its beginning, its middle, and its end before he had anything to do in public affairs."[23] It was, of course, one thing to be diminished in these calculations; quite another to be excluded from them altogether.

Aaron Burr found himself falling out of this pantheon of the founders in 1805. Dropped from the vice presidency for Jefferson's second term, Burr presumed a continuing right to high public rank and took little definition from success as a brilliant lawyer; he was all too suddenly a private citizen without portfolio. All of Burr's schemes in the West can be read as attempts to regain a former footing. His last discussion with Thomas Jefferson, a year after he had been pushed out of the vice presidency, opens a window onto his predicament. The report of the meeting comes from the president's pen, but even allowing for animus, the interview meant humiliation for Burr in the role of supplicant. Jefferson wrote his account of the interview in his daybook, or *Anas*, on April 15, 1806, a month after the fact:

> Colo. Burr called on me, & entered into a conversation in which he mentioned that little before my coming into the office I had written to him a letter intimating that I had destined him for a high employ, had he not been placed by the people in a different one; that he had signified his willingness to resign as V[ice] President to give aid to the adm[inistratio]n in any other place; that he had never asked an office however; he asked aid of nobody, but could walk on his own legs, &

take care of himself: that I had always used him with politeness, but nothing more: that he had aided in bringing on the present order of things, that he had supported the adm[inistratio]n, & that he could do me much harm: he wished however to be on a differ[en]t ground: he was now disengaged from all particular business, willing to engage in something; should be in town for some days, if I should have any thing to propose to him.[24]

Jefferson's condensation of the meeting surely made the contradictions more blatant than they would have been in conversation, but the passive-aggressive stance ascribed to Burr rings true. Burr admitted rejection by the people even as he claimed a significant role in the present order; he insisted that he had never solicited an office while in the act of asking for one; he claimed to have been loyal to Jefferson while openly threatening him; and he argued for his own importance within the disclosure that he had nothing to do and found himself at loose ends. His great need was "high employ." Jefferson may have exaggerated Burr's desperation, but the desperation was there. The former vice president seemed to say, "Help me, or I must help myself, and I can do that now only by harming you." Jefferson certainly saw the danger, and his account must be read with that realization in mind.

The president didn't hesitate to twist the knife in response. Burr, Jefferson told him, had "lost the public confidence" not in the newspapers, as Burr believed, but through "the late presidential election; when tho' in poss[essio]n of the office of V[ice] P[resident], there was not a single voice heard for his retaining it." Burr had failed either because of a lack of support or because of his incompetence while vice president. His political peers had condemned him. Jefferson used the opportunity to read Burr out of any alliance structure, adding in passing that he "feared no injury which any man could do me." Always the pedagogue, the president could not resist the temptation to lecture: "I observed to him . . . that he must be sensible the public had withdrawn their confidence from him, & that in a government like ours it was necessary to embrace in its adm[inistratio]n as great a mass of public confid[en]ce as possible, by employing those who had a character with the public, of their own, & not merely a secondary one through the Ex[ecuti]ve." The insertion of the adverb *merely*—"merely a secondary" reputation—must have cut deeply.

Jefferson, the most powerful man in America with no end in sight to his power, had dismissed Burr's assumed importance against Burr's own experience of personal popularity in the western territories. Left with only that popularity, Burr decided to use it. His armed recruits never numbered more than one hundred men, though rumor would run it to a legion of twenty thousand!—a stupendous number for the times. Whatever their number, Burr's men were the focal point for a groundswell that would wrest territories from Spain as the United States declared war on that country. If Burr's own actions precipitated such a war, he knew that many westerners would celebrate his initiative, and the result would be the same. Both outcomes served the former vice president's purposes. Either way, Burr would be the hero with a new base in the western United States or just beyond it, but everything depended on war with Spain, and there the schemer's miscalculation began and ended with Jefferson.

Tensions between Spain and the United States were high enough for war in 1806, but Jefferson foiled Burr's expectations by hanging fire for many months and avoiding open conflict at the last moment. His decision left Burr dangling—a private citizen, on an unlawful military venture, against a peaceful neighbor. Thus far, however, Burr's plan could not be characterized as a treasonous plot against the United States, and so Jefferson waited. The president moved to have Burr arrested only after receiving a letter ostensibly from Burr to General James Wilkinson, military governor of the northern portion of the Louisiana Territory. The letter delivered to Jefferson by Wilkinson urged in cipher that Wilkinson join his official forces to Burr's volunteers under Burr's command in an armed expedition.

The articulated version of Burr's intentions in the Wilkinson letter came much closer to the line of treason, and Burr clearly *spoke* like a traitor at times in 1805 and 1806. Still, by definition, the crime of treason required an overt act *against* the United States, and for that purpose it had been useful to keep Burr from all semblance of official representation in the West. From the moment of their interview in March 1806, Jefferson's purpose had been to lock Burr out of a formal capacity. The nature of Burr's fallen rank would come up again and again in the Richmond courtroom, and to that extent the trial for treason, like *Paradise Lost*, revolved around the theme of lost status.

Burr's grandiose behavior in the West had been possible as a Revolutionary personage with enough continuing standing or legitimacy in the early Republic to convince others of his ability to carry the Revolution into a new dimension. Only such a figure could have hoped to gather a meaningful force around him to take Mexico or build a separate empire. But which way did the claims of personage cut at trial? They cut in every direction, and each claim led to a further magnification of Burr for good or ill.

Even insignificant defendants appear larger than life at trial because of the intense focus placed upon their behavior. In Burr's case, the liminality of the defendant in abeyance between guilt and innocence yielded unusual extremes in narrative projection. The one-time Revolutionary hero was either a complete knave in 1807 or the truest champion of the moment, depending on whom you asked. No one could ignore who he had been or what his previous status as a Revolutionary icon meant. He was, as the prosecution liked to claim, "a man heretofore distinguished" (1:402).

The formality of a trial transcript is a useful indicator for exposing larger uncertainty, and this one contained language that brought the problem home to everyone. Burr was at once the defendant and a defense attorney in his own trial, a vexed circumstance that the transcript recognized in a curious detail. Burr the subject at trial took regular title through the lore of his Revolutionary past. He was "Colonel Burr" as the defendant, but when speaking as his own counsel, he was simply "Mr. Burr."

The awkwardness of dealing with both identities came up with frequency in the trial, most famously in Burr's sensational attempt to drag Jefferson into court with him by asking the court to issue a subpoena against the president (1:113–14ff.). The prosecution complained loud and long about "Mr. Burr's" legalistic adventurism. The man in the dock—but also out of it—had "with unexampled dexterity contrived from the very start, almost invariably, to quit his situation as an accused" with "the purpose of escaping the effect of the prosecution carrying on against him." Through some "strange manner," Burr had seized "the high ground of public accuser and assailing others" (2:28). There was a mysterious and dangerous brand of magic in the makeup of the defendant as defense counsel in his own case.

There was no way around the enlarged figure, and so it had to be made to serve. Prosecuting attorneys had the difficult task of proving that Burr was the principal actor and not an accessory in the events with which he was charged. Burr's absence from Blennerhassett Island during those events compounded the difficulty and encouraged a magnification in capacities that would obviate the distance between man and event. Burr, after all, had been more than two hundred miles away in geographical terms (2:209). To cover that distance, the prosecution made him "first mover of the plot," "the *Alpha* and *Omega* of this treasonable scheme," "the very life of this treason," "the abominable instigator," "the daring, aspiring elevated genius who devises the whole plot," "the great actor," and, in a particularly clever response to the problem of distance, "the sun to the planets which surround him" (2:39, 66, 95).

These efforts joined physical prowess ("a soldier, bold, ardent, restless, and aspiring"), to intellectual cunning beyond the norm ("for no man has a more comprehensive knowledge of human nature"), and on to Burr's overreaching sense of entitlement ("no man's talents are more competent to distinguish and assert his rights, than those of the accused") (2:39, 33, 28). These traits were easily borrowed from the image of the Revolutionary hero and recast for present purposes. The prosecution relied on them to argue for Burr's prowess in conducting the conspiracy from afar.

There was, however, an even better way to convey Burr's absent presence on Blennerhassett Island, and the prosecution was not at a loss for words. If shining presence at the scene of conflict defined the Revolutionary hero, subterfuge and evasion were the stock and trade of a traitor who would act in secret and, therefore, logically from afar. The prosecution raised this possibility through the negative imagery of cunning that would forever stick to Burr as a personage who had embraced diabolical means. How did one measure the presence of an absence? Once again, the spiritual world could be made to serve for an ordinary understanding. Freed of mere physical presence as the Alpha and Omega, Burr could be everywhere at once. He could, the prosecution argued, "secretly wander, like a demon of darkness, from one end of the continent to the other" (2:65).

The defense worked even harder to inflate Burr's identity. Their client was a leader of men, as his record in the Revolution proved. Luther Martin dared to compare Burr in the West to the greatest warrior of all, George Washington. In both men, "plans were most meritorious, predicated on principles of an honourable war" (1:467). Edmund Randolph raised yet another dimension, that of the stellar politician. The "censure and obloquy" heaped on Burr could be accounted for without any logical explanation of crime. False accusations came upon every leader, and Burr was no different than Jefferson or Washington or other heroes in this regard: "Many other great and eminent characters have been in like manner assailed." Randolph knew a noble figure when he saw one, and this one had been sacrificed "at the shrine of faction and persecution" (2:391, 397).

Everyone was embarrassed to find a founder of the Republic and recent vice president of the United States in the dock. Caesar Rodney, attorney general of the United States, said so in court. He pointed to the man "whom he once considered as his friend, and treated as such in his own house," lamenting the discrepancy between "transcendent talents" and "the most heinous crime" (1:8). The prosecution openly admitted that the former vice president lived "perhaps the second in the confidence and affection of the people." It eschewed the intrusion of these facts as prejudicial popularity at trial and, in an awkward reversal, then used them to insist that Burr's "circumstances rather aggravate than extenuate his guilt" (1:450–51).

The defense played its own cards with equally feigned gestures of regret. Why had the president of the United States "let slip the dogs of war, the hell-hounds of persecution to hunt down" an innocent man and virtuous ally (1:128)? Accusations of prejudice, general alarm, and danger for the country came frequently from both sides (1:62, 78, 163, 233, 239–40, 409, 411), and, as frequently happens in a high-profile trial, insults grew sharp between opposing counsel (1:232, 263, 331, 386, 585).

Courtroom conflict notwithstanding, three things became clear to both sides and received confirmation from neutral observers and reporters. Everyone agreed that neither the larger situation nor the reputation of Aaron Burr could remain where events had left them. More positively but also ominously, they assumed that the decision reached in Richmond would have national repercussions that no one could fathom, and, finally, all eagerly awaited the outcome at trial on these terms.

Consensus on these points entered the communal imagination in a special way and beyond the event itself. For the first time and as something of a precedent, Americans conceded and then welcomed the larger impact of a courtroom event as a legitimate barometer for gauging their collective situation. Whatever happened, early republicans accepted that the trial would shape communal perceptions and perhaps the direction of the country. Here, without anyone quite realizing it, was the birth of a ritual in the republic of laws.

After what would be a thousand pages of printed transcription of argument, the formal decision proved to be the simplest part of the case. John Marshall followed the lead that John Wickham had handed him on August 20 and 21 and gave the country a sharply restrictive definition of treason, partially reversing himself on an earlier decision in the process. It would be the longest opinion and the most detailed scholarly presentation that Marshall would ever write as a judge, and it took three hours for him to deliver. The gist can be given in a sentence. "In conformity with principle and authority then," Marshall announced, "the prisoner at the bar was neither legally nor actually present at Blennerhassett's island; and the court is strongly inclined to the opinion that without proving an actual or legal presence by two witnesses, the overt act laid in this indictment cannot be proved" (2:432).

With the answer predetermined, Marshall then instructed the jury to apply his finding in law to the facts, and the jury, after a brief retirement, returned with its verdict on September 1, 1807. "We of the jury say that Aaron Burr is not proved to be guilty under this indictment by any evidence submitted to us. We therefore find him not guilty" (2:446). There was a last flurry. Burr and his attorneys struggled to remove the deliberately grudging tones in this statement, but the chief justice refused them the simpler verdict of not guilty, perhaps in recognition of something else that had transpired in court.

Burr may not have committed treason, but his behavior had been unacceptable, and the more it was talked of in court, the more unacceptable it became. The demonic image remained in place because it exorcised a national threat. Not for the last time, a high-profile trial brought an inchoate problem into sharp focus. The possibility of a hostile nation rising in the western part of the North American continent worried many in 1807. Separate nations might duplicate the patterns of bloodshed then ravaging Europe.

As late as 1804, Jefferson as president had faced the prospect of a separate empire with equanimity. "Whether we remain in one confederacy or form into Atlantic and Mississippi confederacies," he wrote to Joseph Priestley in triumph over the Louisiana Purchase, "I believe not very important to the happiness of either part."[25] The specter of Aaron Burr loose in the West changed this complacency into alarm. Jefferson would denounce the decisions in Richmond and predicted dire consequences from them. "They are equivalent to a proclamation of impunity to every traitorous combination which may be formed to destroy the Union," he wrote of the court's actions.[26]

Burr had shown how a bold leader with attractive credentials might delude others into forming a competitor nation. The trial raised frightening prospects for all to see. As one of those who claimed to have been misled by Burr said of him in court, "The distinguished rank he held in society, and the strong marks of confidence which he had received from his fellow citizens did not permit me to doubt of his patriotism." In a disquieting moment for the listening nation, the speaker, an armed and ready veteran, asserted that he could find "none within the United States, under whose direction a soldier might with greater security confide his honour than colonel Burr" (1:474).

The overblown image of Burr had its impact on communal thinking. Some of those involved recognized the process at work. Speaking of Harman Blennerhassett at trial, Edmund Randolph complained, "He is to be called small in guilt because that of Mr. Burr is to be magnified" (2:387). Each side exaggerated the figure of Aaron Burr for argumentative purposes, and everyone was left with its enlarged scope and no clear sense of what to do with its puzzling dimensions. In the end, all of the hyperbole would clarify the pantheon of the founders through counterexample. Burr as Satan was the perfect type for a fallen angel, one subject to parallel distortions in appearance, intention, and negative power. The contrast reinforced what it meant in other founders to have acted correctly. The now thoroughly misshapen figure of Burr would frighten early republicans into a tighter conception of civic identity. Seduction of the Blennerhassetts had been a timely warning for all to heed.

Concepts of evil in a culture identify the blamable other, circumscribe it, and then hold it up as a spectacle for all to see. Aaron Burr, like the Miltonic Satan, had conscripted followers into a false cause.[27] As more and more Americans envisaged a providential continental republic, the trial of 1807 dramatized where fault could be assigned if the preordained expansion of the United States went awry.

Early republicans worried a great deal about how they should behave as public citizens in a changing nation.[28] Burr provided the object lesson in how *not* to behave—a lesson that brought new urgency and definition to westward expansion. The ultimate accusation leveled at Burr in his trial for treason charged him with dividing East against West in sectional strife (1:447–48). The demonic image of him at trial, a representation of communal danger, would continue to flourish as the risk of a divided nation grew more likely across the antebellum period. In the most graphic account of him ever written, Aaron Burr would come to stand for the horrors of civil war.

"THE MAN WITHOUT A COUNTRY"

Most Americans first encounter Aaron Burr through a short story entitled "The Man without a Country" written by Edward Everett Hale in 1863. Hale's biographer notes that the "combination of immediate success and enduring emotional relevance" made the story "unique among American stories written for magazines," and he doesn't exaggerate by much when he places its protagonist, Philip Nolan, alongside Rip Van Winkle as a recognizable character in American literature. At Hale's death in 1909, the *Nation* would call "The Man without a Country" "probably the most popular short story written in America." Within a year of its first appearance, the story sold half a million copies, a stupendous figure for the times. It has been frequently republished and anthologized ever since.[29]

Hale's parable on patriotism can be summarized in four sentences. Aaron Burr and other indicted "big flies" escape conviction in 1807, but the youthful Philip Nolan, a minor U.S. Army officer seduced by Burr, is found guilty, and in frustration, he shouts out at his trial: "D—n the United States! I wish I may never hear of the United States again!" His judges, Revolutionary War veterans all, decide to grant this wish and sentence the defendant to spend the rest of his life at sea on government ships under the singular injunction that he "never hear the name of the United States again." A lifetime of penance in total ignorance of his country gradually teaches Nolan the lesson of patriotism. Still under sentence after more than half a century at sea, he dies in the middle of the Civil War but only after developing the deepest devotion to his country and its meaning.[30]

Hale wrote his story in 1863, the darkest moment of the war for the Union cause, and his stated purpose was to teach Americans, particularly the young, "what the word 'Patriotism' means,—or what one's Country is." When he saw that his story was "copied everywhere," he felt justified: "It met the taste of the patriotic public at the moment." He also revealed what he expected in his reader through his own recorded reaction. Hale engaged in careful research to surround his fiction with accurate historical detail, but he wrote the actual story "almost without a break," pausing only to check with his editor and finishing it in one sitting. He would argue that spontaneity in the act of writing should control the act of reading. "The sentimental reader may be interested to know," Hale confided, "that my own tears blotted the paper of the original manuscript."[31]

The image of Aaron Burr in "The Man without a Country" flows from the one that William Wirt created. Burr is a "gay deceiver," "a disguised conqueror," the clever lawyer who "had defeated I know not how many district attorneys," and finally the mythic figure of fantastic rumor with "an army behind him and an empire before him." When he meets "little Nolan," it is "as the Devil would have it" and to "seduce him." A first encounter leaves the "fascinated" Nolan bored and restless with ordinary life, much like Blennerhassett before him; the second meeting binds Nolan "body and soul" to Burr, and from that moment "though he did not know it, [Nolan] lived as A MAN WITHOUT A COUNTRY" (666).

As in Wirt's account, Hale's Burr conquers through the magnetism of his rank and personality. He possesses mysterious powers. The fictional narrator of the story, a retired naval officer, condemns Burr but notably admits that he has no idea what Burr intended to accomplish or did in his western jaunts. "What Burr meant to do I know no more than you, dear reader," this narrator admits, in one of many direct addresses that control the emotional timbre of the narrative. "It is none of our business just now" (666).

Why can the narrator say with such confidence that Burr's guilt or innocence is none of our business? Burr, a cameo figure in "The Man without a Country," functions as a stage prop in support of a familiar lesson. The prop works so well because Hale duplicates the picture that the trial of Aaron Burr has already imprinted on republican culture. The narrator must confess his ignorance of Burr's intentions because every court that tried Burr came to the conclusion that it could not convict him of anything, and so the phrase used over and over again in the narrator's description of Burr is "I know not" (666).

This refrain repeats the jury's finding in Richmond while the pejorative connotations of the trial remain in place. The combination means the narrator need not explain the connotation of a "gay deceiver" in league with the devil. It is enough that Aaron Burr, the mythic figure with "an army behind him and an empire before him," has betrayed the future vision of America—more than enough, in fact, to condemn him outright. The image of Burr is less clarified than fixed in Hale's story, and it serves a particular purpose. The original United States, a confederacy of republics defined by the right of revolution in the eighteenth century, has been replaced by a modern nation-state in which the test of membership is going to be loyalty. Its explicit goal by 1863 is complete continental union.

"The Man without a Country" facilitates the shift from early Republic to modern nation-state for those caught in the crucible of civil war. The story, while simple, unfolds with this ideological shift in mind. Philip Nolan's disastrous cry against the United States occurs because he has kept to himself in his feelings of outrage (not an infrequent impulse in the early Republic) instead of accepting a national identity or his assigned place in his military unit, where a greater sense of membership might have saved him from his mistake (666). Poorly educated in citizenry as a boy by "an Englishman" in the then-disputed territory of Texas, Nolan chooses affiliation incorrectly, "body and soul," when the need for membership takes hold of him. He is undone by his ignorance and failure to recognize national values: "To him 'United States' was scarcely a reality" (667). That reality hardly existed in its full definition by 1807. The Burr conspiracy is useful to Hale precisely because it hastens the shift in perspective on the national question. Hale would admit the chronological problems in this evolving conception of the nation but only in a much later comment on his story:

> The Civil War has taught its lesson so well that the average American of the year 1896 hardly understands that any such lesson was ever needed. The United States *is* a nation now. And there is not left any one, living in the Northern, Middle, Western, or Pacific States, who ever thinks that the United States *are* a confederacy. The War settled that.[32]

Plurality was a dangerous conception for the fighting Union in 1863. Hale wrote to demonstrate the need for cohesion and to offer dramatic proof that his own definition should never have been in doubt.

The story pulls the reader into its claim of national unity in three ways, only one of which has been firmly identified. The first and frequently noted means of control involves Hale's use of *vraisemblance* to establish authentication. The fictive narrator of the story, a retired captain in the American navy named Fred Ingham, speaks in sailor's jargon but somewhat incongruously with high literary tones as well. Although the story appeared anonymously, this speaker secretly identifies the author by bearing parallel initials once removed: Officer *F*red *I*ngham follows author *E*dward *H*ale. The story works through Ingham's "half-confidence" with Nolan. Narrator and character learn from each other; they grow "confidentially intimate" and are "very kind" to each other (675, 677). As symbiotic creations, Ingham, the boy midshipman, first learns from the adult Nolan's example in a series of sea adventures. Now as an old man from the sea, this narrator writes to warn the American youth of 1863 "of what it is to throw away a country" (666, 677).

Ingham is a partially unknowing but thoroughly reliable narrator who must piece his story together from many accounts: "From one and another officer I have learned, in thirty years, what I am telling" (675). Just as sea voyages would have been regularly spaced, so each successive officer in the story informs the reader of another pattern in shipboard custom, which, in turn, connects with the history of the American navy. The clincher in this series comes when a final officer, named Danforth, writes to Ingham of Nolan's repentance and death. The internal narrative of this letter is festooned with the name of the writer's ship and its longitude and latitude as Nolan dies (677–79). Hale succeeds so skillfully with these authentications that some nineteenth-century readers would write to him with confirmations and corrections on the life of his fictional protagonist![33]

Hale's second device in unifying the nation reaches back to the jumble of rumor and fact that defined Aaron Burr in the early Republic. Like the first historian Herodotus, the narrator distinguishes between what he saw and what he heard, between conjecture and fact, between the reliability of one source and the fallibility of another, and he is similarly quick to confess an uncertainty. These gestures guard an inner truth where all before has been mystery. Many sentences in the story begin with phrases like "I have reason to think," "I have always supposed," "It may have been." They allow Ingham to step forward at other times with the firmer claim "But this I do know." These assurances culminate in absolute certainty over Nolan's final and utter repentance (665, 666, 667, 670, 675).

The narrator clarifies Nolan's life beyond "the mysteries that we boys used to invent" and wields this new precision to define the nation. "These are the traditions," he tells us, "which I sort out, as I believe them, from the myths which have been told about this man for forty years. The lies that have been told about him are legion" (677, 671). The biblical reference—Jesus casts "an unclean spirit" in the form of "devils" out of a madman and its "name *is* Legion"—reaches obliquely toward the demonic, but this time in elimination of confusion.[34] The narrator's careful distinctions between his previous ignorance and current knowledge parallel the ideal of education that the good citizen must undergo.

The same mystery and confusion apply to accounts of Aaron Burr. Hale draws the connection by dismissing a rumor that Nolan later met Burr on one of his cruises. There was no fortuitous meeting, no "tremendous blowing-up." Nolan never gets to ask Burr "how he liked to be 'without a country.' " The narrator's dismissal of this fantasy allows Hale to secure the rest of his imagined account as fact. Ingham first calls the meeting with Burr "a lie" but immediately corrects himself, turning it more deftly into "a myth, *ben trovato*," one so well said that people will believe it (675).

Hale wants his readers to know that the dangerous self-interests in history welcome exaggeration and distortion. The problem, of course, is that similar fabrications now threaten the nation. The Southern Confederacy has adopted a false narrative of national origins to break up the Union, and its deluded leaders, in their ignorance, deserve "all the agony of Nolan's" (676). Accuracy becomes the prime virtue of correct national identity. Hale's sequential storytellers replace exaggerations with negative truths, a device that guards their reliability for the positive truth of defining the nation.

A third authenticating device secures the psychological dimension. The plotline of "The Man without a Country" is highly sentimental. Reader after nineteenth-century reader followed Hale's example in weeping over his pages. We must look to an emotional progression to explain these reactions. Too harshly punished, Nolan undergoes six formative crises during a half century of captivity aboard ship, and they gradually lead him to *accept* his incredible sentence as just. Each incident teaches a different part of the lesson to be learned and imbibed vicariously by "the sentimental reader."

In the first lesson, Nolan breaks down in public while reading aloud from Sir Walter Scott's "Lay of the Last Minstrel." Scott, an early symbol of literary nationalism, reminds Nolan of his isolation. Dispossessed of "my own, my native land," Nolan has become a "wretch, concentrated all in self" (670). A second incident—in which "a celebrated Southern beauty of those days," "a splendid creature," refuses to talk of home to Nolan during a ball held aboard ship—completes his isolation, this time in social terms. It also gives an image of the true South through a potent symbol of that culture, the Southern belle (670–71). The third crisis, Nolan's heroic participation in a battle at sea during the War of 1812, teaches him and everyone else that courage has never been the issue; it therefore brings no change in punishment (671–72). The fourth incident, which begins at the center of the story and is by far the longest, requires more careful treatment. Set in the 1820s, it entails the capture of a slave ship, the freeing of the slaves on it, Philip Nolan's first public repentance, and the definition of citizenship that Hale wants to impose (673–75).

Brought aboard the slave ship as an interpreter, Nolan experiences "the horrors of the Middle Passage," a "nastiness beyond account." "Nolan's agony" develops as he translates for the freed slaves who plead: "Take us home, take us to our own country, take us to our own house." These events trigger a confession to Midshipman Ingham as they return by boat to their own ship. "Youngster," Nolan begins, "let that show you what it is to be without a family, without a home, and without a country." Family, home, country are all one in Nolan's new conception of country. Ingham hears "forget you have a self, while you do everything for them!" By the end of this soliloquy, the conflation is complete: "Remember, boy, that behind all these men . . . there is the Country Herself, your Country, and that you belong to Her as you belong to your own mother. Stand by Her, boy, as you would stand by your mother" (675). Turning into "a sort of lay chaplain" of nationalism, Nolan realizes in the subsequent and fifth lesson that his previous home, Texas, must have joined the Union. In a phrase that will come to mean everything, he discovers "Texas is out of the map" (676).

The sixth and concluding vignette reveals that the dying Nolan has built "a little shrine" to country in his stateroom aboard ship (677–79). His place of worship is complete with the Stars and Stripes, a picture of Washington, and the American eagle. "Here, you see," he explains, "I have a country!" This profession, if nineteenth-century accounts are to be trusted, brought endless tears.[35] "There cannot be a man who loves the old flag as I do, or prays for it as I do, or hopes for it as I do," adds Nolan, and he means it quite literally. In a ritual performed twice a day, he has knelt to thank God "that there has never been any successful Burr" and prayed that God will "behold and bless Thy servant, the President of the United States, and all others in authority."

The truly striking discovery in the cabin is, however, Nolan's empty map. Early republicans lived with the iconographic anxiety of territory beyond their definition and grasp. Nolan in his ignorance in 1863 remains an early republican held in suspension, and he has tried to fill the emptiness with imaginary categories. The first thing he asks for, the gesture that means the most to him, comes when Danforth agrees to "take down his beautiful map and draw [the new states] in as I best could with my pencil." Nolan turns "wild with delight." His shock of recognition reveals in emblematic form the trial of Aaron Burr better than any narrative. The problem is not just a question of boundaries. The uncertainty in unboundedness and the ensuing inability to imagine a satisfying spatial coherence led the first republicans to behave in ways and beyond the ken of later Americans.

The legal implications of Nolan's cabin take shape in an epitaph that he has left for his tombstone. These last words, also the final words of Hale's story, are "He loved his country as no other man has loved her; but no man deserved less at her hands" (679). Trials ask a defendant to accept punishment while enduring it. When a defendant actively refuses the legitimacy of a court's finding, uneasiness lingers over the process like a bad smell. Nolan has been too severely dealt with, no question, but his love of country overcomes whatever hesitation he may have felt on that score. As he says of his country, "Never dream a dream but of serving her as she bids you, though the service carry you through a thousand hells" (675).

A defendant overly punished deserves sympathy; one that rises above the fact receives admiration. The nobility of Nolan comes through his growth in punishment, just as the presumed ignobility of Aaron Burr lies in his unwarranted escape. Nolan's one moment of anger in death comes when he learns that Burr was never tried again. The narrator tells us that Nolan "ground his teeth" over this travesty. The moment leaves us with two questions that Edward Everett Hale expected his reader to take for granted (678). Did Aaron Burr deserve punishment? What is more, did he really escape it?

JUDGMENT AT RICHMOND

The continuum of publication around a trial is of particular use in gauging what is often called "public justice," the compensatory reaction when a community acts through its own conclusions about what has taken place in a trial. Public justice develops into a serious matter when a discrepancy exists between official findings and communal perception. It becomes acute when a verdict of not guilty fails to convince a community that the defendant has deserved the benefit of the doubt just received.[36]

A verdict of not guilty is entirely appropriate in a close case. The legal system assumes that defendants do not have to prove their innocence; they need only raise a reasonable doubt to avoid a determination of guilt. But not guilty also leaves persistent questions unanswered in a legal contest that has attracted great attention and much speculation. If the defendant is not guilty when a crime has been committed, then who is guilty? This question invariably becomes an angry one. Communities expect the clarification that a trial can bring them and grow annoyed when a crime or other form of deviance remains unresolved. When negative decisions are reached, perspectives still change. Reputations are made and lost. All of these conditions applied in the trial of Aaron Burr, and they can be used to delineate a larger shift in historical understanding.

Of the reputations involved in the Burr trial, only that of John Marshall emerged fully intact. The chief justice, acting as a circuit judge, was criticized at the time, but the opinion that he delivered in Richmond on August 31, 1807, represents one of the finest hours in an illustrious career. Marshall conducted the trial under enormous pressure from all sides, and the greatest pressure came from above. Marshall presided under a threat of impeachment from his chief political enemy, the president of the United States.

Thomas Jefferson oversaw the prosecution of Burr from Washington. He justified every expense, sent scores of letters with suggestions about strategy, and offered blanket pardons to co-conspirators who would cooperate as witnesses. Six months before the trial, Jefferson had declared that Aaron Burr was "the principal actor, whose guilt is placed beyond question."[37] He needed a conviction. Threats of impeachment against Marshall if he rendered an unfavorable decision were first raised obliquely but then explicitly by both sides in court, and the threats had substance. Attempts to intimidate Federalists who sat on the bench during Jefferson's

Figure 6. James Reid Lambdin (after Henry Inman), *John Marshall* (painting after 1831). Oil on canvas, 35 ⁷/₁₆ x 28 ¹⁵/₁₆ in. (NPG.65.54). National Portrait Gallery, Smithsonian Institution. Gift of the A. W. Mellon Educational and Charitable Trust. Chief Justice John Marshall, presiding in the Circuit Court of the United States in 1807, prevented the conviction of Aaron Burr by confirming the restrictive definition of treason written into the U.S. Constitution twenty years before. Marshall held his ground against veiled threats of impeachment from his longtime adversary and president of the United States, Thomas Jefferson. The opinion he wrote was one of the most courageous and learned of an illustrious career; it remains a vital gauge of American liberty and judicial independence today.

administrations included impeachment proceedings as well as legislative plans to curtail the judiciary.[38]

Worried by the government's tactics, the defense added to Marshall's discomfort by hinting that he had slipped in the temple of justice. "The floor of that temple is slippery," observed Edmund Randolph, questioning Marshall's resolve: "He who means to stand firm in that temple must place his hand on the statue of wisdom; the pedestal of which is a lion."

Randolph wondered whether Marshall had the courage, symbolized by the lion since antiquity, to act appropriately, and he left none of the negative implications to chance. "In the conflicts of political animosity justice is sometimes forgotten or sacrificed to mistaken zeal and prejudice," Randolph concluded (2:400). This rather pompous lecture on professional courage included the last words that Marshall would hear before sitting down to write his opinion on whether or not the prosecution would be allowed to proceed with what amounted to a constructive theory of the crime of treason.

Strain is unavoidable in a high-profile case. The population of Richmond doubled during the trial, and newspaper coverage exploited every moment of the proceedings with speculation about individual performances and particular scrutiny given to Marshall. The chief justice faced serious procedural challenges over the fairness of his proceedings. He had to make crucial distinctions between questions of fact, which should be given to the jury for decision, and questions of law, which the court would decide.

How, in the first place, could one come up with an impartial jury in Richmond, where most potential members of the voir dire pool admitted some prejudice against Burr through newspaper commentary and their willing acceptance and support of the president's comments against Burr? Jefferson, after all, was a fellow Virginian complaining about a New Yorker. When the jurors finally took their assigned places on August 17, they did so only after two weeks of wrangling and a careful analysis by Marshall setting forth the reasonable limits on jury impartiality (1:414–20). Everyone understood that the twelve men selected would lean against the defendant (1:427–30).

The legal contest depended absolutely on the choices that Marshall would make. The prosecution wanted as many issues as possible brought before the favorably inclined jury, while the defense asked for judicial decisions out of jurors' hands. What did it mean to "levy war"? Was this a question of fact for the jury or of law for the bench? Was Aaron Burr's constructive presence at Blennerhassett Island a question of fact or of law? Was Burr an accessory or a principal in the events that took place on the island, and was this question, too, one of fact or of law? Marshall found himself in the uncomfortable position of having to deal with his own loose words about treason from just a year before.

In *Ex parte Bollman*, a case that touched on others in the Burr conspir-

acy, Marshall had declared that "if war be actually levied, that is, if a body
of men be actually assembled for the purpose of effecting by force a treasonable purpose, all those who perform any part, however minute, or
however remote from the scene of action, and who are actually leagued in
the general conspiracy, are to be considered traitors."[39] Did this seemingly
broad construction of treason decide the issues of principal versus accessory and the degree of activity for war to be levied? The legal questions
were far more complicated than the public discourse on Burr's behavior
wanted to allow.

The chief justice knew better than to rely on his customary use of
broad principles. He took up the same tangle of arcane cases and statutes
in English and American law that counsel had argued before him, citing
more authorities than in any other opinion that he would ever write.[40]
Then, claiming "the most temperate and the most deliberate consideration," he came down hard on the side of a strict construction of treason,
one that held the government to the literal meaning of article 3, section 3,
of the Constitution (2:401, 443). Marshall noted, "There must be a war or
the crime of levying it cannot exist," and he found there had *been* no war
by the evidence shown (2:402). An "assemblage of force" to which the
defendant could be tied directly by two witnesses was an indispensable
condition in an assessment of guilt (2:421–22). English doctrines of constructive treason were "inapplicable to the United States," which meant
the overt act of treason could not be stretched to include one "who counsels and advises it," as Burr seemed to have done (2:405, 439).

Not content with the theory of the matter, Marshall came perilously
close to questions of fact in a final crushing blow to the prosecution's
case: "In conformity with principle and authority, then, the prisoner at
the bar was neither legally nor actually present at Blannerhassett's island"
(2:432). It seemed hardly necessary to add more, but Marshall did: "The
court is strongly inclined to the opinion that without proving an actual
or legal presence by two witnesses, the overt act laid in this indictment
cannot be proved" (2:432).

Leaving the jury with nothing to decide, Marshall turned next to his
tormentors at the bar. The final words of his opinion established a touchstone of judicial independence against the intrusions of executive and
legislative authority. Earlier, when defense counsel "plainly insinuated
the possibility of danger to the court" through threats of an impeachment proceeding against him, Marshall had held his own peace, blandly

refusing to find "any personal allusion" in the language cited (2:238–39). Now, with the case decided, he moved to demonstrate just how solid his footing had been on the floor of justice that counsel had so glibly derided as too "slippery" for him.

The opinion had been carefully prosaic up to this point, even matter-of-fact, in careful contrast to the "degree of eloquence" that Marshall already had thanked counsel for exhibiting (2:401). At the very end, though, the chief justice lifted his own language, choosing cannily but quietly from the same registers of religiosity that the lawyers before him had wielded with such bombast. "That this court dares not usurp power is most true," he began. "That this court dares not shrink from its duty is not less true." He then gently chided the lawyers in front of him. His stance had never deviated "to the one side or the other from the line prescribed by duty and by law," even though "on each side" they had tried to "press their arguments too far," had been "impatient at any deliberation in the court," and had come to "suspect or fear the operation of motives" (2:444).

These negative propensities of counsel against the court could be dismissed as "perhaps a frailty incident to human nature," but a judge had to operate above such tendencies while also controlling them. The references to frailty then took a compelling form. Marshall had been hurt by the veiled accusations bandied about him, and he said so, not hesitating to use the language of Christ to present his situation. He had not enjoyed finding himself "in a disagreeable situation." What person would? "No man is desirous of becoming the peculiar subject of calumny," he reminded those who had abused him, including the president of the United States. "No man, might he let the bitter cup pass from him without self reproach, would drain it to the bottom." Marshall wanted everyone to see that he had persevered after being forced to drink deeply. A conception of duty beyond the view of those around him had sustained him and guided his conduct throughout (2:444–45).

Marshall had seen right away what dangers an expansive definition of treason could bring. "As this is the most atrocious offence which can be committed against the political body," he observed at the beginning when committing Burr for trial, "so it is the charge which is most capable of being employed as the instrument of those malignant and vindictive passions which may rage in the bosoms of contending parties struggling for power." Sensibly, the American people had "refused to trust the national

legislature with the definition," fixing it instead in the body of the Constitution (1:13–14). Only a severely restricted definition could possibly hold
unwarranted passions in check. In effect, *United States v. Burr* would secure that result but at a price. Soon there would be an ugly stepchild
to circumvent the difficulties in proving a charge of treason: the crime
of conspiracy. Marshall would even show the way as, once again, Aaron
Burr served as a catalyst in thought.

The arch conspirator in the Burr conspiracy was clearly identified in
Marshall's opinion. The chief justice made the connection repeatedly but
with a vital distinction in mind. "However flagitious may be the crime of
conspiracy to subvert by force the government of our country," he reasoned, "such conspiracy is not treason" (2:416). The plotter of a crime
could be a "blacker criminal" than the physical actor, but "moral guilt"
could not convict Burr of treason by reason or authority (2:440–41). If
Burr had been up to something, it was nonetheless true that "the law does
not expect a man to be prepared to defend every act of his life" (2:424).
Could one who procured a treason be found guilty under the Constitution? Possibly, but the Supreme Court had not yet said so; Marshall
distinguished all earlier cases on the subject, including *Ex parte Bollman*
(2:439). Had Burr been an accessory to treason? Marshall handled the
question tongue in cheek:

> Pleading to an indictment, in which a man is charged as having com-
> mitted an act, cannot be construed to waive a right which he would
> have possessed had he been charged as having advised the act. No per-
> son indicted as a principal can be expected to say I am not a principal.
> I am an accessory. I did not commit, I only advised the act. (2:442)

No one could miss the schemer in these descriptions of Burr. Marshall
seemed to say that the government had bungled its case more than Burr
had won it. Timing and precise wording were everything in his view of
the matter. It was only "the present indictment" that had failed (2:443).
Could there be others? Marshall implied that was possible (2:444). If Jefferson had been listening carefully, he might have realized that Marshall
was fulfilling the basic goal of the prosecution. Everything in the chief
justice's demeanor toward the man he frequently called "the prisoner"
implied unacceptable behavior at the source. The implication though
muted would carry the day. It was not necessary to convict and execute

Aaron Burr to punish him. Better far to avoid even the hint of martyrdom. The personage who still carried a political threat would suffer more from his release.

PUBLIC JUSTICE

The subsequent life of Aaron Burr would prove the point. His career in American politics was over the moment he left the courtroom, and Marshall's handling of the trial had much to do with that result. The restraint shown in letting a seeming rascal go enhanced the dignity of the legal process and left Burr with none. No longer a founder who had shared in the creation of the Republic, Burr was now and forever the conniver who tried to tear it down: "the destroyer comes" (2:97). At trial he had turned out to be what no success story in America could ever tolerate: a bungler.

Nothing that Burr had attempted had worked, and, long before the creation of Philip Nolan, he became the man without a country. For the four years following his trial, he wandered in exile through Europe, where his moods would swing between grandiose plans and realization of what he had become. As his journal from those years indicates, Burr led an aimless life organized around constant travel, frustrated ambitions, shallow acquaintances, compulsive womanizing, and grinding poverty. He described it once as "too long a story to tell, and worth nothing when told."[41]

Always resilient, Burr struggled against a fate that he could not change. He went to Europe with major ambitions, and, as always, he made friends easily. In Europe those friends would include Jeremy Bentham, Charles Lamb, William Godwin, and Johann Wolfgang von Goethe, but the former vice president was shunned everywhere by Americans abroad, and every attempt to reestablish himself as a personage led to further humiliation. Burr's dreams bore no relation to his new reality. "I sit down to recollect the trifling incidents of the last six days," he wrote from Stockholm in 1809. "Trifling indeed. But if the operations of my head and heart could be delineated, each day would fill a volume." Final realization would come in Paris in 1810, where he grandly "hoped to do the emperor [Napoleon] and myself so much good." Once there, however, and spurned when not harassed by officialdom, he found "no prospect but that of starving in Paris."[42]

Social slights of all kinds came thick and fast. Dining at the Baron d'Albey's in Paris, Burr discovered that he "was of so small account that neither chair nor plate was provided," and "he stood a minute after all were seated." At another noble house, he was denied admission altogether, "not being on the list of receivables." With the Duke of Rovigo, he was one of forty-seven beseechers in a semicircle; the duke kept him waiting for hours before a thirty-second interview that accomplished nothing. Poverty would eventually drive Burr completely "out of society." Toward the end of his European sojourn, he found himself too poor to keep a fire in the dead of winter or to reclaim his boots from repair. Hunger was now a reality instead of a metaphor, and it led to new levels and kinds of degradation. "Better than starving," he turned translator. "The book in question," he discovered on one occasion, "contains a quantity of abuse and libels on A. Burr."[43]

The journal became the record of a man fighting depression. Burr complained of "great torpor." He slept too much and remembered no dreams from his prolonged slumbers. "Home at six," ran an early entry, "a little stupid or so." "I had to go sauntering about the streets of a strange place, alone and unarmed, on Christmas Eve," ran another from Birmingham. "It is no easy matter to determine how to dispose of myself," he wrote from Stockholm in 1809. "Why stay here? The summary is that I am resolved to go without knowing exactly why or where." A sojourner in Europe, Burr had no word from home for years at a time. By his own admission, he grew rude and irritable.[44] When he did hear from his beloved daughter, Theodosia, to whom he addressed his journal, it could not have helped that she expected some great thing of him. "Tell me," she wrote in October of 1808, "that you are engaged in some pursuit worthy of you." Reading the newspapers from America, he looked for "some consequence to me, if, indeed, anything be of any consequence." This was punishment indeed for a fastidious socialite driven by ambition and the quest for fame.[45]

Rarely reflective, Burr knew what had happened to him. His experience in Europe became a pointless and prolonged exercise in misery. Early on he described the consequences. His life had become a "sort of non-existence." The founder's fall had been from a great height, and like his accusers, he described it in religious though mocking terms. "I have often heard that great sinners have relieved their consciences in full confession," he wrote late in 1808. "Let us try." In Paris the military man toured the Hôtel des Invalides, the hospital and memorial to France's own military heroes. As Colonel Burr, he naturally went to pay his respects to the fallen Duke of Montebello, a hero mortally wounded in battle the year before as one of Napoleon's valiant field marshals. Honored in every way, the duke, in Burr's description, "lies in state" amongst "lamps innumerable hung with black." The American outcast admitted that he went for personal reasons: "What I was most desirous of seeing was the process of getting a soul out of purgatory."[46] Even as a joke, the contrast to his own living purgatory could not have been without recognition and pain.

Another sacred building in Paris brought full-fledged despair. Burr visited the Panthéon early in 1811. He was impoverished and in hiding from his creditors as well as the French authorities at the time. All of his vaunted projects lay in ruins, and he was without either the means or the official papers to leave France. The account written down in his journal is worth quoting in full:

> Thinking of other things as I walked; got to the Panthéon without thinking whither I was going. I then stood some minutes to discover who I was. In what country I was. What business I had there. For what I came abroad. And where I intended to go.[47]

The symbol of French national glory, the Panthéon stood for everything that Burr had tried to achieve and failed to accomplish. It, too, contained the honored dead, and the motto above its portico read: "AUX GRANDS HOMMES LA PATRIE RECONNAISSANTE." The impoverished translator would have had no trouble rendering the English: "To Great Men the Grateful Country."[48] Burr was no longer great and his country was certainly no longer grateful. No similar arrangement awaited him. The scene so represented lost status and absent prospects that he paused to wonder who he was and where he could possibly go from there. Burr was an eighteenth-century man. His life as an ostracized exile lacked all meaning before the monument of civic coherence before him. Here, if anywhere, was the man's recognition and acceptance that he no longer belonged in the story of American formations and receptions. None of Aaron Burr's enemies could possibly have wished for more.

Lingering over Burr's descent serves a purpose. The grip of a high-profile trial can lead to permanent change when the circumstances are right, and there are lessons to learn from the phenomenon. This trial stripped a prominent figure and successful defendant of all identity—even in his own mind. Burr would return to America in the middle of 1812 to live out a private life of legal practice, but nothing changed in the way that his country regarded him. It made no difference when Texas broke from Mexico in 1836 and declared itself a separate empire as the conspirator had wished many years before. "*There!*" Burr is supposed to have claimed, "you see? I was right! I was only thirty years too soon! What was treason in me thirty years ago, is patriotism now!!"[49]

Not so. The charge of treason held mud that stuck. National understanding would never entertain another conception. Burr's trial for treason occupied a permanent niche in the conception of national formations. Burr remained too valuable an example of forbidden behavior for the still-expanding United States to revise its opinions of the man who lived on and on but never beyond his fixed moment in history.

One cannot lose caste; only status. Permanently enlarged but ignored, Burr sought a return to respectability in one final act that reached back in principle to the Panthéon and the Hôtel des Invalides. He asked, as a matter of right, to be buried with honor in the Presidents' Plot of the college burial ground at Princeton beside the graves of his forebears, President Jonathan Edwards and President Aaron Burr Sr. Would Princeton deny him that right? In a final twist of negative mythology, the college granted the wish while thwarting the desire. On September 16, 1836, Aaron Burr received burial with full ceremony in the appropriate place, but the grave itself went unmarked for decades. Today a simple marker identifies the deceased as "colonel in the army of the Revolution" and "vice-president of the United States," Burr's primary patriotic identifications.[50]

The graveyard is worth the trip. To see Burr's marker you must search for it. Princeton has shrouded the tombstone on three sides with a bush that separates it from the other graves in the Presidents' Plot. The separation is complete. The bush around the stone obscures Burr's grave from every position except straight on. To take up that position, to see the inscription, you must stand outside of the Presidents' Plot and look within. No other headstone in the plot is surrounded in this manner. Aaron Burr, not guilty of treason, is still damned for it into the twenty-first century.

CHAPTER FOUR

John Brown: Defendant on the Loose

THE FIRST MODERN COURTROOM EVENT

Arguments at trial convince through different rhetorical features, some more obvious than others. The trial of Aaron Burr in 1807 responded to an anxiety in national formations through the mechanism of story. When a modern Satan sought to destroy happiness in the American garden, available parallels to the biblical tale were convincing enough to carry beyond a strict application of law. The high-profile trial of John Brown in 1859 drew upon another national anxiety, the paradox of slavery in a democratic republic, and it, too, changed the way Americans would think about a central issue in their midst. But Brown's trial, held in the Virginia State Circuit Court of Jefferson County in Charlestown, tapped into the collective imagination in a more subtle way. It altered thought through the form of story rather than the tale itself. Generic conventions helped to make John Brown a paradoxically successful defendant in the moments of his conviction and execution.

Ralph Waldo Emerson summarized the complex nature of John Brown's appeal in a single sentence. "For Captain Brown," Emerson wrote on the second day of Brown's trial, "he is a hero of romance & seems to have made this fatal blunder only to bring out his virtues."[1] Emerson's words are familiar today, but we no longer quite comprehend what they meant at the time. We accept Emerson's appraisal but without an informed sense of the assumptions at work in his language. What did it mean to be a romantic hero who blunders into virtue? Hidden from view in Emerson's comment are literary recognitions that controlled American thought processes on the brink of civil war.

Ironies abound when a community contemplates the actions of its legal system. Burr, a distinguished citizen and leading public servant, was found not guilty of treason in 1807 but lived out the remainder of his long life as the unquestioned villain of republican culture. Brown—a ne'er-do-well who failed in every major venture of his life, a loner on the fringes of antebellum politics—was found guilty of crimes against his country in 1859 and emerged as an American saint, even though he bungled his plans worse than Aaron Burr and used violent tactics that left innocent blood on his hands. In both trials, observers placed value on something other than the legal decision, and yet the legal process was crucial in shaping opinion.

Had Brown been killed during his raid on Harpers Ferry, as he nearly was, he would almost certainly have been dismissed as a fool and an aberration in the midst of sectional strife. It was what happened to John Brown *during* his trial that made him a byword in history. To understand how Brown materialized as a national figure is to see how a major trial creates personality and changes public opinion in dramatic ways. The image of Brown that emerged from his trial was of the first white man in America to risk himself for black people held in slavery, the first to actually sacrifice his life for universal application of the principle that "all men are created equal." Even so, there were other narratives afloat during Brown's trial, and few white Americans in 1859 were prepared to accept blacks as their equals. Why, then, did the narrative of Brown's sacrifice dominate reception so immediately, and why did other accounts fall just as rapidly by the wayside?

Generic recognitions flooded immediate communication about the trial and enabled its proponents to interpret a complex event a certain way. Resonances between courtroom performance and the genre of the American romance turned Brown into Emerson's "hero of romance" and Brown's life into a national story of mythopoeic proportions. Reiteration through familiar form imprinted both manifestations on the American mind in a remarkably short period of time. The nature of that transmission remains with us today, and its peculiar power foreshadowed things to come. Brown's trial became the first modern courtroom event. It would be the first to claim daily multimedia validation—from newspaper journalists, from leading essayists, from poets, from occasional orators, and from the greatest invention of the times, what was then called "the voice of God," the telegraph.

Much against its own purposes, the Virginia courtroom in Charlestown brought implicitly condoned ideological inconsistencies about
slavery to the surface. Brown's unprecedented attack on Harpers Ferry
pitted region against region through force of arms, but it was the defendant's mode of presentation at trial that forced new recognitions about
slavery through a specific frame of interpretation. On trial for his life,
John Brown achieved imaginative power in the same way that the prosecutors in the trial of Aaron Burr did. He mixed legal artifice with religious
language. But if Brown spoke as he did through personal conviction as a
deeply religious man, he convinced his most important auditors, the less
religious writers who would establish his reputation, on another plane
of reference.

Media recognition came through the rhetorical license that the
nineteenth-century romance gave Brown. The reigning genre in antebellum fiction, the romance, so-called, was "conceived in terms of the
fanciful and idealistic, rather than in terms of observation and faithful
description of fact."[2] Never one to be tied down by facts, Brown wielded
his own facts loosely and for maximum melodramatic effect. But how
did this propensity fit the unlikely setting of a courtroom? How could
the contrasting proclivities of the romance and legal narrative come together at all in a trial? Where did "the fanciful" apply in a legal forum
committed to "faithful description of fact"?

"CAREERING ON THE VERGE OF A PRECIPITOUS ABSURDITY"

The failure of the raid on Harpers Ferry had everything to do with John
Brown's ultimate success as a public figure. The fatal blunder, to paraphrase Emerson, brought out Brown's virtues and repressed his vices.
The raid, in narratives of the event, became an "ultimate triumphant
failure," and Brown himself came to understand his role in these terms.[3]
"The great bulk of mankind estimate each other's actions and motives
by the measure of success or otherwise that attend them through life,"
he wrote from prison after the raid. "By that rule, I have been one of
the worst and one of the best of men." Two days before his execution, he
added, "I have now no doubt but that our seeming disaster will ultimately
result in the most glorious success."[4]

The raid as planned could not have succeeded, and many said so at the time. Be that as it may, the significance of failure to later cultural formations has not been appreciated. The raid broke down as soon as it began on October 16, 1859. John Brown and his twenty-one followers held their objective, the U.S. Arsenal at Harpers Ferry, for less than thirty-six hours before federal troops under Brevet Colonel Robert E. Lee easily overwhelmed them. Not a single local slave chose to join Brown's attempt "to free the slaves."[5] Of the seventeen who died at Harpers Ferry, ten belonged to Brown's party; two were his sons. The project was ill-conceived and poorly executed. Harpers Ferry, in the Blue Ridge Mountains of northern Virginia, had no large slave plantations nearby to call upon, and free whites outnumbered slaves in the surrounding counties by a ratio of almost seven to one. None of the circumstances at hand were propitious for a slave rebellion. Moreover, the raiders neglected to bring so much as a day's rations to sustain their enterprise, and their first shots killed a black railroad worker who was already free.[6]

These facts could be ignored only because every failure contributed to another kind of success. The act of imagination behind the raid stimulated reactions that still need to be explained and that suggest much about the intellectual sensibilities of antebellum Americans. In a series of reversals, the attack on Harpers Ferry held nineteenth-century minds in part because it did *not* hold physical terrain. There was, in consequence, little need for anyone except the court to dwell on the messy and often absurd details of Brown's actual performance. Instead, imagined possibilities dominated all accounts on every side of the event. Unconfined levels of fascination spiraled away from reality but—and this was the crux—in a strangely familiar and, therefore, enjoyable way.

John Brown loomed large because of his capacity to dare. He roused competing visions in the American psyche: dreams of cultural fulfillment and purification vied with nightmares of armed invasion and racial warfare. Each side constructed an extreme fictional protagonist out of Brown. He was either the hero or the villain of history—never anything in between. Neither vision had much to do with the facts at Harpers Ferry. North and South both gave way to entrenched patterns of thought in which political, religious, and racial perceptions welcomed exaggerated possibilities.

Rhetorical excess transfigured Brown from lifelong bungler, bankrupt, narrow extremist, murderer, and border ruffian into a cultural icon.

No other transfiguration of character in American history compares in speed, power, and acceptance, even though no one has bothered to trace this phenomenon to its ultimate source. Thematically and historically, the transfiguration of Brown belongs to the development of a literary form that reached its highest expression in what critics have come to call the American Renaissance, the great outpouring of fiction, poetry, and intellectual texts amidst the sectional strife of the 1850s.

The parallels between John Brown's appeal and the genre of the American romance can be seen in the comments of one of the greatest practitioners of the form, Nathaniel Hawthorne.[7] No supporter of Brown, Hawthorne expressed a prevalent communal reaction when he said that the leader of the raid on Harpers Ferry had "preposterously miscalculated the possibilities."[8] The remark is useful because Hawthorne also knew that the preposterous described an essential form of comprehension and literary expression in his time. As he told his publisher in 1850, "The fact is, in writing a romance, a man is always—or always ought to be—careering on the verge of a precipitous absurdity, and the skill lies in coming as close as possible, without actually tumbling over."[9] John Brown appeared on such a verge, and his tumble turned into an extraordinary ascension. His transformation would correspond to the license, disengagement, symbolism, and performative dialectic that Hawthorne brought to the craft of fiction. Unmistakably, nineteenth-century Americans exalted or vilified John Brown for some of the same reasons that they were titillated by romancers like Hawthorne.

That John Brown contributed to his own figuration has long been recognized. Historians refer to Brown's "remarkable sense of words" and his capacity "to create an image of himself as a man." The best of them recognize that "this strange disguised romanticist," in "holding the mirror up to art," "had romanticized himself quite as much as others romanticized him." Missing from these accounts, however, is a precise understanding of how Brown's words in court and from prison worked, how they electrified his countrymen through popular forms of expression.[10] Missing, as well, is a realization of how strategic these uses were for the times. Brown may be the first figure in American culture to have controlled the perception of a major event through self-dramatization and media awareness. As he put the matter himself in pondering his own execution, "I have been *whipped* as the saying *is*; but am sure I can recover all the lost capital occasioned by that disaster; by only hanging a few moments by the neck; & I feel quite determined to make the utmost possible out of a defeat."[11]

Success from failure supplies the stuff of the romance, and quantum shifts in the opinions of contemporaries show how Brown used his trial for just this effect. Students of the raid and its aftermath agree that the apotheosis of Brown would have been mitigated, perhaps obviated altogether, if Brown had received a prison sentence instead of the death penalty at trial. They also agree that most antebellum Americans were not in sympathy with Brown's goals. North as well as South feared a slave insurrection of the kind that Brown tried to instigate at Harpers Ferry. That the slaves did *not* rebel was a relief everywhere in white America, and this, too, provided one of the levels on which failure functioned as a license for the imagination.

It was Brown's strange performance at trial that led so many to identify with him. In the first hundred years of the Republic, only the deaths of leading presidents—of George Washington in 1799, of John Adams and Thomas Jefferson prophetically together on July 4, 1826, and of Abraham Lincoln on Good Friday in 1865—matched the paroxysms of emotion unleashed by the death of John Brown. In 1859, between October 18 (the day of Brown's capture) and December 2 (the day of his execution), the public image of the man moved from an outlaw on the edge of abolitionist politics to a moral touchstone for all in American life. How did these shifts achieve such range when the vast majority of Americans, North and South, remained suspicious of Brown's goals at Harpers Ferry? How did they reach such a level of intensity over a relatively obscure figure in a mere six weeks?

The answers to these questions remain complicated even after we acknowledge that they can be found in Brown's words and behavior during his six-day trial in the Circuit Court of Jefferson County. Some of the explanation lies in the extensive reportage given to colorful eyewitness accounts of the trial and to the peculiar nature of Brown's performance in the eyes of the press. In 1859 the media were just reaching the technological capacity to narrate the immediacy of daily events on a national scale, and Brown made good regular copy through his bold but careless attitude toward his own peril under court counts of conspiracy, treason, and murder. While a long string of witnesses under the direction of special state prosecutor Andrew Hunter supported all three grave charges with vivid accounts of the raid during the first three days of the trial,

Brown managed to keep himself at the center of attention by challenging his own lawyers and forcing several changes in them.[12]

Part, but only part, of Brown's movement from marginality to "the greatest and best" and "the most American of us all," to use Henry Thoreau's phrases, came through the willingness of the press to concentrate on Brown's courtroom theatricality in newspaper lead after newspaper lead.[13] Reporters repeated the essential facts of the raid every day but through the lens of Brown's perspective and trial experience. Constant repetition imprinted the story—what has since been termed "the story line"—turning the trial itself into a synecdoche of Brown's achievement. Meanwhile, recognition of the story line taught a national press that a local trial, like the outlier Brown himself, could make good regular copy. Newspapers about the trial sold everywhere and on a daily basis.

ABOLITIONISM UNGAGGED

What happened in the trial of John Brown changed antebellum attitudes toward a stance in the republic of laws. Brown used his right to be heard at trial to dramatize a contradiction in the culture around him, that of slavery in a society where all men were declared to be equal. The contradiction was hardly new in 1859. Americans had recognized the problem in 1776, and they had accepted a presumed inconsistency between republicanism and slavery when they included the "peculiar" institution in the act of national formation.[14] Brown and other abolitionists repudiated that acceptance, but they had been a minority in antebellum politics to this point and faced great difficulty in finding a forum at once congenial and official for articulating views that most of their contemporaries regarded as extreme.

Brown's trial brought a suddenly unavoidable focus to the debate over slavery. Before the trial, Congress and state legislatures managed to evade radical abolitionist polemics through informal or formal "gag rules" that kept antislavery petitions from being heard. Ordinary citizens could, in consequence, ignore or repress the ideological inconsistency in slavery by consigning their frustrations to the dysfunctional political sphere.[15] In Brown's trial, the context of exchange was neither occasional, nor consensual, nor even loosely political; it was official, adversarial, efficacious, and, above all, legal. Scrutiny of slavery was imposed in the courtroom by

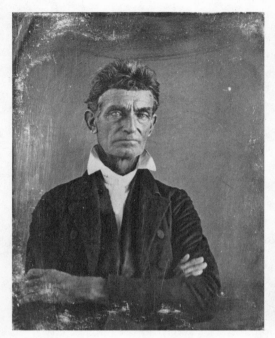

Figures 7 & 8. (*Left*) Anon., *John Brown* (1856). Portrait. Sixth plate daguerreotype, bare plate. Accession #1942.1. Photograph: UTB 6/5.4/Bro.j. (no. 1). Boston Athenaeum. (*Right*) Anon., *John Brown* (1859). Engraving. Photograph courtesy of Columbia University Libraries. In the first high-profile trial to depend on pictorial representations in press coverage, John Brown's beard was a public relations triumph. Beardless in 1856, the hard-faced, fanatical, and notoriously difficult Brown became instead the wise sage of abolitionism and an Old Testament prophet on trial for his life when fully bearded in 1859. This second, more benign image of Brown was copied from a full-length photograph by J. W. Black in the same year. It figured prominently in the first public transcript of the trial, also published in 1859 by Robert M. De Witt, and it appeared everywhere in the Northern press during Brown's trial. The hagiography of the martyred Brown would be formalized in a romanticized life-sized oil portrait by Nathan B. Onthank, using the same photograph as his guide.

the rigor of procedure. For once, the issues of universal rights and protection of property were starkly joined. Duty to conscience challenged obedience to law in prolonged debate, and the life of a man who was inordinately loved and hated hung in the balance.

Although Brown suffered discrimination as an abolitionist under arrest in a Virginia courtroom, he achieved advantages for his cause when he entered into the formal protections of trial ritual. The exclusive focus in the courtroom on charges resulting from the events at Harpers Ferry enabled Brown to erase unseemly events in an unheroic past. On trial for his life, he became what he appeared to be in the moment, the courageous leader of a doomed but exciting mission. Gone from view were earlier incidents of personal cruelty, his vocational failures, previous legal difficulties in which he was clearly and inexcusably culpable, his limited standing in the political circles of abolitionism, his inept role as a military commander, and his unprovoked murder in their homes of five pro-slavery men just three years before in "bleeding Kansas."[16] In their place arose a righteous man willing to die for his cause.

When they did appear in the publicity surrounding the trial, Brown's weaknesses ended up as strengths. His insensitivity appeared as fixed principle, financial failure grew into superiority to material concern, the atrocities he had committed in Kansas were excused as the veteran warrior defending freedom. Everything combined to prepare the defendant for the final role he chose to play. Humiliated for years by constant litigation and bankruptcy proceedings over fifteen business failures in four states, Brown knew his way around an American courtroom.[17] In 1859 he turned those bitter lessons to account, manipulating trial ritual (the procedural sense of formal, collective participation) into a confrontation of moral issues and competing discourses. Helpless in previous trials, he was on top of this one. Even the intimidating question of guilt or innocence suited his moralistic temperament; the courtroom appealed to his tastes better than the nuance of political compromise ever could.[18]

Brown translated innocence and guilt into good and evil, evoking powerful rhetorical themes—themes familiar and persuasive in themselves but much more powerful when woven together. By resisting the charge of guilt through appeals to higher truth and by trying to destroy the evil of slavery in the name of good, Brown followed his penchant for religious explanation and moral certitude. He simultaneously activated affinities in the literary modes of the romance, where good and evil battle toward conclusion in a narrative freighted with symbolism and exaggeration. The mixture of legal and religious frames of reference with the added elements of the romance proved explosive in awakening sympathy for Brown and in magnifying his cause. Thereafter, whether as diabolical invader of the peace or first martyr of republican freedom, he was always larger than the life he led, always above the legal decision to take that life, always somewhere beyond the facts.

"A SHORT STORY OF A CERTAIN BOY"

Not known as a master rhetorician, John Brown nonetheless belonged to a generation that made a singular contribution to American literature. Tracing that connection is essential in any understanding of the man who spoke and wrote so much better than he knew. Brown made himself a cultural symbol overnight, and language was his primary tool. Granting, for the moment, that the man on trial surpassed himself, what were the skills and cultural affinities that supported his effort? Brown's own writings and comments outside of the courtroom are especially useful in responding to these issues; they reveal congruencies with the writers of the American Renaissance and allow us to avoid the tautology of explaining Brown's impact through his impact.

When, for example, investigators explain John Brown's appeal by concentrating on his seeming prescience about the evolution of sectional strife and the eventual destruction of slavery, they conflate his ideas in support of his actions with his later ideological achievement. The result, while not always inaccurate, is a circularity of explanation that leaves out of the equation Brown's immediate influence in 1859. Lost in these emphases is the separate importance of his trial and Brown's role in it. Long before he showed that he could die well, Brown held the nation through powers of expression. Earlier writings demonstrate his literary capacities, his relationship to available literary forms, and the nature of his eloquence at trial.

A deliberate even meticulous care with language comes through in Brown's short autobiography, written on July 15, 1857, in the form of a letter to the thirteen-year-old son of a financial supporter, the wealthy Massachusetts merchant and abolitionist George Luther Stearns. This letter would be widely circulated during Brown's trial, and it had its own impact then.[19] Simply but shrewdly crafted, the letter must be read with the historian David Potter's warning in mind: "Hardly anything can be said with certainty about John Brown."[20] Brown, in fact, couched the autobiography as a fiction. "[I] have concluded to send you a short story of a certain boy of my acquaintance," Brown tells young Harry Stearns, "& for convenience & shortness of name, I will call him John." A fabrication, the writing is meant for several levels of understanding. Written simply as boy to boy, it is a man's tale in admonition of youth, a sophisticated narrative pitched to the influential father behind the son, and, overall, Brown's communication to the world of what he wanted it to know about him.

The idea of fabrication, inscribed here in the notion of story, was not necessarily a pejorative concept for Brown's several audiences. Antebellum Americans were taught to look for a higher truth in what they read, and they learned to accept and engage in distortions of mundane reality to achieve that goal. As Ralph Waldo Emerson described his own reading style, "[I read] for diversion & a mechanical help to the fancy & the Imagination. I read for the lustres as if one should use a fine picture in a chromatic experiment merely for its rich colours. It is not Proclus but a piece of Nature & Fate that I explore."[21] A thirst for drama, for imaginative projection and the crystallization of effect, and particularly for the possibility of self-dramatization were part and parcel of the American Renaissance. John Brown and his publicizers could craft a mythic persona out of the ruins of failure because their countrymen accepted Emerson's performative strategies for reading.

Brown's autobiography takes the problem of fabrication as a central concern. The boy John's greatest fault in Brown's story, one to which he is "somewhat addicted," consists in "*telling lies.*" The same penchant continues in the man as Brown finds himself "[in later life] obliged to struggle *so long* with so *mean* a habit." The implication is that Brown, "so often guilty of this fault," has managed to overcome it, and yet the storyteller frequently hides the truth for larger ends. The man of many failures brags of "the degree of success *in* accomplishing his objects," of "his close attention to *business*; & success in its management," of how "he rarely failed in some good degree to effect the things he undertook."[22] If this need to appear successful is understandable in any autobiographer, the strain shows in Brown's own arranged definition of success.

To Benjamin Franklin's formula of frugality, unceasing industry, and emulation of the virtuous, which he admires, Brown adds consistency of conduct and character in the name of "*some definite plan,*" "plan of life," or "greatest or principal object." Elsewhere, the formulation took a more melodramatic and decidedly un-Franklinian turn: "Death for a good cause was glorious," he told one family friend, in words that revealed Brown's "capacity to become greatly excited when his mind fixed on one idea."[23] Success as a consistency of high purpose lay within Brown's ken in a way that evidence of material advance did not. His sense of lofty aspiration fit both abolitionist purposes and a monomaniacal personality, and it set a standard that was difficult to measure, much less refute. In the words of his autobiography, Brown had decided to live in "the consciousness that our plans are right in themselves." The idée fixe encouraged a dramatically represented sense of self that did not have to conform to the realities of daily life or to its own unexciting past.[24]

In keeping with the flexibility in a constructed self, the autobiography juxtaposes competing images. Brown is not only the serious young businessman on the road to success, but an isolated, swashbuckling Western adventurer dressed in buckskins, one who consorts with Indians and who takes on the persona of "a rambler in the wild new country." Then again, he is a descendent of Revolutionary warriors, a pacifist whose "disgust . . . with military affairs" leads him to get "along like a Quaker," a humble shepherd ("*it being* a calling, for which *in early life* he had a kind of *enthusiastic longing*"), an imperious leader of men (" 'A King against whom there is no rising up,' " who is "much disposed to speak in an imperious or dictating way"), and, inevitably, the abolitionist and religious zealot ("believer in the divine authenticity of the Bible"). Each of these images entered the larger mythology of John Brown. The more immediate point, however, is that Brown felt rhetorically free to serve up any one of them, or any combination, when it suited the integrity of his "principal object."

A revealing subtheme of the autobiography balances the conventional topic of success. Over and over, Brown stresses the fact of loss in his life. The losses of a toy, of a pet, of another favorite animal; and each reversal leaves the subject of this narrative in a "protracted *mourning season*." All are then transmogrified in the trauma of his mother's death; John at eight is "left a Motherless boy which loss was complete & permanent." Of even the least in this series of catastrophes, a marble lost by the boy of six, Brown tells us, "*it took years to heal the wound*." This mournful figure appears as a willful loner, an isolato by both inclination and circumstance: "To be sent off through the wilderness alone to very considerable distances was particularly his delight."

Unremitting loss fuels the obsessive personality of this writer. His grief and anger interact and feed upon each other. The unresolved grief of the child finds a home in the undifferentiated and permanent anger of the adult ("his haughty obstinate temper"), and both emotions fix on abolitionism. Only one figure, in a telling parallel, appears less fortunate than young John in the autobiography. Forced to watch the beating of a "*negro boy* (who was fully if not more than his equal)," John is led "to reflect on the wretched, hopeless condition, of *Fatherless & Motherless* slave *children*." The psychological repercussions are fierce identification and a tenuous social equilibrium. Brown is helped by the fact that loss operates as a pervasive and dominant theme in early America.[25] Although his compulsive rendition of "*sore trials*" borders on the grotesque, he achieves balance by channeling his sorrow and anger into protest against the acknowledged grotesqueries of slavery.

These passages reveal Brown for what he was in another sense, a primitive writer who depended on standard literary conventions for the appeal of his prose. Virtually every strategy used in the autobiography appeared prominently in the popular literature of the times. Brown's calculated appeal to separate audiences (one reading a surface narrative and the other probing beneath), his stress upon intensity or excess of feeling, his claim of spirituality in conscious righteousness, his intrusive and openly manipulative narrator, his selectivity and willingness to exaggerate event through symbolism, his readiness to inflate a represented self through a bewildering range of character traits and alternative experiences, and, above all, his assumption of a rhetorical license to mix and match—these were the conventional characteristics of the American romance.

While Brown brought no special craft to these devices, he understood them well enough to enrich a capacity for self-dramatization. The same intuitive awareness applied to his use of corresponding themes. Here again, Brown's autobiography resembles the nineteenth-century romance and its folkloric corollaries, the tall tale and the ballad. The narrator recounts the boy adventurer's triumphs in "the school of *adversity*," he celebrates the isolated but dedicated individual, he resists the commonplace, he summons the sorrows and the terrors of death, he relates cruelty to children and the healing domesticity of the virtuous woman, he yokes the romantic hero to the responsible citizen, he conjures up the Revolutionary past as well as the Wild West, and he purveys the timeless battle of good against evil (in his "*Eternal war* with slavery"). These themes were ready preoccupations in both the historical and the domestic nineteenth-century romance.[26]

Brown was no accomplished romancer. He gave no single theme a unique rendering and offered no imaginative equivalents of the tortured Dimmesdale and demonic Chillingworth in *The Scarlet Letter*, nor of the multifaceted Holgrave in *The House of the Seven Gables*, nor of the monomaniacal Hollingsworth and inquisitive Coverdale in *The Blithedale Romance*. He could only register such figures in embryonic form, but the nineteenth-century reader recognized them for what they were, familiar types. Brown as well as Hawthorne realized, each at his own level, that the issues of the time demanded the language and the psychology of spiritual engagement.

As Hawthorne was on the periphery of what remained a Bible culture, so Brown was steeped within it, and each saw—Hawthorne with irony, Brown with conviction—that the link of secularization to religion in America encouraged a rhetoric of excess in which materiality and spirituality could mingle.[27] Symbolism, in particular, took on double meaning in the material and spiritual worlds. Brown, with Hawthorne, assumed that he was "allowed a license with regard to every-day Probability." He accepted that a rhetorician could look for "an available foothold between fiction and reality," that fact and invention could intersect in search of a higher truth, that the ultimate integrity of a narrative lay not in the details but in the quality of abstraction, "the authenticity of the outline."[28]

"THIS NEGRO QUESTION I MEAN— THE END OF THAT IS NOT YET"

Brown reached at trial for a "moral" similar to one offered by Hawthorne in *The House of the Seven Gables*. When captured at Harpers Ferry, he immediately reconfigured the event from military into purely ethical terms, and the means he chose were typically half political and half spiritual in scope. As Hawthorne had voiced that moral, "The wrong-doing of one generation lives into the successive ones, and, divesting itself of every temporary advantage, becomes a pure and uncontrollable mischief."[29]

The threat of a curse and the necessity of sacrifice and expurgation to alleviate it were underlying concepts, and for Brown, they reached just as easily across levels of reality and into an abolitionist's understanding of the evils in slavery. Lying painfully wounded on the floor of the armory at Harpers Ferry with his dead sons around him, Brown raised himself physically and spiritually through the "available foothold" between fiction and reality. His grasp of a rhetoric that bridged spiritual and material venues allowed him to address his furious captors with perfect equanimity and simple eloquence. "You may dispose of me very easily," he told them calmly; "I am nearly disposed of now; but this question is still to be settled—this negro question I mean—the end of that is not yet."[30]

This speaker could have appeared as a character in *The House of the Seven Gables.* "God will give him blood to drink," warns Matthew Maule from the gallows, and John Brown, on the way to his own execution, would sound a similar note. "I John Brown am now quite *certain* that the crimes of this *guilty land will* never be purged *away*; but with Blood."[31] Crime, guilt, and purgation conflated legal and religious explanations with Brown fused in the roles of prophet, judge, and sacrificial object.

The Civil War would remove the ironies from these identifications and instruct others in their use. The trope of sacrifice would reach ultimate expression in Abraham Lincoln's Second Inaugural, where again the language, neither entirely religious nor specifically political, would operate through a concurrence of possibilities: "If God wills that [this mighty scourge of war] continue until all the wealth piled by the bondsman's two hundred and fifty years of unrequited toil shall be sunk and until every drop of blood drawn with the lash shall be paid by another drawn with the sword, as was said three thousand years ago, so still it must be said, 'The judgments of the Lord are true and righteous together.'"[32]

Where Brown predictably fell short of Hawthorne was in the romancer's orchestration of the variables. Hawthorne was an artist. His romances, combining ingenuous and ironic ways of reading, crossed boundaries between the domain of the senses and the world of imagination, exercised dark inner drives, explored inconsistencies between the ideal and the real in American life, and conflated the spectral and human qualities of experience.[33] Ironic discrepancy was the common element in these procedures, and Hawthorne used it to stress disjuncture in the name of the grotesque. The grotesque was Hawthorne's calling card, his method of alerting and holding his reader.[34]

Brown could lack Hawthorne's talent and still achieve the same effect. Character and circumstance supplied the grotesque at Harpers Ferry, and they needed no orchestration. The discrepancy that arrested antebellum Americans depended on the aura around slavery—Northern horror of it and Southern fear of insurrection from it—but the affect of the grotesque requires concreteness, and the events at Harpers Ferry supplied that ingredient in abundance. Take, for example, John Brown under siege pacing the armory with two sons dying around him and responding to

one's cries of agony with the rebuke "If you must die, die like a man."
See the enraged local populace slicing off the ears and beating one dead
raider, Newby Dangerfield, with sticks before allowing hogs to root at the
body. Consider the mob seizing and slaughtering Will Thompson, another raider held captive, and using his corpse for target practice. In eyewitness accounts, "the cries and screams [of the dying] made one's flesh
creep." Watson Brown, for one, was shot through under a flag of truce.
Later his body was taken to the Winchester Medical College, where it was
"skinned, and the skin varnished, after which a dispute arose whether it
should be kept whole or stuffed, or cut up for game pouches."[35] There was
no shortage of the grotesque at Harpers Ferry, and over it all impended
the bizarre, uncanny personality of John Brown himself.

The figure of Brown occupied the boundary line between worlds: "an
angel of light" to his supporters; "the foe of the human race" to his ex-
ecutioners.[36] The defendant's skill at trial and during punishment came
in his recognition and use of this normally helpless form of liminality.
A transgressor by definition, he turned the courtroom into an explo-
ration of whether the ideal and the real should change places and whether
the spiritual could supplant the merely legal. Response to transgression
forces either a rearticulation of values or an enunciation of new ones. The
relation to literary expression in this game of levels did not go unnoticed.
Henry Thoreau's appraisal in "The Last Days of John Brown" insisted on
Brown's literary character. Brown's commentary from prison and on trial
formed "an American book" like no other. "I do not know of such words,
uttered under such circumstances, and so copiously withal, in Roman or
English or any history," Thoreau observed.[37]

Literature operated as more than an analogy in Thoreau's explanation
of Brown's importance. "See what a work this comparatively unread and
unlettered man wrote within six weeks," observed Thoreau. "Where is
our professor of belles-lettres, or of logic and rhetoric, who can write
so well?" Brown succeeded because he knew "the *art* of composition is
as simple as the discharge of a bullet from a rifle." His transition from
lawless raider to legal defendant turned "a material weapon, a Sharp's rifle" into "the sword of the spirit." The power of Thoreau's images should
not disguise their standard place within the literary parlance of the times.
The goal of standard interpretation was self-dramatization (words as bullets), and the writer's hope was for a transformation between material
and spiritual realms. The ascendancy of the spiritual within the material,

Thoreau argued, was precisely the quality that allowed Brown to "answer more wisely than all his countrymen beside."

Brown, again like Hawthorne, resolved the competition of realities into higher truth, but where Hawthorne relied on aesthetics and artistic control, Brown emphasized the exercise of principle in action. What was it that separated Brown from others with him who attempted to rescue slaves and were executed for it? Thoreau answered by emphasizing the "devotion to principle" in Brown's words at trial. Brown "forgot human laws, and did homage to an idea." In this stress on principle, "the North, I mean the *living* North was suddenly all transcendental," where "transcendental" meant the courage to see past the limits of human law in recognition of "eternal justice and glory."

For Thoreau, any inability to accept Brown's words as higher truth indicated a failure of comprehension in the reader. His terms of reference were again ones of literary interpretation. Those who thought of John Brown "as an ordinary felon" had lost their spiritual way and their aesthetic bearings. It was no coincidence that Thoreau's condemnation of the merely material opponent in "The Last Days of John Brown" paraphrased Hawthorne's similar mockery of insensitivity in "The Custom-House" of *The Scarlet Letter*. "They have either much flesh," wrote Thoreau of those who did not understand Brown, "or much office, or much coarseness of some kind. They are not ethereal natures in any sense." The true reader of Brown, like Hawthorne's romancer, should "live throughout the whole range of his faculties and sensibilities" and would know how to explore higher worlds in the name of the spirit. Internal and external realities had to meet. "How can a man behold the light who has no answering inward light?" Thoreau asked the country.[38]

In transcendentalist circles, deciding for or against Brown reflected directly on one's literary capacity. "Show me a man who feels bitterly toward John Brown, and let me hear what noble verse he can repeat," sneered Thoreau. "He'll be as dumb as if his lips were stone." For the same reason, mutual recognition of Brown's achievement supplied literary, political, and social solidarity. Thoreau, Ralph Waldo Emerson, Bronson Alcott, Louisa May Alcott, Lydia Maria Child, Theodore Parker, and others lionized Brown because they found in him an intellectually and emotionally kindred enterprise. They wanted to see him in their own terms, and Brown's trial gave them the means.[39]

When Thoreau wrote that he knew "of nothing so miraculous in our history" as the "meteor-like" last six weeks of Brown's life, he meant that communal responses acclaimed Brown's actions and thoughts in an unprecedented act of recognition as his trial and punishment proceeded. "No theatrical manager," he concluded, "could have arranged things so wisely to give effect to [Brown's] behavior and words." The trial, a providential stage, tested moral affinities best appreciated by turning to the actual juncture of theatricality and legal procedure practiced in Charlestown, Virginia.[40]

THE BLACK FLAG ON VIRGINIA SOIL

The Circuit Court of Jefferson County labored under an enormous strain in the trial of John Brown. A community is always on trial in the courtroom of a republic of laws, but when the extended community is seriously divided, as this one was, the pressure placed on courtroom procedures increases geometrically. The raid on Harpers Ferry by abolitionists had unleashed local fears of rampant illegality against the South—so much so that more than a thousand armed troops were guarding Brown in Charlestown from the twin terrors of the lynch mob and the rescue party, each rumored on a daily basis with the possibility of a slave insurrection thrown in. Criticized from all sides, local leaders feared that Jefferson County was about to become "the seat of war."[41] They were thus doubly anxious that legal decorum be maintained in Brown's trial as the test of a functioning community.

Judge Richard Parker, speaking for the circuit court on October 21, claimed the crucial connection between legal decorum and communal identity when he first charged the grand jury of Jefferson County to provide "a fair and impartial trial" for Brown and his men. "We owe it to the cause of justice as well as to our own characters," he observed, "that such a trial should be afforded them."[42] Scrutinizing every move, the *New York Times* spelled out the implications of Parker's words in the North:

> We know of no better test of the civilization and soundness of a State than the tone of her judges and Bar, in dealing with a case of this kind in a time of great popular excitement. . . . The world will always take it for granted that a community which produces judges, who preserve

their composure, their honor, in the midst of tumultuous passions, is sound at the core.[43]

Composure was indeed a struggle for any Virginian on October 21, 1859, just two days after Brown's raid. As Judge Parker told the grand jury:

> I will not permit myself to give expression to any of those feelings which at once spring up in every breast when reflection upon the enormity of the guilt in which those are involved who invade by force a peaceful unsuspecting portion of our common country, raise the standard of insurrection amongst them, and shoot down without mercy Virginia Citizens, defending Virginia soil against their invasion. (50)

These words shed light on the relation between decorum, fairness, and communal identity in Judge Parker's courtroom, and they help to explain how decorum there became the necessary term *between* fairness and identity. Parker wanted to exclude from deliberation the potent emotions that Virginians possessed on the issue under investigation ("those feelings which at once spring up in every breast"). By the same token, his personal denial ("I will not permit myself") attested to negative emotions supposedly banished from the courtroom. When the judge spoke of "the enormity of the guilt" and of those who "invade by force," characterizing the defendants as those who "raise the standard of insurrection" and "shoot down without mercy," his feelings were more than clear; they were instructive. The narration for conviction was already in place before the grand jury heard a shred of evidence.

Decorum, in this construct of denial and assertion, signified not the absence of emotion but a hermetically sealed zone of restraint and order. Legally speaking, it meant confining public behavior within sanctioned norms and established formal conventions. Local authorities feared that anything less would induce communal breakdown one way or another. The acceptance by all participants of constrained roles and adherence to formal ritual was an absolutely essential first step. It would be followed in courtroom deliberations by an insistence on fairness that would keep the extraordinary circumstances of the raid under control while rearticulating the values of a community under threat.

In typical expressions of this theme, Judge Parker appeared "desirous of trying this case precisely as he would try another, without any reference at all to outside feeling" (83). The prosecution, in turn, promised "to avoid anything by way of argument or explanation not immediately connected with the particular issue to be tried" (67). In this way, everyone could expect Brown's trial "to vindicate the majesty of the law" as it moved toward conviction (93). Communal patience was essential, said prosecutor Andrew Hunter, "in preservation of the character of Virginia, that plumes itself on its moral character, as well as physical, and on its loyalty, and its devotion to truth and right" (93).

Virginians realized, in other words, that their state had joined Brown on trial in Charlestown, and that awareness led them to act out the strictest rule of legal decorum in defense of their collective reputation. A minor incident recorded in the trial transcript underscored the punctiliousness that all felt on this score. As Brown, easily the most hated man in Virginia on November 2, received the sentence of death, the "perfect quiet" of the courtroom was broken by "the clapping of the hands of one man in the crowd." Officialdom and all others in attendance were horrified that proprieties had thus been shattered, and a gloss by the trial stenographer immediately minimized the fault. The celebrant, it turned out, was "not a resident of Jefferson County," and his unfortunate misbehavior had been "promptly suppressed" with "much regret . . . expressed by the citizens at its occurrence" (95). Elsewhere, the transcript would congratulate the audience in attendance for hiding its emotions in respect for "the forms of the Court" (93).

Every courtroom depends upon the observance of protocol and ritual, but the standard established in Charlestown left the Circuit Court of Jefferson vulnerable from two directions. First, the idea of excluding from the legal process the imaginative thrust of events that totally absorbed the community was unworkable. Virginians, even official Virginians, needed to express the very feelings they sought to suppress, as Judge Parker's own statements before the grand jury illustrated. Second, proper decorum requires the participation of everyone present, and Brown, who openly sought martyrdom through the court's ultimate capacity to punish, had few incentives to cooperate on anything but his own terms—terms that happened to be distinct from those imposed upon him. Just as the Virginia court wished to protect the events in the courtroom from outside pressures, so Brown's goals led him to open those events to the largest possible communal debate.

Several consequences followed from the vulnerabilities of the court, and they all favored Brown's capacity to make the most of his situation. When intrusions from the outside inevitably came, they reinforced questions about the fairness of Brown's trial. Officialdom's accent on decorum also turned Brown's occasional disruptions of proceedings into effective episodes. Only Brown could *be* dramatic in the courtroom. The court already had assigned itself as mundane a role as possible ("without any reference at all to outside feeling"), and Brown made it clear that any display of emotion at all by the prosecution or the court would trigger disengagement or further disruption on his part.

The results were functional and rhetorical imbalance. Brown lost his case at each stage of the decision-making process, both procedurally and substantively, but his repeated threats to disrupt proceedings, balanced by otherwise good behavior, led to concession after concession from the prosecution and the court, both of whom were anxious to obtain and maintain Brown's minimal cooperation. A defendant without fear of sanction can disturb the delicate procedures in advocacy. Using this purchase, Brown gradually became an independent agent left to pursue his ulterior purposes at trial. By the fourth day of the adversarial process, he was freely instigating "a general colloquy" with witnesses and the prosecution. "No objection was made," runs the transcript of these moments, "to Brown's asking these questions in his own way, and interposing verbal explanations relative to his conduct" (80).

Brown's performance was part of his cultural transformation. Crossing boundary lines and assuming control amidst the unimaginative rigidities and official constraints of the courtroom, the defendant became the active figure of romance that Ralph Waldo Emerson described. He entered that "medium the most suitable for a romance-writer" of Hawthorne's description, "a neutral territory, somewhere between the real world and fairy-land, where the Actual and the Imaginary may meet, and each imbue itself with the nature of the other."[44]

Neutrality, in the Hawthornian sense, meant divergent possibilities that could inform each other, and it matched another similarity between courtroom event and the romance narrative, the held ambiguity of opposing arguments. The decorum of the courtroom was a baseline for the imagination to rest upon while it searched through levels of reality for answers to the fantastic in Brown. Of course, his disruptions of decorum encouraged such speculation. People in favor of Brown made the most of the exaggerations of his effect. Those ranged against him found plenty of scope for casting him back into the outer darkness from which they thought he had come and to which they wished to consign him again.

The normal extremes in advocacy took on new meaning. When the prosecution wanted to demonize Brown, its documents confirmed every hyperbole.[45] Brown's indictment for treason specified that the raiders had acted "not having the fear of God before their eyes, but being moved and seduced by the false and malignant counsel of other evil and traitorous persons and the instigations of the devil" (59–60). The prosecution of Aaron Burr had not been able to resist the opportunities in this opening in 1807, and neither could its counterpart in 1859. Brown was evil incarnate.

The prosecution sought to punish "those who have raised the black flag on the soil of this Commonwealth" (66), a crime after which "there could not be a female in this country who, whether with good cause or not, was not trembling with anxiety and apprehension" (83). Brown had invaded Virginia as a diabolical agent of destruction. "He glories in coming here to violate our laws," warned the government; he came "with the deadly purpose of applying the torch to our buildings and shedding the blood of our citizens"; he wanted to make Virginia another racially ravaged Haiti (92–93). Even Brown's unknown Northern attorney, still to arrive, got swept into this rhetoric of overblown possibilities. "We know not," warned prosecutor Hunter, "whether he is to come here as counsel for the prisoner, or whether he wants to head a band of desperadoes" (65).

This backdrop of desperadoes and frightened maidens magnified Brown further and so did artifacts offered as evidence by the prosecution. Brown's provisional constitution, written out for an abolitionist state, proved his malignancy; there was simply "too much method in Brown's madness" (92). Doubly horrifying as symbols of slave rebellion were the 950 spears that Brown brought to Harpers Ferry to arm those whom he freed. These pikes were substitutes for narrative in the case against Brown. They held the attention of the South like no other aspect of the Brown raid, and regional firebrands fueled the flames by sending samples as warnings to the governors of the fifteen slaveholding states.[46] "When you put pikes in the hands of the slaves, and have their masters captive," the prosecution argued, "that is advice to slaves to rebel, and punishable with death" (92). The duty of the court was clear, though even death proved but a temporary measure in the prosecution's scheme of things. As Hunter told the jury, "Let retributive justice, if he is guilty, send him before that Maker who will settle the question forever and ever" (93).

From the other side of the case, the defendant figured as God's agent. Brown set the tone himself in the first moments of the trial by announcing that God had "always been at his side." Placing "full confidence in the goodness of God" also removed any need for a confession of criminal action. The defendant, the transcript noted, "knows God is with him and fears nothing" (58). Brown always referred to his courage in this spiritual register, and his worst enemies granted its significance.[47] Even Virginia governor Henry A. Wise had to admit that Brown was "the gamest man I ever saw," in a colloquialism of honor as well as respect. "He is a bundle of the best nerves I ever saw . . . a man of clear head, of courage, fortitude and simple ingeniousness," Wise observed. "He is cool, collected and indomitable . . . and he inspired me with great trust in his integrity as a man of truth."[48]

With the connection between courage and integrity acknowledged by all, the next step, from integrity to the superiority of the spirit, became automatic for Brown's defenders. Crucial moments at trial would then confirm these assumptions and turn supporters into believers.[49] The transcriber's description of the verdict, "terrible to look upon," made Brown "the only calm and unruffled countenance" in the entire assemblage: "there he stood, a man of indomitable will and iron nerve, all collected and unmoved even while the verdict that consigned him to an ignominious doom was pronounced upon him" (93). This equanimity on October 30 would hold for the doomed man on December 2. Completely "calm and cheerful" on the way to the gallows, Brown bid "an affectionate adieu" before taking the final plunge.[50] "I am waiting the hour of my public murder with great composure of mind and cheerfulness," he had explained in a last letter home, ". . . in no other possible way could I be used to so much advantage to the cause of God and of humanity."[51]

Martyrdom marks the ultimate boundary between flesh and spirit, between grotesque bodily humiliation and the sublime aspiration of eternal life. Brown's courage allowed supporters to predict his martyrdom from the moment of his capture, and their knowledge contributed to his own performance. "Let Virginia make him a martyr!" cried Henry Ward

Beecher in a sermon on October 30, 1859. "Good," wrote Brown on his own copy of the newspaper report.[52] The press helped Brown to discover and act out the touch points in how he should behave. As he wrote letters made public in the weeks before his execution, Brown located himself within established hagiographical traditions. He was Peter armed with the sword, Samson overturning the house of slavery, Paul in prison, even Christ on the cross. Lest a biblical allusion be missed by readers, Brown supplied parenthetical references.[53] These last letters reached for station as God's chosen servant—and for something more. With a newly developed humble demeanor that would help Emerson to compare the gallows to the cross, Brown concluded: "Let them hang me; I forgive them, and may God forgive them, for they know not what they do."[54]

The dramatic impact of such language was immeasurable in the religiosity of antebellum America, and Brown wielded it in personal purification. At work in the borrowed words of Jesus—"for they know not what they do"—was a timely signification. An earlier Calvinist age might have found presumption in Brown's appropriation, but by the 1850s Americans imbibed their religion in a rhetoric of excess. Brown as Christ was a theatrical effect for contemporaries rather than a blasphemous gesture. His confirmed courage represented physical presence in a world that still believed natural facts prefigured spiritual truths.[55] No one in America in 1859 believed that such bravery could be accidental or merely characterological, and religious parallels appealed to friend and foe alike. One way or the other, the display of Brown's courage was going to have another meaning, and his followers would use the assumption to enact a transfiguration of colossal dimensions.[56]

"I AM READY FOR MY FATE"

Brown was *in* but not *of* the world of his trial, *in* but not *under* the constraints of legal procedure. "I am ready for my fate," he announced on his first day in court, a pro forma preliminary hearing before a magistrate's court. Five times in this short appearance, he asked "to be excused from the mockery of a trial" (55). The opportunity for him to speak came because the court had to inquire if the prisoner had counsel, and Brown seized the occasion. "If you seek my blood," he answered, "you can have it at any moment, without this mockery of a trial" (55). His only other formal request was also rhetorically pointed: "I have now little further to ask, other than that I may not be foolishly insulted, only as cowardly barbarians insult those who fall into their power" (55).

No strategy could have been better calculated to put Virginia authorities on the defensive. Because the larger perception of fairness was to state leaders a symbol of their own civilization, Brown could challenge both claims at once by belittling their procedures. "If we are to be forced with a mere form—a trial for execution," he volunteered, "—you might spare yourselves that trouble" (55). Seeking martyrdom, Brown needed the ritual of the trial as much as his accusers did, but first he had to secure the event for his own purposes.

Indifferent to the actual procedures leading toward his execution, Brown challenged them closely with an impunity born of indifference in order to put himself above them. Virginia wanted to prove criminality in the defendant's attack on Harpers Ferry. Brown responded with a legal non sequitur: he proclaimed the selflessness of his actions. Of no use as a defense, this strategy was crucial to the martyr. Brown realized he could succeed only by extracting an extralegal right of flexibility from the court, and his early challenges set guidelines for resisting all charges of irrelevancy.[57]

A sentence from the transcript captures the essence of Brown's position and his awareness of officialdom's vulnerability in Charlestown. "I wish for counsel if I am to have a trial," he observed in the first stage of a continuous battle over the assignment of counsel, "but if I am to have nothing but the mockery of a trial, as I have said, I do not care anything about counsel" (56). He feared, as he was quick to admit, that if he accepted counsel, he would "not be allowed to speak himself" and agreed to cooperate only after the court and assigned counsel, in the first of many concessions, promised to "give him the advantage of every privilege that the law will allow" (58). Brown used these debates over the right to counsel to serve notice: any "insult," any challenge to his own rectitude, would trigger a public challenge to the fairness of the proceedings and authority of the court.

Brown disrupted proceedings once each day he was in court—just often enough to maintain the threat. Quiet most of the time, he chose his moments carefully, and his restraint is suggestive since violations of due process and other opportunities for protest occurred in the course of the trial. Afraid of the incendiary atmosphere in Charlestown, Governor Wise ordered the prosecution of Brown and other raiders within a week of their capture, and this was done even though Brown, wounded in four places during the raid, could not stand unassisted at his own arraignment and had declared himself incapacitated (58, 62).[58] Grounds for challenge were everywhere. Brown had no real chance to consult with his attorneys before trial (55), defense counsel changed three times during the course of the six-day event without benefit of recess (55, 72, 78), and the governor's special prosecutor, Andrew Hunter, had clear conflicts of interest.[59] The defense raised these issues, except the last, but did not emphasize them, and Brown ignored more routine opportunities (55, 62, 63, 65, 66, 76). He failed, for instance, to challenge a single person during the selection of his jury.[60]

Brown's motives for disrupting the trial had nothing to do with due process. He wanted the trial to dignify his spiritual mission and for legal procedures to allow the narratives useful to him. A hostile courtroom had to serve his communal interests in the face of complaints from the other side of "out-door effect and influence" (75). There was a fine line to be walked here. Brown proceeded just reasonably enough to keep the court from sustaining the prosecution's objections to tactics "outside of what the laws recognize" (65). His most blatant manipulation fed the claim of martyrdom. Brown exploited the wounds he had received from the fighting at Harpers Ferry at every turn. Forced to stand trial while suffering from painful sword cuts and loss of blood, he reacted by refusing to walk into court. The ensuing compromise gave him the right to be carried into the courtroom on a cot, and it would be an arrangement that the prosecution soon learned to regret (63–64, 66).

Whether languishing or rising in rejoinder, Brown used his bed of pain to repossess the extraordinary circumstances that the court tried to exclude from its considerations. The cot was an emblem of current affliction as well as a symbol of final suffering to come, and it turned Brown's presence at trial—"laid down on his cot at full length within the bar" (64)—into a visible act and reminder of his courage. Inherently theatrical as a prop, the cot in the courtroom became the tool of a knowing performer. In trial moments that questioned or criticized him, Brown lay prostrate, exhausted, and seemingly indifferent to proceedings. Such moments included his indictment (66), the march of prosecution witnesses (68–71), and the closing arguments of counsel (84, 93). Brown could disregard whatever he pleased. Sometimes he dismissed the trial altogether—covering himself completely, closing his eyes, and, after one dramatic outburst, feigning sleep (63, 93, 77).

More than a prop, the cot was a pulpit for guarding Brown's sense of mission from challenges in the courtroom. On the second day of trial, when assigned defense counsel tried to introduce evidence of insanity in their client, Brown apprehended the threat that it contained to his plan of principled sacrifice, and he moved quickly to refute it.[61] "Brown then raised himself up in bed," runs the court transcript, and declared, "I reject, so far as I am capable, any attempt to interfere in my behalf on that score." He "disdain[ed]" the plea and those who made it: "I look upon it as a miserable artifice and pretext of those who ought to take a different course in regard to me . . . and I view it with contempt more than otherwise" (64–65).

References to his own helplessness were peculiarly accessible to the man on the cot, and they tempered an anger that was now poignant rather than offensive. Thus, when hostile witnesses boasted of shooting "those villainous Abolitionists," Brown, weeping for his dead followers, staggered dramatically from his mattress to do battle. A consciously doomed man "ready for anything that may come up," he was a formidable adversary in the role of wounded warrior. When he rose to complain, he did so without fear or hope, and his physical plight was its own comment on the procedural imbalances around him (75–76).

Brown knew what would upset the court most. He also understood that his own counsel supplied the best target for proving "that nothing like a fair trial is to be given me." Whenever events at trial were not to his liking, he exercised that option. "I have no counsel, as I before stated, in whom I feel that I can rely," he exclaimed when frustrated on the third day of his trial. Rising feebly once again beside his cot, he was the iconographic verification of the complaint that followed: "I am myself unable to attend to [my defense]. I have given all the attention I possibly could to it, but am unable to see or know about them [the witnesses], and can't even find out their names; and I have nobody to do any errand, for my money was all taken when I was sacked and stabbed, and I have not a dime" (76). As it was intended to do, this outburst overwhelmed the court. Brown's appointed lawyers immediately resigned over his public claim of "no confidence" in them. For his own part, Brown ignored the furor that he had caused by collapsing back on his bed while Judge Parker postponed proceedings until the next day (77–78).

This incident underlines an important point dealt with abstractly in earlier chapters: namely, the fragility of all courtroom procedure. Adversarial in form, trials depend on a very high level of cooperation in practice, and any substantial disregard of that cooperation brings the interactive mechanism to a halt. The Circuit Court of Jefferson County asked for the trouble it received by rushing Brown to trial in prejudicial circumstances; it coped, against Brown's rejections of its forms, by doing everything possible to induce him back to the level of cooperation needed for the trial to proceed.

Desperate to continue, the prosecution helped by backing down whenever necessary. It withdrew its objections to the submission of pointless evidence by the defense, granting the latitude that Brown needed to present himself in his own spiritual terms: "We are perfectly willing to admit these facts in any form [the defense] desire[s]" (77). The facts in dispute involved "the conduct of Captain Brown in the treating of his prisoners with leniency, respect, and courtesy" during the raid (77). Irrelevant as proof against any charge, these facts and their submission in court helped to create the impression of Brown as an efficacious moral force at Harpers Ferry in place of the confused raider who crouched indecisively in the armory on October 17 with no idea of what to do next.[62]

The concessions continued. On the morning after Brown's outburst, the prosecution withdrew every document that Brown's new team of lawyers disputed (79). The state also agreed to forgo cross-examination of any witness called by the defense. Incredibly, it even offered to pass on a final summation before the jury if the defense would do likewise (81, 83). Nothing in these acquiescences influenced the formal judgment against Brown, but the change in narrative outcome for the listening nation was immense. Imbalances in the adversarial process helped to inflate the image of Brown from both directions. While the defense emphasized Brown's restraint, his bravery, his kindly attentions to his hostages, his high moral character, and his indomitable will (79–81, 89), the prosecution magnified the scope and importance of the raid by stressing the threat in Brown's fanatical purpose (92).

Lost in both presentations were the petty and ridiculous sides of Brown; in their place, a consensus emerged that Brown's actions had momentous consequences for all Americans. A blend of these embellishments entered the popular imagination, and it would be what history would bestow on John Brown—not, however, before Brown gave the blend a final stir.

"I SAY LET IT BE DONE"

The foundations of legal procedures—their arcane forms, their avoidance of surprise, their insistence on repetition, their claim upon regularity, and their complexity—are undramatic trial ingredients, but they give way to moments of high tension and vital suspense, and the highest, excepting the verdict, comes in the moment of sentencing. Only here does the public trial allow the person or persons under scrutiny free rein. Here defendants receive the right to speak within but beyond the forms of the law. It is the final liminal moment for all concerned. The defendant, found guilty, is passing from the community that made the negative determination into a separate state of punishment. The moment also distills emotion otherwise foreign to the rationality of the legal process. In every other phase, defendants are encouraged to protect themselves from the world, to hide even from themselves, if necessary, protected by the right against self-incrimination. Asked at this point why sentence should not be imposed upon them, they enter a different realm of presumed candor and conscience without intermediaries and unimpeded by the intrusion of counsel.

John Brown made himself the timeless master of this moment. He had prepared for it. Throughout the trial, he had been striving to speak without benefit of counsel, to separate himself from others, to dwell on the meaning of his punishment, and to engage in revelation. The spiritual resonances that he had struggled to create elsewhere in the legal process were now his for the asking. As much as the gallows, Brown's speech at sentencing provided a platform, and he made the most of both.

Emerson would later place Brown's words alongside Lincoln's Gettysburg Address as "the two best specimens of eloquence we have had in this country."[63] Much earlier, Emerson had summarized what real eloquence meant. "The high prize of eloquence may be mine, the joy of uttering what no other can utter & what all must receive," wrote Emerson in 1834.[64] Brown seized that prize in Charlestown on November 2, 1859. He uttered what no other person could and what all had to listen to and could not help but receive—no matter where they stood on the issues at hand.

Brown's oration is best examined as living speech. His words are all the more remarkable in that they begin and end in falsehood. Brown uttered twenty-six short, very simple sentences; they fill less than a printed page, and ten contain fifteen words or less.[65] Yet no less than eight of Brown's most declarative sentences, including five of the first six, assert that he never planned an insurrection of the slaves, a claim that contradicted all of the facts. His sincerity notwithstanding, Brown had talked at length about his plans to instigate a slave uprising. His intentions at Harpers Ferry made no sense without the hope of an insurrection.[66] Why would a small but heavily armed band of raiders take an additional armory with them and seize another one unless they were supplying weapons for other people? Brown, at trial, admitted that he possessed sufficient weaponry to arm 1,500 men, a figure that included the 950 sharpened pikes that he had brought to Harpers Ferry for freed slaves to handle until they gained familiarity with firearms (71).

A second puzzle in the speech helps to explain the first. With his trial nearly over, Brown abruptly disowned all former statements about it. "I feel entirely satisfied," he announced, "with the treatment that I have received on my trial." This overly generous admission recalibrated his previous strategy of confrontation. Brown reached now for universals. With his objective in sight and the whole nation in mind, he spoke as the guardian of freedom everywhere rather than as the raider and nightmare of the South. "I never had any design against the liberty of any person," Brown told a riveted audience. Mission and sacrifice, not insurrection and anger, were to be his closing messages for the scaffold.

The speaker's realization took all sting and querulousness from his tones. Elegiac power and stately acceptance replaced acrimony and argument in this last moment before the bench that was now a sacrificial altar. Brown held his own life in his hands and told why he must die. God's law in the injustice of a slave land required it of him! This explanation, cast in the simple language that biblical cadence allowed, lifted the speaker and his subject above court and country. It was from the spheres that Brown delivered his firmest rebuke:

Had I interfered in the manner which I admit, and which I admit has been fairly proved—for I admire the truthfulness and candor of the greater portion of the witnesses who have testified in this cases—had I so interfered in behalf of the rich, the powerful, the intelligent, the so-called great, or in behalf of any of their friends, either father, mother, brother, sister, wife, or children, or any of that class, and suffered and sacrificed what I have in this interference, it would have been all right, and every man in this Court would have deemed it an act worthy of reward rather than punishment. This Court acknowledges, too, as I suppose, the validity of the law of God. I see a book kissed, which I suppose to be the Bible, or at least the New Testament, which teaches me that all things whatsoever I would that men should do to me, I should do even so to them. It teaches me further to remember them that are in bonds as bound with them. I endeavored to act up to that instruction. I say I am yet too young to understand that God is any respecter of persons. I believe that to have interfered as I have done, as I have always freely admitted I have done in behalf of His despised poor, is no wrong, but right. Now, if it is deemed necessary that I should forfeit my life for the furtherance of the ends of justice, and mingle my blood further with the blood of my children and with the blood of millions in this slave country whose rights are disregarded by wicked, cruel, and unjust enactments, I say let it be done.[67]

Americans, Brown wanted his audience to realize, had been listening to the wrong stories. Their popular tales of injustice had concentrated on the rich and the powerful, the so-called great, or on the domestic circle of protection, to the exclusion of the greatest story, Christ's willing sacrifice for humanity transferred into the greatest injustice of the day, slavery in America. Brown's reprimand, like his autobiography, cataloged the themes of the romance but for a new reason. Something was missing from the injustices that his fellow citizens had been willing to entertain in stories.

America had cast aside its spiritual empathy for those human souls in most naked distress. This much of Brown's rebuke was aimed at all regions of the country, and his own story came as a counterweight. Brown had "interfered" with the mundane reality of the moment in the name of high spiritual reward, and he would accept low secular punishment for it. Here was the integrity of national narrative recovered. The moral conventions of that narrative had been debased all through the land, but Brown restored them to their proper place. The ignored slave undermined every other story worth telling.

The doomed speaker understood that even his supporters lacked respect for the essential personhood of the African American. Few white Americans in 1859 would have disagreed with Emerson's brutal summary of his own priorities in 1851: "The absence of moral feeling in the white man is the very calamity I deplore. The captivity of a thousand negroes is nothing to me."[68] Nothing? The real calamity was deeper than Emerson's generation could see, and Brown, knowing that, reached for all of its implications by insisting on metaphors of attachment that linked him to black men and women. He was "bound with" those in bonds and agreed "to mingle" his blood with theirs in integration with those "whose rights are disregarded." Both conceptions, the victim bound and the mingling of blood, evoked Brown's claim to the sacrificial altar. He would become what he had suffered for. "I say let it be done," he concluded quietly, turning his own death into a logical step toward legal and spiritual emancipation.

Brown never forgot that the clash of peoples around him was a clash of levels and worlds. Like other speakers of the period, but in under four minutes before the court, Brown presented the spiritual continuum through which the ambiguities of high and low could explain each other. Here, too, dramatic effect relied on levels of reading. The Bible glorified God's "despised poor." Brown, by referring directly to the golden rule in the Sermon on the Mount, drew attention to the message in its most eloquent form.[69]

Unfortunately, a correct reading of that message was not possible in the Virginia courtroom or, by extension, in an America that tolerated slavery. If the court acknowledged the law of God, it was not following it. The witnesses at trial who sealed their oath of testimony with the Bible could not possibly know its contents. Therefore, Brown could only guess at the nature of the "book kissed" in front of him. ("I see a book kissed, which I suppose to be the Bible.") The qualifications marked Brown's rejection of Christian authority in a slave state. "There are no ministers of Christ here," the condemned man wrote of Charlestown, rejecting the services of several.[70]

Brown made each of these points with a delicacy foreign to his usual imperious manner and writings. There may be no better indication of how completely he had risen to the occasion. Not rigidity but a gentle awareness now pervaded his understanding of the forces around him. In his preparation for death, spiritual mission and courtroom decorum merged. The quality of his recognition would be mirrored in the acceptance that came after him. In a conjunction of legal ritual and consummate literary expression, Brown's final courtroom speech touched the highest aspirations in the culture.

"A ROMANTIC CHARACTER ABSOLUTELY WITHOUT VULGAR TRAIT"

It would be a mistake to leave the last word to John Brown on the matter of his significance, a common-enough shortcoming in interpretations of his mythological status in American culture. Our concern in this chapter has been the power of understanding revealed in the generic conjunctions of law and literature—the power, and also the license, in the cultural formations that the conjunctions inspire. Brown's presentencing speech may live on its own, but the circumstance of transcription and its subsequent transmission have enhanced his original eloquence. The important thing to remember from the example is that the connection of law and literature is an inevitable one and deserves attention as an intrinsic and sometimes controlling aspect at trial.

Anyone who has scanned a court record understands how the repetition, the circularity, the technicality, the occasional opacity, and the sheer minutia in transcription inflict a special burden on the reader. Some kind of burden always exists in comprehension. Contemporary critics talk of "horizons of expectation" in a reader's interaction with a text and of the "tenacious" search for "textual unity or wholeness."[71] These problems of expectation and unity proliferate in the looseness and impossible bulk of a trial record. In the case before us, the transcript of Brown's trial and the capstone of his final speech welcomed internal generic appropriations that gave them larger meaning.[72] Left for demonstration is the process by which these appropriations took on a life of their own.

We have seen that John Brown's behavior and words in the Circuit Court of Jefferson County invited generic reconstruction of his place in American culture. Ralph Waldo Emerson, returning to the idea of the romance a month after Brown's execution, saw the likelihood of further imaginative production clearly. "Thus was formed a romantic character absolutely without vulgar trait," Emerson observed of Brown's trial, "living to ideal ends, without any mixture of self-indulgence or compromise. . . . And, as happens usually to men of romantic character, his fortunes were romantic. Walter Scott would have delighted to draw his picture and trace his adventurous career."[73] Emerson realized that the character "formed" of and by Brown in the courtroom would be formed again and again thereafter through the imaginative requirement of "living to ideal ends."

Emerson could intuit this much because he already had measured the impulse in himself. In speaking of Brown, he and others "delighted to draw his picture." There is no need to rehearse again how Brown's words summoned responsive language beyond the trial, but it *is* important to comprehend how one discourse comes to dominate all others, consolidating and simplifying a complex trial event for reception in the popular mind. John Brown, like the prosecution in the trial of Aaron Burr, spoke words that managed to subsume and hold all other narratives; his language redirected all others like a magnet sweeping across iron filings. The phenomenon should be studied. Something like this unmistakable power, admittedly to a lesser degree, happens every time a community is drawn to a courtroom.

The trial and execution will always remain the backdrop of the picture drawn of John Brown, but the seeming finality of legal ends was refashioned and extended in 1859 through the construction of Brown "living to ideal ends." In his final speech, Brown emphasized that "the law of God" would take account of what he had "suffered and sacrificed" and would turn his punishment into reward, his death back into life. In nineteenth-century thought, these words translated into Emerson's "romantic character absolutely without vulgar trait." So powerful was this construction as narrative desire that even vulgar forms would be altered to serve it; nowhere was that more apparent than in the mode of memory most frequently summoned, the popular song "John Brown's Body."

Irony in the most frequently voiced lyric in American history lies in its lost origins. The song still sung today invokes John Brown's last speech at trial. Just as the courtroom defendant framed physical defeat in a claim of spiritual victory, so, in balladic terms, the phrase "John Brown's body lies a'mouldering in the grave" receives exultant qualification in the refrain "his truth is marching on." But the parallel must be understood against a startling discrepancy. The original figure in "John Brown's Body" was *not* the legendary raider of Harpers Ferry but Sergeant John Brown of the Second Battalion, Boston Light Infantry, Massachusetts Volunteer Militia, in 1862.

The song originated in an army jibe from the ranks at the expense of a feckless noncommissioned officer of the same name. Spreading narratives of the abolitionist hero then seized the song in an appropriation of meanings and subject matter. Lost in the shuffle is the low humor and comic incongruity, antihero against hero, that launched the original jingle. Sergeant Brown of Boston died pathetically rather than in pathos or for a purpose. Not sacrifice but the grim hilarity of men who faced slaughter and sudden death from all sides explained the song. This Brown drowned quite by accident, even ludicrously, while attempting to cross the Rappahannock River with his regiment on June 6, 1862.[74] Union soldiers first sang in an attempt to laugh at their own probable fate.

The transformation from earthy tune into triumphant marching song serves as a final illustration of the urgencies that turned John Brown into something that he had not previously been. To understand what he became requires a dual move in interpretation. The official legal narrative of treason, conspiracy, and murder, on the one hand, competed in Charlestown with the superimposed narrative of cultural meaning, on the other. "Narrative," Roland Barthes has argued, "is first and foremost a prodigious variety of genres, themselves distributed amongst various substances."[75] Legality, which needs a monological level of discourse for the authority of a decision reached and enforced, must always grapple with the "prodigious variety" that advocacy and surrounding commentary will produce in the continuum of publication around a major trial. What happened so dramatically in Charlestown happens on a more mundane scale whenever litigants argue in court.

In these transformations of a trial record, genre represents a hidden presence. The literal transcription of everything said is an ingredient of the legal process, but observers accept through the familiar form of stories they understand. The massive record of what *has actually been said* at great length demands a simpler answer to what critics have called "vacancy within the referential field."[76] Form must supplant the vacancy of impossible bulk. Courtroom speakers use the generic forms available to them to explain a case to a particular audience, the jury; trial observers then impose their own selective recognitions on what they hear in order to make sense of the event, and if they care about what they have heard, the recognitions they choose can change their thinking. These changes are mostly subtle, but as the trial of John Brown indicates, they can lead to wholesale shifts in communal thought for good or ill. Both for and against these tendencies, a knowing culture should learn to prepare itself.

CHAPTER FIVE

Mary Surratt on the Altar of National Identity

"SHE DOESN'T DESERVE TO DIE"

When the state executes a woman, more than punishment figures in the act. Women represent only 2.8 percent of the total number of confirmed executions in the English colonies and the United States from 1608 to the present. Percentages drop further when restricted to the modern era. The rate since 1973 has been 1.2 percent, and media coverage has been intense whenever it has happened. Comparatively few women end up on death row (an annual average of 51 women out of a population of 3,499, or 1.45 percent in the first years of the twenty-first century), and as slight as those numbers are, the figures for condemned women who are "screened out" still exceed the overall rate of those removed from death row. The low numbers hold up even though women account for 10 percent of murder arrests.[1] A decision by the state to kill a woman occurs only in extraordinary circumstances, and nowhere is that premise plainer than in the first woman to be legally executed by the government of the United States.

Mary Surratt was the most peripheral of the four convicted defendants who, on July 7, 1865, faced the hangman's noose for the assassination of Abraham Lincoln. "Mrs. Surratt is innocent," claimed Lewis Payne, who stood beside her on the scaffold and was the most active member of the conspiracy after John Wilkes Booth. "She doesn't deserve to die with the rest of us." But no one in authority wanted to hear those words from anyone in the summer of 1865, much less from an assassin like Payne.[2]

In rejecting Mary Surratt's innocence, most Americans also refused to contemplate the possibility of a lesser role in the crime. Melodramatic events called for stark explanations, and so Mrs. Surratt loomed large in state accusations and newspaper coverage in the joint trial of the conspirators across May and June, and she remained the focal point during and after her execution in July. An obscure landlady, Mary Surratt would become the most photographed woman in America in 1865.

The trial transcript opens with a graphic demonstration of the state's assignment of importance to Surratt. A photograph of the nine convicted defendants arranged in a circle introduces the official court record. Appropriately enough, John Wilkes Booth, the already-dead assassin who shot the president, and Payne, the conspirator who seriously wounded Secretary of State William Seward on the same night, occupy prominent positions in the photograph at the top of the circle. The unaccountable placement is Mary Surratt's. Her image appears *inside* the circle of the other conspirators, and both her photograph and the representation of the person in it are significantly larger than those of the eight men around her. Circling her photograph, again in the center, come defining words: "The Conspirators."[3] Anyone glancing at this official rendition will see Mrs. Surratt first and, before reading a word, logically identify her as the ringleader of the conspiracy.

Although many have noted the symbolism in this first federal execution of a woman, the deeper manifestations of the event remain to be plumbed. Three *intertexts* (writings from the period with close affinities) reveal how Mary Surratt came to serve her country's needs. The transcript of the trial in which she was found guilty of "*maliciously, unlawfully, and traitorously*" conspiring to murder Abraham Lincoln deserves first priority in any investigation.[4] A second text, a trial transcript of another female defendant tried for murder at the same time, gives added perspective on women as criminals at the time. Forgotten today, *District of Columbia v. Mary Harris* involved a sensational murder trial in the same city during the very week that Mary Surratt stepped on the scaffold, but unlike Mary Surratt, Mary Harris would be found not guilty of any crime, even though witnesses watched her gun down her former lover, Adoniram Burroughs, in the Treasury Building at the end of a busy working day on January 30, 1865.[5] A third text, also forgotten in everything but name, offers background on the circumstances in play. *Our American Cousin*, written by the English playwright Thomas Taylor in 1858, was popular in America, and Abraham Lincoln watched it with his wife on the night he was shot in Ford's Theatre, April 14, 1865.

Historical episodes coded by gender norms join these three texts and clarify the ideological lines of force that brought Mary Surratt to the forefront of trial concerns. First, Abraham Lincoln died laughing at the most misogynistic moment of *Our American Cousin*, and the timing was no coincidence. Second, the funeral of President Lincoln and the execution of Mary Surratt were rigidly marked ceremonies of patriarchal assertion in response to a national crisis. Third and related, Northern media accounts regularly turned the Confederacy into a foolish woman at the moment of its defeat in 1865. Fourth, contemporaries believed that every woman connected no matter how remotely to the scene of the assassination had been marred for life and could never be quite the same person again.

These moments of gender marking were so intrinsic to thought at the time that they went unnoticed. But if other patterns of thought offered more visible threads of explanation as the nation tried to recover from war and the trauma of the assassination, stereotypes regarding women dominated considerations when it came to Mary Surratt, a woman with Southern sympathies on trial for conspiring to kill the president of the United States. More complicated than they first appear, these stereotypes lowered the standards of proof required to execute an unfortunate middle-aged Maryland landlady who found herself in the wrong place at the wrong time.

Studies in cognition show that "a widely held stereotype" reduces the level of information that a decision maker needs, or asks for, in rendering an opinion. Stereotypes operate across levels of consciousness, with more reflexive aspects controlling "silent arguments" and perceptions below the level of articulation.[6] An illustration from the case can clarify these premises. Andrew Johnson, as the new president, would reject an appeal of clemency for Mrs. Surratt by saying that "she kept the nest that hatched the egg" of conspiracy. The open part of this claim stipulates that Mary Surratt can be held responsible for the workings of her domestic sphere. Conventionally, Johnson could relegate Mrs. Surratt to that sphere and make her responsible for it. But a "silent argument" guides the stereotype, and it is deadly for the interstice in proof that it allows to go unrecognized. Mrs. Surratt was culpable for failing to keep her domestic sphere free of crime. But how far did culpability extend? "Silent argument" does not require an answer to that question. Mary Surratt had raised a nest of vipers in her boardinghouse, and that fact shaped all further knowledge of the conspiracy in her. She had perverted her womanly obligation by

Mary E. Surratt

Figures 9 & 10. (*Left*) Anon., Mary E. Surratt (1865?). Photograph courtesy of Columbia University Libraries. (*Below*) Alexander Gardner's photograph of the hanging of Mary Surratt, Lewis Payne, and co-conspirators, Washington, D.C., 1865. Library of Congress, 1977, no. 0837. Digital ID: cwpb 04230.

Figure 11. The ring of the convicted Lincoln assassin conspirators. Photograph courtesy of Columbia University Libraries. Alive and dead, Mary E. Surratt, an obscure Maryland landlady, was the most photographed woman in America in 1865. She was certainly peripheral and probably innocent in the assassination of Abraham Lincoln, but an angry nation made her the central figure in the trial, conviction, and execution of the conspirators. The photograph that presents Mrs. Surratt as the literal ringleader of the conspirators adorned the frontispiece of the published trial transcript in 1865.

failing to nurture an innocent home; it was enough to prove what the president called "female crime."[7]

Other factors pushed attention on Mary Surratt. The outpouring of grief and religious assertion over the death of Lincoln on Easter weekend did nothing to ease an embarrassing truth. Federal authorities had failed to protect the president. It had been an easy matter for John Wilkes Booth and his pitifully small, dysfunctional band of conspirators to kill the president, attack the secretary of state, and disrupt the government for weeks on end, even though everyone knew that the wartime capital was filled with Southern sympathizers and that escape to enemy territory lay just across the Potomac River. Worse, John Wilkes Booth had escaped in precisely that way after shooting the president. He had even taken the time to make his Southern sympathies clear by shouting the Virginia state motto, *Sic semper tyrannis*, from the stage of Ford's Theatre, and he had managed to remain at large for twelve days before federal troops could hunt him down and kill him near Port Royal, Virginia, on April 26.

How could such a thing have been allowed to happen? It relieved pressure on authority to find a domestic conspiracy of betrayal at the center of things, to label that level of conspiracy unforeseeable, and to fit it within the larger and thoroughly visible treachery of secession. The government wanted to show that a hundred people had been involved in the conspiracy under the deceptive cover of a small eight-room boardinghouse at 541 H Street, and it bolstered its claim by throwing scores of suspects into prison in the weeks before the trial. John Ford, the owner of the theater in which Lincoln was shot, was himself imprisoned for more than a month.[8] Amidst the confusion and blame of assassination, numbers had to substitute for the absence of personages.

The government's parallel desire to link the conspiracy to the leaders of the Confederacy demanded inclusive strokes of the imagination, and again it helped credibility to tie everything to the particularity of a place. Mrs. Surratt's boardinghouse fit neatly, even crucially, into a theory of spreading guilt. "Jefferson Davis is as clearly proven guilty of this conspiracy as is John Wilkes Booth by whose hand Jefferson Davis inflicted the mortal wound upon Abraham Lincoln," argued the prosecution in its summation at trial. Mrs. Surratt, a Southern sympathizer, had cloaked a vast military operation under the impenetrable respectability of her home. The final charge in the many against her, delivered in soldierly terms by her military panel of judges, began with the words "her house was the headquarters of Booth." In tacit agreement, *Harper's Weekly* would run a picture of that house alongside the photographs of Surratt's body hanging from the gallows.[9]

The reigning ideological metaphors against rebellion made it easy to pinpoint Mary Surratt. The familial notion of brother against brother aptly described the clash of armies in this civil war as in others. Abraham Lincoln had tried to counter the prospect in 1858 with a version of the same idea. "A house divided against itself cannot stand," he said then.[10] Seven years later, in the summer of 1865, the house of the Union had been saved but with internecine hatreds unbearably heightened by fratricidal war. How was the family in that house supposed to come back together again? How was the broken authority of the home to be reconstituted? These were not easy questions in the prospect of "reconstruction," a term that could mean either return or change. What was to be put back and what designed anew in the house of the Union? The North would find it convenient to think of the defeated South as a disobedient child in the family of the Union or, better yet, as an erring woman in need of correction—*not* as brother to brother with the equality that the sibling relation naturally implied.[11]

Mary Surratt found herself swallowed in these vortices. The military tribunal that convicted her put the matter directly: it believed, without any apparent need for further explanation, that "the execution of Mrs. Surratt would have a wholesome influence on other Southern women." There had not been "women enough hanged in this war," added President Johnson in his refusal to reduce Surratt's sentence. Johnson claimed to fear an explosion in crime by women if he pardoned in this case. "It would be a mercy to womankind," he concluded, "to let Mrs. Surratt suffer the penalty of her crime."[12] What could possibly justify such thinking? It was intellectually easier for authority to kill Mrs. Surratt than to let her live in the troubled summer of 1865.

No court system is at its best in a time of war. The value in explicating the trial of Mary Surratt comes not in painting the errors that occurred, nor in exposing injustice, nor in complaining about the stereotypes that doomed the defendant, although there is plenty of room for complaint. The aim of interpretation must be to show how stereotypes about an unpopular defendant work at different levels to overwhelm reflection. For while stereotypical thinking is unavoidable as a mental process, unfair manifestations of it must be guarded against in legal advocacy. Trouble

begins when a courtroom uses stereotypes beneath the level of articulation to bond with communal thought in promiscuous ways.[13] No matter
how peripheral, every relevant assumption in persuasion should be subject to proof at trial. Unpacking the layers of thought in stereotypes is the
first step in resisting their imposition.

A LANDLADY ON TRIAL FOR TREASON

The facts of the case can be summarized briefly. Mary Surratt was tried
with seven others before a special commission of military officers (seven
generals and two colonels). The tribunal presided in the penitentiary
where the alleged conspirators were held in solitary confinement. The
accused appeared in court under heavy guard and chains. Early in the
process, they were made to wear hoods. All eight were charged with "*maliciously, unlawfully, and traitorously, and in aid of the existing armed rebellion against the United States of America . . . to kill and murder, within
the Military Department of Washington, and within the fortified and in-
trenched lines thereof, Abraham Lincoln, late, and at the time of said combining, confederating, and conspiring, President of the United States of
America and Commander-in-Chief of the Army and Navy thereof.*"[14] The
military cast to these charges—Lincoln is killed as commander in chief
within battle lines—was deliberate. It justified martial law and the looser
standards of proof that a wartime tribunal could allow itself.[15] Mrs. Surratt faced an additional charge of conspiracy as the one who "did . . . receive, entertain, harbor, and conceal, aid and assist, the said John Wilkes
Booth" (20).

The three defendants who would share Mary Surratt's fate on the scaffold could be shown to have acted with knowledge aforethought in the
assassination. As part of the plan, Lewis Payne had knifed and come close
to killing Secretary of State William Seward on the same night as the
assassination. David Herold aided and accompanied Booth during his
escape to Virginia and was captured with him. George Atzerodt accepted
the assignment of killing Vice President Andrew Johnson but lost his
nerve at the final moment. Nothing of the sort, whether in knowledge
or participation, could ever be assigned to Mary Surratt. Moreover, the
government suppressed exculpating evidence that would have severely

complicated its case against Mrs. Surratt. It held back all mention of the diary that it had seized from John Wilkes Booth. Booth's entries revealed that he made the decision to kill the president alone and only on the actual morning of the assassination.[16]

The court officer best placed to sift through all of the evidence was the courtroom reporter who also took down every witness's testimony during prior interrogation. He left a stunning summary of what he had learned. "That Mrs. Surratt, who was hanged with the three male conspirators who were concerned in a plot to assassinate President Lincoln and other high government officials, was entirely innocent of any prior knowledge of or participation in those crimes, is, to my mind, beyond question," Benn Pitman, this official stenographer, would write later. Pitman would detail his reasons and conclusions on several occasions, and he would add: "I again affirm my solemn conviction that Mrs. Mary Surratt was innocent of the crime for which she was hanged."[17]

Why, then, were the officers of the Military Commission that convicted her and the president who refused clemency so convinced of her guilt? The evidence presented to prove Mary Surratt's involvement in the conspiracy was ambiguous and circumstantial but also suggestive. The government made the following case: Mary Surratt rented rooms to two conspirators, one of whom was her son; the conspirators met occasionally in her house; she held conversations with Booth and had a picture of him and of Jefferson Davis, president of the Confederacy, in her house; she made two trips to Surrattsville, her farm and tavern in southern Maryland, in the week of the assassination; the second trip occurred on the day of the assassination; she met briefly with Booth on the morning of the assassination when he came to her house to ask her to carry a package for him (binoculars) to Surrattsville (the assassin would pick up the binoculars with other supplies while in flight); she benefited from ten dollars in travel expenses that Booth had given to the tenant who took her to Surrattsville; she may or may not have left instructions with a tenant in Surrattsville about firearms deposited there; she may or may not have talked at her door in Washington with an unidentified man linked to the conspiracy on the night of the assassination; finally, she failed, along with others, to identify Lewis Payne, a conspirator, when asked by government officers to name a man who arrived at her front door on the night that she was arrested (392–94).

The defense had an answer for each incriminating fact and insinuation. Mrs. Surratt's son, John, had escaped to Canada, and he was the one who brought the conspirators into his mother's house. Where was the evidence that he had confided in her? Available letters proved that Mrs. Surratt went to her farm in Maryland on legitimate business on both occasions. It was hardly surprising that a landlady on the margins of society would treat a leading figure like Booth, a well-known actor from a famous family on good terms with official Washington, with respect when he entered her modest home.[18] How could she deny such a figure the common courtesy of taking a package to a destination on her route? It was a custom of the times routinely granted by many.

More to the point, there was not a single word on record of conversation between Booth and Mary Surratt. The photographs of Booth and Jefferson Davis were not hers; they were the property of her grown daughter, and there were similar photographs in the house of Union generals (including Ulysses Grant, Joseph Hooker, and George McClellan). The meeting that took place with Booth on the day of the assassination happened completely by chance on her part; Booth arrived and asked his favor of her only after Mrs. Surratt had made her own plans to go to Surrattsville (292–99).

There were other explanations to counter the accusations of complicity. Booth was notoriously prodigal with his money. The ten dollars from him proved nothing about the defendant's knowledge of his intentions. In any case, the money had been given to another person, and that person testified Mrs. Surratt knew nothing about the money at the time (117). The farm tenant who provided innuendo regarding Mrs. Surratt's knowledge of firearms for the conspirators at Surrattsville told a story with many contradictions. His reliability was also open to question: He had been drunk when Mrs. Surratt visited the farm and intoxicated again on the stand; he was clearly an intimidated witness who cooperated only under the threat of prosecution for his own role in conveying supplies and firearms to the assassins in their flight.

Mrs. Surratt's failure to identify Lewis Payne could also be explained. She was extremely nearsighted, the hallway where Payne stood at some distance was dark, Payne had changed his appearance drastically since previous meetings, and Mrs. Surratt was under arrest. Why should she speak when anything she said would be used against her? Others in the house also failed to identify Payne. All of the facts were "explainable so as to exclude guilt," and, facts aside, "where was the guilty knowledge" required to convict? By law in a conspiracy case, defense counsel reminded the court, "the intent or guilty knowledge must be brought directly home to the defendant." The prosecution had failed to prove its case beyond a reasonable doubt (292–99).

Hysteria over the assassination may have been enough to convict on such evidence, but the words used at trial always count, and they did here.[19] The prosecution concentrated on Mary Surratt's activity outside of her home and on her conversations with men beyond her family. As the indictment read, she had agreed to "receive" and "entertain" beyond her natural circle. "Persons were in the habit of coming from the country and stopping at her house," ran the testimony of one prosecution witness. "Mrs. Surratt was always hospitable, and had a great many acquaintances, and they could remain as long as they chose" (115). Many of these visitors were critical of the government and a number seemed "disloyal" (140–43). Why would an honest woman so involve herself in politics? Then, too, a woman who received money from a public figure like John Wilkes Booth surely had to have an intimate connection of some kind with him (117).

The government sneered at the thought of Mrs. Surratt away on private business; it was "the pretence" for other purposes. Why would a landlady spend so much time on the public roads? Why would she whisper in low tones in "*secret* conversation" with a man outside of her family while on that road or hold a "secret interview" with Booth in her own parlor (392–96)? The unstated basis of suspicion in these claims is not hard to find. Mary Surratt's actual situation disappeared in the conventional wisdom that a good woman belonged inside the domestic sphere taking care of home and family.[20]

Against that ready domestic image, there were the following realities. Surratt was a widowed businesswoman who ran a boardinghouse in Washington and a post office, tavern, and farm with tenants in Surrattsville (twelve miles south of Washington). She dealt regularly with all kinds of people in consequence. Wartime disruption had destroyed much of her livelihood from the farm in Maryland, and she managed to make ends meet only by moving back and forth between her two locations. She traveled often on business. However, operating outside of the home on the day of the assassination and in proximity to the conspirators could be and was construed as improper conduct in an honest woman. The prosecution argued on either side of an unarticulated line between socially questionable behavior and illegal conduct, using available constructions of female identity to control the variables.

The defense did not help its client by inserting her into its own version of the domestic sphere. It argued that Mrs. Surratt was "an innocent and guileless woman not knowing what was occurring in her own house" (294). She was "a *mater familias*, the good genius, the '*placens uxor*' of a home where children had gathered all the influences of purity and the reminiscences of innocence, where RELIGION watched, and the CHURCH was MINISTER and TEACHER." It was "monstrous" to think that such "a Christian matron" would "associate in crime" with her very own son. Yes, she was "a daughter of the South," but a "guileless-hearted woman" could not go against "maternal solicitude." Like Lady Macbeth, she would have "unsexed herself" by engaging in such a plot. It was not conceivable. "*This woman knew it not*," exhorted the defense (298–99).

More of such blather followed. Imprisoned, Mrs. Surratt sat "widowed of her natural protectors" and away from her now "desolated hearthstone," where "wretchedness and unpitied despair have closed like a shadow around one of earth's common pictures of domestic peace and social comfort." The defendant deserved to be "restored to her sex." "Remember *your* wives, mothers, sister, and gentle friends, whose graces, purity, and careful affection ornament and cherish and strengthen your lives," defense counsel implored the nine military judges. "Not widely different from *their* natures and spheres have been the nature and sphere of the woman who sits in the prisoner's dock to-day." The defense asked for "the aegis of impregnable legal justice which circumvallates and sanctifies the threshold of home and the privacy of home life against the rude irruptions of arbitrary and perhaps malice-born suspicion, with its fearful attendants of arrest and incarceration" (298–99). This strategy asked for too much and explained far too little.

The defense's assertions belonged to the times but did more harm than good in the situation. Hyperbole about *mater familias* played to stereotypes already leveled against the defendant and forgot that her main hope lay in mundane reality. Neither version of the broken domestic sphere offered in court fit Mrs. Surratt. The truth lay between on an entirely different plane of discourse, and that truth, if properly told, fell short of a basis to convict, but no one in 1865 could find a way to tell it, and this left the Military Commission with a dilemma.[21] The nine military veterans on the tribunal had to choose between sentimentally overblown arguments from both sides. Parsing between extremes on the same theme, they found the story of the prosecution more believable. The defendant, a peripatetic landlady, had carried parcels between her two homes for conspirators whom she knew, and one of them was her son. She did not appear entirely guileless, as the defense claimed. Whatever she did, she certainly had not been at "domestic peace and social comfort" by her hearthstone.

If the judges had qualms, they received no mediating narrative, an alternative of *some* guile. Advocacy failed everyone here, as it frequently does, by indulging in the sharpest edges of guilt and innocence. The Military Commission accepted the contention that Mrs. Surratt *should* have known what was happening in her own home and *should* have realized what at least her son was up to, and these assumptions allowed it to accept the prosecution's imaginative leap; she *must* have known. Even so, the hard evidence against Mary Surratt fell short of the standard needed to convict, much less to execute. How could such circumstantial evidence create the certainty that capital punishment required? The answers lie in the stories that wartime America told and heard about its women.

OUR AMERICAN COUSIN AND THE PROPER WOMAN

The story that Abraham Lincoln listened to on the night of April 14, 1865, was well known to theater people. The actor John Wilkes Booth knew *Our American Cousin* and chose the moment of loudest audience reaction to shoot the president. The play is a comic farce with resolving marriages at every social level. It features stock characters who misunderstand each other across the Anglo-American divide.

Asa Trenchard is a hard-drinking, straight-shooting, down-to-earth American hero who must cut through the machinations of two English villains threatening the inheritance of his lovely female cousins in England. Of course, he must also choose the right cousin for himself. A Davy Crockett figure, he brings the house down in the last act when he exposes the duplicity of the female villain, the refined but insufferable, gold-digging Mrs. Mountchessington, who seeks wealthy husbands for her daughters. "Don't know the manners of good society, eh?" barks Asa. "Wal, I guess I know enough to turn you inside out, old gal—you

Figure 12. The actress Laura Keene from the frontispiece of John Creahan's *The Life of Laura Keene* (1897). Photograph courtesy of Columbia University Libraries. Playing the leading role in *Our American Cousin* as Abraham Lincoln was shot in Ford's Theatre, Laura Keene rushed to the stricken president's assistance, where she showed more presence of mind than anyone else in a night of total confusion. Keene remained a prominent actress, writer, and entrepreneur for another ten years. Even so, the conventions of the time made her a ruined woman because of the traumatic experience that she had endured. Used negatively, the same stereotypes would control accounts of Mary Surratt in the dock.

sockdologizing old man-trap."[22] "Sockdologer" denotes a knockdown blow. The use of it in finally open combat between the sexes always led to prolonged applause, stamping of feet, shouts, hoots, and whistles in nineteenth-century American theaters. Booth the actor knew exactly what the reaction would be and waited for it to cover the sound of his pistol and to help him escape in the bewilderment and uncertainty that would follow his attack.[23]

The comically arranged confusions across national, social, and gender lines in *Our American Cousin* never perplex a watching audience. Everything is clear because stereotypical guidelines for each character are firmly in view. The English aristocrats suffer from overcultivation. Asa Trenchard counters as an American bull in the English china shop. He is ready to fight at all times, uses violent language at every turn, constantly bumps his refined English hosts onstage, and likes to use his "yankee key"(an ax) to open things. He also has a heart of gold and can be tamed by the right woman.

The leading female character, played by the famous actress Laura Keene, is Florence Trenchard. She serves as her father's "little clerk and person of all work" but not in financial matters, which exasperates her (I.i). Florence's superior ability, wit, and knowledge are clear, but they don't keep Asa from finding her "small potatoes." He chooses her cousin Mary Meredith, a milkmaid who turns out to be an English heiress in her own right (II.ii). Asa prefers Mary because of her contentment in domestic chores; she is "as bright and clean as a fresh washed shirt," a telling simile in what a husband will expect. "Wal, darn me," Asa tells Mary in the presence of Florence, "if you ain't the first raal right down useful gal I've seen on this side of the pond" (II.ii).

Asa's marriage proposal to Mary in act 3, scene 2, typifies the interplay between violence and tenderness. Abraham Lincoln never got to hear it, but he would have been familiar with similar tales. Mary is Asa's "sunbeam in a shady place." "Give me yourself," he pleads. "I know what a rude, ill-mannered block I am; but there's a heart inside of me worth something if it's only for the sake of your dear little image." The service of that image is not left in doubt:

A S A: You needn't fear that I'll ever be rough to you. I've camped out in the woods, Mary, and seen the wild bear who in her savage fury would tear the bold hunter piecemeal, as gentle, and loving to her young as a mother to her child. I've seen that claw that would peel a man's head, as a knife would open a pumpkin, as gentle to them, as if it was made of velvet. Which I'll be with you, Mary. And if ever harm should reach you, it must be over the dead body of Asa Trenchard.

MARY: I know it, Asa. And if I do not prove a true and loving wife to you, may my mother's bright spirit never look down to bless her child.

The bargains in this exchange contain implicit understandings. Mary will be Asa's protected child as wife, and in that role she will curb his tendency toward violence. The sudden absence of dialect in his proposal of marriage already reveals improvement in him. Mary maintains the blessings of her heritage and sex as long as she is loyal and obedient to him. The qualifications in this marriage contract are absolute ones: violence or disloyalty can and will destroy her and everything that she stands for.

Farce in the play belongs to the female personality. Mary puts the socially inclined Florence in her place: "I thought you never had any graver business than being very pretty, very amiable, and very ready to be amused" (II.ii). A minor character, husband-hunting Augusta Mountchessington, exposes the triviality in this possibility when she complains: "I am so tired, Ma, of admiring things I hate" (II.i). Her sister, Georgina, plays the fragile lady who faints at every opportunity and lives on air alone (II.i). Even their avaricious mother must admit her daughters are fools (III.vi).

These caricatures have to do with essential balances. When does proper amiability and deference become subservience for the woman in society? When, if at all, can she protest? When does the innate frailty of the wife turn into sham and narcissism? The answer to these problems lies in loyalty actively exercised in the domestic sphere. Mary, an "everlasting angel of a gal," describes such a scene in her vision of the good life: "I can see men and boys working in the fields"; "we lasses bustle about to prepare supper"; "the fire burns on the hearth, while your good old mother cooks the slapjacks" (III.i; III.ii).

The "most celebrated comedy" of an established English playwright, *Our American Cousin* played well for years on both sides of the Atlantic.[24] It did so because its characters corresponded to conventional types in the leading magazines of both countries. In 1864 and 1865, *Harper's New Monthly Magazine* published story after story on the proper arrangement of the domestic sphere: a woman's work in the home, her absolute duty and responsibility for the domestic good of her family, the pleasures of the hearth, the good woman who makes her man better than himself, the importance of her faith and charity, her frailty without them, her husband's authority in exchange for sustenance and protection, and her honored role of wife in the names of industry, obedience, and loyalty.[25]

To follow these linked precepts of domestic virtue never guaranteed success. Nineteenth-century readers liked to cry over undeserved misfortune. On the other hand, to ignore or challenge domestic virtue meant certain ruin in popular fiction. *Harper's* expressed its editorial alarm over the dangers: "There is scarcely a lady in the land who will not tell you that it is as difficult again to rule well her household as it was years ago." Too much education could be a problem. "Schools are good, but so much school and so little home is very bad." A woman's education had to make "common cause with the good mother or housekeeper."[26] Florence Trenchard loses out to Mary Meredith in *Our American Cousin* because she has interests *beyond* the home and *too much* education for her own good.

Magazines specifically for women, like *Godey's Lady's Book and Magazine*, hit these themes even harder and with specific warnings in the crisis of 1865. Business and the integrity of the home required separate spheres, as readers learned in stories like "Cupid *versus* Kerosene." In "Minus a Bonnet," a woman who puts herself into the public arena knows she is courting danger. "The Family Circle" finds all-consuming duty in "the sanctities of home," where home signifies "the nursery and preparatory school of the affections and moral sentiments of our nature." Every good home depended on the gender hierarchy celebrated in *Our American Cousin*. "Our training for immortality," preached *Godey's*, "begins with our first recognition of the right to command which the tones of a father's voice express, with the first appreciation of the love which plays in a mother's smile." In "The Wife to Her Husband," a poem that Tom Taylor's dairy maid might have written, the speaker clings to her husband in "holy woman's trust," obedient to her bridal vow.[27]

The editors of *Godey's* insisted on absolute differences between men and women. Men were the strength and honor of the Republic; women its grace and glory. Sons were growing plants; daughters, the frozen corner of the temple. Crucially, "woman is not undeveloped man." As something entirely of another kind, "she should not ask his place, nor his pay, nor covet his wealth, nor usurp his title." Sacrifice and the care of others were the woman's sacred lot. "Her rewards are rarely in any material gains for herself," the editors intoned; "a true woman finds her best recompense in the good she does." Most important of all, the pressing demands of the world could be fatal, and a woman under such strain would be "much more fertile in capacities of suffering than a man." "We would not change the stations of the sexes, or give to women the work and offices of men," the editors concluded. They welcomed newly established Vassar College's emphasis on "*Domestic Education*" but only to "maintain a just appreciation of the dignity of woman's home sphere."[28]

DISTRICT OF COLUMBIA V. MARY HARRIS

The same story controlled American courtrooms in 1865. On the day that Mary Surratt lost her life on the scaffold, the attorneys of another Mary, the accused murderer Mary Harris, began "to plead the cause of woman—gentle, lovely, virtuous woman," on behalf of a client who had traveled a thousand miles with a loaded gun in her purse and a plan to use it. On arrival, and after hiding in wait for hours in the Treasury Building, the accused killed her former lover with two careful shots as he left work. Despite clear proof of these facts, the jury in *District of Columbia v. Mary Harris* would listen for two weeks to courtroom debate and find Mary Harris not guilty of any crime whatsoever after five minutes of deliberation.[29] The defense argued that Miss Harris, while of sound mind, had acted out of "paroxysmal insanity from moral causes." The moral cause was "disappointment in love," an excusable but temporary source of mental disturbance in women (69, 99, 144).

The ostensible victim, Adoniram Burroughs, had known the defendant since childhood but had broken off their relation of seven years to marry another woman when he moved from Chicago to Washington, D.C. "We know that among the moral causes of insanity, disappointed affection is one of the most frequent," the defense contended, using medical experts to prove its case, "and we know that among physical causes, uterine irritation is one of the most frequent" (51). Mary Harris had suffered from both. Through "painful disease peculiar to her sex," she became, though only momentarily, "a human being totally transformed" (152). Luckily, all of that was in the past. As she sat in court, Mary Harris was again "the delicate, gentle being" she had been before her attack. To look upon her was to see that she was guilty of "no crime at all" (138, 123). Improbable as "these demonstrations of science" may sound to the modern ear, they convinced a jury of twelve men through the stereotypical story of womanhood already outlined (158).

The defense succeeded by insisting on the "holy flame" peculiar to the "woman's sphere of happiness" when love was given and returned. Love created "a season of bliss" in domestic life that every virtuous woman deserved to find. Mary had trusted Adoniram Burroughs, and he had violated that trust in two horrific ways: "He had wronged her, cruelly wronged her, and taken her from her home" (140, 57). The mantra of the defense raised this dual standard: betrayed trust and loss of home. "Though without sin, yet she was cast out from her place of blissful abode." Adoniram Burroughs "had lifted her up almost to celestial heights, only that her fall might be sufficiently great to dash her to pieces" (142). So great was *his* sin that he actually deserved death! "Who is to punish the betrayer of female honor?" wondered the defense. "Who is to punish the serpent that with his slimy track pursues from early girlhood into budding womanhood the unfortunate girl, separates her from her friends, her family, and leaves her alone and isolated, without father or brother to defend or protect her, and then throws her heartlessly upon the world?" (125).

Never without an answer to its own questions, the defense stressed their client's "natural" response against the one who "carried off her happiness." Yes, Mary had brought the gun with her from Chicago, but God himself had completed the act, choosing "as the instrument of his justice, in this particular case, the unfortunate girl." "Had not the bullet been guided by the finger of an all-wise Providence," the defense reasoned, "it would have passed him by harmless as the wind" (133). Women needed God's help to shoot straight! Whether agent or instrument, "whether she acted with cause, or under a mere delusion," whether sane or insane, Mary Harris deserved an acquittal from the jury (28). "Restore her by your verdict to the soothing influence of friends, of home," the defense demanded (161).

This strategy worked off of traditional formulations. Mary Harris had not entered the public sphere out of choice; she had been forced into it by the destruction of her home. She was "taken," "cast out," "separated," "lifted," "isolated," "carried off," and then thrown "heartlessly upon the world." Each verb form turned on the dead victim's violation of the defendant's sacred sphere. That sphere of domesticity belonged to *all* virtuous women, and they had a right, even a duty to protect it. To convict would be "a slander on Mary Harris" but in a clever extension, "equally a slander upon the truth, fidelity, and virtue of womanhood" (141). All of femininity would be slurred and maligned by a conviction.

Washington society heard the plea of *District of Columbia v. Mary Harris*. More fashionable ladies flocked to the trial each passing day. They visited Harris in prison and, expanding the iconography of the courtroom, many of them sat *beside* the defendant within the well of the courtroom (54, 75, 112). They were there, the defense confirmed, to protect "what the proudest, the purest, and the best have done in all countries and at all times." A woman had to trust her man when she "turned her back on home" (141). They were also there, if they read *Harper's New Monthly Magazine* and *Godey's Lady's Book and Magazine* and listened to the defense, to confirm "the susceptibility of the female mind to insanity when laboring under grief from disappointed affection." The stock nature of these patterns were repeatedly confirmed in court. "Why, gentlemen," exclaimed the defense, "we are simply following a broad, sorrowful, well-beaten track" (143–44).

The trial of Mary Harris has been worth pursuing because it clarifies the conviction of Mary Surratt. The helpless prosecutor of Mary Harris touched on a truth when he denounced "all this nonsense about insanity and moral justification"; it was "a pretext" to find "a pretty, delicate, little woman" not guilty (179). Mrs. Surratt aroused no such sympathy. She was a stout, rather dour, middle-aged widow shrouded in a veil and drab clothing. But if neither young nor attractive, Mary Surratt's appearance hardly explains why the language of pretext, always part of advocacy, ran so decisively against her. A better answer lies in a legal similarity between the two defendants.

The cases of defense for Mary Surratt and Mary Harris come together in their repudiation of middle ground. The lawyers in both trials refused to consider partial explanation, wrongdoing at any level, and their refusals required utter rejection of the concrete facts before them. Just as Mrs. Surratt's lawyers refused anything but a "guileless" defense, so their counterparts for Mary Harris insisted it was "very plain from the evidence in the case here, that the prisoner at the bar is guilty of willful murder, or else she is not guilty at all" (119). How could it be so very plain? After all, the undisputed physical evidence against Mary Harris indicated *some* degree of at least manslaughter. She had shot an unsuspecting man to death after planning that very act.

Extreme defenses were employed in both cases because of other binaries at work in the construction of nineteenth-century womanhood. The voiced assumption of the age held that women had to be either much better than men or "infinitely worse" if they went bad. When identified as criminals, women were understood to be "more ferocious" than men and capable of falling much further. The female criminal, it was thought, had greater capacities for vengeance and brought a more "refined, diabolical cruelty" to her pursuits.[30] In 1865 the woman defendant in court dared not be a little bit bad. The ruling hypothesis of complete purity or total depravity denied all possibility of middle ground and ran against the customary defensive incorporation of alternative arguments.

Mary Surratt had to be "exemplary and lady-like in every particular," and "all the time from the 1st of November up to the 14th of April 'doing her duties to God and man,'" *or* she was the complete reverse, the companion of Lady Macbeth, Nero's mother, and Catherine de Médicis. The defense risked raising these negative alternatives, all dreadful examples of the sex, to insist on their inapplicability to Mary Surratt. She was not one of those women with "demoniac ambitions" who "could harbor, underneath their terrible smiles, schemes for the violent and unshriven deaths" of anyone (295, 298–99). Or was she? Such talk made sense at trial only if the extremes of good and evil dominated the reality of womanhood. In comparable narratives in her own trial, Mary Harris had been "endowed by her Creator with the highest capacity for enjoyment or anguish" but no possibilities in between. Moderation was not a stance that her lawyers would entertain. With "but few, if any medium traits," Mary Harris lived in "a land of sunshine or a land of darkness" (143). To admit intermediate points in the spectrum of either defendant's actions invited an admission of complete guilt.

Mary Surratt's practical situation could not sustain the wildly optimistic side of this binary construct. The landlady's active life contradicted the sentimental tableau assigned to her at trial. The presence of the Lincoln assassin in her parlor further tainted the stock image of an innocent and happy hearth. Nonetheless, it would be another characteristic in the stories noted that would lead to her death. The ultimate impulse in narratives of womanhood, whether in magazine story or legal narrative, revolved around the theme of loss. Every woman in these nineteenth-century narratives devolves into something less and also different in the absence of her man.[31] The assassination of Abraham Lincoln would kill Mary Surratt in more ways than one. She was the victim of a twice-told tale: she represented the mournful end of the woman when the best of men is lost.

TRAPPED IN THE PUBLIC SPHERE

The Washington landlady was not all that unusual, but those like her also found themselves in an uncomfortable situation in the spring of 1865. Women in numbers had joined Mary Surratt in the workplace, particularly in Washington, either in government service or charitable institutions or support capacities indirectly linked to the war effort and its booming economy.[32] The end of the war and the trauma of the assassination would begin to change that with renewed expectations in domestic life.

The funeral of Abraham Lincoln and the trial and execution of Mary Surratt unfolded as fierce ceremonies of patriarchal right, and they were accompanied by derogatory figurations of women. Just 7 of the 600 invited guests who attended the official funeral in Washington were women, and one of them was a domestic servant. No women accompanied the entourage of 300 dignitaries on the train that carried Lincoln's casket on its thirteen-day journey across the country for burial in Springfield, Illinois, a distance of 1,700 miles with display of the president's body in nine cities. The absence of women could only be called peculiar, given the province of mourning allotted to the female role. Only one woman, Mary Walker, the lone female doctor in the Union army, witnessed the carefully photographed execution of Mary Surratt, which took place before 200 ticketed spectators and 3,000 soldiers on guard, and Dr. Walker would be criticized for her presence despite her professional standing.[33]

The prominent "other woman" of the times was the fallen South. Using the feminine pronoun, Northern newspapers saw her as defeated but unrepentant. The *Nation* described the Confederacy as "childishly" entrenched in the face of its cruelty and treason and "hugging this infamy like an only babe to its breast."[34] A traveling reporter who wrote a series of articles on "The South as It Is" gave particular attention to the slovenly nature of the domestic sphere of the region and to the women in it. The Southern woman's bitter opposition in the poverty of defeat gave her an unacceptable masculine aura. In one such account, a woman from North Carolina typified the South:

I have seen a great many women on the roads and in the houses of this region whose appearance resembled hers. She was barefooted and wore a man's hat, from beneath which escaped some locks of tangled hair; her sallow face was thin and dirty, and stained at the corners of the mouth with the juice of tobacco, which she chewed. The original colors of her cotton dress had run together and faded, till it had become of a uniform dingy white or clay color, and matched her complexion, and it clung about her as she walked with long strides. . . . [H]alf-a-dozen children were crying and fighting on the floor, so that nothing but their noise could be heard.[35]

The Southern women chronicled in these Northern reports spoke in rude dialect, smoked when they did not chew, and mismanaged a messy home full of misbehaving residents; many of them regarded Yankee visitors with a bitterness beyond their men. The correspondent of the *Nation* dwelt on the extent to which the sphere of womanhood in the South had broken down. "It would have been useless, I suppose," he wrote after one encounter, "to counsel her to cleanliness or industry, or decency of manners and morals, and I had to decline the difficult post of her adviser."[36]

There was, however, one visible area of industry in Southern womanhood, and it was a disturbing one. As another writer for the *Nation* revealed, "Every Southern matron is bringing up her children to hate and despise the Federal Union."[37] Presumed guardians of the home and first educators, Southern women were using their sacred stations to distort the young in moral growth and patriotic duty. The tones of violence in the speech of the fallen Confederacy could be traced to women and allowed Northerners "the right to treat Southern language as an important and alarming symptom of the social and political condition of the country."[38]

The tendency to feminize the South took a specific turn as the trial of Mary Surratt began. At daybreak on May 10, the day after proceedings opened, federal troops caught up with the fleeing president of the Confederacy in Irwinville, Georgia. Surprised in the semi-darkness, Jefferson Davis tried to elude his captors by rushing from his campsite wrapped in his wife's shawl. Northern media sources gloated for weeks over the implications. "Jeff Tries to Escape in Women's Clothes," blared the *New York Daily Tribune* on May 15. "Who Is President of the Confederacy?" mocked the *New York Times*, insisting that "Mrs. Davis is the legitimate successor to her husband's duties." "When he ran off with her petticoats," the *Times* chortled, "she had no alternative but to put on the breeches."[39]

Newspapers also stressed acerbic remarks supposedly made by Varina

Davis as her husband was captured. Crowed the *New York Times*, "In view of the language she used on the occasion, we venture to predict that foreign nations will make all haste to recognize her as a belligerent." *Frank Leslie's Illustrated Newspaper, Harper's Weekly*, and other journals carried cartoons of Jefferson Davis decked in female dress and bonnet. Frequent sketches of Davis in drag with comic captions ran throughout the trial of the conspirators.[40] All of this fun over the feminization of Davis eased identifications of him with the conspirators. A presidential proclamation on May 2 had accused Davis of being a co-conspirator in the assassination, and the *New York Times* had followed with a bold headline: "JEFFERSON DAVIS IS THE HEAD OF THE ASSASSINS."[41]

Guilt by association and the assumption of a warlike nature in Southern women appeared everywhere in print, and the spreading web of accusation along with Northern complaints about the unladylike behavior of Southern women could not have come at a worse time for Mary Surratt. One of the few attempts to answer the invective heaped upon her revealed the extent of that abuse and the difficulty in defending against it. "It is customary to represent [Mrs. Surratt] as a monster, with an unlimited amount of cunning and cruelty in her face," a female correspondent wrote in to the *Pittsburgh Commercial* in a letter widely quoted, "but she is simply a representative Southern woman, no better or no worse than the majority of Southern women."[42] What did it mean to be a representative Southern woman? The "better" aspects of womanhood in the region were suspect, and the worst fit the wishes of Northerners eager to punish a traitorous South. The linkage of the defendant to this general identification was an inevitable one. As the *Chicago Tribune* would describe Mary Surratt, she was "the perfect type of venomous Southern woman."[43]

The language of monstrosity used to describe Mrs. Surratt rested on another rhetorical foundation as well. Horror over the assassination seemed to disfigure all of the women connected to it, no matter how tangential or innocent their relation to the event. Because nineteenth-century ideals of womanhood maintained that female sensibilities suffered more than the male in a crisis, the unprecedented murder of an American president with women present invoked extravagant possibilities.

Eyewitness accounts of the assassination from ladies in Washington strengthened the convention. One woman in a nearby theater that night confessed the "terror" she shared with a female companion when their escorts, "wishing to join the throng, quickly took us home, leaving us frightened women to console each other"; "there was no sleep or rest until the men came home."[44] Another witness, actually in Ford's Theatre on the night, described how "delicate women stand clinging to the arms of their protectors." Forced "with shuddering lips" to regard " 'our President's blood' all down the stairs and out upon the pavement," she acknowledged that "sleeping or waking, that terrible scene is with me," and she was still "a frightened child" two days later, adding, "I can't bear to be alone."[45]

The closer a woman came to the martyred president, the greater the presumed negative impact upon her. The president's wife, Mary Todd Lincoln, gave the image of the destroyed (and destructive) woman plenty of reinforcement. Always temperamental and given to outbursts of public anger, she fell into prolonged hysterics at the scene of the assassination and total collapse immediately after, taking to her bed for more than a month. Her "uncontrolled anguish" on the night of the assassination "irritated the all-male watch of government officials, generals, and doctors" who sat at the dying president's bedside. The command given from there after one particularly loud outburst applied figuratively to all women in the aftermath: "Keep that woman out of here."[46]

Mary Lincoln's words in her new situation confirmed the stereotype of womanhood in crisis: "Alas! All is over with me!" The few visitors allowed to see Mrs. Lincoln in the days after the assassination found her "more dead than alive—broken by the horrors of that dreadful night." For the remaining seventeen years of her life, Mary Lincoln lived in seclusion with the full trappings of mourning and weeds of widowhood in place. Her occasionally bizarre behavior allowed the world to challenge even rational claims as the work of disturbed womanhood. When she thwarted the plan of Springfield, Illinois, to bury her husband in the center of the city, Mrs. Lincoln earned its enmity and much criticism for insane obstinacy, but she had good cause to resist. She realized that Springfield's plan would prevent her, as a woman, from receiving burial next to her husband, and she acted in recognition of operating proprieties ("such would be out of the question in a public place of the kind"). Her insistence on semi-official prerogatives brought censure in sharp gender terms. "If Mrs. Lincoln had studied her true mission as a mother and wife," the *Columbus Sun* wrote in denunciation, "she could not have discredited her sex and injured the name and fame of her country and husband."[47]

· But if Mary Lincoln conformed to the stereotype, Laura Keene was forced into it. The lead actress in *Our American Cousin* rushed to aid the stricken Lincoln in his theater box and showed more presence of mind than anyone else in Ford's Theatre on the night of April 14. No amount of composure, however, could save her from stock representations. Keene appeared in accounts as the distracted "incarnation of tragedy." In the words of one eyewitness, "Her hair and dress were in disorder, and not only was her gown soaked in Lincoln's blood, but her hands, and even her cheeks where her fingers had strayed, were bedaubed with the sorry stains!"[48]

A bold entrepreneur as well as an actress of note, Laura Keene would perform on the stage for another decade while managing Chestnut Street Theatre in Philadelphia and writing a book on the fine arts. It made no difference. Her biographer would find she was never the same again: "A crime which distracted strong men everywhere, did much to physically ruin a woman of Laura Keene's gentle and entirely feminine composition." The reasons for her decline were also made clear. Her "true sphere, after all," was "as a woman." She could never be that "strong-minded creature, or that horror of our mother, wife, sister, or daughter, and detested generally by manly men—the 'he-she,' who cannot even by way of apology command the respect of men, while ever abhorred by women."[49]

A woman caught in the public sphere at the wrong moment had something to answer for in 1865; a woman with Southern sympathies, a lot more. The first received pity, if hurt; questions, if not. The second endured scorn and required correction. The options for a woman exposed in public were limited. She could explain the right to her presence through a more subtle articulation of proper spheres, she could engage in tacit withdrawal, or she could mount a full retreat if the situation called for it—all standard patterns of conduct in the behavior of nineteenth-century women who wished to avoid criticism.

By way of contrast, Mary Surratt found herself held there against her will; she was a stationary target first in the dock and then on the scaffold. None of the available avenues of retreat presented themselves. Trapped outside, uncovered in public, she underwent what every cultivated American woman of the age sought to avoid in both life and death: the prolonged gaze and negative scrutiny of her culture. It was an extraordinary situation, and it would serve extraordinary purposes. The unsexing of Mary Surratt in the public sphere would contribute to an ideological transformation of national proportions.

"FEMALE FIEND INCARNATE"

A high-profile trial becomes an irresistible force when the language used there defines how general behavior must be understood. As early as May 3, the *New York World* concluded that the other conspirators were really Mary Surratt's disciples. Three days later the *New York Tribune* agreed, arguing that the accused landlady was "entitled to a place in the front rank of the most active and dangerous plotters." The *Boston Journal* knew on May 9 that Mary Surratt had "unquestionably nursed the plot with malignant care." Not to be outdone, the front page of the *New York Times* on May 12 found a "female fiend incarnate."[50]

The singular progression in these accounts toward a female conception of evil reveals the kind of journalistic momentum that takes over in a high-profile trial. The compulsion to embellish a story line within a common frame of competitive reference emphasizes an attribute that can be assigned to the targeted figure. In this case the frame was guilt, and the main attribute that could be assigned to the utterly silent Mary Surratt was her femininity. Accordingly, in imitation of the penalty to be exacted, an angry press sought to destroy that femininity.

There was no appropriate stance that Mary Surratt could assume on trial for her life. She already had failed as a woman. "Mrs. Surratt is to be much blamed," concluded the *New York Daily Tribune*. "She should have exercised a woman's influence and a mother's love, and then she could have prevented all."[51] In one of its most unfair strokes, the *New York Times* made the Washington landlady a poor housekeeper. Ignoring the fact that soldiers had ransacked Mrs. Surratt's house while looking for evidence on the night of her arrest, the *Times* observed the next day that "the house was found in a very disordered condition, the beds all unmade, the clothes piled on chairs, and everything in confusion, showing very plainly that the inmates had other business on hand than the usual business of housekeeping."[52]

When Mrs. Surratt remained passive in the courtroom, the *New York Daily Tribune* criticized her "stoical indifference"; if she cried, it assumed she was showing "signs of contrition." If instead of remaining passive she formally exercised her right by seeking counsel, the same paper complained that her decision "evinces her boldness."[53] Defendants on trial in most jurisdictions in nineteenth-century America were not allowed to address the court. Unable to speak, Mrs. Surratt had to be interpreted entirely through her behavior. Newspapers across the country used her every action and non-action to find her "guilty."

Reporters were not above inventing what they could not find. Forced to look for signs, they disputed among themselves over how Mary Surratt looked. They agreed she was "the most prominent of the accused," and their coverage kept her that way. Debate centered on whether the defendant's "cold gray eyes" contained a "cruel gleam" or were merely "lifeless." As one of "the chief instigators," she had to have eyes filled with "crafty, implacable spirit" or "gross stolidity and defiance." However, as a woman, the same eyes had to be filled with tears, and the debate over these elements of status and display continued even though the defendant always appeared in court heavily veiled.[54]

Surratt's conviction sharpened the contradictions in press coverage. On July 8 the *New York Times* found "a cold eye that would quail at no scene of torture" as well as "a close, shut mouth, whence no word of sympathy with suffering would pass." Found guilty, Mrs. Surratt offered "a square, solid figure, whose proportions were never disfigured by remorse." That was the criminal, but what of the woman who faced execution? Incongruously, the *Times* would declare that Mrs. Surratt "for a moment forgot the Surratt in the woman, and felt the keenness of her position. Fainting, she cried aloud in the bitterness of her woe, wailing forth great waves of sorrow; she fell upon the floor and gave vent to a paroxysm of grief, partially hysterical, and wholly nervous."[55]

The problem of the female defendant's qualified visibility figured in two other ways. Reporters debated the question for weeks over whether or not Mary Surratt had been forced to wear chains in the courtroom like the other accused conspirators. The defendant's long skirts prevented direct verification. Interviews were not allowed, and the government was not talking. At least one reporter claimed to hear telltale clinks on the rare occasions when Mrs. Surratt moved in court. The issue was important because of the disgrace that fell on a freeborn woman in chains and the imputed cruelty of captors who would enforce such an unnecessary measure. The other defendants were clearly and awkwardly in heavy irons in court. Was Mrs. Surratt in smaller ankle chains? Should co-conspirators be treated differently? The debate raged long after the event and was still a topic in the 1890s.[56]

The second issue involved the much-photographed execution. Criticized for killing John Wilkes Booth needlessly and burying him in secret—criticisms that led to claims that Booth might still be alive—the government had an official photographer, Alexander Gardner, on hand to take sequential pictures of the execution. Without ceremony, it then buried the four executed conspirators in full view, also photographed, right next to the scaffold in the prison yard. The awkwardness of the occasion supplied another instance of how the age constructed the female body as at once sacred and profane. "I took charge of Mrs. Surratt myself," the chief executioner detailed, "not being willing that any hand should desecrate her. I lifted her tenderly in my arms, her limp body bending as I held it. I removed the noose from her neck, and with my own hands and alone placed her in the box." It was much too late for such delicacy to reign. Descriptions and photographs of every aspect of Surratt's execution were detailed, close-up, graphic, and widely disseminated.[57]

Was it shameful to hang a woman? Many felt and said so. The problem could be solved, however, by making Mary Surratt less of a woman. In court the defense had agreed that a guilty woman would have "unsexed herself' " (298). Found guilty, Mrs. Surratt began to disappear in sexual terms except in the assignation of her failures in the home—failures that translated easily into physical terms. Her counsel noted that the trauma of prison had caused her to suffer from "the womb disease." Another defense lawyer who visited her in prison found that "her sickness was change of life" and that "her cell by reason of her sickness was scarcely habitable." By the time of her execution, the officials close to her agreed that she was already dying anyway. "I doubt whether she knew much of her execution," claimed the same lawyer. "She behaved as one that was three-fourths dead."[58]

Well before death, Mrs. Surratt had been effectively removed except as a residual object. The proprieties called for nothing less. A devout Catholic, the doomed woman pleaded for a public hearing in her final confession. "*Holy father*," she asked, "*can I not tell these people before I die that I am innocent of the crime for which I have been condemned to death?*" When it came, her priest's response confirmed the marginal posture of the ideal woman in nineteenth-century culture: namely, silence in public.

"No, my child; the world and all that is in it has now receded for ever," he answered. "It would do no good, and it might disturb the serenity of your last moments!"[59] In a curious juxtaposition, the newspapers continued to write that Mary Surratt had to be "one of the most active and energetic of the conspirators."[60] There could be no real resolution between these extremes except that each, in its own way, encouraged the act of taking Mrs. Surratt from life to death.

Acceptance of the execution would come less easily as time passed. Questions began with the trial of Mary Surratt's son in June 1867. John Surratt, who clearly had been involved with the conspirators, escaped to Canada and then to Europe. When he was caught and returned for trial two years later, it would be in the regular criminal court of the District of Columbia; in the interim, the Supreme Court declared military commissions of the kind that Andrew Johnson had authorized in 1865 to be unlawful in peacetime.[61] John Surratt would go free when a jury of laymen could not decide on his guilt over the assassination, and his trial verified a fact that had been suppressed. Five of the nine military judges of Mary Surratt had secretly urged clemency in 1865 on the basis of her sex. Notably, the trial in 1867 also impugned the testimony of the two main witnesses against Mary Surratt when they were called to testify again, this time against her son.[62]

Recriminations over the execution increased with the revelation of John Wilkes Booth's suppressed diary and grew bold in 1880, when prolonged debate between the officials who had allowed the execution to take place began to surface in articles of the prestigious *North American Review*. Everyone saw in retrospect that the charge of an official Confederate conspiracy in assassinating Lincoln had been completely false, and this knowledge turned the procedures of the Military Commission into an open embarrassment. Forty percent of the government's witnesses, 60 out of the 147 summoned, had been called to testify about the character of the Confederacy under the assumption that its leaders had been complicit in the assassination. Witness after witness described the Confederacy's worst atrocities during the war, and while these accounts were irrelevant as testimony, they contributed to an atmosphere of prejudice against Mary Surratt.

Just as significant were the accusations that emerged between Judge Advocate Joseph Holt, who had overseen the prosecution for the government; James Speed, who had been the government's chief lawyer as attorney general at the time; and Andrew Johnson, who had refused to reduce Mrs. Surratt's sentence as president. Who was to blame for Mary Surratt's death? Holt attacked the ex-president for "base falsehood," for being "a treacherous Executive," and for taking "craven refuge from accountability for official action." He turned James Speed into President Johnson's "moral accomplice." Speed had acted with "the stench of [Johnson's] baseness in your nostrils." No one in the 1880s wanted to take responsibility for refusing the tribunal's gesture of clemency.[63]

Former attorney-general James Speed fueled the flames again in 1888 by claiming rather incredibly that "Mrs. Surratt had a fairer trial before a military court than she would have had before the civil tribunals"; he compared her to the biblical Jezebel, "who stirred up Ahab, and incited him to commit the foulest murders."[64] Many late nineteenth-century Americans disagreed and found instead that Mary Surratt had been the victim of "a wild cry for legal vengeance." Her trial illustrated "the pitfalls that commonly surround court-martial or civil trials during scenes of popular excitement," and her execution had put a "stain which time can not efface" on the legal history of the country.[65]

But if one generation had been enough to condemn the errors of 1865, these later reassessments still rested on the cultural work that the execution had served. The year 1865 had been much more difficult than 1861 when it came to defining the Union. Up against that difficulty and uncertain about how to proceed next, the vast majority of Americans favored the execution of Mary Surratt in 1865. More than conviction, sentence, and death had been at stake in the rituals that led to photographs of a dangling female body on the scaffold.

CONSTRUCTING THE NATIONAL "WE"

One of the more interesting comments in the *New York Times* during the vexed April of 1865 raised the whole nature of national authority and how Americans should talk about it. Abraham Lincoln had been a much-criticized president before martyrdom turned him into the greatest American of all, and the *Times* noted that fact in an article entitled "License of Speech and Assassination."

The newspaper drew a direct connection. Booth had killed in the belief that Lincoln was a tyrant, but how had he come to hold this mistaken belief? It was only because others had planted the idea by irresponsibly writing of the president in such negative terms. The lesson to be drawn was obvious. Fair criticism had to be allowed. "But we do most earnestly hope that this assassination will restrain license of speech," the *Times* concluded. Everyone in the country, North and South, had to take some responsibility and learn "to avoid all such excess of evil-speaking."[66] Loyalty to one's country had begun to mean acquiescence as well as allegiance to those in authority.

Every witness and officer before the Military Commission at trial had to endorse the new ideal of loyalty. Each participant took a loyalty oath as the price of participating in the trial of the conspirators, and accusations of disloyalty figured prominently and promiscuously in the courtroom debates that followed.[67] Taking the lead, the commission moved obedience to the federal Constitution to higher levels of stringency and devotion. The war had transformed the Constitution into a sacred document, one "so divine in its spirit of justice, so beneficent in its results, so full of wisdom, and goodness, and truth, under which we became one people," that it deserved to be taken on faith. Faith, in this connotation, meant more latitude for authority and the court to deal with the crisis of union.

Courtroom speakers for the government vied in their professions of obedience. The clear winner in this contest of patriotic ardor was the assistant judge advocate for the prosecution John Bingham. "I will yield to no man," Bingham declared, "in reverence for or obedience to the Constitution of my country, esteeming it, as I do, a new evangel to the nations, embodying the democracy of the New Testament, the absolute equality of all men before the law, in respect of those rights of human nature which are the gift of God and, therefore, as universal as the material structure of man."[68]

The proclaimed links between national and religious worship, and there were many of them, had nothing to do with proving the guilt of Mary Surratt. Their purpose, rather, was to draw suspicion toward anyone who failed to make similar associations. Pharisaic displays of loyalty in court had three purposes: first, they presumed a more rigorous standard of civic allegiance in the claim that God supported existing authority; second, they left people who questioned the court open to the criticism of disloyalty; and third, they tarred anyone who failed to use such rhetoric with the brush of tepid allegiance in a national crisis.

As the victorious North took stock of victory, it faced two questions that it was inclined to fuse into one. How had the "European crime" of assassination found its way to American shores? And what was to be done with the defeated South? The conflated answer, repeated to the point of tedium in court and in Northern newspapers during the summer of 1865, worked through parallels. Its proponents maintained that secession equaled treason equaled assassination. Whether the leaders of the Confederacy were *directly* involved or not, the South's lack of true patriotism led to the murder of Abraham Lincoln. The prosecution argued at length that assassination represented only the latest strategy in a long enumeration of deliberate Confederate atrocities.[69]

Northern newspapers carried the same message. "Every possible atrocity appertains to this rebellion," the *New York Times* noted, and it listed "massacres and torturings, wholesale starvation of prisoners, firing of great cities, piracies of the cruelest kind, persecution of the most hideous character, and finally assassination in high places" as the main elements in a natural continuum. Assassination was "the logical and legitimate ending of a long series of outrages," and it was only what the North should have expected from a slaveholding society. "The barbarities practiced on the black man prepared the way for the barbarities since practiced on the white."[70] The plot of assassination planned by "the conspicuous rebel chiefs," echoed *Harper's Weekly*, "is no more atrocious than many of which they are notoriously guilty." "The real murderers of Mr. Lincoln," chimed the *Atlantic Monthly*, "are the men whose action brought about the civil war." A clear and, therefore, deliberate path could be traced. "Booth's deed was a logical proceeding, following strictly from the principles avowed by the Rebels and in harmony with their course during the last five years."[71].

Several things followed from the assumption of general Southern culpability in the death of Lincoln. It meant the South was unrepentant in the face of defeat and that it could not be trusted to behave with minimal decorum in peacetime. What, then, was to be done with the rebel states? The editors of the *Nation* presented the issue squarely to its Northern readers. "One of the most singular incidents of the reconstruction process is the difficulty which President Johnson, *as well as most other people*, seems to have in deciding whether the rebellious States are in or out of the Union," they wrote. "He holds firmly to the theory that they are in, but he as firmly acts as if they were out."[72]

Here was the nub of the problem. Could the Southern states simply renew prerogatives that they had never lost? After all, the driving policy of the war effort had been that a state could not *leave* the Union. Thaddeus Stevens, the leading abolitionist in Congress, was also chair of the crucial House Ways and Means Committee, and his scornful answer to the predicament captured the mood if not the policy of the North. Stevens thought the problem should be handled by reducing the states "lately in revolt" to the status of territories "until such time as the rest of the country shall consider it safe to re-admit them to the Union." The Southern states belonged in roughly the same category as the conquered cities of Latium when under the military thumb of ancient Rome.[73]

Few agreed with Stevens's analogy, but most Northerners accepted the undercutting corollary in his logic. Since the South remained dangerous, its status could not be quite what it had been, and it deserved to be chastised. It followed that the federal government needed extra power to accomplish these ends. The *Nation* expressed a growing frustration in the North with a thunderous interrogative. "IS ANYBODY TO BE PUNISHED?" President Johnson had said as soon as he took office that "*the principles of public justice*" and "*sound public morals*" required punishment. "*The American people must be taught*," he exclaimed to a delegation from Illinois less than a week after the assassination, ". . . that *treason is a crime and must be punished*; that the Government *will not always bear with its enemies; that it is strong*, not only to protect, *but to punish*."[74] The government wanted to use its victory to extract new levels of loyalty from all concerned—not just the South.

Naturally choleric, the new president had spoken too rashly. To defeat the South was one thing; to change an entire region with its set ways and solidarity, quite another. Punishment as an ideological tool also sounded better in Washington than it could operate on the ground. The desire to rectify in the North meant simple retribution in the South, and no one in either region had a workable calculation on where to stop such measures once they began. At what level in the ranks of Confederate political and military leaders did the charge of actionable treason lose its force? Northern politicians soon realized that symbolic punishment would have to satisfy the overblown rhetoric of castigation that they themselves had created. Thus, and despite countless accusations of Southern atrocities, Captain Henry Wirz, the commandant of the Confederate prison camp at Andersonville, would be the only person tried and convicted by the Union for war crimes.[75]

In this atmosphere of rhetorical inflation, the official deaths of the convicted Lincoln conspirators served a very important mediating function. Here at least was the punishment called for. Hanging, "that mode of death to which a peculiar stigma is attached by the common consent of mankind," branded the South with an appropriate measure of disgrace.[76] The executions allowed the North to encapsulate its anger and move on. "The bloody deed of the 14th of April has been expiated, after the lapse of almost three months," the *Nation* editorialized. "Public opinion rests satisfied with the finding of the Court, satisfied with its verdict, and satisfied with the execution of four of the conspirators in assassination."[77]

The terms of address in the *Nation*'s summarizing editorial were "expiated," "rests," and especially "satisfied." The editors congratulated the tribunal, the American people, and by implication themselves. "The public mind had grown calm and dispassionate in the interval, and the patience which has endured the tedious process of the Court is a guaranty of the absence of vindictiveness in sanctioning the usual penalties." Of Mary Surratt, the editors added, "It is less repulsive to see a woman strangled where a man would be, than for her to have participated in the most atrocious murder of our time." Any remaining uncertainties and distress could be allowed to disappear in the exchange of blood for blood. Repugnance in hanging a woman answered the revulsion over assassination.[78]

No important source in the North disagreed with these findings or the means of resolution. Everything about the execution was affirmed in 1865. Like the *Nation*, *Frank Leslie's Illustrated Newspaper* congratulated trial officials and hailed the "real relief" of the execution: "the last act of the tragedy, beginning with the assassination of President Lincoln." The nation could now forget the worst. "Men seek to draw a veil over an incident which is without parallel in our history." In a telling metaphor, the execution "dropped the lid of the coffin and shut the bolt of the prison between the nation and the constant contemplation of the participants in the most revolting crime known to history." An act of oblivion, use of the scaffold encouraged a new burst of nationalism even as it fixed the "natural sequence" from rebellion to assassination on the defunct Confederacy.[79]

Acceptance of the trial and execution included a new national picture. In chapter 3, we saw how Edward Everett Hale's story from 1863, "The Man without a Country," replaced a republic defined by the right of revolution with a nation-state where the test of membership would be loyalty. Americans in 1865 used their anger to work out that new construction. As the *Nation* saw it, "The new wine of impartial liberty which the nation has trodden out of the red wine-press of the rebellion" could never be put back "into the old bottles of State rights."[80] A stronger, a more imposed and imposing union was emerging.

Nationalism works through the plural of the first-person pronominal form. "The crucial question relating to national identity is how the national 'we' is constructed and what is meant by that construction."[81] In 1865 the "we" of national identity somehow had to reconstitute itself *with* the return of the South but *without* the threat that the South still presented. The trial of the conspirators provided a useful ideological prop in managing this tension creatively. Exposure and punishment of the assassins, all of whom were Southern sympathizers, warranted retention of wartime binaries: "us" against "them."

The infinitely expandable charge of conspiracy and the extensive publicity given to it held the South in partial abeyance. Even if most Southerners deplored the assassination—and many in the North were not willing to grant that much—it was not enough. The error of rebellion had given birth to the sequence of secession, treason, and assassination on American soil, and that could not be forgotten nor, in any legal conception of blame, easily forgiven. Trying the conspirators routinized Northern insistence on punitive status for the defeated and suspect South until it could once again prove its loyalty to the Union, and no one was in a hurry to decide what such proof might entail.

The prosecution had argued at trial that authority had "to redress every wrong and to avenge every crime" with implications well beyond the conspirators.[82] Less formal venues had made these claims, but it was another matter to have a general spirit of censure legitimized in a high-ranking courtroom and disseminated in public every day from May 9 to June 30, a period of seven weeks. The prolonged intensity of the trial and national interest in it educated the public through its observation of punishment.

Theorists describe this social process of indoctrination as one of "*enhabitation*." Through repetitions in a highly charged event, exceptional circumstance gives way to a newly established pattern of habitual or routine belief.[83] The prosecution's winning discourse at trial wrapped the anxiety of the assassination in two assumptions, one comforting and the other directive. It kept the Southern states in suspension while logically holding them to national stipulations through punishment, and it made reflexive allegiance the gauge of true citizenship. These premises became credible when the official "we" of the patriotic voice in court assigned regional blame for the murder of the president.

Mary Surratt could not be expected to survive these thought processes. Her death was too crucial to them. But where does that realization leave us? Communal anger and momentums toward conviction notwithstanding, trials are supposed to protect a defendant until *proven* guilty. Instead, the limitations placed upon Mary Surratt at trial molded her into a communal narrative at her expense. Present but absolutely silent, visible but thoroughly cloaked, a female defendant left entirely to male voices, she fed the familiar stories of the time, and those stories embraced stereotypes that could not reach the life she actually led. Would the result have been different if more of the real Mary Surratt had appeared at trial? Perhaps not, but the guilty verdict would at least have been more difficult to reach.

A rule of law is always vulnerable to other communal needs, and all too easily run over by them. In 1865 an already-aroused community imbibed the court's proceedings through inflammatory and manifestly unfair newspaper accounts. Caught up in the patriotic moment, even leading defense counsel spoke to the ages and for the state instead of for the client he was engaged to save. Attorney Fred Aiken's final esoteric appeal could have meant little to the hard-headed military veterans in judgment, but his words gave some notice of what was actually happening in court. "Let the heralds of PEACE and CHARITY with their wool-bound staves follow the fasces and axes of JUDGMENT and LAW, without the sacrifice of any innocent Iphigenia," he implored the Military Commission, "let the ship of State launch with dignity of unstained sails into the unruffled sea of UNION and PROSPERITY."[84] Arguably, just such a sacrifice was taking place. Mary Surratt was more than a scapegoat in 1865. She was Iphigenia slaughtered on the legal altar of a new national launching.

Figure 13. Michael Schaak, *The Execution* (detail) (1889). Engraving. Published by F. J. Schulte & Co., Chicago, IL (ICHi-03675). Photograph courtesy of the Chicago History Museum. Chicago was an armed camp consumed with false fears of an insurrection during the execution of the Haymarket defendants on November 11, 1887. The execution itself was badly botched. Thousands of policemen stood guard while 170 observers watched the doomed men slowly strangle to death on the scaffold.

CHAPTER SIX

Traitors in Name Only:
The Haymarket Defendants

WHAT HAPPENED IN THE HAYMARKET?

Four men were hanged in Chicago in 1887 for an unsolved crime. The execution itself, on November 11, was bungled badly. All four men died by slow strangulation on the scaffold instead of receiving the quick death by broken neck that the mechanism should have given them. A fifth condemned prisoner ended his life even more horribly the day before the execution by exploding a hidden dynamite cap in his mouth; mutilated beyond recognition, he succumbed only after five hours of appalling agony. Two others, who had pleaded for executive clemency over crimes they never committed, had their death sentences commuted to life imprisonment hours before their scheduled executions. These gruesome details and many more like them belong to what is called the Haymarket trial, "one of the most unjust in the annals of American jurisprudence."[1]

Eight men in all were convicted of murder and conspiracy to commit murder after a bomb from an unknown assailant was thrown into the ranks of policemen who had come to break up a peaceful labor rally near Haymarket Square in Chicago on May 4, 1886. None of the eight defendants could be connected to the bomb that had been thrown, but all were anarchists organizing the labor force against deplorable conditions in the workplace, and seven of the eight were foreign-born. The evidence against them proved so weak in retrospect that a subsequent governor, John Peter Altgeld, would grant full pardons in 1893 to the three remaining defendants in prison. The accused had been convicted as a political group for the ideas they held and for their differences from native-born Americans—not for anything that they might have done or planned on May 4.

The inclination when thinking about a shameful event like the Haymarket affair is to cast it into the fallible past. Modern accounts document the injustices involved, but with few exceptions, they treat the case as a period piece, the by-product of growing pains during the country's industrial development. Labor in the 1880s fought for better conditions in factories, the eight-hour workday, and the right to unionize—goals it would slowly achieve through protest, organization, and legislation. Success of this kind tends to sugarcoat history. Through the cause of labor, the eight Haymarket defendants have become farsighted martyrs with an honored place in progressive views of history. The law, however, cannot afford to think in such terms, and neither should any citizen who wants to know the vulnerabilities of the legal process when it copes with controversial situations.

The important point to take away from the Haymarket trial and executions is not what happened, but how and why something like it could happen again. The circumstances that led to injustice in 1886 remain useful indicators for today because they point to breakdown within the structure of the legal system. What were the impulses that destroyed eight innocent defendants and countless others associated with them?

The relevant conditions included fear of the foreign, anxiety in the face of a limited but dramatic threat, the demand for quick answers to terrors aroused, the need to identify an immediate enemy, resort to patriotic discourse in seeking punishment, demands from authority for national solidarity in support of actions taken, and evasion of the conditions that led to aberrant behavior in the first place. Who can deny that similar preconditions exist today or that they might lead again to breakdown? We are what our ideological predilections have made us. Communal pressures against the values in a rule of law are permanent parts of the social condition, and they enter easily through the open door of the public trial.

What happened in the Haymarket is now a matter of common record except for one all-important detail. Labor rallies by mostly immigrant factory hands led to violent clashes between strikers, strike breakers, and police as the weather turned warm in Chicago during the spring of 1886. On May 3 police broke up such a gathering by firing indiscriminately into a crowd of strikers who had begun to fight with scab workers at the McCormick Reaper Works factory on Blue Island Avenue. Several workers were killed and many more wounded.

The next evening, at a peaceful rally held near the Haymarket in protest of police brutality during the Blue Island incident, an unknown assailant threw a bomb into the ranks of policemen who had come to break up the meeting. One policeman was killed outright, the only death that can be traced directly to the bomb; six others would die along with many more civilians in the mayhem after the explosion, and scores on both sides were wounded. Under orders to "Fire and kill all you can!" the stunned policemen retaliated wildly with volley after volley. Studies now show that the overwhelming number of dead and wounded in the Haymarket, including the other officers, fell under gunshots and clubbings from the disordered ranks of the police.

Accounts at the time ignored the police role in the violence that had occurred. Initial reports turned the orderly gathering into "a Haymarket riot" of irresponsible riffraff. The label would stick, and it continued to dominate all subsequent narratives against available evidence that the police had provoked panic in the square and inflicted most of the damage after the bomb was thrown. Media coverage, official commentary, and intellectual circles joined in blaming the organizers of the meeting. All leading channels of information made the anarchist leaders the perpetrators of a riot, and many accused them of fomenting open rebellion.

The long-range result would be a nationwide backlash against radical politics, organized labor, and immigration that would fuel American politics and public opinion for decades. More immediately, animosity would dictate biased coverage and overthrow normal codes of professional conduct in court when the anarchists, only two of whom could be placed anywhere near Haymarket Square on May 4, were brought to trial on June 21, less than two months after the bomb attack.

Failure to identify the primary culprit is, of course, the crucial missing detail in this and every other account of the Haymarket. Who threw the bomb? Theories about the unknown assailant abound, but theories notwithstanding, no one has found an answer that would satisfy a court of law, and arguments over the possibilities have obscured the legal predicament of 1886. Courts are supposed to orchestrate the conflicting accounts of an event during advocacy with the objective of bringing them toward one answer in truthful judgment. To achieve this goal, they must explain the crime that occurred to general satisfaction. The greater the communal interest, the more confidently a court must project its knowledge of the crime. Regrettably, the events of 1886 did not lend themselves to the usual sequence. Ignorance of a controlling fact, the identity of the bomb thrower, left the Haymarket court with procedural and rhetorical gaps that could not be ignored.

How could the law proceed so severely against defendants as accessories and co-conspirators when everyone knew that the criminal responsible could not be identified, much less found? Compelled to find an answer, the trial court responded by demonizing the anarchist defendants as a group and by making the nameless bomb thrower a minor figure somewhere within the defendants' ranks. It replaced the criminal act with conjectures that became legal assumptions. It assigned culpability to ideas it could not prove led to the crime. The law, in a word, lost its balance.

When a court visibly loses its objectivity, judgment loses its legitimacy, other voices take over, and those new voices claim the event. Dispute then turns on the law itself, which loses credibility in the process. Blame, the reflex reaction in all trials, shifts from the judged toward those who have judged erroneously, and competing claims attract ever-more dramatic narratives in cycles of explanation and continuing controversy. In this way, recognized lapses in the rule of law take on a profound literary dimension.

In the face of such acrimony, society still needs to think well of itself, and when it cannot, it tries to come to another understanding. It finds other ways to defend its sense of righteous well-being. When these conditions arise, as they did in the Haymarket affair, diverging points of view become a pivotal tool of interpretation across legal and literary dimensions. There is, however, an important difference. What the law holds separate—its methods of proceeding remain sequentially distinct from the conclusions it reaches—literature conflates with complete license to shape opinion in any way it wishes.

Competition over points of view between law and literature grew fierce over the Haymarket affair because the official perspective could not explain the facts. The absence of the bomb thrower (the unknown that had to be known) exposed the judgment in court to conjecture, and writers of all kinds benefited. With the law trapped in its own ignorance, the Haymarket affair entered the communal imagination, where creative literature could dominate through its more flexible use of perspective. This ability to dominate must be understood carefully. The realm of fiction creates a *knowing* reader by making a world instead of receiving one, and in so doing, it projects its own desirable answers and understandings on the history that it seeks to correct.[2]

Three leading novelists of the period in particular were sufficiently vexed by the uncertainties and travesties they found in the Haymarket affair that they turned to fiction to explain their views. Frank Harris, Robert Herrick, and William Dean Howells each reinterpreted the case of the anarchists, each writing from a dramatically different point of view about the unacceptable in what happened. Together they present a composite of the versions of how later Americans would cope with the injustice in their midst.

An erratic Irish raconteur and radical spokesman, Frank Harris gained attention by pretending to solve the central mystery. *The Bomb*, published in 1908, tells the story of the Haymarket from the imagined perspective of the missing bomb thrower. Harris's mystery man turns out to be a tenderly loving, well-educated protagonist who sacrifices his own happiness in the name of principle. Admirable in every way as a kind of Robin Hood, he belongs to the only group in the novel that shows any real integrity, the radical wing of labor protest. The Haymarket affair is everyone's calamity, but it emerges in *The Bomb* as the tragedy of an idealist who acts to correct the ignored social conditions of the industrial poor.

Robert Herrick, the novelist as academic, offers a similar but much cooler first-person narrative couched within the same specifics of the event. This time, however, the Haymarket story is told from the perspective of a juror who sends the anarchists to their deaths without a second thought. His guilty verdict helps the juror to become a robber baron in the meatpacking industry and eventually a corrupt United States senator. The rise of this glib speaker is Herrick's real story, and it turns *The Memoirs of an American Citizen* from 1905 into an allegory of the price paid for national prosperity. Herrick's amiable but thoroughly amoral adventurer accepts unfair influence as a matter of course. He is the American everyman who takes what he can get and ignores injustice in the name of success.

A far more distinguished writer and member of the cultural elite, William Dean Howells uses omniscient narration to project a wider and more complicated sphere of concerns. In *A Hazard of New Fortunes* from 1890, the protagonist is an ironic literary journalist on the edge of the fray, and yet Howells, who was closest to the Haymarket event, cuts nearest to the bone; it would be his best novel. Overview is the tool of satire. Howells offers up a detached critique of hand-wringing intellectuals who are themselves detached as they watch labor strife from the relative ease and security of the sidelines. The titular claim of "hazard" thus contains a rebuke over risks not taken. Howells is asking a larger question in *A Hazard of New Fortunes*, one that continues to haunt the American scene. What will a citizen hazard for justice in a society geared to the making of "new fortunes"?

CHICAGO AND THE NATION IN 1886

A certain passive fatalism over what happened in Chicago is the common thread in all three novels, and we must begin by understanding why that was so. The Haymarket affair stands out for the immediacy, the universality, the power, and the virulence with which an entire nation turned against the falsely accused. In effect, each of the writers examined here trips over that fact in a different way.

What can be said about the levels of denunciation that killed innocent men in 1887? Can anything be done to avoid a comparable reaction sometime in the future? Once a decision had been rendered at trial, the law seemed helpless when it came to rectifying its own error. An elaborate appeal process reached to the Supreme Court of the United States, but none of the official efforts changed or even qualified an original decision that history soon found to be unjust. Why not? The answers to these questions require a closer look at the times, the nature of legal remedies, and deeper impulses in the country itself.

The poet Carl Sandburg grew up in Galesburg, two hundred miles south of Chicago, and he experienced the trial as a boy of eight. "We heard about it, read about it, and talked about it, from May 5 on through every day of that year," he wrote later of the anarchists, or "arnashists," as the term of choice for the eight men on trial. "We saw in the Chicago papers black-and-white drawings of their faces and they looked exactly like what we expected, hard, mean, slimy faces"; they "were not regular people and they didn't belong to the human race, for they seemed more like slimy animals who prowl, sneak, and kill in the dark."[3]

These words, the nub of a child's nightmare, bespoke an adult reality. "This I believed," Sandburg recalls, "along with millions of other people reading and talking about the trial. I didn't meet or hear of anyone in our town who didn't so believe." Galesburg wanted a world where there *were* no anarchists, and it was "more than happy" when the execution took place. Adults "sang it out with a glad howl." Years later the poet would change his mind. "The feeling grew on me that I had been a little crazy 'off my nut,' along with millions of people like myself gone somewhat crazy."

How did an entire population come to lose its balance in 1886? Newspaper articles like the ones the young Sandburg read made a difference, but they were symptomatic of registers already at work in communal thought. Media coverage across the country was as spontaneous as it was uniformly negative. The *Detroit Tribune* immediately saw the accused as "a loathsome and a hideous set of law-breakers and murderers." The *Duluth Tribune* called them "red-mouthed devils" and "splendid targets for militia rifles." "What Chicago needs just now is a police that will kill," noted the *Kansas City Journal*, and the city was "fortunate enough to have that sort."[4]

Everywhere the reaction was the same. The *New York Mail and Express* tarred the accused with a more sweeping brush. The arrested anarchists should have been stopped before they "openly threatened war against property and every institution that native-born Americans have been taught to regard as sacred." The *Bloomington Pantograph* wanted *all* anarchists and socialists "hunted down . . . and brought to punishment." Alarmed at how easily the accused had gained "the upper hand" in Chicago, the *Globe-Democrat* in St. Louis ordered them met with "the crank of the Gatling gun." The *Omaha Herald* agreed with the same image: "Bring out the troops and sweep the streets with Gatling guns of the inhuman devils." The *New York Times* urged "the promptest and sternest way of dealing with such outbreaks as that among the Chicago anarchists." The *Alton Telegraph* warned that "this foreign invasion of the dregs of humanity . . . must be stamped out swiftly and sternly, or social chaos will result." The *Telegraph* actually used the word "exterminate." What the law would do was preordained in the press. Anticipated executions of the anarchists appeared in editorials and cartoons before the defendants were even charged in court.

The media immediately assumed and dispensed the whole truth about a still mysterious event. All of the comments just noted were *initial* responses, and the *Chicago Tribune* reprinted them within three days of the bomb explosion, not that it needed confirmation for its own views. The *Tribune* had been against organized labor long before the Haymarket incident. The leading newspaper in the city, its standing policies condemned the right to strike and traced all labor turmoil to "the vile utterances" and "inflammatory harangues of a lot of rabid Anarchists," also known as "a Rabble of Imbecile Foreign Fanatics."[5] The bomb, never mind who threw it, turned these certainties into something worse. The *Tribune*'s editors claimed to be glad that a physical contest had been irrevocably joined. "Perhaps some such monstrous act as this was needed to arouse public opinion," they explained. Their disagreements with labor could now become direct attacks on the accused and on any sympathizer who dared to maintain support in any form.[6]

The immediacy of these attacks implied assumptions already engrained in the reading public. The *Tribune* distinguished between "Americans and Americanized foreign elements of the working classes," on the one hand, and "alien and un-American elements in the working population," on the other, and it used the distinction to argue that "the amount of disorder, the commission of crime, the defiance of the law, and the use of brute force are in exact proportion to the numbers of this un-Americanized, ignorant, alien class of laborers." Arrested shortly after the explosion, the anarchist leaders were "political mad-dogs" and should be chained like animals until "punished according to law." The *Tribune* demanded full punishment without "mercy or regret." Ideas about "the sacredness of free speech" could be dispensed with as "popular but delusive and misplaced notions"; radical newspapers were "to be suppressed by the police"; protest meetings had "to be broken up and the leaders sent home if need with broken heads." The anarchist defendants were serpents from another world who struck with "poisonous fangs" at the true Americans who had taken them in. "STAMP OUT THE ANARCHISTS," ran an editorial headline on May 7.[7] The *Tribune* did everything it could to arouse its already-conditioned readership.

Most contemporaries believed the bomb was the harbinger of a massive plot by "un-Americanized foreign elements." It was generally assumed that rioting workers murdered everyone who died in the Haymarket, that the fabric of the nation was in a precarious state, that another extraordinary attack would follow, and that anyone even re-motely involved deserved the severest punishment. The newspapers bol-stered these impressions by falsifying facts to conform with popular opinion. In its first lead article on May 5, and against the eyewitness ac-count of its own reporter in the Haymarket, the *Chicago Tribune* claimed that "the Anarchists and rioters poured in a shower of bullets before the first action of the police was taken." It also claimed that "wiry whiskered foreigners" had been overheard planning the attack under instructions to "aim low."[8] The *New York Times,* under the banner "ANARCHY'S RED HAND," followed suit. "Then from the Anarchists on every side, a deadly fire was poured in on the stricken lines of police, and more men fell to the ground."[9]

Only part of such commentary can be explained on its own terms. Influxes of immigrant workers in the 1870s and 1880s did lead to exag-gerated reactions against "wiry whiskered foreigners." A depression of three years' duration, deteriorating labor conditions in factories, and an attempt on May 1 to mount a nationwide strike in support of the eight-hour workday were all contributing elements, but more disruptive ear-lier protests did not lead to such excessive reactions. It was peculiarly the Haymarket affair that "raised xenophobia to a new level of intensity, pro-voking the worst outburst of nativist sentiment in the entire post–Civil War period."[10]

Something more subtle than economic conditions was at work, and the root of the matter lay in the fact that the anarchists were collective defendants in an extremely visible dock. Targeted as a group, they faced levels of abstraction in accusation that seemed to need no proof and, in requiring none, resisted efforts at counterproof. The accused were un-done by arguments that were irrelevant to the formal charges but touched on deep-set communal fears and needs—the kind of fears and needs that cannot be met without creating more damage than the responses are worth. The heightened zone of scrutiny that always goes with accusation in court gave new focus and articulation to those anxieties, and only a designation of guilt was going to resolve them.

One of several arguments that could not be challenged in the Hay-market courtroom had to do with the claim of communal well-being, or, as the prosecution asserted in its closing address to the jury, "We live in Chicago, the metropolis of the great Northwest: the very center of the highest and best civilization on earth."[11] To the extent that the prose-

LIBERTY IS NOT ANARCHY.

Judge

THE FRIEND OF MAD DOGS.

Governor Altgeld of Illinois in freeing the Anarchists bitterly denounced Judge Gary and the jury that convicted them.

Figures 14, 15, & 16. (*Upper left*) Thomas Nast, "Advice to So-Called American Socialists: 'You had better not attack this club,'" *Harper's Weekly* 30, no. 1523 (February 27, 1886), New York, NY. Engraving (ICHi-03660). Photograph courtesy of the Chicago History Museum. (*Lower left*) Thomas Nast, "Liberty Is Not Anarchy," *Harper's Weekly* 20, no. 1550 (September 4, 1886), Haymarket Riot, Chicago, IL. Engraving (ICHi-31344). Photograph courtesy of the Chicago History Museum. (*Above*) "The Friend of Mad Dogs" (New York: Judge Publishing, 1893). Cartoon (ICHi-31336). Photograph courtesy of the Chicago History Museum. Highly pejorative depictions of unpopular defendants are a frequent phenomenon in high-profile trials. These cartoons from the period portray the Haymarket defendants as demons, collective vermin, and mad dogs. When a community thinks of its enemies as less than human in this way, it loses some of its own humanity. The figure shown unleashing the dogs on Liberty and her children is John Peter Altgeld, the once-popular governor of Illinois who knowingly sacrificed his political career by pardoning the remaining defendants in 1893.

cution's paeans to progress held the floor, the defendants could only be wrongheaded, unpatriotic troublemakers, and yet to counter the assertion, to expose Chicago's sordid side, would hardly serve a jury taken from a proud community under unwarranted attack. The claim that there could be "no such thing as an *American* anarchist" created another rhetorical bind for the defense. If such alienation never came from indigenous Americans—if, as so many said, "the American character has in it no element which can under any circumstances be won to uses so mistaken and pernicious"—then blame for Chicago's turmoil had to rest with "un-Americanized" elements subject to the leadership of foreign-born leaders.[12] One did not have to throw the bomb to be caught within the web of this logic.

A parallel contention, the claim that private property secured national prosperity, was similarly difficult to counter. The "sacred" principle of private property usually came with the charge that anarchist leaders had either violated it or failed to understand it. Most Americans in 1886 could not accept the fact that their prosperity depended largely on the hidden fact of cheap labor—labor *kept* cheap by the regular importation of immigrant workers into factories and mines under contract labor agreements.[13] The ideology of prosperity asked immigrants to be patient in "the *land* of promise," which by definition was "a region on the earth's surface where a few days' unskilled labor will purchase the fee-simple of an ample farm."[14] Mass immigration by subsistence-wage earners in factories offered no such trajectory, but the cultural finger of accusation could again assign the source of failure to anarchist leaders. Rabble-rousers with no understanding of property, anarchists spoke in ways that diverted their own kind from accepting the American dream.

To think otherwise required a reassessment of the changing circumstances in the nation, and it was a reassessment that most American-born citizens were either unwilling or unable to make in 1886. A majority resorted instead to what has been called "the paranoid style in American politics." Its tendencies ("heated exaggeration, suspiciousness, and conspiratorial fantasy," especially regarding foreign elements) have always been strong in a culture where the need for constant adjustment has led citizens in each generation to feel "dispossessed" of their heritage. The formulations of the paranoid style include apocalyptic terminology, a threat of catastrophic proportions, an identified enemy who can be held responsible for every problem, and a crisis mentality that brings "fundamental fears and hatreds, rather than negotiable interests, into political action."[15]

The paranoid style translated easily into the Haymarket situation. Chicago in 1886 was a city where dispossession touched everyone. "Anglo-Saxon Americanism," "a kind of patrician nationalism," remained the frame of reference, but other ethnicities were a majority of the population by the 1880s, and the percentage of foreign-born was rising with each passing year. To keep the upper hand, the holders of Anglo-Saxon Americanism looked with suspicion on any immigrant who brought "a divided heart" to Chicago. Americanization demanded "a process of elimination" through "denationalization of non-English descent." Immigrants were to strip themselves of previous affiliations as the price of acceptance. "The real Americans were Anglo-Americans." Sophisticated immigrants could challenge these pressures, and most brought coherent cultural affiliations with them, but to argue from them in an American courtroom meant "a divided heart" or worse.[16]

Too much was ideologically at stake for anarchist claims to be tolerated by the dominant culture. Acceptance of the plight of the immigrant in 1886 required an admission that the American experiment had gone awry. It was so much easier to extol an endangered heritage and blame present ills on alien ways of thinking and acting. The physical bomb in the Haymarket brought an intellectual explosion of nativism in reaction. Dynamite, newspapers and communal leaders announced, was the weapon of the foreign-born. It had been a European attack on American values, and an enraged citizenry was more than happy to have their designated enemies dragged into court.

Not the least tragedy in the Haymarket affair lies here. Communal animosity grew fat on the legal context. Already portrayed as despicable extremists in the press, the defendants suffered further harm from the exaggerations that always come in courtroom advocacy. They appeared as fiends and traitors in the arguments of the prosecution, and daily coverage of the prosecution's case fueled more communal hysteria. Victims on this level, the defendants contributed to their own downfall on another. Courts dislike arguments about sociological process. They assign responsibility for particular behavior in the individuals who are brought before them. In their radicalism, the Haymarket defendants could accept neither the thrust nor the legitimacy of this orientation. They saw themselves in an international struggle against capitalist oppressors, and the particularities of the law ran against their most cherished ideological imperatives.

When the anarchists responded in court, it was with the assumed superiority of their own theoretical stance. They treated the trial court with disdain as the tool of the power elite, a view that left them ill-equipped for the give-and-take of trial performance. Automatically shrill as professional protesters seeking to be heard, they saw no reason to adjust their language as legal defendants. Ideological needs and group solidarity would prove especially disastrous as the legal process continued its ominous march after trial. Five of the convicted men on death row would refuse to plead for a pardon that required a tacit admission of guilt.

The idealistic defendants clearly hurt their own case. Even so, why were they not saved by others in a better position to understand their legal situation? The guilty verdict at trial is easy to explain. It was the logical, even automatic consequence of communal outrage. The Haymarket jurors listened for two months to complicated arguments based on an indictment that contained sixty-nine counts on eight very different defendants, and they convicted all eight men in less than an afternoon. But if juries reflect communal thought, they depend even more on trial performers and professional conduct, and that was the case here.

Questionable judicial and prosecutorial behavior contributed to the hasty verdicts in the Haymarket trial, and both were serious enough to require higher review. The most troubling questions come on appeal *after* trial. Were the defendants easily convicted? Yes, they were. But why were their convictions upheld? Why were four wrongly convicted men executed despite the cognizance of two higher courts, including the highest court in the land?

THE HAYMARKET ON APPEAL

Leaders of the Chicago bar immediately saw what needed to be done through assigned error on appeal, and proper applications were made to the Supreme Court of the State of Illinois and then to the Supreme Court of the United States. Public opinion remained an intimidating force at these levels, but the law is not a consensual process, even though it breathes in a consensual culture; its leaders pride themselves on their objectivity, their fairness, their special knowledge, and their professional immunity from outside pressure. Nevertheless, the upper reaches of the legal system ratified decisions that would soon be seen as unjust, and they ratified them unanimously. The trial of the Chicago anarchists has many facets, but the insidious vitality of injustice once committed may be the darkest.

The grounds for reversible error in the Haymarket trial have been described by others.[17] On August 20, 1886, the Criminal Court of Cook County, with Judge Joseph E. Gary presiding, found all eight defendants guilty of murder as accessories before the fact in the death of Mathias J. Degan, the one police officer who clearly died from the bomb on May 4. August Spies, Michael Schwab, Samuel Fielden, Albert Parsons, Adolph Fischer, George Engel, and Louis Lingg all received the penalty of death, while Oscar Neebe was given a sentence of fifteen years in prison under the same verdict. Judge Gary's handling of the case would receive so much criticism that he took the unusual step of publishing an article in defense of his actions.[18] One disinterested and highly respected member of the Chicago bar left the following description of what took place:

> Every principle and precedent of Anglo-Saxon law was outraged by the rulings of Judge Gary, and he so confessed in the remarks he made when overruling the motion for a new trial. He said, "This case is without precedent. There is no example in the law books of a case of this sort." He manufactured the law and disdained precedent in order that a frightened public might be made to feel secure.[19]

The specifics that higher courts were asked to review can be summarized quickly. Judge Gary showed hostility to the defendants and their attorneys on numerous occasions, comparing the men in the dock to horse thieves and dismissing objections to his rulings with derision and contempt. He allowed a special bailiff to handpick the jury pool. His rulings during the selection of the jury led to biased individuals serving on the panel. He allowed the state to present inflammatory evidence beyond the scope of the charges before the court. Worst of all, he gave an overly broad definition of the crime of conspiracy to the jury as it retired to make its decision. Under Judge Gary's instructions, the defendants could be found guilty of murder as accessories without identification of the bomb thrower, and the defendants' words *at any time or place*, whether in print or speech, could be used to convict if their language encouraged other individuals, left undefined, to commit murder.[20]

These instructions were unprecedented. They allowed the jury to *guess* at the affiliations and motivations of the unknown bomb thrower, they encouraged the jury to assign specific agency to words spoken loosely in an abstract context, and they tied all of the defendants to the crime through the language of any one of them. Judge Gary's further insistence on a joint trial over the protests of the accused—men held together only by membership in the International Association of Workingmen— insured that the standard for conviction would be set at the level of the most radical of the men on trial, Louis Lingg. Nothing in the Haymarket could be traced to Lingg, but he was openly defiant and dangerous looking. He could be shown to have made bombs with the threat of using them, and he openly challenged the validity of the court. Speaking in German, he would tell the court: "I despise your order, your law, your force-propped authority. Hang me for it!"[21]

The prosecution also engaged in prejudicial conduct. State's Attorney Julius Grinnell promised to show the court who threw the bomb when he knew that he could not do so. He roiled emotions unnecessarily by waving the bloody uniform of the victim, the dead policeman, in court. He reached beyond the indictment to pin *all* deaths in the Haymarket on the defendants, assuring the jurors that if he could only get them to "see the dead and mingle with the wounded and dying," it would "*steel [their] hearts against the defendants.*" Grinnell used inappropriate terms about the defendants; they were "loathsome murderers," "organized assassins," "infamous scoundrels," and "revolutionists." He said the accused were "on trial *for treason*," when they were not, and he compounded the impropriety by insisting that treason meant "no mitigation, no palliation, no chance for the jury to hedge on the offense." Finally, he intimidated jurors by warning them. Their responsibility was "greater than any jury in the history of the world ever undertook." They had to act. The Republic itself was at stake. "Law is on trial," Grinnell told them. "Anarchy is on trial."[22]

On appeal, the defense would prove how these and other irregularities crossed the line of fairness, but not one of the issues raised convinced either higher court to overturn or qualify the Haymarket decision. Part of the explanation can be traced to the narrow scope of the appeal process itself. In acknowledging restraint, higher courts filter an appeal through all of the reasons for denying one. A refusal to act can be substantive or procedural, linguistic or strictly legal, professional or prudential, political or technical, or simply evasive. Appellate judges recognize that rulings of error undermine the credibility of the system. They work hard to guard the discretion of a trial judge, and there are good reasons for doing so. Protecting flexibility in the court of first resort allows justice to be done on the facts in individual cases. Thus, in one of the least understood elements of the legal system, real energy and power lie with the trial judge, and they almost always stay there.[23]

The Supreme Court of Illinois deliberated for six months before upholding the trial court in every particular, and when its unanimous decision finally came, it left the defendants with less than two months to live. A close execution date was set for November 11, 1887. At the same time, the court admitted it could not "approve all that was said by the trial judge." Nor did its members find the trial record "free from error."[24] How, then, could the highest court in the state appear so certain in a flawed capital case based on circumstantial evidence and involving so many different defendants?

Justice Benjamin Magruder, speaking for his six colleagues, quoted extensively from the prosecution's collection of anarchist materials. He agreed that the International Association of Workingmen sacrificed some protections of the law as "an illegal organization, engaged in the making of bombs." He granted without question the unproven contention that the bomb had been the first step in a concerted attack in the Haymarket: "*First*, a bomb was thrown among the policemen; *next*, shots were fired into their ranks by armed men, belonging to the organizations heretofore described." Taken as facts, these assertions gave prima facie evidence of a conspiracy, and they allowed the Illinois Supreme Court to confirm the right of the state to prove its case in any way that it chose.[25]

Samuel McConnell, a skilled lawyer and a judge himself soon after these events, would write that the Illinois Supreme Court "ignored the major questions involved in the case."[26] Appellate courts control their decisions by what they will allow themselves to see, and in this regard, the foregone conclusion of a guilty verdict seems to have weighed heavily with Justice Magruder. The decision to try the defendants jointly and the instructions given the jury were matters of discretion for the trial court.

The rhetoric of an official point of view took care of the rest. The Illinois Supreme Court disagreed with some of what Judge Gary had said but found "no such error" as "would justify a reversal of the cause." Justice Magruder handled the largest problem with a statement supported only by itself: "We cannot see that the remarks of the state's attorney were marked by any such improprieties as require a reversal of the judgment." Reliance in this way on an animate point of view—no institution actually *sees*—gave the court the power to adjust its priorities just as individuals see near or far depending on the occasion or whim. In this case, it allowed seven judges to push the line of error away from them; it kept them at the distance they needed to avoid the appearance of injustice.[27]

The U.S. Supreme Court had even less difficulty in rejecting the defendants' writ of error on November 2, nine days before the scheduled executions, and its language shows again how high the bar can be set on appeal. Chief Justice Morrison Waite delivered the opinion for a unanimous court. On the question of whether prejudiced jurors had been allowed to sit on the panel, he quoted precedent, saying: "It must be made *clearly to appear* that upon the evidence the court ought to have found the juror had formed such an opinion that he could not *in law* be deemed impartial"; nothing could be done "unless *the error is manifest*." To overcome the judgments of two state courts, the error complained of had to be "*so gross* as to amount *in law* to a denial by the State of a trial by an impartial jury to one who is accused of crime." The Supreme Court refused to look beneath the surfaces. There were no questions "on the face of the record" for it to decide.[28]

The roadblocks set up on appeal are necessary ones, but they also reveal that the best place to cope with injustice is at trial. A disturbing story unfolds in the upper reaches of the Haymarket case. Since facts are generally not reviewed at higher levels, a trial court that misuses them presents a difficult problem for the legal system to handle. Even when a judge bends the law, as Judge Gary did with a loose definition of the crime of conspiracy, the standards for reversing a trial decision remain narrow. Legal error must be apparent; "it must be made *clearly to appear*." Reversible error must be "manifest"—"so gross," in fact, as to amount to a denial of justice *in* law and not *as* a matter of fact. The constitutive metaphor of sight allows an appellate court to see only what it cannot avoid by holding to "the face of the record." The privilege given to ostension below (*showing* at trial) qualifies point of view above, and most problems remain, in consequence, "a matter of discretion in the lower court."

The Haymarket trial from more than a century ago remains legally useful today because it illustrates two elements of continuing importance. On the technical level, appeal processes in the legal system are an essential but insufficient safety valve, and the nature of the insufficiency points toward a second and more tangled level of concern. Injustice flourished in Chicago in 1886 because communal angers with media encouragement infected "the court of first impression" and because fixed impressions are difficult to change. The subsequent appeals failed for additional reasons. There is great institutional energy and momentum behind a legal decision once reached. All the same, when a decision is flawed and sustained anyway on appeal, something else happens: the energy and momentum shift back to the community that triggered injustice in the first place. Debate over the Haymarket trial did not end with the death of the defendants in 1887.

As more and more people realized that eight admittedly unpopular men had been convicted when they were nowhere near the crime and that, despite every uncertainty, four of them had been executed on the flimsiest evidence, reactions set in. The legal system had failed to protect the innocent until proven guilty. One at a time, outside narrators began to appear with their own descriptions of the event. Trials that are perceived to have gone wrong in a republic of laws provoke acute responses. Is it helpful to measure a community by how it reacts to injustice in its midst? The imaginative literature of the Haymarket affair comes alive in the awkward responses it delivers to this question.

FRANK HARRIS WRITES *THE BOMB* (1908)

Frank Harris, the Anglo-Irish writer and radical journalist, "dictated three-quarters of *The Bomb* in one night," and aspects of the novel read that way. He could compose at such speed by forcing a familiar chronology of events through formulaic religious parallels.[29] Louis Lingg, the most radical of the Haymarket defendants and the man who committed suicide in his cell to cheat the hangman, serves as a Christ figure for Harris, with the words "one man should die for the people." This outsize characterization calls "for one of us now to do what Jesus did with the cross, and by sheer loving-kindness turn the hangman's noose into a symbol of the eternal brotherhood of men." Harris's Lingg enjoys the devotion of a Mary Magdalene (Ida Miller), knows he will be betrayed by a Judas, receives "reverence" even from his enemies, and names his judge Pontius Pilate. Harris's wish fulfillment of a bomb thrower, Rudolph Schnaubelt, narrates this radical version of the Haymarket affair as Lingg's disciple. They are bomb maker and bomb thrower acting in mutual sacrifice for humankind.[30]

The excesses of *The Bomb* are what make it interesting. Harris writes a promiscuous jumble of reality and fantasy that joins court transcripts and newspaper accounts to fantastic characterizations and his own "confession of faith."[31] The novel falters in these crossovers, caught between romance, history, and personal projection. Rhetorically, Harris's story is the negative to the photograph of prosecutorial bombast in 1886. Everything evil in the official and semi-official narratives surrounding the Haymarket affair appears in obverse as innocence in *The Bomb*. All of the praise for law and order in the *Chicago Tribune* becomes a source of iniquity here. The facts that drive the novel are ones that the Criminal Court of Cook County refused to consider when it punished the anarchist defendants.

Harris's protagonist, the escaped bomb thrower Rudolph Schnaubelt, is the prototype of the disillusioned immigrant. He comes to America believing that hard work will lead to success and finds himself trapped by vicious cycles of poverty and prejudice. His experience, chapter by chapter, exposes the dimensions of immigrant labor in nineteenth-century America. Child laborers, women, and other factory workers die horribly from disease and unsafe conditions. Capricious layoffs occur, and starvation stalks the urban ghettoes. Police suppress legitimate labor protest. The courts protect oppressive capitalist interests, and newspapers attack labor at every turn through patriotic rubrics.

In these conditions, responsible protest turns into "ineffective speech," and the logic of the situation demands radical action (75–76, 93, 97). The theme is important because it figures prominently in all of the novels that deal with the Haymarket affair. In every case, contempt for mere words lends a vital tension and a scene of extremism to what the novelist has written. Predictably, Harris saves his harshest criticism for the trial of the Haymarket defendants, where words are understood to have maximal importance and where the articulation of justice is supposed to be a controlling aspiration: "It seems only natural to expect human beings to be at their best in a trial where life and death hang in the balance." Instead, the trial unfolds as "a horrible revelation of man's innate brutality" (263).

The Bomb reverses the ethical positions of the historical defendants and their accusers. Courage defines the anarchist defendants; "cowardice and stupidity" reign in court (258). The trial is "a cruel farce," and the narrator's realization is significant. In fact, it is this legal travesty that destroys first the idealist and then the man (265–66, 288). Injustice meted out by the Haymarket courts triggers a personal spiral into complete disillusionment, and the rest of the novel becomes a critique of the radical temperament in decline. Corruption in the legal process has hurt the most because of the bomb thrower's original belief in it. If the law can be just and is not just, what then?

The sharpest proof of the power in injustice comes through an especially depressing source: the "indecent and shameless delight" of the multitudes who welcome the Haymarket death sentences. "That seven out of the eight men were entirely innocent seemed to concern no one, and interest no one in particular," the narrator of *The Bomb* remarks as he enters a dismal world of "cold looks, unwilling attention, shrugging shoulders." He sees that "the number of people in this world who care for justice or right, apart from their own interests, is very small," and the recognition leads him to condemn humanity altogether, a step that drains him of all meaning (278, 291).

Early on this narrating persona declares that "the misery of mankind is as infinite as the sea" (26). His additional discovery is that no one cares enough to examine that misery, and so the misery spreads while the truly miserable suffer alone. In the end, everyone seems to deserve or at least receive some kind of punishment in this perspective, and the bomb thrower descends into an abyss of endless malevolence. "Nature comes and strikes our fingers one after the other," he concludes, "till, unable to endure the punishment any longer, we loosen our hold and fall into the void" (26, 316).

Frank Harris's novel is valuable for the way it dramatizes a radicalism of despair. When protest becomes hopeless, it turns violent. *The Bomb* tells that story, and it is one that every complex society with a modicum of injustice in its midst had better hear. The task of law is to respond fairly to complaint, violence, ill-treatment, accusation, objection, infringement, violation, oppression, and discrimination. As the main locus of meaning in a secular world, law is the civil religion of the state, and there is great ideological danger when it fails. *The Bomb* depicts the collapse in meaning when faith in a legal regime disappears. Harris records a form of disruption that annihilates everything in its wake and anything it can reach, including, quite willingly, itself. Any twenty-first century reader of *The Bomb* will recognize this appalling phenomenon and must fear the prospect of coming to know it too well.

ROBERT HERRICK WRITES *THE MEMOIRS OF AN AMERICAN CITIZEN* (1905)

The Memoirs of an American Citizen is at once a more sophisticated and a more parochial novel than *The Bomb*. A cosmopolitan journalist, Frank Harris attacks injustice in the capitalist system everywhere, with the Haymarket trial as a convenient example. Robert Herrick tries instead to write the great American novel, and as a displaced New Englander teaching at the University of Chicago, he cannot avoid the Haymarket as a comment on fundamental communal identity. He writes more subtly but with a simplistic dichotomy in mind. His America is "the most brilliant exponent of the democratic principle" but also "a hideous Shylock, obese, heavy-jowled, cynically selfish and callous, incapable of understanding even its own best interests." Herrick tries to bring this double-natured beast to life in a unified work of literature. What, he keeps asking, are Americans doing to America?[32]

Harris and Herrick differ most strikingly in their treatments of the Haymarket defendants, and the contrast is an alarming one in light of Herrick's nationalist perspective. Harris, the amoral international adventurer, sympathizes with the downtrodden and falsely accused in his depiction of the anarchists and the laboring poor. Herrick, the national moralist as intellectual, remains aloof from all poverty and squalor in his eagerness to depict American idealism under siege.[33]

The difference stands out because of other similarities. Herrick and Harris agree about the nature of injustice in the Haymarket trial. The judge is just as biased, the jury just as handpicked, the capitalist influence just as manipulative of opinion, and the defendants even more innocent in *The Memoirs of an American Citizen*. "Few stopped to think of justice, and no one of mercy," Herrick writes in his version of the trial, but his outrage never translates into sympathy. His defendants are cardboard figures without personalities and "misguided fools" in court. Notably, Herrick chooses his protagonist from the other side of the fence. The comparable first-person narrator of his novel is a juror who convicts men he knows to be innocent.[34]

It is telling that both writers make the courtroom the essential forum for shaping character development. The juror as protagonist, like the bomb thrower, receives his most important lessons from the law. Herrick's first-person narrator, Edward Van Harrington, first encounters the law as an Indiana farm boy mistreated by a corrupt local judge. Innocent of wrongdoing, his attempts to get back at the judge land him in jail as a "good-for-nothing" and "a bit of a hoodlum," and he escapes prosecution only by a lucky turn of events (21–30). In Chicago as an angry young man, Van Harrington runs afoul of another judge, and again he escapes through happenstance. These experiences lend an ugly wisdom. Van Harrington recognizes that he has been "a plain fool" acting on "sorehead feeling" (30–33). Energized rather than defeated, he begins a ruthless climb to fame and fortune. He has "the stomach to do the world's work" and no need for further reflection until his boss in the meatpacking business makes him serve on the handpicked Haymarket jury (50, 68–71).

Enforced idleness in the jury box brings introspection: "There in the courtroom, and later shut up in the jury quarters, day after day, cut off from my usual habits, I thought over some of the real questions of our life, and made for myself a kind of philosophy." No fool, Van Harrington sees that the judge has manufactured the law to convict and that the defendants are innocent except for being "kickers who tried to upset the machine," but he knows that capitalism controls the court, and he votes guilty anyway. Life in his point of view is "a struggle between sensible folk who went about their business and tried to get all there was in it— like myself—and some scum from Europe, who didn't like the way things are handed out in this world." Hanging the anarchists completes a new identity. "[The trial] coming as it did, when I had my foot placed on the ladder of fortune, had something to do with making me what I am to-day." A sincere but unreliable narrator throughout, Van Harrington makes this admission cheerfully and without a touch of regret (72–77).

The Memoirs of an American Citizen renders the narrator's thought processes about the Haymarket affair in painstaking detail for a reason, and the tones of the speaker are the key. Herrick, high above his morally obtuse narrator, injects slang to undercut depth in the mentality that he has created. He uses this element of vulgar speech to control another point of view in the novel: the negative reaction of the reader. "It was a fine thing to live and hustle with your neighbors for the dollars," Van Harrington says as a Haymarket juror. "I had done my part to make the game go on smoothly" (76). No reader, regardless of political affiliation, can sympathize with the flippant manner of Van Harrington as he describes his participation in the Haymarket tragedy.

Curiously, though, Herrick confirms the philosophical trajectory of his speaker, and this decision eviscerates every potential crisis of awareness in the novel. Those who join Van Harrington in his rise to wealth and status are invariably hurt by the ride and say so, but they have no impact on him. Humorless behind the veil of his own censoriousness, Herrick supplies no growth in his leading character, no breakdown, no relief from a picaresque march through similar incidents. The same Van Harrington moves through scenes and solves difficulties. His philosophical epiphany as the Haymarket juror—"Suddenly a meaning to it all came to me like a great light" (75)—has no sequel. True, he occasionally realizes "the fight I was waging with fortune was as cold as these ashes and doomed to failure." But nothing really fazes him. An emptiness around the narrator never interrupts the new American citizen's enjoyment of his rightful success (266–79).

The result is an even deeper fatalism than found in *The Bomb*. Van Harrington thrives because Herrick validates his character's division of the world into the weak and the strong. A monotony of patterned contrasts fills the novel. Every strong character takes a weak mate in *The Memoirs of an American Citizen*, with the victory of the strong performed and cataloged. Herrick's major example of strength on the side of American idealism is beaten down by Van Harrington and the new economic order.

This idealistic figure, Van Harrington's first love May Rudge (rhymes with drudge), jousts with him throughout the novel over moral and religious principle, but she marries Van Harrington's pathetic older brother and dominates her husband while losing all influence in the major contest. Van Harrington, in turn, marries the fragile socialite Sarah Gentles, while his equally weak, querulous boss, Henry Iverson Dround, takes cues from another strong figure, his wife Jane, who inspires Van Harrington in dirty dealing. "She is so strong, and I am so weak," moans Sarah, fearing for her husband while acting out Herrick's major theme, but there is nothing to worry about (96). Herrick's women are sexless. The novelist cares only for power, not physical relation. Couples invariably present a ruler over a weaker ruled, and their children turn the pattern into a natural principle of selection (241).

The source of these patterns is also unsettling. Like many of the writers of his generation, Herrick takes his philosophy from Charles Darwin and Herbert Spencer. Van Harrington is no intellectual, but he is made to read both authors avidly (52). Spencer is particularly valuable because he takes Darwin's theory of evolution and applies it to human relations in works like *The Study of Sociology* (1873) and *Principles of Ethics* (1879). Survival of the fittest in Darwin becomes in Spencer the capacity to adapt through the recognition of force in all phenomena. The Spencerian synthesis makes individual action worthy only when it recognizes power effectively; evolutionary force turns into morality when filtered through utilitarian ethics.[35]

In the economics of *The Memoirs of an American Citizen*, a Spencerian stance requires "a strong hand" that will use power ruthlessly in speculation (219). Words like "better" and "worse" figure as "childish" anachronisms and are replaced with an evolutionary spirit of adaptation. "Every age is a new one," Van Harrington pontificates, "and to live in any age you have got to have the fingers and toes necessary for that age" (114). Now on the other end of the law, he doesn't hesitate to bribe a corrupt judge of his own when opposing forces have him cornered politically (154, 166–67). Force must be met with force by whatever means that will identify the strong; or in Harringtonian slang, "it's dog eat dog," and "the big dog will eat up the rest" (94).

Herrick obviously disapproves of this voice, but he provides no alternatives to the logic it lives by. *The Memoirs of an American Citizen* tells the story of "strugglers on the outside of prosperity, trying hard to climb up somewhere in the bread-and-butter order of life" (41). It *is* dog eat dog in the world of the novel. Struggle is the novelist's theme, and irony over his character's moral obtuseness changes neither the nature of the struggle nor the fascination that success breeds. Elsewhere, Herrick bemoans "the relentless pressure in economic laws" as a force that obliterates the past and causes public discourse to be "almost insanely preoccupied with American wealth," but he also concedes that "it is a waste of time" to deplore these conditions. In this, his best novel, he proves the point over and over again. Ironic disapproval, yes; but real protest seems to be useless.[36]

The narrator-protagonist's "gospel of man against man" disarms even the ultimate enemy, an anarchist who has cornered him physically and prepares to kill him on the spot. Van Harrington saves himself not with threats but by persuading his adversary that capitalism controls the world. Convinced and depressed, the "loose-minded" anarchist vanishes from the novel as suddenly as he arrived, never to appear again (160–62). The inability of anyone to answer a character who builds his philosophy around a moment of injustice troubles the novel. Intellectual bankruptcy would not be too strong a term.

All of these problems can be traced directly to Van Harrington in the jury box. The casual nature of his decision shocks at all levels: "The world seemed to me so good a place to hustle in that I couldn't rightly appreciate the complaint of these rebels against society," and so "guilty or not, these men must suffer for their foolish opinions, which were dead against the majority" (74). Rightly suffering whether guilty or not? A philosophy of inevitable force in the hands of the strong destroys innocent men who are at fault for being too weak and impoverished to defend themselves. The novelist gives us a new kind of American citizen, and it is one defined by prosperity through whatever means it takes.

In thinking about the role of law in this world of force, Herrick underscores the loss in values through Van Harrington's lawyer. Jaffrey Slocum is "a man of learning and a lover of the law for its own sake" from a line of distinguished New England judges. He represents American idealism but turns himself into "a trained prostitute" when he bribes the courts for Van Harrington. His sacrifice of legal meaning symbolizes the demoralization of law when courts act unjustly, and the worst of it is that Slocum acts not for gain but in acceptance of the new order in things. In Van Harrington's breezy account, "He sold himself to me, not just for money, but for friendship and admiration" (255–58).

Herrick's upright but embittered symbol of integrity, May Rudge, explains why the Haymarket affair will happen again. "I say, Van," she accuses, "you are the devil's instrument! You and those like you—and there are a good many of them—are just plain big rascals, only the laws can't get hold of you" (192). Later in life, and sounding a little like May, Herrick will attempt to rekindle "the old urge of justice, the old cry of freedom from tyranny—the desire of the individual man or woman to prove life under tolerable conditions," but the younger and better novelist has already grasped a darker reality.[37] Steeped in the tawdry details of the Haymarket trial, he cannot avoid an awful conclusion. If the pursuit of happiness is defined by wealth, what the law cannot help it will join.

WILLIAM DEAN HOWELLS WRITES *A HAZARD OF NEW FORTUNES* (1890)

William Dean Howells congratulated Herrick for the "carefully guarded unconsciousness" of Van Harrington in *The Memoirs of an American Citizen*. Herrick had given life to a " 'pal' of Providence" and deserved praise for keeping emotions in check and avoiding any sign of a "hectic flush" in his critique of American society. Howells's words indicate how much he agreed with Herrick in remaining high above their created characters. Both writers valued a quiet objectivity and understatement that would supply "an ethical impulse effecting itself by means of truth to life."[38] Realism demanded restraint and an unsentimental observer. It resisted excess. "Even with vice and crimes," Howells declared, "[the novelist] should not be *directly* moralistic."[39] But what if a novelist felt excessively about a particular situation? What if truth to life had to challenge truth itself? What if life required more of the writer than the display of an ethical impulse?

Howells's approval of Herrick exposes the dilemma in his own treatment of the Haymarket affair. No other event in a long life, not even the Civil War, upset "the Dean of American Letters" as this one did. The trial of the anarchists had been "the cruelest wrong that ever threatened our fame as a nation." Howells delivered his "very strong feeling in the matter" to anyone who would listen, including the newspapers, the courts, and the governor of Illinois. He would be the one major literary figure to protest in public and received heavy criticism for it. Normally matter-of-fact in his view of the world, he agonized over the execution of the anarchist defendants. "Annie," he told his sister, "it's all been an atrocious piece of frenzy and cruelty, for which we must stand ashamed forever before history."[40]

There could be no holding back. Engulfed in "the helpless grief and rage which seems to be my part in this business," Howells claimed that the

Haymarket affair would never end for him. "All is over now," he explained after the executions, "except the judgment that begins at once for every unjust and evil deed, and goes on forever." He could not put it aside. "That is the devil of it," he observed; "the train of evil seems to warp and twist all things awry as it goes on, when once its infernal impetus is given." Undone, the writer confessed frustration and more. "It's no use. I can't write about it," he admitted after trying. "Some day I hope to do justice to these irreparably wronged men."

That day of reckoning came sooner rather than later with the publication of *A Hazard of New Fortunes* in 1890. Howells wrote in direct reaction to the Haymarket affair, and it would be his greatest novel, the hardest for him to write, and his most misunderstood work of fiction. Howells himself tied the book to "the bombs and scaffolds of Chicago." He called it a "remission of sins" and "the most vital of my fictions."[41] *A Hazard of New Fortunes* became all of these things through an inner contest that dominates its pages. The distraught observer of 1887 vies with the aloof writer who proceeds from the distance of hindsight. When the book appeared, its recipients found the same wry, detached, even remote point of view that the writer brought to all of his novels of manners. Tonally, *A Hazard of New Fortunes* belongs to the genteel tradition of nineteenth-century American letters.[42] Thematically and in its dialogues, it is a fierce satire of national values with the scars of the Haymarket trial all over it.[43]

Howells's radical early education in an abolitionist family had prepared him for a protest that could not be avoided in 1887. "*They died in the prime of the freest Republic the world has ever known, for their opinion's sake*," Howells cried in bitterness and alarm over the anarchist defendants. He had to write about them. "It is useless to deny this truth, to cover it up, to turn our backs upon it, to frown it down, or sneer it down. We have committed an atrocious and irreparable wrong."[44] The fact of irreparable wrong deserved to be shouted to the rooftops. The health of the country depended upon it and so did Howells's integrity. If the cooler tones of the novelist never quite reach this level, there was a philosophical as well as an artistic reason for the difference.

The writer as realist has not forgotten the citizen-observer's mission, the promise "some day to do justice to these irreparably wronged men," but he has added a larger question beyond protest. After all, protest had failed. *A Hazard of New Fortunes* never deals with the Haymarket trial directly, but its characters are arranged to answer the writer's larger query about it. How could such an injustice take place in the prime of the freest republic the world had ever known? How could it happen *in America*? The question would not go away, and it held major ideological significance because Howells, even in protest, remained the clinical observer. He made himself see the largest truth about the execution of the Haymarket defendants. "I say, we," Howells wrote, blaming everyone in 1887, "because this deed has apparently been done with the approval of the whole nation."[45]

The man who had believed in a moral governor of the universe with the United States of America at the forefront of providential thinking changed his mind between 1887 and 1889, and it shows in the writing of his novel. The democratic idealist cannot be found in these pages. When Mark Twain wrote to Howells enraged over another political issue in 1889, Howells responded in measured tones. "I have just heated myself up with your righteous wrath," he admitted as cool as ice. "But it seems to me that you ignore the real reason . . . which is that there is no longer an American republic."[46] These are strong words coming from one who consorted with the leaders of his day.

In the place of a once-shining beacon to the world, Howells announced that "an aristocracy-loving oligarchy" ruled the United States, and it had ruthlessly rejected the democratic agenda. "Why should our Money-bags rejoice in the explosion of a Wind-bag?" Howells asked Twain, over a deposed dictator in Latin America. "They know at the bottom of the hole where their souls ought to be that if such an event finally means anything it means *their* ruin next; and so they *don't rejoice;* and as *they* mostly inspire the people's voice, the press, the press is dumb." Like Herrick and Harris, Howells blamed the media for much of what took place in the trial of the Haymarket defendants. More polite than they were about it, he would also be more subtly artistic and devastating in depicting it.

Howells's revulsion turned inward. If he and his wife, Elinor, were "theoretical socialists," he knew full well that they were "practical aristocrats," and the discrepancy filled him with disgust as he wrote *A Hazard of New Fortunes* in 1889. He wondered how it could be "a comfort to be right theoretically" when it was necessary "to be ashamed of one's self practically."[47] In his most famous letter from the period, written to Henry James, Howells unleashed an orgy of loathing over his own social hypocrisy, and his distress came from a progressively negative view of American culture:

I'm not in very good humor with "America" myself. It seems to me the
most grotesquely illogical thing under the sun; and I suppose I love it
less because it won't let me love it more. I should hardly trust pen and
ink with all the audacity of my social ideas; but after fifty years of optimistic content with "civilization" and its ability to come out all right
in the end, I now abhor it, and feel that it is coming out all wrong in
the end, unless it bases itself anew on a real equality. Meantime, I wear
a fur-lined overcoat, and live in all the luxury my money can buy.[48]

In *Annie Kilburn*, published in 1889, Howells described an unbridge-
able gap between rich and poor in modern America and dramatized the
failure of philanthropy to do anything about it. Immediately after, in *A
Hazard of New Fortunes*, he turned on the upper-middle class to which
he belonged for its own failure to act. The placid acceptance of class differences by his own kind, their blithe dismissal of labor unrest, and their
evasion of the desperation they saw in the urban poor were fixed in his
sights.[49]

A *Hazard of New Fortunes* opens with an alter ego of the novelist moving from Boston to New York to work on a magazine amidst labor unrest, just as Howells had done in 1888. Each character in the novel connects to this magazine venture in some way. Phonetic parallels on the
names William and Elinor Howells, Basil and Isabel March are joined
by Mr. Fulkerson, a fast-talking managing editor; Jacob Dryfoos, an up-
start millionaire from the Midwest who finances the magazine for his
unworldly son, Conrad; Berthold Lindau, the radical German socialist
who translates for the magazine; Angus Beaton, a self-absorbed artist
who provides layout and design; Alma Leighton, who drafts covers for
the magazine; Margaret Vance, a socialite who entertains the others; and
a former Southern Confederate, Colonel Woodburn, who writes for the
magazine.

These characters and their appendages enter into the predictable conflicts we would expect of them, but in all of their careful differences, they
are as one in their hopeless attitude toward the deteriorating social fabric
of the city. The figures who care for social justice are peripheral and are
either killed off (Conrad Dryfoos and Lindau, the socialist) or consigned
to a nunnery (Margaret Vance). The omniscient narrator reveals that his
characters will "grow too well satisfied with themselves, if not with each
other." In an omen of how his creatures will vacillate between self-interest

and principle, Howells gives the literary magazine at the center of his plot an ironic title: *Every Other Week*.[50]

Most critics make the mistake of tying Howells's point of view to that of the character patterned on his own life, Basil March—a fair assumption when applied to Howells's use of Basil in an earlier novel, *Their Wedding Journey*, but Howells explicitly rejected the connection here.[51] He makes brutal fun of Basil and Isabel March in *A Hazard of New Fortunes*, hitting them hard at every turn. They are precisely the kind of people who will fret quietly, if they fret at all, when authority hangs radicals like the Haymarket defendants. Basil is "a man who had always been too self-enwrapt to perceive the chaos to which the individual selfishness must always lead." He recognizes "the fierce struggle for survival, with the stronger life persisting over the deformity, the mutilation, the destruction, the decay of the weaker," but he feels abstractly with "nothing definite, nothing better than a vague discomfort, however poignant, in his half recognition of such facts" (184).

Howells builds his novel around these half-recognitions. A good man, if not an especially courageous one, his protagonist Basil March would be on the side of the angels if there were angels to follow in *A Hazard of New Fortunes*, but there are none. Basil never knows quite where to turn in consequence. His "whimsical shrug for the squalor," as he walks through a poor neighborhood, permits an ocean of condescension "It's curious, isn't it, how fond the poor people are of these unpleasant thoroughfares?" he asks rhetorically. Lest one miss the point, the narrator announces that Basil "sentimentalized the sweltering paupers who had crept out of the squalid tenements" (299).

The scene of poverty leads Basil to "pine for the society of my peers." Half-jokingly, he asks to be "taken somewhere to meet my fellow-exclusives" but then finds them dull and wonders why. Howells uses the moment to skewer "the vast, prosperous, commercial class, with unlimited money, and no ideals that money could not realize." Half-aware once again, the Marches want to know "whether this were the best that a great material civilization could come to" (299–302). Their supercilious responses are indeed the stuff of satire. Tentatively and sharply by turns, Howells is the first American novelist to fully see and send up the liberal temperament in urban life.[52]

Howells disarms the Marches on precisely the topics that he cares most about in the late 1880s. Basil admits that "his own life of comfortable reverie" has left him without a moral compass. Asked about his convictions, he replies: "I don't know what they are" (194, 441). He and his managing editor, Fulkerson, agree that people of principle are "cranks" to be avoided (410). The two men laugh at Conrad Dryfoos's efforts at charity. Basil chuckles again when the radical socialist Lindau rages against the capitalist owner of the magazine for breaking a strike of workers by force with armed Pinkertons. Howells gives his protagonist an "American ease of mind about everything," and this means that Basil approaches poverty and the other social problems of his day with "impartial interest" (190–91). "The burden of all the wrong in the world comes on the poor," responds Lindau, but this and other cries of injustice are mere "ravings" to the literary editor of *Every Other Week* (300–301). When a policeman treats him rudely in the culminating scene of labor unrest, Basil identifies with the people but quells the anger that might lead to involvement: "He struggled with himself and regained his character of philosophical observer" (412).

Ridicule at Basil March's expense is also Howells's despair. Asked what he would do himself about repression of the transit strike that dominates the climax of the novel, Basil answers, "Do? Nothing." "I find that I can philosophize the situation about as well from the papers, and that's what I really want to do." His interlocutor in this scene is more chilling. Fulkerson, the huckstering managing editor, actually welcomes the butchery taking place. He is the symbol of the modern commercial temperament in *A Hazard of New Fortunes*, and because he identifies with "unalloyed prosperity," he welcomes the "iron hand" and "splendid courage" of the police against the strikers (95, 406–8). Howells gives his characters neither the vision nor the capacity to cope with the unfairness around them; instead they are part of it. In the scene of police brutality that follows the exchange just noted, the good (Margaret Vance) increases the danger of the just (Conrad Dryfoos) by her presence. The good and the just are equally helpless, and the just sacrifices himself unwittingly, killed by a policeman, when he enters the conflict in the name of the good.

A typical exchange between the symbol of the artist, Angus Beaton, and Howells's representation of unaided goodness, Margaret Vance, indicates how satire works through dialogue without further comment on it:

He could not help saying in natural rebellion, "Well, the man of one idea is always a little ridiculous."

"When his idea is right?" she demanded. "A right idea can't be ridiculous."

"Oh, I only said, the man that held it alone. He's flat, he has no relief, no projection." (396)

Accurate at the expense of the supercilious Beaton, Margaret has been thoroughly mocked herself in a previous scene: "She had a repute for good works which was out of proportion to the works, as it always is, but she was really active in that way, under the vague obligation, which we now all feel, to be helpful." Women like Margaret Vance, Howells tells us in identification of social complicity, "are the loveliest of the human race, but perhaps the rest have to pay too much for them" (246–50).

The speaker of these last words, Isabel March, receives her own come-uppance with astonishing regularity. She's the butt of Howells's sharpest sarcasm. To take only the nastiest dig, she objects to the radical Lindau as a tutor for her children because her son and daughter "had been nurtured in the faith of Bunker Hill and Appomattox as the beginning and the end of all possible progress in human rights." Isabel reprises Howells's self-flagellating letter to Henry James: "She was naturally an aristocrat, but as an American she was theoretically a democrat; and it astounded, it alarmed her, to hear American democracy denounced as a shuffling evasion. It shocked her to be told that the rich and the poor were not equal before the law in a country where justice must be paid for at every step in fees and costs, or where a poor man must go to war in his own person, and a rich man might hire some one to go in his." In the hilarious denouement to this scene, the mother in Isabel deserts her love of equality as soon as it counts: "She had been comforted by the thought that if there ever was another war, and Tom were drafted, his father could buy him a substitute" (292–93).

Howells searches so mercilessly for targets because he is his own best source. After the Haymarket affair, he tried to teach himself "patience with conditions that I believe wrong," even as he admitted, "I do not think there is any final hope of justice under them." "I am neither an example nor an incentive," he realized, and the insight left him staring at "my ugliness and fatuity and feebleness."[53] In *A Hazard of New Fortunes*, a pinch of authorial self-abasement appears in every character with the closest parallels in the figures who behave the worst. Jacob Dryfoos sounds like the people who executed the Haymarket defendants when he shouts that a foreign protester is "a red-mouthed labor-agitator" who "ought to be hung!" (347). Yet, in the death of his son and wallowing in sorrow and guilt, Dryfoos resembles no one more than William Dean Howells, who grieved in similar terms over the death of his daughter Winnie while writing the novel.[54] In an acrid moment that makes the identification especially raw, Basil March puzzles dryly over Dryfoos's bereavement. The literary man who lives vicariously wonders whether anyone is ever changed by "tremendous sorrow" (485).

Howells never lets up, and no one is safe. The artist, Angus Beaton, appears as the most despicable narcissist imaginable, which is perhaps why the novelist leaves him dithering over the same fur-lined overcoat that Howells spoofs in depicting his own hypocrisy to Henry James (382). Alma Leighton, the colorless sketcher of magazine covers, is a lively type for Howells's other daughter, Mildred. Both the real and the imagined daughters spend their time in one art school after another with little hope of anything more.[55] Alma, meaning soul, comes just before Angus in the characterological alphabet, but the novelist as father allows her to resist the connection. He renders Alma just wise enough to reject Beaton's proposal after the most tedious courtship in modern literature.

The world of New York in which these figures move verifies their limits in scope, ambition, and social consciousness. More whimsical than Herrick's protagonist in *The Memoirs of an American Citizen*, Basil March comes to the same conclusion. "Some one always has you by the throat," he complains to his wife, "unless you have some one else in *your* grip" (436). Only the terms of reference improve as Howells moves up the ladder. The pinnacle of class status in *A Hazard of New Fortunes* argues that civilization "would go to pieces, if people acted from unselfish motives." Polite society wears a mask. It is, in fact, "a painted savage" offering favors that turn into merciless bargains. All of Howells's characters act out the cost of these propositions in one way or another. "You get what you pay for," an aunt coaches her too-gentle niece. "It's a matter of business." The niece, in turn, has no chance because the testing ground is tepid when not corrupt. As the narrator reveals, "She almost had opinions and ideals, but really fell short of their possession" (254).

The problem in this satiric vision is that the writer doesn't know quite where to stand on his subject, the lost efficacy of American idealism. Great satire requires a confident point of view as well as faith in a better possibility. Derision succeeds only if it accurately gauges the distance between a fallen reality and the ideal that the target has failed to achieve.[56] Dismayed to find injustice thriving unchallenged in America, Howells was too philosophically disoriented in 1889 to find a fixed platform.

This instability in point of view becomes clear in the one character who speaks as Howells himself wrote in his letters of disillusionment over the Haymarket affair. Berthold Lindau presents a special case as the solitary radical thinker in the novel. A foreigner in speech and thought, Lindau is the only character to have sacrificed anything of importance for the ideal of equality. He has lost a hand as a Union soldier in the Civil War, and he lives among the urban poor by choice while others conduct their well-meant observations from a convenient distance. Lindau never quibbles or dissembles on intellectual issues in the way that every other character in the novel does, and he invariably speaks his mind. It is hard to avoid the conclusion that Howells wanted to be such a man but knew he could not manage it.

The radicalism of Lindau functions outside of the drollery and idle wit on almost every page of *A Hazard of New Fortunes*. The philosophical edge in the plot also comes from him. "How much money can a man honestly earn without wronging or oppressing some other man?" Lindau asks Basil March. The question gives substance to Basil's vague anxiety about how everyone seems to be at each other's throat (191). "What is American?" Lindau asks again, and he concludes there *is* no America "any more!" No man who works with his hands, he tells Basil, has the liberty to pursue the vaunted happiness promised in American thought. Working and living conditions for the urban poor have become impossible, and the courts as well as the newspapers have been bribed to keep matters that way by the countinghouse of commerce (318). When Basil speaks patriotically of country, Lindau replies with brutal candor: the poor have no country (94).

Basil March comes out worst in every exchange with Berthold Lindau. He manages, nevertheless, to evade the negative ideological implications by relegating them to Lindau's faulty reading habits, a defense mechanism that compounds his own ignorance. The omniscient narrator describes how Lindau lives by practical experience, which is more than any other character in the novel can claim (194). In the end, Basil will betray his friend Lindau even in death. When Basil's son Tom, tutored by Lindau, asks whether the German socialist in defending strikers had died in "a bad cause," Basil responds, "Why, yes . . . he died in the cause of disorder; he was trying to obstruct the law." Tom listens and then delivers the most devastating line in the entire novel. If Lindau has died in a bad cause, Tom reasons, speaking as the representative of the next generation, "what's the use of our ever fighting about anything in America?" (451). The last line of the novel reifies Tom's conclusion. As Margaret Vance, the symbol of goodness, retreats into a nunnery instead of challenging the world, the Marches decide to trust not her works but "that look of hers" (496).

Howells sees the implications that his characters do not, and he means to convey them, but he cannot help pulling his punches. The novelist has almost as much trouble with Berthold Lindau as Basil March, and he shows his discomfort by undercutting his presentation of the power in radical thought through a cheap linguistic device. The character with the most ideas, the German Lindau, speaks in pidgin English so thick the reader must pause over just about every sentence. He asks:

> What iss Amerigan? Dere *iss* no Ameriga any more! You start free and brafe, and you glaim for efery man de righd to life, liperty, and de bursuit of habbiness. And where haf you entedt? No man that vorks vith his handts among you hass the liperty to bursue his habbiness. He iss the slafe of some richer man, some gompany, some gorporation, dat crindts him down to the least he can lif on, and that rops him of the marchin of his earnings that he might pe habby on. (318)

This passage literally bespeaks the prejudice at the root of the Haymarket trial. Lindau's broken English conveys what many felt then: only a foreigner could think in such terms. Many realists of the day handled dialect to great advantage, but Howells's use of it here is an artistic failure of sizable proportions. Coleridge pinpoints the mistake in a discussion of Wordsworth on "*low or rustic life.*" Giving speech "from the mouths of men in real life," Coleridge observes, does not admit the diction of "the cottager." Bad language means "doubtful moral effect." Rude speech encourages "the reader's conscious feeling of his superiority awakened by the contrast presented to him."[57] Lindau suffers this fate in *A Hazard of New Fortunes*, and it seems to have been a deliberate strategy. Other characters, the omniscient narrator included, ridicule Lindau's fractured English and the gravity of his "brincibles" (319–21).

The execution of the anarchists left Howells with "questions that carry

beyond myself," and he admitted that his "horizons have been indefi-
nitely widened by the process," but it was also true that the new perceptions frightened him. "I don't know yet what is best," he wrote queru-
lously to Hamlin Garland, adding, "I am still the slave of selfishness,
but I no longer am content to be so."[58] There is more to this discontent
than meets the eye. As Howells's perceptions changed, they came to fit
a mysterious pattern in the nature of American thought. Protest in the
United States tends to grow out of the melodrama of particular situations rather than all-purpose, theoretical complaints about society, and
a favorite zone for the social particular has always been the American
courtroom.

Authorial distance from the poor in *A Hazard of New Fortunes* reveals
a great deal in this regard. Howells did not turn protester over urban
poverty. Nor did his disillusionment flow from any awareness of unfair
treatment suffered by foreign workers in Chicago in 1886. It was the perception of injustice *in the courtroom* that changed him. Four months after the bomb exploded, Howells could still reject all "profoundly tragic"
elements in American fiction as "false" and "mistaken." Novelists were
to concentrate instead on "the more smiling aspects of life, which are
the more American." Serious writers needed to achieve literary success
through "the individual rather than the social interests."[59]

As late as the summer of 1887, Howells saw the economic situation as
a cultural strength rather than a weakness to be addressed. "It is worth
while, even at the risk of being called commonplace, to be true to our
well-to-do actualities," he advised in a gesture toward American prosperity. On the very edge of psychological transformations, he could even
talk of writing "a labor-question romance" with a casual joke about anarchists.[60] Alarm, when it finally came, drew powerfully from another
source, and it would be intensely traumatic. Just before the execution of
the defendants, Howells wrote in despair: "It has not been for one hour
out of my waking thoughts; it is the last thing when I lie down, and the
first thing when I rise up; it blackens my life."[61]

What exactly was it that blackened the life? Howells's moment of self-
recognition came when he realized that capital sentences had been imposed unjustly in an American courtroom and that no one was going
to stop them from taking place as legal events. The first casualties in the
actual Haymarket affair raised a tragic aspect, but it was the inexorable
approach of another kind of death, wrongful death under official sanc-

tion, that changed Howells. Debasement of the law was the real problem. Howells reacted only after reading a pamphlet on the procedural irregularities and judicial misconduct of the Criminal Court of Cook County. Sometime in the summer of 1887, he received a copy of *A Concise History of the Great Trial of the Chicago Anarchists* by Dyer Lum, a Chicago journalist. Through detailed reference to the trial transcript, Lum proved that the defendants had been convicted for their political protests rather than for anything done in the Haymarket.

Lum's pamphlet also underlined comparisons between John Brown's trial and that of the Chicago anarchists, and these resemblances struck home in Howells, the reader of them. "They are condemned to death upon a principle that would have sent every ardent antislavery man to the gallows," Howells cried in support. Within two months of the execution, the Dean of American Letters was calling for a "new commonwealth . . . founded in justice even to the unjust, in generosity to the unjust rather than anything less than justice."[62] The reiterated term explains what had happened to him. The demoralization of William Dean Howells came through twin sources that would not go away. The republic of laws had been unjust, and the vast majority of Americans had enjoyed it.

THE PEOPLE DO NOT BELIEVE IN MERCY

There is no silver lining in the Haymarket tragedy, and no end to it. From irreparable injustice what recovery? On June 26, 1893, the first foreign-born citizen to be elected governor in the United States, John Peter Altgeld of Illinois, made the amends that were possible by commuting the prison sentences of the three remaining defendants. Altgeld's executive pardon cut through the legalese that kept the higher courts from reversing on appeal. His assessment of the record ran to eighteen thousand words, and it revealed that "much of the evidence given at the trial was a pure fabrication." Altgeld reported that "prominent police officials" had terrorized ignorant men into false testimony, that witnesses had been bribed, and that the prosecution failed to show any connection between the defendants and the bomb thrower, who remained unknown seven years after the event.[63]

The governor's report left no stone unturned. He proved that a prejudiced jury had been selected to serve in the case; that the presiding judge misstated the law ("no judge in a civilized country has ever laid down such a rule before"); that the same judge "conducted the trial with malicious ferocity" while "pressing for conviction"; that "it was debatable whether the evidence tended to show guilt"; that "the verdict should not have been allowed to stand, because the law requires that a man shall be proven to be guilty beyond a reasonable doubt"; and that, in sum, "the trial was not fair." The degree and extent of error in the legal process could not be ignored. "I am convinced that it is clearly my duty to act," Altgeld concluded, and he granted "an absolute pardon," without reservations of any kind, to Samuel Fielden, Oscar Neebe, and Michael Schwab.

Altgeld's decision would make him a hero of law and literature to future generations. Vachel Lindsay immortalized him in "The Eagle That Is Forgotten." Justice William O. Douglas extolled Altgeld as "a symbol of the clean, powerful force that we call American idealism."[64] At the time, however, the practical politician in the governor's mansion knew better and accepted a different reality. "If I conclude to pardon those men," he told Clarence Darrow, "it will not meet with the approval that you expect; let me tell you that from that day I will be a dead man politically." When the predicted storm broke over his head, Altgeld would nod and observe, "[The people] do not believe in mercy; they love revenge; they want the prisoners punished to the bitterest extremity."[65]

Outrage over the pardon filled the country's newspapers. The *Washington Post* reviled Altgeld as "an alien himself" with "little or no stake in the problem of American social evolution." Most accounts questioned Altgeld's patriotism and even his right to remain a citizen. "It is Altgeld's un-Americanism which unfits him for the office which he holds, or even for citizenship," ran a typical passage from the *New York Times*. "He cannot forget that he is of foreign birth, and foreign ideas are at all times dominant in his mind." "The American portion of this community feels outraged," the *Times* concluded, arguing that "no rational lover of law and justice" could accept the governor's decision. Altgeld had become "an enemy to the safeguards of society" and "a reckless demagogue who is incapable of understanding the spirit and temper of the people of this Republic."[66] The pardon would indeed destroy Altgeld's career, as he had predicted it would.

Anger over a memorable trial can reappear in an instant. Fury over the release of the remaining Haymarket defendants became a major campaign issue three years later in the presidential election of 1896. Condemnations of "Altgeld's anarchistic policies" helped William McKinley defeat William Jennings Bryan and cost Altgeld reelection as governor in Illinois. A popular choice in 1892, Altgeld was trounced in 1896. McKinley's vice-presidential running mate, Theodore Roosevelt, led the smear campaign. "Mr. Altgeld is a much more dangerous man than Bryan," Roosevelt charged. "Mr. Altgeld condones and encourages the most infamous of murders and denounces the federal government and the Supreme Court for interfering to put a stop to the bloody lawlessness which results in worse than murder." A vote for Bryan or Altgeld would bring "a red welter of lawlessness" upon the land.[67]

When defeat came, the *New York Tribune* announced "cause for national rejoicing." The country was free of "Altgeld the Anarchist" with his "blood-imbued hands." The *Chicago Tribune* reported that the voters had recognized Altgeld's "criminal sympathies, his anarchistic tendencies, his fostering of evil, his industrious, sedulous efforts to breed social discord." *Harper's Weekly* made Altgeld "the most dangerous enemy to American institutions of all the ruffianly gang which has broken out of the forecastle of the ship of state." This festival of censure at Altgeld's expense teaches a sober lesson.

What, in the scheme of things, had Altgeld done? He had freed three wrongly convicted men after seven years in prison, but he also had asked the American people to return to a scene of legal shame. It was too soon, and his contemporaries hated him for it. Altgeld's careful document in justification of the pardon gave the clearest evidence of a miscarriage in justice, but it went unread. No one who urged the execution of the anarchists, a huge majority in the country, wanted to hear his arguments. Even neutral observers found it psychologically more efficient to turn the governor into one more victim of the Haymarket. The law so poorly rendered in Cook County would continue to dominate public opinion. Anarchism had been identified as the enemy to be fought, and punishment of it would remain a trump card of political opportunism for the foreseeable future.

The spread of intolerance from the Haymarket affair remains its most extraordinary contribution—also, for the reader of today, its most disturbing effect. Blunders of the law in one local courthouse led to a national deterioration in intellectual exchange, a debasement in general political discourse, and a collapse in fundamental levels of public civility everywhere. How could one legal decision cause so much damage across an entire nation? Courtrooms are the visible platforms that bolster or undermine the American rule of law, and the price of failure in them can be incalculable. It is hard to avoid a blunt conclusion. Once released, the genie of injustice does not return to the bottle willingly or easily.

Figures 17 & 18. (*Above left*) Julius and Ethel Rosenberg as a married couple (ca. 1940s). © Michael and Robert Meeropol, reprinted with their permission. (*Below left*) The Rosenbergs as convicted defendants (1951). Photograph courtesy of Picture-History (item #1950.0036, Washington, D.C.). The far-fetched seemed real and the mundane impossible in the trial of the Rosenbergs. The ordinary lives of the Rosenbergs had no meaning next to the exciting story told by the prosecution of nerveless traitors who had stolen the atomic bomb. The photograph of the convicted couple on their way to prison satisfied deep-seated ideological fears. It was the only image Americans could see in 1951.

CHAPTER SEVEN

Killing the Rosenbergs

THE CRIME OF THE CENTURY

Julius and Ethel Rosenberg were not executed for conspiring to throw a bomb, as in the case of the Haymarket defendants, but for conspiring to steal one, the atomic bomb. When he delivered the death sentence in the United States District Court for the Southern District of New York on April 5, 1951, Judge Irving R. Kaufman condemned their offense with dramatic certainty. "I consider your crime worse than murder," he told the Rosenbergs. "Plain deliberate contemplated murder is dwarfed in magnitude by comparison with the crime you have committed." He then added, "I believe your conduct in putting into the hands of the Russians the A-bomb years before our best scientists predicted Russia would perfect the bomb has already caused, in my opinion, the Communist aggression in Korea, with the resultant casualties exceeding 50,000 and who knows but that millions more of innocent people may pay the price of your treason."[1]

It had been, in the phrase that J. Edgar Hoover made famous, "the crime of the century."[2] The Rosenbergs were electrocuted two years later on June 19, 1953, when President Dwight D. Eisenhower refused clemency while repeating the same claims: "I can only say that, by immeasurably increasing the chances of atomic war, the Rosenbergs may have condemned to death tens of millions of innocent people all over the world."[3] Judge Kaufman, still in his early forties, presided over the trial as the most brilliant new addition to the federal bench. Hoover had directed the Federal Bureau of Investigation for more than a quarter of a century. President Eisenhower was the most trusted man in the country. If these

national leaders had the facts and spoke the truth, only a person who rejected capital punishment on principle could object to the electric chair
for the Rosenbergs.

But the accusations as stated were not true. They were false and on a
variety of levels. The atomic bomb was *not* stolen from the United States.
If stolen information accelerated Soviet development, it came from the
British scientist Klaus Fuchs, a fact that American authorities knew full
well at the time. Atomic scientists did *not* predict a long-term American
monopoly; the best of them warned that the Russians would soon develop a bomb on their own. Military and political leaders, *not* scientific
experts, were surprised when the Soviet Union exploded an atomic bomb
on August 29, 1949, four years before the earliest estimates of the Central
Intelligence Agency.

These inaccuracies were general; deadlier ones applied directly to the
defendants. The Rosenbergs did *not* put the bomb in the hands of the
Russians. Their actions did *not* cause the Communist aggression in
Korea. They were *not* found guilty of treason but of conspiracy to commit
espionage, and they contributed to *no one's* death except their own. Recent ex-Soviet revelations and declassified American sources now suggest
that Julius Rosenberg did spy for the Soviet Union and that he may have
passed information regarding the development of radar systems, but the
same sources find only the most peripheral role in Soviet atomic espionage. It is virtually certain today that Julius Rosenberg did not convey
nuclear secrets of any value to the Soviet Union.[4]

The most discussed and controversial courtroom event of the twentieth century, the *Rosenberg* trial has won these laurels through the exaggeration, vituperation, and mutual suspicion that dominate all aspects of
the case. The defendants appear in debate as either the leaders in a massive Communist conspiracy or as relatively innocent victims of a modern
witch hunt. These extremes dominate mundane realities in "the hidden
Rosenberg case," and the reason is clear. Middle ground, much closer to
the truth, holds distasteful implications for both sides. Yes, Julius Rosenberg was probably a Soviet spy at some point and probably could have
saved himself and certainly his wife from the electric chair by divulging
what he knew, though it will never be known how much he knew, nor
whether it would have been enough to satisfy the fertile imaginations of
the FBI in its vain search for an enormous spy ring that didn't exist. From

the other side, the trial was manifestly an unfair one, and the Rosenbergs did not deserve the punishment that they received.[5]

The prosecution acted unjustly, the presiding judge helped them, and their mutual efforts would prove unfortunate even in victory. Officialdom's stringency in seeking the deaths of the Rosenbergs won a huge public relations victory in the Cold War, but it won it for the enemies of the United States. The executions would damage the national interest and international reputation of the country more than anything the defendants had done. Mutually embarrassing truths—some guilt, on one side, and professional irresponsibility and stupid politics, on the other— complicate every discussion of the case.

Most accounts attribute the hyperbole around the *Rosenberg* trial to the atmosphere of the Cold War between 1949 and the middle of 1953. Events during those years brought American anxieties to a fever pitch. In August and September 1949, the nation learned that China, along with much of Eastern Europe, had fallen under Communist rule; also that the Soviet Union had exploded an atomic bomb much sooner than most citizens had been led to believe could be possible. Domestic events also contributed. On January 21, 1950, a jury in a New York federal court convicted former State Department employee Alger Hiss of perjury for denying under oath that he passed government documents to a Communist agent named Whittaker Chambers. Then, in February and March, Klaus Fuchs, who worked on the Manhattan Project of the atomic bomb during World War II, confessed to giving information about the bomb to the Soviet Union; as a British subject, he was tried as a spy and sentenced in England to fourteen years in prison. The information given by Fuchs was clearly valuable or at least confirmative to Soviet efforts, and it is usually thought that Fuchs got off lightly for the damage he, and not the Rosenbergs, had done. However, it is often forgotten that there was no law available for extradition to the United States and that Fuchs received the harshest penalty that the laws of England would allow for his offense at the time.

In the same months, Joseph McCarthy, the junior senator from Wisconsin, began to accuse the State Department of harboring hundreds of Communist spies, and Fuchs fingered an American chemist in Philadelphia, Harry Gold, as his courier to the Russian vice consul. Gold's own confession led in June to the arrest of Ethel Rosenberg's brother, David

Greenglass, a lower-level machinist in the Manhattan Project. The arrests of Julius and Ethel Rosenberg followed in July and August from Greenglass's disclosures. Meanwhile, between the arrests of Greenglass and Julius Rosenberg, Communist North Korea invaded the South, and the Korean War would go badly for the Western allies through the trial of 1951 and into the appeal process of 1952.

Later commentators have attached such importance to the negative accumulation of these events that they wonder whether the Korean armistice and the congressional resolve to censure Senator McCarthy in July 1953, a month after the executions, might have saved the Rosenbergs from the electric chair as "the climate of the Cold War shifted."[6] But if standard assumptions about the impact of Cold War mentalities apply, they still do not suffice as legal explanations even if it is true that anti-Communist fervor had everything to do with the execution of the Rosenbergs in 1953.

A rule of law must deal on its own terms with mistakes made, and the effort is doubly important given the propensity to exaggerate for effect in high-profile trials. We have seen how trials magnify the personalities involved; how a good story, whether true or false, can capture a trial; how generic recognitions convince on their own; how submerged intertextual relations control subliminal understandings; and how advocacy tends toward excess and melodrama beyond the facts. All of these elements worked against the Rosenbergs and remain a worry in all trials that capture the communal imagination.

The defendants were undone by vivid claims about a vast spy ring that could not be seen or found. "Imagine a wheel," the prosecution told the jury. "In the center of the wheel, Rosenberg, reaching out like the tentacles of an octopus." In the realm of storytelling, Rosenberg belonged to the "inner sanctum" of a group holding enormous power.[7] Didn't the trial itself confirm the importance of the Rosenbergs? Even if Julius Rosenberg only ran a very small machine shop, would a just government put him on trial if he wasn't significant? One had to know the intricate workings of the FBI and the Justice Department to realize that, well, yes, the government *would* act in just such a way, but access to that knowledge, like so much of the case, was "top secret" and could not to be challenged in court.

When David and Ruth Greenglass testified against their own family, the intimacy of their betrayal made them just appalling enough to be really interesting, and they had a better story to tell than the blanket denials of the defendants. Mere disclaimer never disarms the melodramatic; nor a recipient's thirst for the bizarre. In the moment that everyone who writes about the case always records, Ruth and David Greenglass testified how Julius Rosenberg made a courier signal out of the separated halves of a torn Jell-O box while boasting that "the simplest things are the cleverest." No minuscule kernel of explanation could have been better suited to suggest a mastermind among lesser co-conspirators. The story was too good, too outré, too wonderfully manipulative of the mundane not to be true in the absence of an equally dramatic response from the Rosenbergs. The prosecution returned compulsively to this incident while quietly improving on the wording ("the simplest things are best").[8]

Conviction in a conspiracy case depends on which story told by co-conspirators you are willing to believe. If the believable witness against the accused also happens to be a relative, some stigma attaches to all parties, but domestic discord is a familiar story and part of the recognized sadness in all things. The prosecution made the most of a hackneyed possibility: "Clearly the breach of family loyalty is that of an older sister and brother-in-law [Ethel and Julius Rosenberg] dragging an American soldier [David Greenglass was on army furlough at the time of the alleged incident] into the sordid business of betraying his country for the benefit of the Soviet Union." A patriotic jury found it convenient to side with the younger Greenglasses. As one member of the panel would note, "Why would a boy [Greenglass] go to this great length to testify against his sister?" She had to be guilty.[9] Never mind that the Greenglasses had incentives to testify as they did. Cooperation with the government eased David's sentence and shielded his wife from prosecution altogether.

An intertext of parallel mentalities complicated matters for the Rosenbergs. Taken together, atomic secrecy and clandestine espionage kept the Rosenbergs from confronting important evidence against them. Emanuel Bloch, counsel for the defense, requested that "top secret" material presented by the prosecution—including the legally potent but technically useless drawings that David Greenglass drew from memory of the plutonium bomb dropped on Nagasaki—be held from scrutiny and omitted from the court record for fear that they could "be used to the advantage of a foreign power." No matter that the untrained Greenglass knew almost nothing about the intricacies of atomic energy. A psychology of concealment dominated both sides in court as well as the bench. No one who counted thought to argue that secrecy is the enemy of light—

light that, in this case, the defense desperately needed. Failure to inspect the crude Greenglass drawings and cross-examine their significance allowed their false importance to stand unchallenged as controlling evidence.[10]

Before concluding that the defense made inexplicable blunders in allowing such secrecy to persist, as most accounts from hindsight claim, we should remember how the intertext of secrecy functioned in the *Rosenberg* courtroom.[11] The decision to exclude David Greenglass's drawings from public scrutiny was thoroughly explicable for the times. "The culture of secrecy that evolved [between 1945 and 1950] was intended as a defense against two antagonists, by now familiar ones: the enemy abroad and the enemy within."[12] The power in the accusation against the Rosenbergs came from joining those two enemies in the charge of conspiracy, and it made the prospect of guilt colossal.

The Rosenbergs, who denied all charges, could only respond by proving their own loyalty, but how? "The concept of loyalty necessarily involved the notion of secrecy. Disloyal employees would reveal secrets; loyal employees would not." In trying to prove that they were neither enemies within nor linked to enemies abroad, the Rosenbergs rather hopelessly sought to demonstrate their own allegiance to country by joining the rest of the nation in the understanding of its universal desire to protect official secrets.[13]

As serious as these handicaps were for the Rosenbergs, a more subtle connection of law and literature clarifies the inevitability of the penalty exacted. Critics mistake the situation when they assert that there were two *Rosenberg* cases: first, the trial and, second, conflict over the executions.[14] There was only one case, beginning on March 6, 1951, in the Foley Square Courthouse in New York City, and ending on June 19, 1953, in the death chamber of Sing Sing at Ossining, New York. The momentum from accusation to conviction to execution was inexorable because of the way narrative transmission related to computation of the crime of conspiracy.

The execution of the Rosenbergs became a certainty when the prosecution's account held narrative desire for the long moment of the trial. The state's master narrative was exciting and deceptively simple in its denial of all other possibilities. It covered contingencies that the Rosenbergs could answer only through mundane claims about their normal existence, but the daily lives of the accused would prove less than satisfying in court and in media accounts. As told, the everyday has no narrative.

It has no structured beginning-middle-end to define itself, and it was no match for the story of a nation plunged into peril.

THE MASTER NARRATIVE AT TRIAL

Narrative works as "the triumph of concordance over discordance." "The pleasure of recognition" holds a listener or reader by movement from disruption to some form of recovery or answer:

> An "ideal" narrative begins with a stable situation which is disturbed by some power or force. There results a state of disequilibrium; by the action of a force directed in the opposite direction, the equilibrium is re-established, the second equilibrium is similar to the first, but the two are never identical.[15]

Legal narrative, by extension, opens with an implied preexistent order as its benchmark of stability. It moves from there through the disturbance of an alleged crime or injury addressed at trial and finishes in a judgment that provides a new stability one way or another. In the context of accusation at the *Rosenberg* trial, the United States had been secure in its nuclear monopoly, but loss of that monopoly through theft had left it vulnerable to the threat of nuclear attack, and this crime required a degree of punishment of the thief that would deter all future thieves and sustain American superiority in the nuclear arms race.

Judge Kaufman refined his version of this narrative in his sentencing statement. As he told the Rosenbergs while reaching for his real audience, the nation, "The competitive advantage held by the United States in super-weapons has put a premium on the services of a new school of spies—the homegrown variety that places allegiance to a foreign power before loyalty to the United States." Death would properly supply "the punishment to be meted out . . . for the preservation of our society against these traitors in our midst" by demonstrating "with finality that this nation's security must remain inviolate; that traffic in military secrets, whether promoted by slavish devotion to a foreign ideology or by a desire for monetary gain must cease." Kaufman cleverly bolstered this master narrative in law with a second one of the spirit. The Rosenbergs had been guilty of a "diabolical conspiracy to destroy a God-fearing nation," and the obvious intertext brought its own measure of comfort.[16] As a God-fearing people already knew, the devil always loses in the end.

The court fashioned a new equilibrium, one that reached back to the security of the first equilibrium while relinquishing a stability that had been lost. All loyal Americans could feel safe again only if they imbibed a lesson in their newly threatening situation. "It is so difficult to make people realize," Judge Kaufman explained, "that this country is engaged in a life and death struggle with a completely different system." Kaufman's sentence of death sought to provide that realization, even as his second equilibrium—a God-fearing people triumphing over diabolical Communism—made national life more interesting than before. Victorious struggle is always more exciting than mere success.[17]

To understand the intricacies of narrative, it is first necessary to see that it has two aspects by definition: account (the chain of events or story) and discourse (the form in language with the strategies by which the account is conveyed). Point of view, generic codes, tonal patterns, symbol systems, rhetorical devices, and the structure of narrative transmission all fall under the designation of discourse. They are the means by which substance is conveyed. To give a legal example of discourse, judicial figures rarely resist a portrayal of anxious decision making in delivering the story of a momentous case.

Judge Kaufman would be no exception in sentencing the Rosenbergs. "What I am about to say is not easy for me," he began. "Every nerve, every fiber of my body has been taxed," Kaufman noted, as he told everyone how he had examined his own conscience, "for it is only human to be merciful." He had searched the record in weary, lonely deliberation "for hours, days and nights" but knew he had to hold himself to the sticking point in the name of duty. "I would violate the solemn and sacred trust that the people of this land have placed in my hands were I to show leniency." By joining the people, Kaufman fused his personal point of view to those of Providence and the nation. An ingenious closure rounded this circle of narrativity. "It is not in my power, Julius and Ethel Rosenberg, to forgive you," Kaufman concluded. "Only the Lord can find mercy for what you have done." The *description* of his decision is Kaufman's story or account; *confirming* his decision *rhetorically* through the absolution of God and country is an example of discourse.[18]

The persuasive aspects of discourse gave unusual impetus to the prosecution and execution of the Rosenbergs, and they could do so because a charge of conspiracy credits the manipulation of narrative more directly than any other accusation of crime. Irving Saypol, the chief prosecutor in the Southern District of New York, defined the government's charge in the following way: "A conspiracy is very simply an agreement and understanding between two or more people to violate some law of the United States." Proof of an agreement usually depends on the informal communications of a conspiratorial group; words exchanged must show that its members formed such a group. The net for catching the conspirators could therefore be entirely linguistic with one exception. There had to be a demonstrable person who had committed an overt act to give life to the charge. [19]

The government made much of the minimum required of it to convict the Rosenbergs. As Irving Saypol explained, "When any one of the persons having entered into this agreement does any such act [to help along the conspiracy], then *all those other persons* who had entered into this agreement and understanding with him *become guilty of the crime of conspiracy.*" Indeed, "proof of *only one* such overt act by *any one* of the conspirators would be sufficient to complete the conspiracy" to find that "*all* are guilty." Judge Kaufman clarified the implications for the prosecution. "I will ultimately charge you," he advised the jury, "that it is not necessary that the defendants actually complete their act or that they have success in their act." [20]

Implicit in such language is the ability to imagine a very large spy ring within the attempt to prove a very small one. The government acted on the vaguer indictment of conspiracy because a charge of actual espionage would have required more elaborate proof and more evidence of actions taken. For the crime of espionage, it would have had to verify that certain individuals passed explicit information to a specifically identified source. As it was, in its charge of a conspiracy to commit espionage, the prosecution could convict by proving an existing *plan* to spy with only the *intention* of giving away privileged information.

Although it did not have the terminology in 1951, the government saw its solution to these difficulties in terms of narrative. Through plea bargains, the prosecution had witnesses who would confess to helping the Russians and implicate the Rosenbergs, but these witnesses had to rehearse their confessions in an order that would reveal the developing conspiracy. Prosecutor Saypol's opening statement went over these priorities in detail. "The evidence, as I have said, best should come from the lips of the witnesses, for you to judge. The plot will be *unfolded* in that way." The government's witnesses would be arranged to speak "*over the course of the time* this crime covered." The jury would "see and hear that the witnesses are telling the truth as *each link in this chain is forged* and *put into place*, by testimony, by documentary evidence, which will be revealed before you, testimony and documentary evidence which cannot be contradicted by anybody or anything in the world, because it is the truth."[21]

Two things stand out in this opening statement beyond the definition of narrative that it provides. First, testimony took priority over documentary evidence in Saypol's description of how he would proceed. Testimony came first because most of the prosecution's case would come from witnesses. Conspirators are usually convicted through the testimony of cooperating co-conspirators, and so it was in the *Rosenberg* case. Physical evidence was extremely limited and circumstantial. The Jell-O box in the case is famous because the prosecution had to place so much emphasis upon its tangibility. The state submitted its own replica of the missing box as government exhibit 4B to solidify the representation of an artifact familiar to all Americans in the 1950s. An alleged signal between spies, the halves of the box gave evidence of a conspiracy at work. The state's Jell-O box could be seen; it was the overt act necessary to convict! Saypol would argue that it "forged the necessary link in the chain that points indisputably to the guilt of the Rosenbergs."[22]

The second rhetorical priority in the prosecution's development of a master narrative turned on Irving Saypol's repeated claims about truth. Every storyteller begins with a problem of credibility, and the prosecution faced an added burden in this regard. The government had to convince a patriotic jury of Americans that some Communists—Communists that it had to admit had placed the country under a nuclear threat—were telling the truth *this* time, even though they had lied repeatedly about their actions before they were caught. Many imaginative convolutions in prosecutorial rhetoric would focus on the imputed trustworthiness of cooperating witnesses. If proving a conspiracy requires a structure of narrative transmission through the stories that co-conspirators must tell to convict, the odium that attached to the prosecution's witnesses made the need critical. Saypol responded by manipulating accounts to make them more believable than perhaps they were.

Clever management became the truth conveyed. Saypol could make his witnesses credible, despite the official untrustworthiness that clung to them as former spies, because of the strength of the master narrative that he created. Technically, the Rosenbergs needed no narrative in response as defendants innocent until proven guilty, but they labored in court under what can be termed a narrative handicap. They faced a charge in which guilt was conveyed through a train of commentary more than through facts presented. Much blame has fallen on the defense counsel for not mounting a positive counternarrative in response, but neither the times nor circumstance encouraged that possibility. The rhetorical ingenuity of the prosecution in court will help to explain why.

THE MASTER NARRATIVE AT WORK

We've seen the themes, but how exactly did the prosecution's master narrative work within the legal process of the *Rosenberg* case? When U.S. attorney Irving Saypol told the jury once again that "each link in the chain will be put in place by my colleagues and myself" and that "the issue is a simple one," the overtones in repetition spoke to both the cyclical nature of narrative and the circularity of a charge of conspiracy as it incorporates all parties into a common crime.[23] Proof of conspiracy leans heavily on suppositions about mutual intent against contested testimony. Conviction depends on the imagination of jurors who are willing to accept a given version of the truth as the common sense of a complicated situation.

Common sense demands simple explanation. Prosecutor Saypol adapted by rendering the complex and vague straightforward and concrete. "Mind you, however," Saypol alerted the jury, "the seriousness of this charge does not make the issue complicated." And why wasn't it complicated? "[A] conspiracy is *very simply* an agreement and understanding between two or more people to violate some law of the United States."[24]

The tone as a guide to argument is important here. Again, "a conspiracy, of course, is merely an agreement between two or more persons to violate some law of this country—in this case the Espionage law." The prosecution emphasized *mere* agreement, *very simply* seen, and *of course* true. Very little extra input was needed from the jury. "The law actually need not be broken, as it was here," Saypol informed it. "The agreement alone to break the law would be enough."[25] These assurances slid over many difficulties. The problems of substantiation in proving agreement in a conspiracy are not negligible. Surface actions in the accused must somehow prove thought patterns, and neither Rosenberg had a record of any kind at the time of their arrests.

Conspiracies rarely generate formal documents to verify their existence because they are "characterized by secrecy in origin and execution." The law responds by giving latitude to prosecutors, enabling them to proceed "by inferences drawn from the conduct of the parties." The license and range of allowable inference are considerable. The law does not require that an agreement be formal, explicit, or written; circumstantial evidence will prove agreement, and agreement can be deduced from a working relationship between parties. A conspiracy does not have to appear reasonable. A conspirator who has not profited from a conspiracy or had any demonstrable stake in it is just as guilty as the rest. The motivation for joining a conspiracy is irrelevant. Proof of agreement and the intention to commit a conspiracy are the only elements needed.[26]

The law also allows the net of the prosecution to be as flexible as it is wide. The "overt act" that the prosecution must prove in any one conspirator to convict all of the others does not have to be physical to be overt. A simple statement will suffice to convict if it has been given in an effort to accomplish a purpose, *any* purpose of the conspiracy, and the statement used need not be in violation of the law or a crime to provide proof. Nor does it matter that a conspiracy lacks a discrete, identifiable structure; it can be loose-knit, haphazard, or even foolish, and still be actionable.

All of this official leeway allows the state unusual room in which to maneuver in court and to present arguments on its own terms and with less interruption. The law agrees that to unmask secrecy in a conspiracy a prosecutor needs scope. The unusual additional element in the *Rosenberg* trial involved the presence of secrecy on *all* sides, a situation that again favored the prosecution. It gave Irving Saypol another layer of adaptability in tailoring explanations to his own independent needs and desires. With a sympathetic judge on its side and the silence of the Rosenbergs construed as secrets kept, the prosecution could use the carte blanche allowed it to create an account of how the Rosenbergs "stole" the atomic bomb. Nothing Julius Rosenberg actually said about the imputed Jell-O box had to be criminal to convict him.

"To steal," very much in personal terms, was the prosecution's frequent verb of choice, and it used every variation on the theme to claim an accomplished fact. "We will prove that the Rosenbergs devised and put into operation, with the aid of Soviet Nationals and Soviet agents in this country, an elaborate scheme which enabled them to steal through David Greenglass, this one weapon, that might well hold the key to the survival of this nation and means the peace of the world, the atomic bomb." Even more specifically, "we *know* that these conspirators stole the most important scientific secrets ever known to mankind from this country and delivered them to the Soviet Union."[27]

Actually, the prosecution *knew* something quite different: it knew that the Rosenbergs were unimportant in passing atomic secrets and that whatever useful information was given to the Soviet Union had come much earlier from the scientist Klaus Fuchs, a convicted spy already punished for his crime.[28] Criticism of this subterfuge under the veil of secrecy on the part of the prosecution fuels much of recent controversy over the trial, but the desire to blame hides another issue, one ultimately of greater importance.

The truly fascinating thing about the prosecution's untrue master narrative is that it dominated the country as well as the court. The government's case gained leverage from political tensions, but something more allowed it to burgeon so instantly into a standard source of Cold War thought. Narrative control is always a vital key, but successful narrative control in a courtroom always enjoys the extra proof of the decision reached and, as such, it can instigate widely held belief. Everyone respects the prompt of victory. Understanding how it worked in the *Rosenberg* case reveals how language reinforced by a popular decision directs a community toward wider applications.

The manipulation of three patterns in narrative discourse contributed to the conviction of the Rosenbergs as a national event beyond itself. The first pattern, emplotment, creates approval through narrative concordance; its devices are completeness (*holos*), repetition, and magnitude.[29] The second pattern, often in tension with the first, encourages momentary discomfort or worried interest over outcomes through disequilibrium, suspense, or seeming insufficiency.[30] The third and related pattern builds suspense through deliberate gaps in narrative sequence to kindle dramatic engagement. The recipient who already knows everything being said loses interest in an account that becomes boring because it requires little in reaction. A good narrator will therefore leave gaps of indeterminacy that stimulate a recipient into imagining more about the subject than is given. All three devices join recipient to narrator in common cause; used effectively, they mobilize the imagination toward a desirable end.[31]

Emplotment or concordance in the prosecution's narrative of the Rosenbergs' guilt reached the jury and the nation through insistence on a "Soviet Communist espionage ring" with the Rosenbergs at its center. The metaphor implied a complete conspiracy to steal the atomic bomb, and the Soviet explosion of the bomb in 1949 gave prima facie evidence of the ring's efficacy. Presumed "mutual devotion to Communism and the Soviet Union" in the defendants offered another concordance, this time in a logical sequence from foreign ideology to betrayal of the nation. Since all Communists were assumed to be alike, to be a Communist meant to betray your country with others. Conspiracies and conspirators are often diverse and complex; all one needed to know about this one was that Communism held the conspirators "together by one common bond"—a bond that in itself was enough to convict.[32]

Magnitude in the crime of the century was a given, but it operated on several levels. "I feel most inadequate to express *to express* to you in words the enormity of the thing," prosecutor Saypol announced whenever he had the chance, "but its seriousness and implications for all of us does not make it a complicated case."[33] The opposite was, in fact, true. It was the complexity of the atomic bomb that dropped a veil of secrecy over every detail and allowed the presumed enormity of the crime to stand alone *for all of us*. The gravity of the situation for the jury supplied another order of magnitude through the implication that its own patriotism was involved. The accused belonged to an enemy seeking "to wipe us off the face of the earth" with "the most important weapon ever known to mankind." Nothing less than "survival of this nation" was at stake, making the case "one of the most important that has ever been submitted to a jury in this country."[34]

Repetition is a procedural given in advocacy, but the nature of prosecutorial reiteration in this case, together with daily media support of it, rendered the "now well-known pattern of espionage" a foregone conclusion in the popular mind.[35] It conveyed that the prosecution had proven a vast conspiracy with an avalanche of evidence when it had not. Noting that one overt act would convict, the prosecution claimed through sleight of hand to have shown twelve such acts, and its overkill had a particular purpose: to kill. Repetition was an intensifier that left no room for mercy: "[Julius and Ethel Rosenberg] stand before you in the face of overwhelming proof of this terrible disloyalty, proof which transcends any emotional consideration which must eliminate any consideration of sympathy. No defendants ever stood before the bar of American justice less deserving of sympathy."[36]

Suspense in the uncertainty of narrative progression, the second influential pattern in narrative discourse, solidified the prosecution's story. Irving Saypol drew on the anxieties of the nation. He announced that the prosecution would withhold part of the evidence for reasons of state and other parts because the extent of the conspiracy remained unknown. These assertions handled a troublesome hitch in the prosecution's argument. The government had complained of a vast espionage ring while indicting only five people and putting just three on trial (with Morton Sobell as a co-conspirator with the Rosenbergs).[37] If you believed the government, it meant that many other and greater conspirators had to be still at large. "The identity of some of the other traitors who sold their country down the river along with Rosenberg and Sobell remains undisclosed," the prosecution noted ambiguously. It implied, however, that it could tell much more than it was safe to say. "We know that such people exist." "We know of these other henchmen of Rosenberg in this plot by him."[38]

The authorities verified the fact of ongoing menace in "the most critical hours of our history." Somewhere out in the country others continued to plot. Taking the Rosenbergs' places were "other traitorous Americans to deliver the safeguards to our security into the hands of a power that would wipe us off the face of the earth."[39] There were no hard details in these sweeping claims, but the nation would ignore them at its peril. The jury had to realize three things in reaching its verdict: a conspiracy that threatened the entire country continued to exist; the government could only punish the *captured* thieves; worst of all, the Rosenbergs remained dangerous even in the dock. The nuclear threat was everywhere. The prosecution's narrative left the gauge of that danger to the untrammeled imaginations of a frightened people that had just heard that it had been betrayed.

Each of these contentions turned with full force on the defendants, insuring their deaths. Just two people in all of the world knew how many more spies remained at work, and they would not speak! "We don't know all the details," Saypol explained, "because the only living people who can supply the details are the defendants. Rosenberg and his wife have added the supreme touch to their betrayal by taking the stand before you, by taking advantage of every legal opportunity that is afforded defendants, and then, by lying and lying and lying here, brazenly in an attempt to deceive you, to lie their way out of what they did." By refusing to divulge the roles of others who were betraying the country, the Rosenbergs sacrificed any right to leniency while protecting "the system which prevails in certain parts of the world where people have lost their freedom."[40] Would they get away with it? Any extension of mercy would allow them to continue to plot with others and add to the nation's risk.

Concordance and discomfort, the first two leading patterns of narrative control, set the stage for the prosecution's handling of the third, its creative use of gaps of indeterminacy. Irving Saypol developed his argument in such a way that loyalty to Communism, worship of the Soviet Union, and disloyalty in the United States would be perceived as the same thing. The spaces in between these categories were ignored. The government argued that loyalty to Communism was disloyalty to the United States. The two states of mind meant the same thing, and that deductive jump allowed another.[41]

Julius Rosenberg, if he helped the Soviet Union with information during World War II, could have thought of himself as an American contributing to the war effort when the Soviet Union bore the brunt of Nazi aggression on the Eastern Front.[42] Painted instead with the brush of postwar Communism, Rosenberg became more than "one of those who have offended against the laws of our land"; he had joined a growing legion "who have dedicated themselves to the destruction of our country," and that difference made mere offense heinous.[43] Crucial in executing the Rosenbergs, the added insinuation of a rise in domestic Communism was also patently false. Historians and government experts have shown that "by the close of the 1940's Communism was a defeated ideology in the United States" and that "by 1950 or thereabouts the Communist Party was essentially neutralized."[44]

A clever narrator in the spotlight of a high-profile trial can turn falsehood into acceptable, even popular judgment without the recipients quite realizing the steps taken. An audience filling in narrative gaps brings its own faculties into play and is held in place by its own enjoyment of belonging to the larger narrative. Conjecture about the real meaning of what has been said gives interactive dynamism to a story in much the same way that speculation during a murder mystery is the reader's real interest. The logic imposed by the narrator becomes the recipient's story through anticipation of its progression before fulfillment.[45] In the *Rosenberg* case, the interactive appeal in condemnation depended on patriotic reflexes in American thought, and the crowning touch, the final gap filled, would come in Irving Saypol's decision to rename the defendant's crime in a way that would insure their deaths.

The Rosenbergs were convicted of conspiracy to commit espionage, but they were vilified in court and in the press as traitors. The prosecution referred to the Rosenbergs as spies, as it had to, but far more often it labeled them traitors performing treasonable acts. It made no difference to the court that the defendants were not charged with treason, could not have been convicted of treason, and faced added prejudice through the prosecution's manipulation of the odious legal category in direct application to them.

Narrative works best when the seams cannot be seen. The ignominy of treason stuck to the Rosenbergs through the imputed stigma of Communism. When prosecutor Saypol first argued in his opening statement that "the evidence will show that the loyalty and allegiance of the Rosenbergs and Sobell were not to our country, but that it was to Communism," Emanuel Bloch protested for the defense, asking for a mistrial. "Communism is not on trial here," he objected. The only charge against the defendants was conspiracy to commit espionage, and the prosecutor's remarks were "irrelevant to the charge before this Court and jury" and "inflammatory in character." But Communism *was* on trial in narrative terms. Judge Kaufman allowed frequent reference to it "for the purpose of establishing a motive for what they [the Rosenbergs] were doing," and he subsequently refused to place any limits on the range of reference allowed.[46]

The defense tried to fight fire with fire, but it had no matches. "May I repeat, and I hope you will forgive me if I repeat, and I hope the Court will forgive me if I repeat at this time," pleaded Bloch, apologetic to a fault, "all we ask is a fair shake in the American way."[47]

Unfortunately for the defense, the prosecution had already been allowed to define what "the American way" would mean in Judge Kaufman's courtroom, and it seized the free rein given at every opportunity. Prosecutor Saypol's attacks on Communism grew more capricious, colorful, and encompassing of "traitorous activities" and "treasonable acts" as the trial proceeded. By the end, a "poison of Communist ideology" had infected the land, and the Rosenbergs were administering it as "traitorous Americans." These would also be the terms of choice in the court's sentencing statement.[48]

It was exciting to have and believe in a big picture. American traitors stealing the atomic bomb for the Soviet Union as part of a diabolical Communist conspiracy made the picayune lives of the Rosenbergs uninteresting and therefore somehow expendable. No one, certainly not the media, was inclined to hear or explore the Rosenbergs' side of the story, such as it was. The government's case was more interesting to report, and the politics of the moment also seemed to justify extreme measures.[49] A judge and jury fearing nuclear attack and wanting to do their patriotic duty had little trouble in finding the Rosenbergs to be the arch traitors described by the government. "I believe that never at any time in our history were we ever confronted to the same degree that we are today with such a challenge to our very existence," Judge Kaufman observed melodramatically as he imposed the death sentence instead of the statutory alternative of a thirty-year prison sentence.[50]

The rest of the official story would prove less exhilarating. Higher courts, the U.S. Court of Appeals for the Second Circuit and the U.S. Supreme Court, wrangled over appeals without altering the legal momentum of the case. In the end, as in the Haymarket appeals, all higher courts refused to take on a combative trial judge who fought back to protect the discretion of his own decisions. The higher courts hid behind similar procedural evasions to avoid the merits of the case.

Certainly evasions controlled for a majority of the Supreme Court. Justice Frankfurter had previously objected to "strangling technicalities" in capital cases, and he objected here. "The Court's failure to take the case of the Rosenbergs," he told his colleagues, "has presented for me the most anguishing situation since I have been on the Court." Despite his frequent pleas, technicalities kept the Supreme Court from reaching the merits of the case. The decision to execute remained in place, and with it the master narrative of the trial court in public opinion. Amidst unprecedented acrimony on the Supreme Court, Frankfurter concluded, "Men's devotion to law is not profoundly rooted."[51]

Wherever and whenever they come up to this day, the Rosenbergs are defined in anger and rancor. They remain the only persons in America ever executed by a civil court for the crime of conspiracy, and that fact never rests. Their deaths still haunt the nation. In the short term, controversies over the Rosenbergs gave a false focus to accusations of treason throughout the Cold War, polarizing domestic politics in the process. Were the Rosenbergs fairly tried? Were they guilty anyway? Was it unjust to execute them? In the long term, no matter what side one argued on these questions, it became clear that it had been unwise to kill them. The price of the executions would be especially high in international politics—higher than anyone in authority could have realized or wanted. The Rosenbergs would "too much disturb the soul" of the nation. Beyond the nation, their deaths would question the executioner's moral leadership in "the free world."[52]

COUNTERNARRATIVE

The most powerful counternarrative of the *Rosenberg* case came much later from a novelist rather than a legal expert, and it emphasized damage done instead of the debate over guilt or innocence. "I didn't want to write about the Rosenbergs," E. L. Doctorow would say later of *The Book of Daniel* published in 1971. "I wanted to write about what happened to them."[53] In effect, the novel uses the *Rosenberg* trial to re-create American civilization in the early 1950s and late 1960s, the two moments in the nation's modern history when radical thought came under closest scrutiny. Doctorow's exercise in periodization also comes with an important warning. The history to be covered cannot be trusted. History, we learn, is a "pig, biting into the heart's secrets."[54]

Doctorow turns to a subversive tradition in American literature for orientation and confirmation. Two of the greatest influences on him, by his own admission, are Edgar Allan Poe, for whom he was named, and Nathaniel Hawthorne, who leads the way. Poe hovers as the guiding spirit over *The Book of Daniel* as "the archetype traitor, the master subversive" who "let the darkness pore through" the American Constitution. "Edgar" Doctorow's main characters, the child who becomes the man in Daniel Isaacson and his younger sister Susan, appear as the son and daughter of the executed Communist couple, and they resemble no one more closely than the incestuous siblings Roderick and Madeline Usher in Poe's story "The Fall of the House of Usher." The parallel is apt because

Doctorow, like Poe, records the utter destruction of a family, including their house.[55]

Nathaniel Hawthorne is even more important to the unusual technique of *The Book of Daniel*. "Hawthorne had an immense impact on me," Doctorow once explained, pointing to the narrative style in the earlier writer that "suited me particularly well." "He did not give you ordinary life but a precipitate of it." Hawthorne encouraged Doctorow to be "interested in imagery as a kind of moral data."[56] The precipitate in *The Book of Daniel* is injustice; the moral data, the *Rosenberg* case; the narrative, necessarily fractured. It is not too much to suggest that Doctorow's mastery of this technique and his emergence as a major novelist came through this bitter work. Looking back four decades later, the writer would himself refer to *The Book of Daniel* as a turning point.[57]

The distorted characterizations of the Rosenberg children are Doctorow's mechanism, his window into awfulness. "Daniel and his sister are survivors of their own holocaust," Doctorow remarked in one interview. They are the spectacularly and unfairly damaged figures who cannot find a way to surmount the catastrophe that defines them. Like Hawthorne, Doctorow looks at America and dares to say, "No! in thunder," or as he puts it himself, "There is always a no inside the yes." He knew that his novel would present a "difficult story for the American public to accept." *The Book of Daniel* writes out the "no" in what happened between 1951 and 1953, and it does it from the forgotten perspective of the defeated through their unavoidably alienated progeny. The novel depicts what its author once called "the terrible injustice of our brutal, ordinary inadequacy."[58]

Aspects of this hell-fired story were too much even for its author. When Doctorow, "thinking about the Rosenberg case," decided "it was something I could write," his plan brought him "as close to total despair as I've ever been in my life." Frustration mounted in particular over narrative terms for conveying the cultural meaning of the *Rosenberg* case.[59] The narrative voice that finally emerges, that of Daniel Isaacson, awakens and flourishes in injustice. The untimely loss of their parents is manifestly unfair to the children of the Isaacson/Rosenberg couple, and that injustice spreads and delves in ever-thickening swarms through every nook and cranny and connection of the children's lacerated lives.

Doctorow's controlling premise is an excruciating one: whatever the parents were guilty of, their children begin as innocents. Soon enough, however, the suffering that they experience as deserted orphans turns them into monsters who pass along their misery with consummate skill. *The Book of Daniel* is about what injustice does to everyone it touches. No one escapes in this book. The burgeoning, upside-down world that comes from injustice resembles that offered in another postmodern novel. As a Walker Percy character reasons in *The Moviegoer*, "All timely and likable people seem dead to me; only the haters seem alive."[60]

Wretchedness, affliction, and perversion thrive alongside cruelty, hatred, and internecine disintegration in *The Book of Daniel*. The raging emotions unleashed are so threatening that Doctorow could only recover by rewriting the family plot in his next major work of fiction, *Ragtime*. In reaction, *Ragtime* offers palliatives to impossible dangers faced. Again a family is sundered, but this time Doctorow circumvents tragedy with an improbable happy ending. *Ragtime* closes with a magically rearranged, multi-ethnic family that is better than the first one in every way.

Critics complained about the sequel as an all too "perfect commodity": "If *Daniel* is open-ended, *Ragtime* is well-nigh seamless and hermetic, finished with packaged slickness."[61] Doctorow once concluded that "there is no fiction or nonfiction as we commonly understand the distinction: there is only narrative." *Ragtime* has been Doctorow's most popular novel because it offers an all-American narrative in conventional terms. *The Book of Daniel*, by far the better book, has sunk into relative obscurity because it wrestles with narrative disjuncture to tell an un-American story that is nonetheless about the nation and its ways. "Doctorow and his narrator are trying to discover what kind of narrative is possible when one stands not only outside but in opposition to the regime."[62]

The unrecognized ingredient in Doctorow's struggle is his preoccupation with the oversimplifying master narrative in the *Rosenberg* trial. The symbiosis between *The Book of Daniel* and the transcript of the *Rosenberg* trial feeds off of a basic recognition. Just as prosecutor Irving Saypol must coordinate and occasionally force variables into line to make sure that "each link in this chain is forged" to form a believable account that will convict and execute, so Doctorow must recover the vitality in those variables by deconstructing each link in the chain.[63] Only in this way can he catch up with the negative impact that followed from the legal and political consequences of the trial.

Doctorow realized that it would not be possible to settle the larger

controversy in fiction. He dwells instead on the aftermath and the un-
foreseen energy of compounded wrong. The interesting thing about this
focus is the writer's recognition that, sooner or later, injustice *received*
will transform itself into injustice *sent*. The abused becomes the abuser.
The decision to shift narrative patterns conveys the nature of this horrifying process and reasserts the fact of human complexity over courtroom
simplicities. *The Book of Daniel* reaches not for exposure, but for something more frightening and appalling. Warped as well as tormented by
life, Daniel Isaacson talks in fractured idioms and out of a bottomless
reserve of ill will and alienation. Every word out of his mouth seeks to
offend. It is the voice of injustice, and Doctorow demands that the reader
imbibe its every permutation.

"IF THIS BE TREASON MAKE THE MOST OF IT"

How does injustice sound? How *must* it sound in all of its twisted misery and distortion? The law doesn't like to think about this aspect of its
subject, but novelists always do. Doctorow is drawn to such questions
in *The Book of Daniel*, and he is equipped to answer them through conflicting goals that he must reconcile as a writer. On the one hand, in "a
kind of parable of the novelist's birth," he learns to be a writer through
the "thrill of transgression." "I believe nothing of any beauty or truth
comes of a piece of writing without the author's thinking he has sinned
against something—propriety, custom, faith, privacy, tradition, political
orthodoxy, historical fact, literary convention, or indeed, all the prevail-
ing community standards together." On the other hand, the philosopher
in the novelist believes the best texts are sacred because they distribute
suffering so that it can be borne, and he assumes, in consequence, an
obligation "to construct a just world."[64]

To transgress, one needs a sense of order. To sin, one must believe
in the sacred. To portray injustice convincingly, one must envisage the
possibility of justice. To think otherwise means that the torments in life
occur just because of the way things are, and if that is the case, no one has
the right to call on a better dispensation no matter what happens to them.
Up against the need for justice, injustice necessarily has both personal
and civic dimensions in *The Book of Daniel*, and the one necessarily codes
the other.

Personal injustice, the moment Daniel enters his own lion's den, comes the day his mother is arrested and imprisoned. Rochelle Isaacson is beautiful to her son as the mother who provides for him; she becomes ugly, "almost waxen," when seen by the deserted child in prison. ("I realized she was no longer pretty to me.") The older Daniel, looking back, describes his pain this way: "She left behind a clean house, and in the icebox a peanut butter sandwich and an apple for lunch. In the afternoon I had my milk and cookies. And she never came home."[65]

There will be many other houses for Daniel Isaacson but never another clean, orderly home. He develops through adolescence incapable of loving anyone or anything. "Heart rejection is a problem," he notes conclusively near the end (293). The initial characteristic offered by the narrating protagonist is designed to horrify the reader: Daniel abuses his wife, Phyllis, as a matter of course. He calls her "the kind of sand dune that was meant to be kicked around" and marries her as his "sex martyr." His ingenuity in abuse of her forces an immediate confrontation with the reader. "And if the first glimpse people have of me is this," Daniel asks, "how do I establish sympathy?" (4–7).

There is no letup in this characterization. Daniel will burn his wife with a cigarette lighter while she pleads not to be hurt, put her in physical danger, strike her repeatedly, torture her in sex, and terrify her by abusing and jeopardizing their baby son. As a boy, Daniel had been a "little criminal of perception" capable of small acts of cruelty; he is now a monster (34). "Who are you anyway?" the domestic abuser asks the reader as he burns "the tender white girlflesh" of his wife. "Who told you you could read this?" Narratological hectoring of the reader is a frequent phenomenon in *The Book of Daniel,* and there is good reason for it. Insisting on the reader's complicity on every page, Daniel figuratively screams: "Look what you have done to me!" The elementary points for Daniel are the pain brought upon him by the reader's world and the loss of identity that this entails. His snarling voice clings to the reader in hatred as part of his sense of self. "If it is that elementary, then reader, I am reading you," he boasts. "And together we may rend our clothes in mourning" (54).

Knowledge of injustice compounds the problem of it in *The Book of Daniel.* It leads the knower not to a higher plane of realization but down into deeper caldrons of delusion and hatred, and the eventual outcome is worse than even the patterns dictate. A frequently used *Portable Guide to Federal Conspiracy Law* describes a conspiracy trial as a play cast in hell where no one should expect angels as actors.[66] Daniel Isaacson is one of those demonic actors. He has created a living hell for himself and those around him, and the basis of his damnation is clear. "Fathers and teachers, I am thinking, 'What is hell?'" asks Father Zossima in *The Brothers Karamazov*. "And I am reasoning thus: 'The suffering that comes from the consciousness that one is no longer able to love.'"[67]

Formal recognition of damnation comes late in the novel when Daniel confronts Linda Mindish, the daughter of Selig Mindish, the character in the novel who betrays the Isaacsons in the way that David Greenglass testified against the Rosenbergs. In an interesting variation on the historical reality, Doctorow makes the betrayer a friend rather than the family member that Greenglass was. As he once put the decision to *not* have a brother send his sister to the electric chair, "No work of fiction could make that believable. It's too incredible and unnatural and hideous."[68] The comment is useful because it suggests that Doctorow is interested in presenting only the more natural horrors that flow from injustice.

Sparring fitfully with Linda Mindish and noting their similarity, Daniel Isaacson sees that "we both live lives that accommodate an event neither of us were responsible for" and that as a result, in a refinement of his earlier perception, "there was enough hard corruption in Linda Mindish and me, flawless forged criminals of perception, to exhaust the fires of the sun." He experiences "the truth of his situation as an equitability of evil" in stock hell-fired terms. There is no relief for anyone. Linda and Daniel, too, are conspirators consigned to the flames. "This is what happens to us, to the children of trials," Daniel observes; "our hearts run to cunning, our minds are sharp as claws. Such shrewdness has to be burned into the eye's soul, it is only formed in fire" (272–75).

The civic dimension of injustice, as opposed to the personal, is easier to identify but harder for the novelist to render in dramatic form, and the difficulty forces him into a series of narrative alternatives. The Constitution appears conventionally enough as the narrator's symbol of "Thrift and Virtue and Reason and Natural Law and the Rights of Man," but the same document unleashes a "scream from the smiling face of America" over the one crime defined therein: treason (177). The bloody birthright of rebellion in 1776 has left the nation receptive to hysteria whenever the charge is made. "No crime can more excite and agitate the passions of men than treason," Chief Justice John Marshall warned in first defining the crime in court for the American nation, and Doctorow uses the insight.[69]

Daniel Isaacson takes up the premise by listing the traitors who have engrossed the national psyche from Benedict Arnold, to Aaron Burr, to the leaders of the Confederacy in the Civil War. He lampoons the most famous moment of reflexive hysteria over treason in American history but with a purpose in mind (177). When in 1765 Patrick Henry proclaimed against the Stamp Act that "Caesar had his Brutus, Charles the First his Cromwell, and George the Third—," the sequence prompted interrupting shouts of "Treason!" from the Virginia House of Burgesses. "And George the Third," countered Patrick Henry above the din, "may profit from their example—if this be treason make the most of it."[70] Daniel's deconstruction of the statement opens into vortices of sadism and self-pity:

> I say IF THIS BE TREASON MAKE THE MOST OF IT!
> If this bee is tristante make the mort of it
> If this be the reason make a mulch of it
> If this brie is in season drink some milk with it
> If this bitch is teasing make her post on it
> If this boy is breathing make a ghost of him (168)

Wordplay breaks down the patriotic response into the speaker's twisted obsessions, but the passage does more; it signifies that every generation will indeed make the most of treason. Here is Doctorow's challenge to the master narrative used to kill Julius and Ethel Rosenberg and their fictional counterparts Paul and Rochelle Isaacson. Rochelle, the more astute defendant, sees the narrative trap that has been set. Although she and her husband have been accused of conspiracy, Rochelle understands that they will really be convicted of treason and then executed for it. "Implications of treason," she remarks, "are fed like cubes of sugar to the twelve-headed animal which is Justice" (201).

Rochelle Isaacson is Doctorow's closest student of the trial transcript, and she observes that "the way questions are asked" have made treason the real charge. The jurors are a "twelve-headed animal" in their passivity. They are easily molded to the patriotic sleight of hand in the prosecution's narrative. Meanwhile, Rochelle fills in the gaps: "traitors, traitorous, treacherous, treasonous, betrayal, treachery," and lest the point be lost, Doctorow has her lawyer admit, "I do not think anyone sitting in the jury box is capable in the present atmosphere of under- standing such a distinction" (201).

Reason hurts those who grasp the truth in *The Book of Daniel*. Ro- chelle, who sees furthest and most carefully at trial, is damaged the most by it. In another and more hidden reference to Edgar Allan Poe, this time to his gothic tale "The Cask of Amontillado," a similarly malicious narra- tor builds a brick wall to bury alive the ironically named Fortunato. Paul Isaacson says the prosecutor and judges "are like bricklayers methodically sealing us up. But their arrogance will destroy them in the end" (197).[71]

Rochelle knows better and intuits their actual fate by watching the court mortise brick after brick. Unlike Paul, she has no illusions of justice. She realizes they cannot outlast the animosity of those who have accused them, and the method of her certainty is especially chilling. She fathoms the death sentence through the anger that she observes around her, "a sharp and penetrating reflection of her own incandescent hatred." In the deepest tragedy of the book, the burden of this knowledge turns a warm and loving woman into a figure of stone. Her name means rock. Most devastating of all, she injects a crystallized version of her hatred into her son and daughter, but what she cannot pass on is her dignity, her "regality of suffering" (189–91, 200–201, 123).

Rage without dignity or meaning explains why Daniel's account splin- ters in confusion. He narrates as a survivor who feels unworthy of res- cue.[72] His story, unleashed in fury and narcissistic self-loathing, cannot be told in a straight manner. It is beyond reason as a counter to the false reason that condemned his parents. In a master stroke, Doctorow makes Daniel a graduate student fruitlessly struggling to find his thesis topic. Much has been made of the ensuing turmoil in narrative strategies that make up the novel. Daniel jumbles fictional modes with the styles of memoir, essay, newspaper article, academic jargon, confession, episto- lary exchange, banner headline, calling card, and historical description. In wild shifts of form and tone, he challenges language itself and the ide- ology that it contains.[73] No one voice can be trusted to convey the face of injustice.

Omnipresent in all of this narrative confusion is the temperament of a middle-class adolescent who believes ghetto profanity is the coolest mode of communication. "You got the picture," Daniel demands of his reader. "This the story of a fucking, right? You pullin out yo lit-er-ary map, mutha? You know where we goin', right muthafuck?" (22–23). It is impossible to like this voice or the person behind it, unless you happen to be the helplessly loving parent, and Daniel has lost the parents who loved him. He is ludicrously proud of his "fuck-everyone persona" (290). Still, the narrating persona holds the reader. Doctorow knows the power in narrative gaps as well as anyone. As he once put his understanding in agreeing with Henry James, a writer must make the reader "guess the unseen from the seen."[74] Through indirection, the novelist displays poignancy in the rage of his narrator. Daniel is the irreducible product of mistakes that have been made by others.

One more narrative continuum, an organizational ploy on the part of the author, defies the master narrative at trial and creates further sympathy for the narrator as victim. A trial transcript is difficult to read straight through as narrative because in its procedural march it sticks to mundane levels and the everyday. The trick of the prosecution in the *Rosenberg* case was to turn the mundane into the extraordinary, a Jell-O box into a successful conspiracy to steal the atomic bomb. Doctorow adopts a counterstrategy. He uses the extraordinary and the celebratory to reach toward the unacceptable in the mundane and everyday, and he does it with a larger philosophical purpose in mind.

Four divisions make up *The Book of Daniel*: "Memorial Day" (1–96), "Halloween" (97–180), "Starfish" (181–258), and "Christmas" (259–303). Three of these smaller "books," as Doctorow labels them, depict savage reversals in the holiday spirit they normally epitomize. The fourth, "Starfish," conjures up the lost thirteenth constellation in the zodiac and stands for "serenity and harmony with the universe" in astrological notions of justice (250). As well, starfish represents the vegetative state that Daniel's catatonic sister Susan has entered on the way to her death. "There are not many degrees of life lower before there is no life" (207). This section features the trial of the Isaacson parents, and so the term also conjures up the injustice of "star chamber." No positive goes without a contrasting negative in a novel about how justice and happiness are lost.

The holiday sections are narrative signatures. "Memorial Day," set in 1967, illustrates the impossible bind of the Isaacson children as knowing adults. What patriotic sacrifice are they supposed to recall and honor? Daniel, the survivor, has been asked *not* to remember what is important to him. "The world wanted you to forget who you had been and what had happened to you." He puts the problem of Memorial Day with great accuracy: "You asked yourself why live in faith or memorial to the people who had betrayed you." The alternative, which the Isaacson children accept for a while, is the passive quotidian of ordinary existence, a new life with a new last name (Lewin) to help them move on. "Daniel and Susan Lewin slipped into the indolent rituals of the teenage middle class" (63). But they cannot relinquish what they are not supposed to remember. Memorial Day exists for them, too, but in an isolating fear from what others celebrate.

The terrifying second section of the novel, "Halloween," returns to 1950 with the arrests of the Isaacsons, the destruction of their home, the trauma of desertion for Daniel and Susan, and their heartrending attempt to return to their lost home on Halloween. This holiday marks the night when the spirits of evil walk the earth unmolested. A night of rampant fear, it is safely contained by the triumph of goodness the following morning, which is always All Saints' Day. Halloween in consumer caricature allows children to imagine the bogeyman and transgress by dressing up like him, a form of play where the extraordinary relieves the commonplace. All of these meanings apply in Doctorow's tale but with his customary twist. In *The Book of Daniel*, evil flourishes unchecked, childish nightmares become permanent facts, and fears run rampant instead of dissolving the next morning. "We are in the mood," the Isaacsons' lawyer states in the light of day, "that someone should pay for what we find intolerable" (118).

The final holiday in the last section of the book explains the message of the first two. "Christmas" puts Doctorow's stamp on the theme of the extraordinary becoming mundane. Daniel visits California to confront Selig Mindish (the David Greenglass figure) over Daniel's "theory of the other couple." He is trying to believe that his parents acted out of selfless heroism to protect another husband and wife, and he seeks verification, but there is no evidence for this assumption. Mindish, who is senile, offers only tears and an inarticulate Judas kiss for "Denny." Doctorow doubles the fantasy in this scene by presenting it as "Disneyland at Christmas." The meeting between Daniel and Selig Mindish takes place in the famous amusement park, which Doctorow describes as "a sentimental compression of something that is itself already a lie." The heart and soul of Disneyland, its cartoon characters, are "the collective unconsciousness of the community of the American Naïve" (285–93).

Disneyland works through artificially induced amazement, but in Doctorow's hands the commonplace constantly interrupts. "When you take the jungle river cruise the plants and animals on the banks betray their plastic being and electronic motivation." Tourists, surrounded by other tourists, find their effort of vicarious participation "thwarted by the mirror of others' eyes" (285–93). Doctorow risks such heavy-handedness to convey the delusion at work in his narrator's quest for importance. Daniel always worries on this score. "I thought we were big time," he notes as a boy. "I thought we were important people." The theory of the other couple is a last attempt to establish a transcendent familial identity, and Doctorow pauses to plow a last furrow of woe. The one positive thing that the trial of the Isaacsons gave their tormented son was a vision of their significance, and it turns out not to have been true. "I could never have appreciated how obscure we were," the older Daniel discloses, and he still cannot bring himself to the ultimate admission (93).[75]

Embedded within the novel through a tough *New York Times* reporter is the grain of a closer reality. Jack P. Fein delivers the primal scene of the Isaacson trial, the drab middle ground of reality in the *Rosenberg* case. A chain-smoking, weary newspaperman, Fein has the briefest of cameo appearances in the "Starfish" section on lost justice, but as the phonetics in the name imply, Jack *be* fine; he *is* fine and also right. "It was a piss-poor trial," Fein begins. "The case against them was nothing." The government's claim, he admits, was "Insane!" There had been no theft of the atomic bomb despite what the government said. "The Russians had everything they needed. They had all that stuff." Even so, the Isaacsons were not innocent. The rest of the story is what the narrator cannot possibly accept:

> In this country people don't get picked out of a hat to be put on trial for their lives. I don't know—your parents and Mindish had to have been into some goddamn thing. They *acted* guilty. They were little neighborhood commies probably with some kind of third-rate operation that wasn't of use to anyone except maybe it made them feel important. Maybe what they were doing was worth five years. (211–14)

Daniel has to ignore this clarification. He cannot afford to respond. If Fein is correct, one of the betrayals that the Isaacsons engage in, perhaps the worst of all, is that of their own children, whom they desert through a wrongheaded sense of self-importance. Notably, and unlike other accounts of the trial, Fein's sits alone and untouched deep within the novel. It is an irreducible concrete block of matter.

The ultimate mischief of injustice lies in the intellectual and social confusion it breeds. Doctorow uses the theme of betrayal, and the twofold reaction it produces to make this point. In betrayal, personal anxieties arise out of abandonment, but a corresponding communal fear stems from the inability to distinguish between kin and stranger, friend and foe, with the stranger predictably figured as foe.[76] Daniel Isaacson imbibes and passes on both forms of betrayal, and Doctorow provides another key to it.

Too much attention is given to the eponymous first name, Daniel the prophet in *The Book of Daniel*; not enough to the last. Daniel's surname *Isaacson* delivers its own multifaceted narrative of betrayal in one word. The biblical Isaac knows that his father tried to sacrifice him and that he was saved, not by Abraham, but by happenstance. Late in life, Isaac will be deceived again, this time by his own son, Jacob, who tricks his father and brother, Esau, out of the regular communal birthright due the eldest son. The circularity of betrayal in the father-son name of Isaacson leaves Daniel no place to stand. He will give his father's name, Paul, to his own son but shows little regard for either. When progenitor and progeny are equally unworthy, how can the speaker find worth or merit in a bewildering world? *The Book of Daniel* is about this problem. Justice cannot be built where such uncertainty reigns.

THE POSSIBILITY IN LAW AND LITERATURE

What can a novelist like E. L. Doctorow possibly accomplish in his desire to "construct a just world"? An unlikable and confused monstrosity, Daniel Isaacson misunderstands the legal workings of justice whenever he talks about them. He derides "American law" as "an institution that constantly fails," and he asks the wrong questions about it (155, 273). For if the law sometimes fails, it does not fail constantly. Only a naive observer would agree with Daniel, when he says, "If justice cannot be made to operate under the worst possible conditions of social hysteria, what does it matter how it operates at other times?" (226). It does matter. Justice in ordinary times is the pearl without price; it is the value to be fought for with life itself when necessary. And what right does Doctorow's puerile narrator have to attach the reader to his own monstrosity? In the manipulative narrative structure of *The Book of Daniel*, "the monstrous writer who places one word after another" captures a "monstrous reader who goes on from one word to the next" (246).

These questions go to the heart of what the connection between law and literature can accomplish and what it cannot. Doctorow claims that a novelist serves as "a Distant Early Warning System in the defense of reality" and that "the artist who displays the elusiveness of historical truth in his work is performing a legitimate function."[77] The law lost sight of reality in the *Rosenberg* case, and the novelist enters the historical situation as an aid to its recovery. When "the investigative apparatus" of a trial fails to "apprehend factual reality," Doctorow believes that such failure enters the realm of fiction in search of what has been lost and must be gained again:

> Using the tested rules of evidence and accrued wisdom of our system of laws we determine the guilt or innocence of defendants and come to judgment. Yet the most important trials in our history, those which reverberate in our lives and have most meaning for our future, are those in which the judgment is called into question: Scopes, Sacco and Vanzetti, the Rosenbergs. Facts are buried, exhumed, deposed, contradicted, recanted. There is a decision by the jury and, when the historical and prejudicial context of the decision is examined, a subsequent judgment by history. And the trial shimmers forever with just that perplexing ambiguity of a true novel.[78]

The novelist claims to be able to speak in such a case not just to a reader but to a collective citizenry that needs to recover discarded realities in order to comprehend what it has done and should not do again.

If the law decides to criticize itself, it does so later, rather quietly, and as constructively as possible. More frequently, it puts aside a result it can no longer help. It is no accident that barely half a dozen articles about "the crime of the century" appeared in American law journals between 1954 and 1977; nor that "most historical surveys of the Supreme Court do not treat the case in detail and some fail to mention it at all."[79] Pragmatic and ever ongoing, the law looks to justice as the condition of its operations. Injustice is "a surprising abnormality" when it appears at all.

It has no philosophical heft in legal thought; it is rather a disturbance or embarrassment to be overcome by its opposite, and it rarely functions as the preoccupation that justice always must be in professional understandings.[80]

In reaction, imaginative literature concentrates on the high price of injustice when law is its subject. Routine justice, the desideratum in court, is boring in fiction, and novelists adjust by eschewing legal normalities for the unrecognized range of individuals hurt by a dubious decision. The transcript of the *Rosenberg* case is a legal, unchangeable fact, but it interests the writer of fiction because it violates the first rule of legal inquiry: *solam veritatem spectat justitia* (justice looks at truth alone). In this vein, *The Book of Daniel* responds to what still needs to be faced in the *Rosenberg* case. It writes out what injustice can do to the legal system, to its performers, to those it judges too severely, and to the surrounding community. We learn that no one wins and everyone loses when injustice is committed.

There is one other contribution literature makes on a legal theme that the law rarely articulates, and again *The Book of Daniel* is an important source. Daniel's insistence on the complicity of his reader registers at a more subtle level. Two thousand years ago the greatest lawyer of antiquity invented a concept that no social system can afford to be without, even though the idea rarely appears in the language of a court. Cicero defined it in an awkward phrase: "quibus infertur, si possunt, non propulsant iniuram": "those, who when they can, do not shield from wrong those upon whom it is being inflicted."[81]

This concept, "passive injustice," is rarely actionable and easily evaded in collective consciousness. Complicity in a wrong allowed to happen requires little or no agency, but it appears frequently in literature, where those who see injustice but do nothing about it can be held up to view and dramatized for the reader. Passive injustice is such a useful idea because it depends on an optimistic premise: it exposes what a community *should have* but *fails* to give its legal system. As a tool of correction and accusation, it assumes *we know enough to be just*.[82] We grant a measure of credence to Daniel Isaacson's grotesque mind because we want to find out where we went wrong as a culture. E. L. Doctorow asks us to examine why and how the country failed to come to its senses in 1951.

Disneyland at the novel's end is an appropriate device for summarizing this problem. The amusement park symbolizes a society wallowing in its material well-being. In Doctorow's words, it is where "the final consumer moment may be said to be complete," where "the ideal Disney patron" receives "his culminating and quintessential sentiment at the moment of a purchase" (289). Doctorow will make the same point more directly in *Ragtime* when he declares the average American citizen "dreams not of justice but of being rich."[83] How true is this observation? *The Trial in American Life* turns next to high-profile trials in the ever-more commercialized consumer culture of today, and there is danger in the offing. When he documented the spread of passive injustice long ago, Cicero wrote: "Avarice is generally the controlling motive."[84]

✶ PART THREE ✶

In Court Today

The trials studied in the last section changed the way Americans thought about their country. Taken together they prove that overwhelming powers of persuasion reach to and away from a courtroom. They also reveal disturbing patterns at work: the greater the controversy in a high-profile trial, the stronger the public desire for a subsuming narrative with victory for one side or the other; also the greater the likelihood of serious competition between legal and nonlegal narratives.

Few aspects of social thought rival the concentration and imaginative expression generated when people care deeply about a legal decision, and we have seen that what is imbibed from that decision is often an indicator of larger ideological change. Gauging similar influences in the present will be more difficult, the present always being tangled to those immersed in it, but there is one advantage in taking that next step. Courtroom events are indicators of timely pressures during their moments of performance.

Previous chapters also have shown that the nature, the intensity, and, above all, the scale of interactions between courtrooms and their communities have increased, bringing heightened pressures to bear on the legal system. Proliferations in the degree, range, number, immediacy, and impact of reportage on courtroom events represent the most obvious changes. From the first national newspaper coverage of a trial with Aaron Burr in 1807, to the far-flung daily accounts that the telegraph allowed in John Brown's trial in 1859, to the impact of news photography on the trial and execution of Mary Surratt after the assassination of Abraham Lincoln, to the excesses of yellow journalism in the Haymarket Riot trials toward the end of the nineteenth century, and on to radio and the edge of the television age with the Rosenbergs in 1951—each new stage in publication brought exponential increases in the degree of exposure with related implications for the nature of a public trial.

The trajectory of these pressures is not just greater now; it is different altogether in the context of postmodern telecommunications. Advances in technology have altered the way we think about a trial, and they have influenced the kind of trial that now captures the imagination of a community. Advances in the electronic tools of observation have improved access to the extent that seeing on a screen can be more intimate than an experience in court. This new vantage point has raised interest but also increased emotionalism as well as the desire for engagement in massive audiences attracted by trial conflict. The ensuing trade-offs between greater understanding and mass appeal are vexed issues in protecting the public nature of a fair trial today, and they are taken up in chapter 8, "The Trial in Television America," for the problems and opportunities they present.

A discerning people must watch even while it trusts the law when it is placed under such pressure, but proper discernment is not easily gauged when the terms of perception change. An electronically fed image culture is complicating previous distinctions between private and public, knowledge, observation and participation, reception as opposed to actual perception. Comprehension of a public trial now comes through video projection with recognition dictated by voice-overs, sound bites, pictorial bombardment, action sequencing, reaction shooting, zoom camera movement, and constant but very selective repetition. Broadcasting reaches a huge but impersonal audience, one in which the sender cannot know the receiver or what has been understood in reception. From the other side, an individual viewer must cope in isolation with a regime of seemingly authoritative appearances but without the benefit of full sensory perception or context.

Under these influences, the right to a public trial has undergone modification without redefinition. Unparalleled media hype, global surveillance, manipulated transmission, and on-the-spot editorializing allow reportage to intrude on the legal process as never before. Reception, too, is unprecedented; it can respond as well as receive through Internet messaging. Anyone with access to computer technology can reach a ready public about a trial in progress, which means that unsettled questions about guilt or innocence now belong to a vast chat room of unguarded opinion and commentary.

The eighteenth-century formulators of the constitutional right to a public trial could not foresee the scope, control, and reactive feasibilities of current reportage, and yet the right, if it is to remain a right on anything like original terms, must serve the same legal priorities established then while adjusting to the unavoidable electronic forms of awareness that determine public opinion today. What should an interested observer of a trial get to see when so much is technically available to be seen by so many and when actual seeing improves insight while also triggering unwarranted engagement?

Chapter 9, "Seeing Justice Done," seeks answers to this question and others brought on by changing conditions. Technology has created a paradox in the perception of courtroom events. Just as courtrooms are vulnerable to media exploitation, so the public trial has never been more available for effective observation, but too often these conflicting priorities get argued out on a level of principle divorced from context. The proponents of free speech and freedom of the press vie with equally righteous guardians of the right to a fair trial, and each side insists on an all-or-nothing proposition: either outright prohibition of television coverage or general acquiescence on more or less media terms.

There are no easy answers to this paradox. Distortions occur when a legal system allows the conventions of television coverage to dominate presentation as it did in the 1994 trial of O.J. Simpson. But if a video presence can exacerbate passions, there is a meaningful distinction between observing a trial and reading about one. The choreography of the legal process, its aggressively visual aspect, assumes that justice must be *observed* to be trusted. But by whom and under what circumstances? Meanwhile, the alternative of restricting observation to courtroom observers with an outright ban on video coverage solves little. No matter what the law does or does not do, a high-profile trial today receives saturation coverage that shapes opinion outside and inside the courtroom. When television is denied access, its reporters shape opinion by focusing on those available to it just outside of a courtroom with all of the added slant that the absence of meaningful controls brings.

Visual reception is the condition of attention in an image-based culture, and the legal system must work with that imperative if it is to maintain an informed citizenry. At the same time, the reflex of entertainment in television culture is not an acceptable standard for following court-room events, and it must be countered despite its pervasive presence. The connections previously drawn between law and literature can be useful because they open the relation between courtrooms and their communi-ties to a more dynamic understanding; the tools of interpretation devel-oped in earlier sections can suggest ways out of the impasse. Whatever is done, a more sophisticated approach to how language works in the nexus of legal procedure and audience reception should improve recognition of the line between public understanding and mere publicity.

A different kind of balance between legal and media rights needs to be struck, even though a meaningful one will draw objections from all sides. It needs to be struck because the haphazard development in cur-rent arrangements is becoming unacceptable against what a trial is sup-posed to do and be. Even the most egregious mistakes in legal history that have been analyzed in these pages can happen again anytime anywhere, and the possibility increases as trials are watched on more careless and promiscuous terms.

In the most alarming development, postmodern coverage of high-profile trials has entered the commercial forum with contingencies that are dangerous for all concerned. For while we accept them in almost every other walk of life, the power and profitability of commercialism have no place in proximity to a courtroom. When justice becomes just another commodity to be marketed between the spot sales of home products and nostrums for personal health, we come that much closer to defining the law by what sells. Just as worrisome, appetites are catered to instead of vigilance maintained.

Legal procedures are inherently fragile. They break down under pres-sure, and then courts find themselves in the dock alongside of defen-dants. Even so, the new pressures are unavoidable. There is no choice but to ride the postmodern tiger of media intrusion. One way or another, the people will watch what is available to them in a high-profile trial when the spirit moves them, as it often does, and what they see changes the way they think. The law hides from this popular gaze at its peril. Safety, as before, lies in an educated citizenry, but for that to be achieved in the existing climate, there must be a more measured control of interests and needs. It is time to react more creatively. We can no longer live with the extreme of outright rejection or, just as dangerously, with a resigned, sup-posedly pragmatic shrug over the momentum called progress.

CHAPTER EIGHT

The Trial in Television America

THE IMPACT OF TELEVISION

There are good reasons for confusion over the impact of television on contemporary life. The omnipresence of TV resists isolation of its effects, and constant shifts in technology complicate analysis at every turn. Commentary also tends toward the histrionic. Although patterns of video reception can be identified, they do not justify sweeping claims that television manipulates how Americans have stopped thinking. Disdainful intellectual elites call television a "boob tube" and "chewing gum for the brain." Programming "dumbs down" thought into "shriveled and absurd" terms, leaving Americans "sillier by the minute." Media specialists reply to these jibes by claiming television is "the foremost medium for cross-demographic communication" and has brought heightened literacy to the culture. "New forms of citizenship" have acquired a "vast, rolling, cumulative oral 'archive' of common knowledge that is both mined and made by television."[1]

These debates are as silly as they are frequent—based, as they are, on a question in need of reformulation. Are viewers "a passive and helpless mass incapable of discrimination," or are they canny eyewitnesses making "their own socially pertinent meanings out of the semiotic resources provided by television"? They are either or both depending on transmission and reception. Powers of observation are enhanced or diminished not by the fact of television but by its modes of presentation. It follows that closer attention to context can minimize pointless controversy. This chapter responds by concentrating on the coverage of well-known courtroom events as a control group—not in another rehearsal of twice-told tales but to illustrate the nature of transmission in the high-profile trial of today.

What are the attributes of television that allow, facilitate, promote—or, alternatively, dictate and control—a viewer's understanding? Recent criticism on the influence of television removes one level of controversy by rejecting a frequent bromide: the claim of objectivity. The eye of television is never neutral; its control of the angle of vision is absolute. The gaze of the camera leaves just one alternative (the option of looking away), and it fights this alternative by threatening the beholder with loss of continuity. The constricted frame of reception, the TV screen, privileges the personal, ignores background elements, and disembodies viewing, all of which rob the recipient of material place. The typical setting of a broadcast can be almost anywhere; we depend on being told where we are.[2]

Television dictates importance through the pictorial. That which cannot be seen is ignored or artificially converted into an image that will serve. Entertainment is a key value. Television is wedded to fascination over moving images, and its compulsions are basically recreational. Rapid camera cutting is used to hold a viewer through surprise and excitement, and the need of that viewer to keep up interrupts reflection until after reception. An emphasis on audience levels naturally increases the focus on entertainment. The number of sets turned to a station are the primary gauge of success. Since advertising and ratings determine what appears, programmers easily conflate what viewers want to see with what sells. Then, too, the intimacy of video imagery blurs distinctions between public and private sensibilities. The need to see closely disregards distance and space, breaking down formalities. Television loves exposure over description, affect over contemplation.

Debate over these attributes tends to falter over which traits are intrinsic to the medium and which are conventions established over time. In so many ways, all of television appears the prisoner of its forms, but even though forms control, programming is contingent on decision making, a point often missed. Even insiders are captured by the conventions they have created, and it is natural and vocationally expedient for them to mistake arbitrary developments for inherent characteristics. When the conveniences in any medium enjoy free rein, they become formulaic urgencies.

Story lines in network broadcasting typify this process of routinization. They are invariably fast moving, certain in thematic assurances of good against evil, and emphatically conclusive; no loose end ever remains untied for long in programming. Television, as it has evolved, welcomes dramatic excess, insists on firm moral resolution, and, in its need for both all of the time, it cannot stand silence for even a moment. Image controls sound in television, but sound sets the scene. To be placed, a viewer must trust a speaker, whether character or voice-over and this need extends to the most nefarious speaker of all, background music. Consider, for example, how frequently a tragic moment in a television story is foreordained by ominous music; with a given tone established, a viewer feels fear even before the designated victim becomes aware of danger.

All of these manipulations are crucial concerns for present purposes, and to the extent that they control perception, they raise questions about the coverage of factual events and official occasions, but not all of the manipulations are on the side of the transmitter. The explosion in cable broadcasting and the Internet have placed stores of knowledge and the ability to respond to them at the touch of a finger in a receiver's home. More people who follow events can find whatever they want to know more easily and quickly than ever before, and they are in a better position to compare sources of dissemination.

The two-way flow of information is unprecedented, and in communal terms, the immediacy of mass reception stimulates a mutual awareness that amounts, at times, to a collective impulse. The minimal channels in original broadcasting have become a plethora of choice. The vast range of options now available empowers subcultures to articulate their inclinations, and if these subcultures remain tenuous, they are sufficiently present to complicate questions about whether or not television consolidates or dissipates power, and they give scope to minority interests.

Attempts to balance the slate between manipulations and opportunities almost always fall back on the side of manipulation. "Among critics and researchers," writes one of the few experts to seek such a balance, "anxiety about the potential of television to hinder the formation and communication of knowledge . . . far outweighs any sense of its positive capacities either in presenting knowledge in new ways or in extending the range of the knowledgeable in different fields."[3] These negative inclinations explain why most professional discussions of cameras in courtrooms end in rejection. The typical account argues that "television trial coverage is inherently at odds with courtroom accounts of the case." Asked recently about televising trials, Associate Justice Antonin Scalia replied: "There's something sick about making entertainment out of real people's legal problems."[4]

These comments and others like them presuppose the dominant patterns used in broadcasting today, and they will continue to control understandings as long as the purveyors of television are allowed to hold to their own industrial norms. No one in the law will argue that standards in entertainment or the use of sound and image bites should dominate appreciation of a trial in progress, and television broadcasting of trials fuels opposition by adhering wherever it can to the practices that have insured success in regular commercial programming. Accordingly, the first step toward a better understanding of media coverage of the courtroom must be away from entrenched positions and toward a more nuanced appreciation of reciprocal needs, issues, and possibilities.

There are flexibilities to be explored on both sides. Many practices in television are *not* inevitable consequences but contingencies born of historical circumstance.[5] The impact of television, however great, does *not* automatically take the act of interpretation away from a viewer. The illusion of reality does *not* prevent a viewer from making calculations about the authenticity of an event. The chatter of "talking heads" does *not* define what a viewer agrees to accept. The proposition that video coverage is "inherently at odds" with courtroom processes is *not* as obvious as one might think. Moreover, seeing is still believing in the law. Louis Brandeis expressed the idea most succinctly. "Sunlight," he wrote in his own discussion of how to correct social ills, "is said to be the best of disinfectants."[6]

THE QUESTIONS IN TELEVISION COVERAGE

If outside opinion can influence a trial, all media coverage becomes suspect at some level. Nightly reporting reaches for the excitement rather than the substance of legal procedure. Can this excitement translate back into the courtroom? Yes, it can. Do comments to the press by participants affect a trial? Lawyers regularly hold press conferences on courthouse steps because they believe their words reach inside. Will a network's fifteen-second segment from a televised trial control what a casual viewer remembers? Probably. Does the slant of that segment, repeated many times in daily coverage, influence participants? Legal counsel watch news segments of their own trials to gauge what plays well, and some admit to adjusting their behavior in reaction. No matter what they say, jury members and witnesses also watch. Does the vast unseen audience in a televised trial change performance in court? Size of audience always alters a speaker's rhetorical delivery. Do the excesses of television broadcasting encourage similar behavior at trial, and does gavel-to-gavel viewing complicate problems implicit in all coverage? Many legal professionals claim that they do.[7]

Even if distortion in a televised trial is somehow avoidable, critics want to know why we should take the risk in the first place. Does a televised trial educate the public or merely stimulate it beyond what it would normally think about an event? The established norms of broadcasting leave plenty of room for doubt over this question. A viewer who comes to a trial with standard viewing expectations can easily come away misinformed. Conventional television, with its focus on personality, turns trial participants into celebrities and generates undue identification with a person who has achieved that status.[8] The eye of the camera—particularly the zoom lens and reaction shots—can bring a measure of soap opera to courtroom coverage. Cameras can also confuse public and private boundary lines through close-ups and sequence shots unavailable to an observer in court.

The identification of good against evil in the quick, know-it-all format of entertainment television lends itself to another misconception. Prime-time series on law enforcement situate a viewer and foretell their conclusions. Good and evil are readily distinguishable early on, and the triumph or at least recognition of goodness occurs in one hour of programming with many shortcuts taken. Shows like *Law & Order* and *Boston Legal* do not always let their protagonists win, but followers of the show receive enough early information—information that would be unavailable in a trial—to know where justice lies. Reasonable doubt almost always translates into absolute certainty on the screen. A trial, on the other hand, strives to hold off preconceptions during proceedings. Jurors are told to avoid the kind of intuitive leaps that are welcomed in the flow of stereotypical television imagery; they must relinquish the omniscient perspective in entertainment programming and give up stock assumptions about behavior and appearances if a fair decision is to be reached.[9]

Critics reinforce these objections by invoking *People v. Orenthal James Simpson*, held in the Superior Court of Los Angeles County and ending only after thirteen months of media frenzy on October 3, 1995. Many of the distortions from conventional broadcasting applied in the televised murder trial of O.J. Simpson. The immediacy of television forced coverage toward tabloid excitement with pandering to celebrity status, gossip, and sexual innuendo. Video coverage also helped to prolong a trial that exhausted and alienated everyone, including a nation that averaged 2.2 million viewers a day. An estimated 150 million Americans, a third of the nation and the largest TV audience ever, watched the verdict, and instantaneous video coverage of the impact of "not guilty" dramatized racial divisions in viewer response. Every major participant played to the cameras, and the intimacy of camera angles impinged upon the usual dignity and ceremony in court. No one knew where or how to stop. There were 121 video hookups, 2,000 reporters, 45,000 pages of transcription, 126 witnesses called, 16,000 objections raised with 7,000 sustained, and daily press conferences by counsel seeking an untoward advantage inside the courtroom.[10]

These excesses affected both local and national understandings during the *Simpson* trial. The celebrity status of the handsome and impeccably dressed defendant and his counsel led to public cheering sections for Simpson's release. Video coverage separated perceptions inside and outside of court when a recording of racist epithets by a perjured police officer received plenty of play in public broadcasting but only brief exposure before the jury. Courtroom cameras fabricated emotionalism through reaction shots of the defendant, the defendant's mother, and families of the victims at disturbing moments of proceedings. The defense would win its case when it drowned the acknowledged complexities of the crime in a television-style melodrama of good against evil. Simpson would be acquitted when racism was unmasked in the Los Angeles Police Department.[11]

Broadcasters, for their part, covered the *Simpson* trial as if it were a sporting event. Daily commentary fixed on who had won or lost ground in each session with projections over what this meant for final victory or defeat. So intrusive were television commentators that other analysts accused them of influencing the outcome, some arguing that a ban on television would have produced a guilty verdict. This and other criticisms leveled against *People v. Simpson* brought a backlash against cameras in courtrooms everywhere. Judge Gilbert S. Merritt, chair of the Executive Committee of the Judicial Conference of the United States, summarized the general view: "Lawyers, judges, and the public have been influenced by the perception that cameras are not good for trial because of the Simpson case."[12]

Everyone thinks first of the problems instead of the learning experience that *People v. Simpson* provided. The video excesses in the case were unfortunate, but there is reason to believe that this trial passed an initial test of relevance in the decision to televise it. What trial, if any, deserves to be televised? Mere voyeurism is not a public interest worthy of protection. Neither the simple desire to see, nor obvious curiosity over the murders of a celebrity-hero's glamorous ex-wife and her friend, nor the wish to watch the celebrity-hero squirm under the charge can justify national viewing. The *Simpson* trial attracted attention for these reasons, but the factors that made the trial noteworthy were of a more substantive nature, and they kindled an intracommunal conflict in which many citizens perceived a threat—surely one criterion for televising a trial already public.

The perceived threat in the *Simpson* case belonged to a legacy that needed to be answered. In one of the shrewdest comments amidst much dross on *People v. Simpson*, the critic Stanley Crouch observed that "race is such a large decoy that it almost always causes us to get very important things wrong."[13] Televising *People v. Simpson* furnished an educational experience for all viewers in this regard. Communal horrors were at work here. The accusation of a crime by a black man against a white woman with whom he has been connected triggered thoughts of long-standing rituals of injustice in American culture. For 350 years the twisted social insight into such a defendant—if indeed the accused had the good fortunate to make it into a courtroom before he was punished—assumed his guilt. The shameful nature of this legacy explains why minority Americans could celebrate Simpson's acquittal.

The verdict of not guilty for O.J. Simpson proved three things: first, that a black man, though perhaps only one with every advantage, might receive a substantial benefit of the doubt; second, that racist attitudes still permeated law-enforcement processes to the detriment of all minorities accused of crime; and third, that an oblivious white culture had to recognize these issues. One can disagree with the verdict and still find that Simpson as a black defendant tied to a murdered white ex-wife functioned beyond the categories of athletic hero, movie star, defendant on trial for murder, domestic abuser, and defendant subsequently found guilty of wrongful death actions in civil court. Significantly, minorities who welcomed the criminal verdict did not protest when Simpson received a subsequent guilty verdict in civil court, and no one has complained since over the "status degradation ceremonies" that the released defendant has suffered from his descent into a communal pariah. Simpson figures now not as a celebrity but as a symbol of the lessons that his trial and the televising of it taught.[14]

An educational function is not the only silver thread in the seemingly gloomy prospect of cameras in courtrooms. Many of the complaints about television coverage can be trimmed or eliminated with careful camera work and a proper sense of restraint. The arrangement of a courtroom relies on familiar forms and rituals that can be duplicated in video transmission, and the same option applies to the choreography of movements in a trial, all of which take place in a carefully defined space that projection can replicate if it chooses to do so. Half of the battle in correct coverage may lie in confining video technology to what is needed instead of allowing it the scope of what it can do.

The affinities that exist between video programming and legal procedure are not as apparent as the differences, but there are parallels to work with, including comparable emphasis on story lines, portrayal of conflict, dramatic presentation, and desire for a clear-cut resolution. Many problems in broadcasting trials begin in the careless transfer of these affinities from commercial programming to courtroom coverage without adjustment to the new forum. Left unplumbed is the degree to which the differences can be minimized with integrity. No one, after all, objects to the simple ability to watch a trial. In the words of a proponent of televised trials, "If you ask real people what was wrong with the O.J. Simpson case they will not say that what was wrong with it is that they got to see it!"[15]

Still another argument for televising trials reaches beyond education and feasibility. Evidence suggests that more people accept a judgment if they have had the chance to watch it take place. We have seen how much damage simple distortion of a trial can cause in the aftermath of reactions. With some justification, proponents of televised trials claim viewers give more credence to solutions that they have actually observed even if they disagree with some of what took place. Although no one liked the accused rapist on trial, "many people who watched the William Kennedy Smith rape case [in Palm Beach County Court in 1991] understood how the jury found him not guilty. The same was true for the hung juries in the [first] murder trials of the Menendez brothers [in Los Angeles Superior Court in 1994 for killing their parents]."[16] Visually conveyed information eases explanation in an image-oriented culture. Television is the provider of *knowing how something happened* along with *what happened* as more and more people take their news entirely from this source.[17]

In effect, courts today have no choice but to reconsider the accuracy, the proper form, and the desired means of video transmission of trials. The reality is already upon us. Subject to judicial discretion, most states allow the possibility. If the use of that discretion has been exercised mostly against broadcasting, the availability of the mechanism reflects a process of change that cannot be ignored.[18] Video transmission offers an ever-cheaper means of recording a trial than manual transcription. Taping will soon be a cost-cutting alternative in all jurisdictions, and as that happens, wider transmission becomes an available resource rather than a special arrangement.[19]

Of course, video recording does not mean general broadcasting, and the puzzle of where to draw the line remains. One can hardly expect a home audience to follow the mundane realities and achieve the perception levels that deference extracts from a live audience in a courtroom. Television broadcasters try to avoid these difficulties by insisting on entertainment modes—voice-over play-by-play and camera cutting—as requirements in holding audiences.[20] But these celebrated means of holding audiences are really part of the ratings game, and they inflame competitive instincts and false investments through their deliberate correspondences to athletic contests. All told, failure to control the reflexive excesses in television broadcasting would seem to tip the scales away from open cameras in courtrooms.

THE HIGH-PROFILE TRIAL AND POSTMODERNITY

Media frenzies during noteworthy trials have become such a staple of our times that dozens of instances will come to mind. Postmodern telecommunication techniques have exacerbated the three characteristics already identified in the makeup of a high-profile trial: *spread of conflict* (the legal issue provokes larger controversy); *surprise* (the unexpected throws the law off balance); and *iconography* (a vivid persona brings added interest). The first event to drive the law across the boundary from modern into postmodern coverage probably took place in 1976. In that year a small-time, lifelong criminal in Utah, an unpleasant and dangerous customer in every social situation, became a national celebrity on the front page of newspapers across the country. Movie rights to his story were fought over; his trite poetry was analyzed in major magazines; and a ballad of his life appeared in *Time*.[21]

Gary Gilmore achieved this status by making himself the first person to be executed in the United States in a decade. Refusing to appeal his conviction for murder, he died on January 17, 1977, before a firing squad, the mechanism that he selected for himself. *Furman v. Georgia*, a decision of the Supreme Court in 1972, had forced a temporary halt to executions, but subsequent decisions, especially *Gregg v. Georgia* in 1976, had outlined procedures for redrafting death penalty statutes for their resumption, and thirty-five states, including Utah, rushed to comply. Three hundred fifty-eight other inmates were with Gilmore on death row in 1977, and he was the first of many to die. Since then nearly a thousand men and women have been executed for crimes committed in the United States.[22]

Gilmore presented a relatively easy case in trial court. At thirty-five, he had spent eighteen of his last twenty-two years in prison on a variety of offenses. His longest stretch of freedom had been eight months at the age of thirteen. He brought a long history of violence into court from episodes in and out of prison, he had tried to escape from prison, he had been a factor in prison riots, he had failed attempts at rehabilitation in optimal situations, and he had declared himself ready to kill again. His trial in the District Court of Utah County for one of two cold-blooded murders in a two-day span—both of subdued, helpless victims during robberies—had been straightforward, careful, and conclusive. The prosecution gained the death penalty not with ideological claims but through reasoned argument: "Nobody who ever comes in contact with him is going to be safe, if they happen to have something that he happens to want. . . . He's a danger if he escapes, he's a danger if he doesn't." If the death penalty made sense for anyone, it made sense for Gary Gilmore.

Controversy over the death penalty, as such, insured a spread of conflict into the community, but it was an element of surprise together with the personality of the doomed convict that took media coverage to unprecedented and unsavory levels of intensity. Gary Gilmore startled everyone after trial by announcing that he wanted to die, and he expressed it with a hip insouciance that made him seem heroic and the courts foolish. "You sentenced me to die," he announced during review processes. "Unless it's a joke or something, I want to go ahead and do it." Arguing more formally before the Utah Supreme Court, he would observe: "I was given a fair trial. The sentence was proper. I'm willing to accept it like a man and wish it to be carried out without delay."[23]

Gilmore knew how to play with the situation. As he asked, "Don't the people of Utah have the courage of their conviction?" Queried about the gory prospect of a firing squad, he answered: "Blood and guts, yeah, man, that really appeals to me. I'm gonna take a spoon." Reporters compared him in court to the movie star Robert De Niro. A nearly successful suicide pact with what *Newsweek* identified as his "twenty-year-old death-house fiancée" and a hunger strike lent added sincerity as well as bravado to Gilmore's assertions and sparked media fires with daily side stories.

A media blitz of this kind can be misleading because it frequently fails to convey the real complexity of a situation, and it can flatten or ignore legal considerations of greater note. Obsession with the story line of a "death wish" in the *Gilmore* case was typical for ignoring an underlying truth. The convicted man sought his own execution for a reason: he could no longer tolerate life in a maximum-security prison—a life that no outsider ever wants to contemplate for more than a moment in the depth of its degradations. "I've spent too much time in jail," Gilmore observed. "I don't have anything left in me."[24]

The approaching execution brought new forms of excess. Movie companies offered lucrative contracts on Gilmore's life—but only if the execution took place. A television station petitioned to cover the execution live; newspapers joined. Denied access, three hundred reporters came anyway, mostly to cover each other; they lobbied to hear the actual shots. Aware that the press would hire helicopters, prison authorities arranged the execution for indoors, and they were not wrong. A news helicopter violated airspace to catch Gilmore as he was transferred to be killed. *Saturday Night Live* televised a parody of the execution. *Time* and *Newsweek* ran a macabre before-and-after: they juxtaposed photographs of Gilmore eating his last meal against others of the stained and bullet-pocked chair in which he had been shot. "In the face of death," Dostoyevsky once wrote, "life has an absolute value."[25] Media coverage of this case reversed that proposition. In the face of Gary Gilmore's death, the living trivialized themselves in a thousand ways.

Can such communal shame be avoided? Probably not. This is what we are. Saturation multimedia, instantaneous coverage—the hallmarks of postmodern communications—debases sensibilities when attracted to an occasional event. Critics who self-righteously claim to rise above it offer no gauge for drawing a line between acceptable and unacceptable publicity. They rely instead on the vagaries of good taste, a sliding scale dependent on context and need. The same sensational coverage, the same voyeurism, the same feeding frenzies, and the same tendency to manipulate news accounts characterized another postmodern trial only to receive praise for the publicity involved. Saturation coverage, it seems, turns into a plus when reception finds a social value in the issue covered.

On January 30, 1989, Joel B. Steinberg, a New York lawyer, was convicted of first-degree manslaughter in the State Supreme Court of Manhattan for beating to death six-year-old Lisa Steinberg, his informally adopted daughter. The trial lasted thirteen weeks with fifty witnesses called, but the testimony of Steinberg's longtime female companion, Hedda Nussbaum, insured the verdict. Nussbaum had herself been severely and repeatedly beaten by Steinberg. At the time of her arrest with Steinberg, she needed treatment for nine fractured ribs, a broken nose, a fractured jaw, and an ulcerated leg barely saved from amputation; her face remained disfigured on the televised witness stand thirteen months later. A contributing factor in Lisa Steinberg's death, Nussbaum testified for seven days. She appeared as a previously charged co-defendant turned cooperating witness and immediately became the video stand-in for the missing victim.

People v. Steinberg is important because it was one of the first trials to galvanize an enormous viewing public through gavel-to-gavel television coverage. The *New York Times* found "brilliant television" while "wallowing in misery" because it was "only human to crave sensation." Perhaps appalled by these admissions, the *Times* would try to extricate itself by positing "a redeeming possibility." Its editors argued that "reliving on television one child's terrible death can arouse in a large audience the will to prevent the deaths of many others." Whether driven by salacious or civic-minded sensibilities, the huge impact of television clearly controlled the importance of the event. Ratings, the *Times* reported, went "through the roof," the reason for writing an editorial in the first place.[26]

What *was* the impact of television on the *Steinberg* trial? Even the participants—judge, counsel, witnesses, jury, and defendant—differed sharply over the influence that cameras in the courtroom had on proceedings. Presiding Judge Harold Rothwax thought the cameras had been neutral or beneficial. Jurors and witnesses confessed their fascination over broadcast segments but resented nightly news coverage. The main defense counsel for Steinberg, Ira London (called "the spin lawyer" by reporters), welcomed cameras. The prosecutors, Peter Casolaro and John McCusker, avoided the press outside of court and regretted cameras in it. Hedda Nussbaum's lawyer, Barry Scheck, predictably bridged both stances in keeping with his client's own liminal status between the prosecution and the defense. He spoke often with the press but only, he said, to improve public opinion regarding his client, and then like the prosecutors, he questioned the cameras. The exposed defendant, Steinberg, naturally believed that cameras kept him from receiving a fair trial. Most startling of all were the differences of opinion of those in court over whether Hedda Nussbaum, the crucial witness, looked better or worse, more or less vulnerable, more or less believable, more or less a victim, on television or in the courtroom.[27]

Television appeared to help or hurt depending on where one stood in the case. Disputes over broadcasting mirrored one's interests, and when they didn't, they reflected the general rhetorical muddle over the influence of television on thought. Did lawyers and the judge engage in immoderate behavior because of cameras, or did they behave better in court? Participants ranged themselves on different sides of this issue. Apparent to everyone, however, was the overwhelming impact of Hedda Nussbaum on the screen. In court you saw her slow and hampered movements; on television the zoom lens made her ravaged face a symbol. Wrote a lawyer officially involved in deciding whether trials should be televised in New York, "Only TV . . . could have imprinted upon us the unforgettable image of puffy, punched-out, disfigured Hedda Nussbaum describing indescribable horrors in her thickened, matter of fact, barely audible voice."[28]

The camera made Nussbaum's face more than a face. A special devastation attached to her mangled features through her status. As a former literary editor and writer of children's books, Nussbaum belonged to the middle class—just like her accused companion, the lawyer Joel Steinberg. The story line of daily coverage stuck on this point. Domestic abuse could be found anywhere: it could no longer be pushed aside as a lower-class phenomenon, and it was prevalent. No one could be sure of protection from its horrors in the secret life of the home; nor, for that matter, was anyone safe from later attack by a criminal who had been twisted by childhood abuse.

The trial underlined ignored statistics. At the time of Steinberg's arrest, "more than 3 children died each day in America, victims of domestic violence, while nearly 2 million women were beaten by their spouses."[29] Hedda Nussbaum's face on television literalized a communal problem of hideous dimensions. Her story, forced out of her only by the threat of prosecution, brought institutional reform. By using that battered face to verify an unbelievable story, television could take some credit for reform. Broadcasting the trial had apparently fulfilled an important social function. But there is always the other side in a court decision, and here it was another face; this one in disguise.

Unmarked and sitting quietly in coat and tie while contributing intelligently to his own defense, Joel Steinberg would be unveiled bit by bit as a monster across thirteen weeks of daily coverage. He symbolized unspeakable crime in the home, an enduring identification from which the fixed gaze of television would grant no later release. At the time, Mayor Ed Koch wanted the defendant "dipped in oil." When Steinberg gained release from prison seventeen years later, Governor George Pataki led the charge of "an outrage." How, asked the governor, could "a despicable child killer like Joel Steinberg" gain early release? "Let him feel every New York eye burning straight through his rotten soul," screamed the *Daily News* in front-page coverage on the same day. Media cars and helicopters overhead chased the "paroled child-killer" from his release upstate to his settlement house in New York City, a distance of 240 miles. His new neighbors complained bitterly.[30] It is not difficult to explain these reactions, though we should worry about them. The merciless imprint of television has created an entirely new brand of generally hostile, permanent, self-informed public justice.

A price is paid in broadcasting a trial, and the emphasis on personalism in televised viewing reveals part of it. Domestic failures and the idiosyncratic wrongdoing of celebrities, what are sometimes referred to as "human interest" stories, attract inordinate media and communal attention today. Recurring patterns of household crime can be counted upon by media sources to stimulate ready audiences with habitual responses to a stock emotional situation. More subtly, they divert attention because they "depoliticize and reduce what goes on in the world to the level of anecdote or scandal."[31] The death of children, the murder of pregnant women, the slaughter of a family member, the fall of the mighty—these transgressions now grip the nation on a regular basis and dominate space in the news as pattern cases with a predictable and therefore welcome appeal to media engines. They represent a disturbing priority. There is a looked-for and sought-after sensationalism in so much of media coverage today, and trials have become their natural resource.

Human tragedy does not demand scale. Nevertheless, something would seem to be out of kilter when the conviction in California of an obscure fertilizer salesman for killing his wife and unborn child receives greater media attention than the death of a controversial longtime world leader, or war in the Middle East, or famine in Africa.[32] Media frenzies have reached their peak in recent years over domestic trials like those of Lyle and Erik Menendez (for murdering their parents in California in 1989), Lorena Bobbitt (for cutting off her husband's penis in Virginia in 1993), Susan Smith (for drowning her children in a lake in South Carolina in 1994), Louise Woodward (for killing the child in her care in Massachusetts in 1997), and Scott Peterson (for murdering his wife and unborn child in California on Christmas Eve in 2002).[33]

So dominant has been the element of iconographic or personal magnetism in current noteworthy trials that the lack of such an attraction can undercut a trial of much greater import. The racketeering and drug trafficking trial of deposed Panamanian ruler Manuel Noriega in 1991 failed to attract as much commentary as it deserved. General Noriega, in uniform throughout his seven-month trial, raised legal issues of great moment. He was the first foreign head of state to be charged in an American courtroom. His trial, over the most devastating narcotic flow into the United States in its history, also required an unprecedented American invasion of another country then at peace.

In "Operation Just Cause," 25,000 American troops attacked Panama to capture General Noriega at the price of 26 American lives, uncounted hundreds of Panamanian lives (the low U.S. estimate would be 516 Panamanians killed), an invasion cost of $163.6 million, and an added $1 billion in property damages. But Noriega remained a passive, unpleasant-looking, and totally colorless defendant throughout his trial, speaking only in Spanish and refusing to testify on his own behalf. Most news sources, observers, and television commentators quickly lost interest and accepted a convenient shift in government rhetoric. Pre-invasion

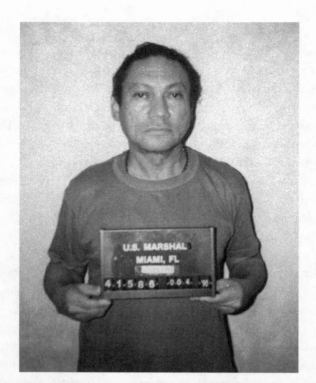

accounts of a major public enemy turned into equally self-serving descriptions at trial of "a small man in a general's uniform," "just another crooked cop."[34]

The most interesting thing about the trial of General Noriega is that it almost immediately devolved into a journalistic afterthought despite the major legal issues it presented. This was the first time, but not the last, that the United States would assume the right to invade another country against its protest and without a declaration of war in order capture a single enemy, take that enemy outside of the country where his alleged illegal acts had been performed, and put him on trial in an American court of law under American law.

Media turned with much greater attention in the same year to the trial of a twenty-seven-year old Manhattan schoolteacher in Westchester, New York. Carolyn Warmus would be charged and convicted (in a second trial) of murdering the wife of her lover in order to marry him herself. Press coverage fastened on *Fatal Attraction*, a movie from 1987 in which a woman stalks a married man with whom she has had a brief affair. Warmus enticed the media for weeks on end as a sexy figure "with a turbulent history of romantic fixations, most often with unavailable men," and it helped that she appeared in court in provocative clothing. Utterly unimportant as a legal or political concern, she struck a salacious communal nerve that Manuel Noriega couldn't match, even though his presence in court represented vital national interests and hers did not. The nation heard much more about Warmus.[35]

Figures 19 & 20. (*Above left*) Mug shot of Manuel Noriega (1990). Photograph: AP Photo (APA1429071). (*Below left*) Carolyn Warmus arriving at the Westchester County Courthouse for trial in 1991. Photograph © by Wilbur Funches / The Journal News. Contemporary coverage welcomes the melodramatic and the sentimental over legal significance. The trial in Florida of General Manuel Noriega, the deposed president of Panama, for drug trafficking, racketeering, and conspiracy across 1991 and 1992, received less attention than trials in the same years of Carolyn Warmus, a twenty-seven-year-old elementary schoolteacher, for the murder of her lover's wife in Scarsdale, New York. Colorless and passive in court, Noriega was an official public enemy. An unprecedented invasion of another country in peacetime with great loss of life and untold expense had been necessary to bring him to justice, and his trial raised novel legal issues over the treatment of an abducted foreign leader in an American court of law. Nonetheless, the *Warmus* murder trials drew more of the popular press. Coverage centered on the sensational defendant, her sexual escapades, analogies to the movie *Fatal Attraction*, and salacious accounts of "open marriages" in Scarsdale.

The discrepancy between media coverage and legal significance is a troubling characteristic of the times. Martha Stewart, America's multi-millionaire diva of domesticity and living well, faced federal charges in 2004 for lying to government investigators over an improper stock sale in which she saved less than fifty thousand dollars. Her trial overwhelmed coverage of more powerful business executives charged with looting hundreds of millions or even billions of dollars from their companies and investors.[36]

Even trials of terrorists in an age of terrorism have not led to saturation coverage in the absence of an evocative profile for domestic consumption. The Unabomber who attacked individuals by mail was significant because of his ideas and elusiveness, but coverage of the court case of Ted Kaczynski in 1997 centered less on his motives and much more on a family drama: betrayal by the brother who had turned Kaczynski in drove most media interest.[37] In the same year, the defendant in the Oklahoma City bombings, Timothy McVeigh, presented the puzzle of a decorated American soldier who claimed to act like one while attacking his own people.[38] In 2004 the Washington sniper, John Muhammad, also depended on U.S. Army skills as a qualified marksman, but once again coverage stressed personal relationships; Muhammad had trained a malleable teenager to kill indiscriminately while hidden in the trunk of their automobile.[39]

Comparable levels of coverage have not developed when arguably graver, more self-proclaimed foes have lacked easy communal recognition and connection. Neither the trial of Sheikh Omar Abdel-Rahman in 1995 for seditious conspiracy to lead a bombing attack in the New York area; nor the trial of Ramzi Ahmed Yousef in 1997, for the first attack on the World Trade Center; nor the trial in 2001 of four Al Qaeda terrorists (Mohamed Rashed Daoud al-'Owhali, Khalfan Khamis Mohamed, Mohammed Saddiq Odeh, and Wadih El-Hage), for the bombing in 1998 of two American embassies in East Africa (leaving 224 dead) would match the public response or media coverage in any one of a number of minor trials where the press could present the participants through familiar sentiment and melodrama.[40] Fascination over a lurid personal crime now trumps offenses of far greater legal significance and impact on people, whether in the form of foreign terrorism or commercial corruption.

The press covers what appeals, and it is not shy about manufacturing added appeal to increase sales. A long-playing trial sells newspapers every day and holds readers and viewers in place. Obviously, a more complicated standard should apply when broadcasting a trial, one that extends beyond simple demand and supply, but the issue is not as straightforward as it first appears. Initial fascination in a "human interest" trial often springs from a more general underlying need. Unstated turmoil in cultural perceptions are often the cause of a spread in conflict, and trials that turn into national events usually succeed at that level when the crime reflects a larger social issue.

Even obviously prurient interests can turn out to have lasting social implications. Lorena Bobbitt, a battered wife, cut off the penis of her sleeping husband with a kitchen knife in Manassas, Virginia, on June 23, 1993. A domestic dispute in a collapsing marriage that no one cared about (including the divorcing couple) quickly became a world event. Newspapers across the country and gavel-to-gavel television broadcasting roused interest around the globe during the successive trials of the husband for marital sexual battery and the wife for malicious wounding. It didn't matter that neither defendant could be found guilty by juries stymied by a domestic quarrel in which both people seemed at fault; nor that the government trivialized both parties. "You might say these two people deserve each other," the prosecutor argued in the first trial. "They are like children. Neither one plays with a whole deck," the same prosecutor added in the second.[41]

The carnal appeal of the *Bobbitt* case was obvious and dominating. Sixteen television trucks with satellite dishes along with dozens of journalists from home and abroad converged on the modest Prince William Virginia County Circuit Courthouse during the eight-day trial of Lorena Bobbitt. Forty-eight witnesses turned her marriage into "one of the most highly publicized and minutely scrutinized ever." Testimony fueled humor everywhere. The Bobbitts were nightly fare on talk shows, where even relatives contributed to the fun. France invented a new verb for the occasion: "bobbiter" went with "bite," French slang for penis. Outside the courthouse, supportive women organized the sale of T-shirts with a reddened knife dripping blood and the caption "Manassas, Va. A Cut Above the Rest."

Where does social value begin and poor taste end? In the *Bobbitt* trial, leading news sources joined the tabloids, dismissing previous standards in their descriptions of sexual matters. The *New York Times* gave daily coverage, photographs, front-page prominence, and several editorials to the case, and it served up the spiciest details—such as John Wayne Bobbitt's practice of shouting out the names of other women he had slept with during sex with his wife. Its editors offered a "Ballad of John and Lorena" complete with humorous asides: "The Bobbitt case is like Madonna dressed in a legal brief: it just won't stop taking its clothes off." But if the hammer of saturation coverage caused the *Times* to rethink its slogan ("All the News That's Fit to Print"), the Bobbitts were news of a kind. The case spoke, as the editors of the *Times* also wrote, "eloquently of our time, in ways we don't even want to talk about." The defendant had been "continually raped, sodomized, and beaten by her husband," and shockingly "her situation was commonplace." The *Times* forced an unpleasant recognition upon its readers. "What happened to Mrs. Bobbitt," its editors concluded, "happens, in varying degrees, to more than a million American women every year."[42]

The *Times* choice of editorial language is illuminating. Trials can become important when they make a community face a problem it doesn't want to talk about. Here, once again, is the element of surprise or the unexpected. Lorena Bobbitt, an immigrant with limited English and less knowledge of American institutions, somehow found the wherewithal to seek help from officialdom two days before her last fight with her husband, but when told by a county counselor that an order of protection would require her to appear in public before a judge, she fell away demoralized. Like many battered women, she said, "I was embarrassed to tell people, and I thought he might change."

Legal issues complicated Mrs. Bobbitt's lonely predicament. The state of Virginia did not recognize that a husband could merely rape a wife. "Marital sexual assault" was the charge against John Wayne Bobbitt instead of rape because "rape applies [in Virginia] only to couples living apart or if the victim is seriously physically injured." Brutalized beneath the plausible level of legal concern, Lorena Bobbitt found herself helpless in a cycle of escalating violence. Her sadistic and physically powerful husband was an ex-marine and former bouncer who knew how to hurt people.

Anyone watching her trial had to ask what could be done about a situation that caused Lorena Bobbitt, a person without any previous criminal record, to strike in such an unacceptable way. For in striking *back*, she invoked "a man's scariest fantasy," the prospect of "feminine revenge," as well as "the awful temptation to admire the crime." The *Times* used the defendant's peculiar situation to advertise general applicability. It gave coverage to a report of the Senate Judiciary Committee from 1992, "Violence Against Women: A Week in the Life of America." It also rued the obstructionist tactics in Congress that were preventing passage of the Violence Against Women Act, a bill still trapped in committee at the time, even though it had been introduced a full three years before the Bobbits' last fight. Policy concerns motivated this stand on the part of the *New York Times*. Still, how likely was it that the *Times* or any other part of the mainstream press would have risen to the challenge without the tawdry details and lewd publicity surrounding the *Bobbitt* trial?

Other sensational trials involving household crime convey similar lessons. In the 1990s, a decade of material prosperity and relative peace, Americans worried more about their well-being than their enemies, and much of their anxiety turned on the perception that the American family had lost strength and control.[43] The rise in divorce rates, births out of wedlock, single parenting, general promiscuity, drug consumption, geographical mobility, and working mothers were thought to have undermined traditional authority and cohesion in the American family—so much so that the nebulous phrase "family values" became and remains a watchword of morality in political campaigning.

Trials like that of Lyle and Erik Menendez for the killing of their parents or of Susan Smith for the murder of her children receive publicity because they focus on a family in disintegration. Most observers of such trials have experienced one or more of the factors presumed to contribute to the erosion of family values. What family in the twenty-first century is without the distractions of geographical mobility, divorce, or two working parents? Everyone also recognizes that legal deterrence has little to do with the sudden swirl of emotion in a family quarrel. Frozen in the spotlight of their courtrooms, figures like Lyle and Erik Menendez and Susan Smith evoke a reflex reaction. Families cannot help but look to their own dysfunctional levels. Who, they wonder, will be next?

The trial of Louise Woodward, a nineteen-year-old British au pair, in the Middlesex Superior Court of Massachusetts in 1997 can be used to clarify how sensationalism, anxiety, and social value come together in postmodern perceptions. Woodward was tried and convicted of murdering Matthew Eappen, the eight-month-old son of her employers, Deborah Eappen and Sunil Eappen, working doctors in the heavily professional Boston suburb of Newton. The trial itself was televised by Court

Figure 21. The nanny child-murder defendant (1997). Photograph: AP Photo / Jim Bourg Pool (APA2325786). Appearances are important at trial. In 1997, when nineteen-year-old Louise Woodward, a trained au pair from England, was found guilty of second-degree murder on the basis of overwhelming evidence in the death of the eight-month-old child in her care, protest over her conviction had as much to do with the way she looked during her televised trial in Cambridge, Massachusetts, as with the sentence handed down. Baby-faced and dressed in simple attire to match, she seemed a child herself. Judge Hiller Zobel quickly reduced her sentence to involuntary manslaughter and time already served, freeing Woodward to return to her home in England.

TV and attracted national attention as no other since the trial of O.J. Simpson in 1995.

Woodward's lawyers adopted an all-or-nothing strategy, refusing the lesser alternative of manslaughter. They insisted that the jury be given just two possibilities, murder or acquittal, and they did so despite considerable evidence that Woodward had been the agent in a fatal case of what the world would learn to call "shaken baby syndrome." Faced with the stark choice and convinced that the defendant had abused the baby, Woodward's jury convicted her of second-degree murder, a verdict that carried a mandatory life sentence. On November 10, 1997, after massive protests against the decision in the United States and Great Britain, Judge Hiller Zobel reduced the verdict and sentence to involuntary manslaughter and time already served, a total of 279 days.[44]

Although the nanny murder trial, as it was called, riveted a huge audience on the issue, much of the outcry can be traced to the appearance and demeanor of the defendant on television. Louise Woodward looked much younger than she was, and she was dressed in court to match that perception. She seemed a child herself. Her emotionalism at strategic points and cries of innocence satisfied a primal need in observers who wanted to identify with the central figure in a melodrama. But Woodward also represented a prevalent nightmare. "Every working parent's deepest fear has a new face," wrote the *New York Times*, "one with a milk-maid's wholesome roundness, clear blue eyes, and a broad serene brow."

The combination of positive and negative responses to the defendant made for a dynamic spread of conflict. How could that "incredible pre-Raphaelite face" represent "the dark undertone, that secret fear in the back of every mother's head that the people she's left her kids with are going to hurt them"? The intelligent mother of the dead child, an ophthalmologist, put the problem succinctly: "The idea that someone who looks 'normal' or friendly or young or—I hate to use stereotypes; a young, white, soft-spoken, British-accented, intelligent girl could harm your child—it's terrifying to people." Yes, it was terrifying, and many observers handled that emotion by blaming the Eappens. The couple had decided to work instead of nurturing their child full-time, and in going for day care they had been careless. How could such intelligent people have left a mere child in charge of a baby?

Indeed. How *could* they? The answer lies in mundane norms and numbers. Despite her childlike video image, Louise Woodward was at nineteen a typical au pair, and she had been vetted by a professional agency, EF Au Pair, before entering the Eappen home. (EF Au Pair would foot the bill for Woodward's defense to the tune of half a million dollars.) The Eappens, for their part, were hardly exceptional in the decisions they made. Nearly half of all families with children had both parents in the workforce by the 1990s. More than 50 million Americans are working mothers today. Almost half of the children in the United States under the age of one receive care from someone other than a parent.[45] Criticism of the Eappens didn't want to accept any of these facts. It sought instead to flush away the communal nightmare over what might happen to children in day care. Scapegoating the Eappens and working mothers eliminated the need to confront growing communal uncertainties over familial norms. Video technology aided these evasions by encouraging viewers to rest in melodramatic sensibilities instead of the brutal facts of the case.

Television encourages a disembodied identification that appears "bodied" through the reality of the image on the screen. Viewers felt they "knew" the sympathetically childish figure of Louise Woodward. "Thanks to television images, we feel able to comment on the moral significance of the behavior of strangers across the globe," the critic Michael Ignatieff has written. "We judge this distanced mediatised behavior as if it were just as familiar as our own."[46] Viewers of the *Woodward* trial assumed a quick familiarity with the facts through the projection of innocence in the defendant, and this presumed familiarity triggered wish fulfillment in a vast population. No one wanted to see the teary-eyed girl ("I love kids") spend her life in jail, and it didn't matter that the image on the television screen belied the facts. One after the other, pediatric experts and specialists in child abuse attested to the manifest presence of shaken baby syndrome during the trial.

Four lines of emotional identification, all hyped by television, turned the nanny murder trial into a spread of conflict, or what the vice president of Court TV happily termed "a big Nor'easter that is beyond any kind of human ability to control or predict." The dilemma of all working parents came first, but it was joined by class resentments (in which the upper-middle-class Eappens became targets of supporters for the working-class defendant). Also at work were high financial stakes for relatively new industries (day care and au pair agencies took a beating) and a national rivalry (England against America).

The Anglo-American divide revealed an interesting flaw in television coverage. British outrage over what the English saw as a more primitive justice system in America exceeded all bounds in part because video transmission had been partial. The satellite television network Sky TV began gavel-to-gavel coverage in England only *after* the prosecution rested. English audiences saw only the sentimental pitch of the defense and little of the technical evidence that supported shaken baby syndrome. Television dramatized an impossible situation. When Judge Zobel released Louise Woodward, the dead baby's father gave this response. "Doesn't he get it?" Dr. Sunil Eappen asked. "Someone killed Matthew." Yes, someone *had* killed Matthew Eappen, but what kind of trial would an impoverished alien have received without the publicity of television coverage?

The horns of the dilemma in television coverage of a trial are sharp. They include heightened competition in press coverage *against* a more available public record, exaggeration of courtroom personalities *against* greater protection for some personalities in need of it, inflated courtroom behavior *against* a check on professional conduct, more melodrama *against* a better view of the trial as it proceeds, false affinity *against* a truer understanding, and voyeuristic satisfaction *against* the articulation of repressed anxieties. As sharp as those horns can be, as inconvenient as they often are for individuals caught in a noteworthy trial, they must not be judged in a vacuum or, even worse, under the assumption that the current system works as long as cameras are kept out of courtrooms. Nothing could be further from the truth. Saturation coverage has brought a wholesale change in the communal construction of courtroom events—with or without television coverage.

A noteworthy trial becomes that way through news coverage, and the fact of coverage will be crucial as long as the guarantee of a public trial is upheld as it must be. Reporters by law, custom, and communal desire have a right to be in court. But few restraints, other than self-imposed ones, apply to the nature and accuracy of the news that follows from the legitimate presence of reporters. Media sources reject the very idea of restraint by arguing that they are the representatives of the public interest. Left unexplored are the terms under which that assertion can claim to be true.

The right of the media to be there notwithstanding, representing the public in court may shift as a viable contention if the people can observe a trial for themselves. What adjustments, if any, should apply to the ever-increasing frequency, form, and intrusiveness of press coverage bolstered by new technological methods? Can distinctions be drawn between reportage geared to communal interest and reportage that generates interest, or is there no meaningful distinction to be drawn between these categories? Does the creation of all news, all of the time have an adverse effect on the procedures that protect a fair trial? To consider these questions, we must first note in greater detail how reporting proceeds in the courtroom of today.

THE MEDIA IN COURT

Democratic society asks media sources to keep the people informed and demands that they remain independent of official interference. Reporters must be free to "educate the public in making political choices." "Being informed" thus requires "freedom of the press." Information is a form of freedom, and it joins "being informed" and "freedom of the press" as inextricable, mutual benefits in a citizenry that must be equipped to favor or reject alternative courses of action.[47] Although quarrels quickly erupt over any attempt to define appropriate information for the informed citizen, critics and social theorists agree that postmodern forms of communications have created new opportunities for exercising and expressing the choices that inhere to being informed. Moreover, proactive response patterns, all duly reported, now appear in everything from sports programming, polls, call-in opportunities, game shows, and computer online venues of all kinds.[48]

Nowhere has this tendency to respond aggressively to events been greater than in observers of high-profile trials. "In an era when each big trial turns us into a nation of jurors," observers in the twenty-first century are eager to believe they "know better than these twelve morons," the twelve who make up the official jury. Twice in the 1990s, "knowing better" actually meant more than an expression of unhappiness. In the trials of the Los Angeles police officers for using excessive force in arresting Rodney King in 1992 and then of Louise Woodward in 1997, "an angry populace has felt sufficiently informed and empowered to revolt against a jury verdict."[49]

Much of the greater volatility in reactions to high-profile trials today can be traced to reporting. Close-up coverage with a focus on emotionalism has been the order of the day, and it induces observers to identify with the person they see most clearly. With imagery a weathervane, the press gives its attention to the animated figure in court over the lost victim. The nanny Louise Woodward received spellbound attention through the desire to find out what she did or did not do, but to answer that uncertainty, observers of her trial had to assume first that they could know *her*. In comparison, eight-month-old Matthew Eappen was a disembodied object in court. No amount of speculation about the dead baby was going to complicate his frozen fate; nothing in him could *further* enlist the observer.

Television observers want to engage and even commit to what they see at trial. Video imagery, whether in court or just outside, pushes coverage toward what is called "emotional humanism, relying on the successful broadcast of scenes of intense emotion to serve as a lubricant for social belonging."[50] How else does one explain the reaction of the retired truck driver who drove for two hours from New Hampshire to join "Free Louise" demonstrators protesting the verdict against her in Cambridge, Massachusetts? "I've never felt this way so strongly about anything," this protester announced on arrival, and he added a telling aside. "I wanted to do something in my hometown, but my town is really small."[51] The engaged spectator reaches for more active participation in the hope of mass identification with those who feel the same way.

Less information delivered more insistently contributes to heightened emotionalism in the courtroom observer. All reporting simplifies a complicated event for the consumption of a mass audience, but the diminished scope and ever-increasing speed and superficiality of coverage simplifies the simplification through shorter articles and more pictures. The front page of the *New York Times* in 1900 carried 10,000 words of text with twelve articles in eight columns of type. Page 1 today offers six articles of 2,200 words with colored illustrations, and those illustrations prompt "human interest" as often as breaking news.[52] Similar or greater reductions apply everywhere in current media coverage. Studies of "the shrinking sound bite," "the rise of evanescent news reports," and the rapid-fire "visual style" indicate that coverage today often "impedes careful thought or calm reflection." The "faster flow" in virtually all of current broadcasting favors "the simple image over the complex, the emotional over the neutral, the conventional over the contrarian."[53]

The influence of entertainment norms on news reportage has reached the point where journalists speak of a new category: "democratainment." Some deplore the descent of their profession into "the bastard child of the entertainment industry." As early as 1977 the then-dean of American broadcasting, Walter Cronkite, warned against "lowest-common-denominator" reporting. "We fall far short of presenting all, or even a goodly part, of the news each day that a citizen would need to intelligently exercise his franchise in this democracy," Cronkite complained then. "So as he depends more and more on us, presumably the depth of knowledge of the average man diminishes. This clearly can lead to a disaster in a democracy." The superficialities deplored by Cronkite and others have increased tenfold during the last three decades, and they dominate the phenomenon of saturation coverage as it has developed in the high-profile trial of today. [54]

More subtle changes contribute to the irony of less news delivered all of the time. The reduction of events to a story line is a time-honored convention and part of the terminology of journalism, but problems arise when the story line congeals into an all-purpose tale. In the business scandal trials of 2004 and 2005, reporters recognized "a Kabuki-like quality" in their reports. From trial to trial, "every person enveloped by the scandal seemed to assume an almost ritualized role." Coverage geared to "a rash of rogue C.E.O.'s" sent reporters in search of ready components: "the fallen giant, the whistle-blower, the dogged journalist, the arrogant lieutenants, the little people left twisting in the wind." [55]

Murder trials of pregnant women devolve into similar patterns: the cad exposed, the victim extolled, the other woman explored, the relatives in grief or anger, and, overall, the family lost. Reporters pressed by deadlines plug in the familiar story in the knowledge that it will play well with editors and a nation already conditioned to express its outrage. "People are not interested in the baroque details but in the moral verities," writes an authority on the impact of legal scandals. [56] The comment should give pause. Trials turn on those baroque details, the fact-specific nature of a case.

Forcing coverage into a well-known story line raises one more danger, a graver one than mere misunderstanding. Use of the familiar tale presages a familiar ending. The teller who imposes a conventional story on a complicated situation threatens the integrity of a trial by implying a standard resolution before the fact of court determination. Plugged in, the stereotypes appeal to equally standard communal biases. Although commentators may gesture toward alternative possibilities as a trial unfolds, they emphasize the answer the public longs to have confirmed.

Reporters know that readers and viewers expect and even yearn for the prearranged forms of melodrama. "The desire to express all seems a fundamental characteristic of the melodramatic mode," writes Peter

Brooks. "Nothing is spared because nothing is left unsaid." In pursuit of this mode (with its indulgence in emotion, its moral certainty over the location of good and evil, and its love of excess), reporters roll out the good, the bad, and the ugly in proverbial terms.[57] Speed rather than accuracy dictates ready-made impulses to satisfy the excitement of the moment. Competition, which forces reporters "to feed the public appetite to know all instantly," reaches for the automatic solution that all others are offering.[58]

A recent sample from patterns of pretrial publicity can illustrate both the problem and the assumptions behind it. When Scott Peterson was arrested in California for the presumed murder of his pregnant wife and displayed in handcuffs on April 18, 2003, the *New York Post* ran a full front-page photograph with the headline "MONSTER IN CHAINS." California's attorney general announced on the same day that it was a "slam-dunk that he [Peterson] is going to be convicted." Even before the arrest, TV commentators like Geraldo Rivera for the Fox News Channel and Nancy Grace for Court TV assumed Peterson's guilt. "There's a profound journalistic question at play here," Tom Rosenstiel, director of the Project for Excellence in Journalism, observed of these inclinations. "Is any speculation or assertion fair game? Or do we have a responsibility to weigh the rights of the accused along with the rights of a fair trial?"[59]

Dan Abrams, a legal correspondent and an anchor at MSNBC, answered these questions by declaring that Scott Peterson became fair game once he "refused to answer certain pertinent questions." Nancy Grace defended her own performances by arguing that nothing has changed. "Before the advent of television, when people were not huddled around the TV," she explained, "they were huddled around the dinner table, the bar, you name it, talking about the murder case at the courthouse." These responses from media figures miss the point. Only in an age of all news, all of the time, where "nothing is left unsaid," can Scott Peterson or any other private citizen be blamed for refusing to answer a press inquiry.

Who gets to decide when a question is "pertinent" and must be answered? Only in court must a defendant answer, and even there defendants are not required to incriminate themselves. Free expression in a rule of law includes the right to remain silent. Court TV commentator Nancy Grace's retort rests on equally dubious ground. She wants to see the press as a stand-in for the people. The people's lawyer as a former prosecutor, she imagines that her commentary as a broadcaster—commentary repeated everywhere on television screens around the globe—replicates a discussion between Mom, Dad, and the kids around the dinner table. But she speaks instead as a public authority, and she leaves an imprint on the public mind from a platform where the standards are presumed to be higher than those allowed in a private conversational or speculative context. Untenable as principles, these media arguments represent something else. They are the new standards of trustworthiness required by the speed, the presumed intimacy, and the range of saturation coverage.

A reporter facing the immediate dissemination of news on a global scale has another problem: news gets old fast. Rapid obsolescence in coverage coupled to the frequency and finger-touch availability of news reports have forced reporters to a frantic level of improvisation in their race "for every scrap of new information, consequential or not." There are, as a result, fewer serious checking mechanisms on coverage; the speed of the need doesn't allow for them. When new information is *not* at hand, the desire for coverage innovation turns instead into "a rush of opinion." Something must be found to fill the gap of "no news" while still maintaining the appearance of novelty.[60]

The media answer, a seamless segue into "opinion coverage," contains a step often missed. This is the moment when coverage leaves the facts in hand and when announcer and viewer implicitly welcome the personal into their understanding. The unending obligation to find something new in twenty-four-hour coverage justifies a desire to jump ahead, to push the envelope. These pressures may be irresistible, but they also demonstrate how "bad journalism drives out good."[61] In context, the way these new parameters of coverage operate in a high-profile trial is particularly important because, as one media critic notes, "[recent decades] have been characterized by a number of media events that have fascinated the American imagination, and notably, nearly all of them have been trials."[62]

Vital affinities reinforce the connection of high-profile trials to saturation coverage and its companion, opinion coverage. Courtroom performers are stationary targets that cannot avoid reporters in a public trial. The predictable march of legal procedures gives the reporter familiar ground for both predicting and recognizing a moment of fresh or breaking news. Everything takes place in a highly visible and reasonably comfortable setting, and the news doesn't grow old anywhere near as fast because the anticipation of a final decision protects speculation. A judgment not yet reached but definitely on the way allows for endless conjecture with room for editorializing and attitudinizing. Everyone knows about these advantages in newsrooms. A high-profile trial is the cushiest assignment in contemporary journalism.

Courtrooms have thus become forums for reportorial flair. The most exciting trial will still have moments of procedural tedium. Momentum slows over tactical moments of dispute, and when it does, the technical matter at hand is rarely stimulating. The reporter in postmodern coverage cannot live with these moments. Saturation coverage adjusts by allowing tabloid mentalities to fill its needs. It worries little about restrictions on its own compulsions, and at the top of the list are "fear of being boring and anxiety about being amusing at all costs."[63] Required to supply news at an unprecedented pace, reporters have learned to create their own substance when not satisfied by the legal incidents in front of them. Interviewing each other is an obvious recourse but hardly the most insidious.

Two recognitions, one philosophical and the other empirical, encourage manufactured news without professional guilt. First, "the power to get one's own social reality treated as truth is one of the most important powers in postmodernity." Created realities are, in fact, the lifeblood of tabloid thinking. "Their truth" (the truth of authority in court) runs against "our truth" (popular belief) to generate artificial excitement.[64] Second, in exploiting the daily predictability of a trial in order to make news, reporters have learned that an irrelevant fact becomes its own truth when fed into the continuous cycles of telecommunications. Once placed, the extraneous but oft-repeated reference on day one becomes a fact in controversy on day two. No source need be acknowledged. The inserted item represents an angle that can be discussed and therefore should be answered by those in authority.[65] A denial by an important face is as good as an affirmation in saturation coverage.

In one of the most unsavory moments of trial reporting on record, the prosecutor in the O.J. Simpson trial, Marcia Clark, became the victim of this kind of extraneous treatment. News of her divorce "filled the vacuum" during a lull; "one tabloid even ran a topless photo of Clark, which they purchased from her obliging former mother-in-law." No news source is immune to these pressures. More respected media engines resist only to follow at one remove. Left with nothing to say at times in the Simpson trial, they speculated endlessly on Clark's personal life, clothes, hairstyles, relations with subordinates, and manner. As news dwindles or dips momentarily in a high-profile trial, journalists vie "to report every leak, giving credence to the wildest rumors."[66]

The reporter's greatest nightmare is no news when on call or, worse, when on view, and so any conjecture that fits becomes a viable source of elaboration. Indeed, there is a worse fate waiting for the television reporter. When times are dull, commentators can always be replaced with the ultimate filler: advertising. All of these propensities, including commercial intrusion, are unsettling ones when ranged alongside the dispensing of justice. The respected press that covered a trial used to have the time and inclination to police itself effectively—checking for accuracy, relevance, and taste before running a story. It no longer does, and the network that controls television coverage has no time for taste in its need for the sound and excitement that will maintain commercial viability.

There is another cost. Lowered media standards have turned the suspicion that court officials always feel toward journalists into a deeper fear and resentment. As a prominent lawyer warned in 2004, "Judicial hostility to the press has reached a tipping point." The situation has changed not because of worry about sporadic misinformation, a given. The courts are incensed because the rise of saturation coverage has begun to control popular perceptions of what they do. Presiding over preliminaries in the trial of pop singer Michael Jackson for child abuse, Judge Rodney S. Melville spoke in exactly these terms from his Santa Barbara County Superior Court. "You need to not mislead the public by constantly indicating that I'm doing something that is not according to the law," he scolded the press.[67] The key to Judge Melville's complaint lies in his adverb: "constantly." Those items selected by the media for continuous video transmission or daily newspaper speculation belong to the postmodern concept of getting one's own social reality treated as truth.

As the poster child of saturation coverage, the high-profile trial exists on a collision course with postmodern journalism. The First Amendment against abridgment of "freedom of speech or the press" is coming into conflict with the Sixth Amendment insistence on "a speedy and public trial, by an impartial jury of the State and district wherein the crime shall have been committed." The Supreme Court has never endorsed prior restraint on the publication of news by the press, but lower courts have begun to seek restrictions that could reshape understanding of the law in this area.

In a decision subsequently reversed in 2004, Judge Miriam G. Cedarbaum, presiding over the trial of Martha Stewart in New York Federal District Court, closed jury selection to the press because of "an extraordinary interest quite beyond the public's right to know." In the same year and city, after newspapers published the name of a juror during a trial, another New York judge ordered the press not to publish jurors' names. Still later in 2004, during preliminary motions over the accusation of rape against basketball star Kobe Bryant in Colorado, the state supreme court ordered the press not to publish information from a transcript e-mailed to them in error by a court clerk. The prosecution of Bryant would end in part because of the unwarranted release of prejudicial pretrial information—information easily disseminated by mistake or design in the electronic age.[68]

When media sources intrude or engage in rumor-mongering or misuse privileged information, they undercut their claim of serving the people in court. They become instead the commercial entities that they are, competing with each other for the most provocative account that will sell their product. By giving priority to the excitement that they can generate, they turn a trial into a sensation for domestic consumption instead of the deliberative process that it is in court. Many have noticed. "In this era of the televised trial and wall-to-wall coverage, the similarities between a legal game show and a major trial send a serious warning signal about our criminal justice system," concluded one observer who experienced this kind of coverage from a trial in 1997.[69]

More sweeping criticisms come from scholars who raise "troubling questions" about the communicative function of the news media. Some now claim that "the media have failed to provide for informed citizenship," that "the accumulated verdict of research is that the media provide an inadequate basis for citizens to fulfill their role," or that "an ever more concentrated mass media . . . does an increasingly inadequate job of fulfilling its role as a facilitator of democracy."[70] These charges sound extreme, and they are, but they make a point that cannot be ignored. Contemporary news disseminators are more intrinsically connected to technological engines and practices that serve commercial momentums, and these momentums have gotten in the way of accurate, inclusive reporting.

It is also possible to see a problem and find no answer to it. Yes, perceptions of justice have been skewed by press coverage. Yes, reporters of high-profile trials have misled public opinion on some larger questions. Yes, media sources highlight emotionalism as much as explanation in their contributions to the understanding of such a case, and, yes, these tendencies are growing. Even so, no defender of liberty would think of restricting freedom of the press at a time when established authority has so many means of manipulating communication to secure its own ends.

Thomas Jefferson, who was subjected to more than his share of scurrilous attack by the press, would speak for his time and ours when in 1787 he wrote, "Were it left to me to decide whether we should have a government without newspapers or newspapers without a government, I should not hesitate a moment to prefer the latter." By 1805, after many more unfair attacks while running a government, Jefferson had not changed his mind, but he attached a pointed qualification to his celebrations of freedom of the press: "the press, *confined to the truth*, needs no other legal restraint."[71] But who decides the truth to which the press should be confined? Who would want the courts to decide "what is truth?" in commentary on a trial when the interests of the courts themselves would be involved in the answer? To ask such questions is to suggest the problem to be taken up next.

CHAPTER NINE

Seeing Justice Done

NOT FALLING IN A FALLEN WORLD

The right to a fair public trial, the right to freedom of speech, and the right to freedom of the press are fundamental coordinates in a free society, but they are ranged on a collision course over publicity in today's courtrooms. When absolute values collide, meaningful solutions are hard to find. Nonetheless, some kind of reconsideration is in order, and the ground that all three rights share—protection of the free use and reception of words in public life—should help in this regard. It also helps that the source of conflict is particular. Technical innovation has turned mere tensions between the law and the press into a battleground of uncertain dimensions. The battleground is uncertain because contemporary communication systems have altered the reception of language and because debate remains fruitless as long as each long-standing right receives a comprehensive priority that cannot be challenged.

Against these seeming incompatibilities, it is worth remembering that the aspirational tones in fundamental rights hide a deeper common truth about them. Rights are fundamental because they reach for the best in human nature while accounting for the worst as the price of social life. This point is not easily understood but any reconsideration of rights must begin with it. Put in more applicable terms, a fundamental right, to remain effective, must engage with how people cannot keep themselves from acting; it must treat the problems in behavior as a never-ending and troublesome variable.

A familiar version of communal origins, the biblical account of Jacob, illustrates the perspective required. Here, in the accessible form of story, is concrete recognition of a peculiar blend, the mixture of aspiration and cunning needed if values are to be sustained in a fallen world that continues to fall. Abraham becomes the father of a chosen people through his innate compassion and hospitality. He is a worthy founder from first to last, but it takes a more flawed figure, Abraham's grandson Jacob, to create the community of people so chosen, and Jacob manages to succeed only through treachery, confusion, and conflict.[1] Son of Isaac and younger brother of Esau, Jacob represents subtlety in human relations and, hence, progress. He is the wily architect of well-being in terrible times.

Jacob begins by betraying his father and cheating the dull Esau out of the latter's birthright of control. A fundamental right has been twisted but seemingly with necessary social ends in mind, at least for the teller of the story. Jacob is a forward-looking leader in the face of change; Esau belongs to a static past. Forced nonetheless into exile by his reprehensible actions, Jacob is cheated in turn by his uncle Laban in ways that induce further struggle and crime down through the generations. There is, in fact, no end to this depressing cycle. Jacob is subsequently betrayed and reduced to misery by the crime of his own many sons, Joseph's brothers. But in the midst of his roles as offender and victim, Jacob has dreamed of God's ladder, a symbol of perspective, and he has wrestled with the angel, an alter ego who typifies the possibility of improvement.

Before he sees God's ladder, Jacob is directed by others; after it, he begins to think on his own and in new ways. Although Isaac has envisaged that Jacob, and not Esau, has "a multitude of people" in him, Jacob's struggle with the angel of possibility legitimizes his leadership. The struggle itself leaves him lame, but it earns the saving name of "Israel," one fit to govern a people, "the sons of Israel." Unavoidably hurt by experience, Jacob grapples with it in the hope of a future better than the unseemly present.

The struggle is worth it because there is a new dispensation for Jacob if he has the wit and the nerve to grasp it. Prosperous even in adversity, he seizes the rising rungs of the possible amidst turmoil and duplicity; never above devious stratagems himself, he understands what others will do to him if left to their own devices. Jacob evades disaster by forestalling it. He meets change instead of accepting it. Creator of the twelve tribes, he redeems understanding and uses it to transform the evil in himself and others.

Nothing so dramatic applies to the problematic trajectory of courtrooms today, but if the story of Jacob seems fanciful, its claim on the reader to a special intellectual terrain in this chapter is deliberate. The issues raised here require a similar risk in perspective, a parallel realization of what people are capable of doing to each other (sometimes without realizing it), and a comparable awareness that change is coming and must be managed if fundamental values are to be maintained.

We are figuratively at the bottom of Jacob's ladder. Only this time the rungs of possibility are legal doctrine, and the angel of technology is the adversarial figure who must be wrestled to a standstill and made to help in the end. We must be more imaginative than we have been if we are to protect the language of the law from canned information, selective repetition, competitive hype, and commercial control.

CAMERAS IN COURTROOMS

One of the most dominant features of postmodernity in American culture involves the continuous bombardment of sound, image, and print from a surfeit of sources, mediums, and directions—so much so that a tenet of the age posits that individuals are now "constructed by the texts surrounding them." The average American now sees three thousand advertisements in a day.[2] The stepping-stones in creating this phenomenon, what we have been calling saturation coverage, have been rapid, steep, and, of course, technologically driven—so driven that it is worth pausing for a moment to consider just how rapidly the welcoming hand of technology has changed approaches to perception from anything that has gone before.

Between 1951 and 1975, the number of television sets in the United States increased from 10 million to 100 million. There are three times that number today. Videotape—the process by which the live transmission of image and sound could be recorded, stored, and repeated effortlessly—was invented in 1956 and refined by 1961 to the point of rendering the repetition and editing of program material "as easy as pushing a button."[3] Even without further refinements, America had become what historians and critics have termed an image culture under the control of new modes of perception.[4]

With these inventions, controlling images of events and opinions could be sent anywhere immediately and hundreds of times without added expense or personal exertion, and soon the image makers themselves could produce their pictures from anywhere. Other developments, aided by the introduction of solid-state technology, reduced the size and maneuverability of transmission equipment in the 1970s, making cameras relatively non-intrusive and portable and leading in the early 1980s to the camcorder, a hand-held camera that a single, relatively untrained person could carry all over the world and wield effectively in the production of video with sound.

The spread of programming encouraged cable reception with an exponential jump in broadcasting opportunities. Satellite transmission opened the world to immediate viewing anywhere on it, and the rate of refinement in instantaneous communication techniques has increased immeasurably since then. Computerization and the introduction of digital video technology in recent decades have dispensed with videotape, allowing previously unthinkable miniaturizations in equipment as well as finger-tip storage, immediate availability of countless pieces of information, the total manipulation of original imagery, and the conjoining of previously separate forms of modern communication.

The explosion and blurring of transmission technologies are especially important for present purposes. Through digitalization and the Internet, processes of telephoning, video broadcasting, musical recording, computerization, and movie projection have come together in the same framework, creating a phenomenon known as "convergence," the "elusive marriage of technology with the flash and dazzle of show business."[5] CNN, itself a combination of reportage and entertainment, piggybacked off of the technological developments just noted to create the first twenty-four-hour cable "news programming" in 1980, and its success led to offshoots at CNN and a flock of other companies—MSNBC, Fox News Channel, and ESPN TV, to name just a few.

Meanwhile, the move from traditional cable to digital cable enabled a second exponential jump in channel broadcasting opportunities. There are now a thousand video channels in the United States up from an original possibility of three. The first clumsy personal computers, invented in 1974, have become miniaturized video cell phones carried everywhere and advertised as "out-of-home entertainment systems" with everything available through an Internet that has expanded beyond individual calculation since its invention in 1969. More than 2 billion people in the world now use a cell phone; 9 trillion e-mail messages are sent, and a billion Google searches for information are conducted in a given year.[6]

The numbing effect of all news, all of the time in such a competitive environment has heightened the need for entertainment in programming. No form of broadcasting is free of these pressures. Everywhere there are more shots of shorter duration, more focal shifting, more angles of vision, more close-ups, more "human interest" asides, more editorializing by experts, more urgent and louder sound to back up every image. Producers plan programming for viewers a touch away from hundreds of other opportunities on the screen. Coverage must be quick if it is to resist the impatient finger on the aptly named "remote."[7]

Enter Court TV. Riding the bubble of saturation coverage, Steven Brill generated the Courtroom Television Network in 1991 by convincing backers that it "would be a cross between C-Span and soap opera."[8] His words were prophetic in their attempt to disguise conflict in the imagined cross. "Created by the cable industry and offered as a public service," the C-SPAN network takes as its mission "access to the live gavel-to-gavel proceedings of the U.S. House of Representatives and the U.S. Senate, and to other forums where public policy is discussed, debated and decided—all without editing, commentary, or analysis."[9] Soap opera, by way of contrast, consists of serialized daytime commercial programming and is "chiefly characterized by stock domestic situations and often melodramatic sentimental treatment"; it is, more simply, "a banal story dripping with sentiment."[10] The only thing these genres share is the technical basis of transmission.

To its vast television audiences, soap opera is much more than the definitions just given, and Steven Brill had all of the addenda in mind. "An invisible nation of more than fifty million Americans watches soap operas" on a daily basis, experts on the subject report. "People don't just watch soap operas; they live with them." The typical serialized soap opera is an intensely personal collection of stories about the "suffering of consequences." As such, it represents "a highly idiosyncratic version of reality," and "the delayed denouement of each subplot allows the viewer to speculate on the outcome of behavior, to imagine hypothetical solutions, to form judgments," and, ultimately, to identify with and gain "an intimate knowledge" of the characters involved. These elements combine to form the telling goal of soap opera: "in this way, the viewer gets addicted."[11]

Throughout the life of Court TV, Steven Brill and his associates and successors have argued for a marriage of these two genres, disinterested public service *but also* affecting entertainment, and their success has led them to discount the differences in these divergent paths. By 1997, six years into its run, Court TV had televised six hundred trials to 26 million cable subscribers with live coverage of trials throughout most daytime programming and spin-off and summary programming at night.[12] Understandably thrilled by this run, Brill talked often of the educational function of Court TV: what he called eliminating "the huge gap between the reality of the law and the legal system and the public perception of it." At the same time, he embraced soap opera mentalities to hold his audiences. "It's about people who are in peril. . . . And they're trying to fight off that peril," he observed in 1994. "And there's a result. Do they win? Or do they lose?" Brill explicitly welcomed the siren call of the soap opera: "It gives people a feeling that we're doing this together."[13]

The idea of "doing a trial together" runs against a legal process dedicated to the idea of keeping each role separate from all others in dispensing justice. The intimacy that Court TV cultivates joins the claim of service to entertainment. Its manipulation of the video focus strives for an affective experience, one *better* than that in the courtroom. In the moment of conception, Brill spoke of the involvement he sought as the overview given a theater audience, but he promised more. "My thought was to . . . not strive simply to put the viewer in the courtroom," he once noted, "but to show the trial, and to make it better than being there by adding expert commentaries and analysis." The "togetherness" of Court TV celebrates an interactive encounter. It wants audiences to engage in decision making, and it has succeeded in the minds of many. Viewers of Court TV, in the words of one admiring critic, are "new-age '*jurors*' for a new-age courtroom."[14]

Other critics challenge these practices. A better view of a trial than one received in court creates the possibility of discrepancies in recognition and understanding. Speculation about winning and losing by on-air experts prejudges issues and encourages rooting sections for one side or the other.[15] Undaunted, Court TV persists in close-up coverage with commentary, and it welcomes the analogy to sports and other forms of entertainment in its advertising. Commercial backing, 60 percent of the network's revenues, drives the educational wheel in Court TV even though its producers claim otherwise. Featured high-profile cases—like those of

Joel Steinberg, O.J. Simpson, and the Menendez brothers—have made Court TV a profitable business, profitable enough for Steven Brill to sell his own interest in the network in 1997 for a sum reportedly between $20 million and $40 million. The Faustian bargains in the network's coverage have not been subtle ones. "Balancing the sensational, lurid, and gory with the evolution of legal doctrine will be the Courtroom Television Network's ultimate test," worried the *New York State Bar Journal* as early as 1992.[16]

Still, there is little point in blaming Court TV for the manifestations of entertainment that it has brought into American courtrooms. In his most articulate defense of his methods, Brill in 1996 offered two justifications for the policies of Court TV: one sound, the other dubious, both instructive. On the one hand, Brill notes that traditional media stoop to "knee jerk" editorializing and tabloid sensationalism over accurate reporting of a trial, and he is right when he says that current coverage hardly represents a standard if truth is the goal. On the other hand, Brill overstates his own solution when he argues that "courtroom cameras always show the truth" and are "above other forms of journalism or court-sponsored public information in existence."[17]

Camera work can deceive as easily as any other mode of controlled perception. The angle of vision, the shot selected for repetition, the exploitation of space by lens control, and the elimination of context manipulate reality as surely as the yellowest journalism in a newspaper, and they tend to manage the deception with greater subtlety. Not that these qualifications bother Brill. His proudest claim, the ease of his adaptation of standard marketing and media techniques, represents the real issue in Court TV, and it points to the larger problem. Because Brill and his successors wield the same video devices in their search for excitement as any other sophisticated program in competitive television, a version of their enterprise was bound to appear with the onset of saturation coverage in video transmission.

Some would even say that there is a simple progression in the highly conventional appropriations of Court TV. After all, excitement has always been the name of the game in courtroom reporting. The most serious difference in moving to TV reportage lies in form, and the new forms matter despite their familiarity through other kinds of TV programming. Reportorial excess in the realms of speed, intimacy, and repetition have turned high-profile trials into mega-spectacles observed by millions of people at a time; both the numbers and the more casual perspective of television viewers are unprecedented concerns.

A new public geared to video immediacy expects closer relations to the visual aspects of trial performance, and the intimate eye of the camera has stoked those expectations by enabling keener identifications and more rapid investments inside of the continuum of publication around a high-profile trial. Indeed, the continuum itself is turning into more of a patchwork of coincident expressions under these pressures. Sequences in the patterns of reportage about a courtroom event have given way to instant replays in cycles of transmission. Media sources now compete with the courtroom over an event *as it is happening*, often using the same image observed in court but from a different angle than seen by those in court and sometimes with a different purpose in mind.

Left to its own devices, television marries narrative to image, sacrificing everything to an affect that can be seen. These are troubling tendencies from a legal perspective. The top-down effect of professional explanation has been weakened, and when image dominates the message, the law loses some of its hold on explanation. Put another way, these heightened immediacies have caused courtroom events to become more intense focal points but without corresponding increases in comprehension.

Television viewers accept more than they can possibly know because their familiarity is apparent rather than actual. To see is to think that one "knows," or to use Hegel's adage, "there is nothing behind the curtain other than that which is in front of it."[18] The enticement of intimacy recognizes few bounds and joins with other trends to change the meaning of "public" in public trial. No one knows how much of a problem these pressures actually present, but there is nothing to stop further encroachment in courtroom coverage, and its momentum will never pause on its own. A spirit of intrusiveness will only grow more promiscuous as interactive communications further permeate American society.

Again, however, it is impractical to think in terms of blame. As messengers with distorting messages, media are the natural scapegoats for every ill in trial coverage, but they are as helpless as anyone in coping with contemporary telecommunications, and criticism of them ignores the technological impositions that dictate press behavior. Compelled to act as they do, reporters have no solutions to their own excesses in courtroom coverage, not that they worry too much about it. In any case, all thought of self-policing disappears in competition for the quickest story.[19] Answers, if there are to be answers, lie elsewhere. They lie in legal thought, but here there is a different kind of problem. Rampant suspicion of the communications industry has left the law in a passive-aggressive stance.

THE LEGAL DEBATE

Illusions have kept the law from dealing with the hidden dimensions of contemporary courtroom coverage. Three related factors have dulled official sensibilities when it comes to thinking about the onslaught of telecommunications. First, the law has shunned each of the new instruments of communication as they have appeared instead of meeting them halfway or testing their applications; second, courtrooms have clung to the professional fable that media influences can be kept outside the door; third, rigidities in doctrines that protect freedom of speech and freedom of the press have kept the judicial branch of government from balancing the interests in courtroom coverage for what they are.

Each of these restricting factors deserves attention, and the third and most important factor, legal doctrine, must somehow be made to yield a better understanding and possible solutions. Is it possible to insure responsible trial coverage through postmodern media techniques without muzzling either free speech or freedom of the press? Most of the disputants on either side of this question will not be happy with the solutions offered in the following pages, but we have to think a different way about familiar things to protect the rule of law in a postmodern world.

As scholars who have studied the sudden emergence of techmatic culture have noted, an "epistemic period shift" has taken place, a "real break with the past": "a deep chasm has been crossed between the 1980s and the present day," one in which "relentlessly self-aggrandizing imperatives of the technological system" have restructured normative values about what is important to know and believe.[20] The law, always a reactive institution from its position of ascendancy, has been notably slower than most frames of reference to recognize the new world in which we live.

Who would sacrifice freedom of the press for vague assumptions about added fairness in some courtrooms? Who, conversely, would sacrifice the prospect of justice to pretrial publicity? No one in either case, but much depends on how harder questions are framed by competing but equally valid interests. When faced with difficulties in a changing situation, the law must respond by rephrasing controversial questions in search of firmer ground and more plausible answers. What if a greater degree of fairness in coverage could be assured *without* limiting freedom of the press? What if publicity, as such, could be *held more distinct* from the public nature of a trial? What if the problem itself could be *lifted out* of the rigidities of present concerns? Not all of these questions will yield meaningful answers, but they set the table.

The original decisions to prohibit the use of radio and television in courtrooms illustrate the reflexive distrust of the law for all of telecommunications. The American Bar Association noted the "impropriety" of broadcasting a court proceeding as early as 1932 and sought to prohibit it in 1937. Intrusive radio and camera work during the sensational Lindbergh baby kidnapping and murder trial of Bruno Richard Hauptmann in 1935 produced Canon 35 in the ABA's Canon of Judicial Ethics: "the taking of photographs . . . and the broadcasting of court proceedings are calculated to detract from the essential dignity of the proceedings, degrade the court and create misconceptions with respect thereto in the mind of the public and should not be permitted." By 1946 Rule 53 of the Federal Rules of Criminal Procedure had formally banished cameras from federal courthouses. The ABA quickly extended its own recommended ban to include television broadcasting in 1952.[21]

Rejection of all electronic broadcasting has dominated legal thought until recently. The Supreme Court gave its own authority to the presumption against in 1965. In *Billie Sol Estes v. Texas*, the Court found that televising a criminal trial against a defendant's objections was "inherently invalid" as a violation of "the time-honored principles of a fair trial"; it dismissed the thought as "a misconception of the rights of the press." Concurring with two other justices, Chief Justice Earl Warren went further. There was "inherent prejudice" in the very idea; "it violates the Sixth Amendment for federal courts and the Fourteenth Amendment for state courts to allow criminal trials to be televised to the public at large." Warren confirmed lower court rulings that "televised criminal trials are inconsistent with the Anglo-American conception of 'trial.' " An American courtroom was a "hallowed sanctuary," and in it "television representatives have only the rights of the general public, namely, to be present, to observe the proceedings, and thereafter, if they choose, to report them."[22]

Whether *Estes v. Texas* remains good law or not today is a matter of dispute. The Supreme Court has changed its tune but arguably not its mind since *Estes*. In *Chandler v. Florida* in 1981, it accepted the right to use cameras in state courts on an experimental basis but with many a cautionary note attached. Following *Chandler*, the right to televise a trial has been raised mostly in the rejection of it by a presiding judge, and the prejudice of the profession against all forms of electronic coverage has changed little over the years.[23]

To be fair, the law has been encouraged in these tendencies by finding little restraint when the media is allowed to proceed as it wishes. Judges and lawyers point to media sources that push against whatever limits are set. Too often, however, that righteous stance has been the end of the matter. Minimal efforts to measure the impact of cameras in court have been inconclusive, and the regular rejection of them has prevented a learning curve from developing as technologies improve. Absolute bans have kept the law from finding out what it needs to know about what it objects to. As a result, there is no current critical context to guide official opinion, and the deficiency has bred further insularity, mistrust, and, in the end, official complacency.[24]

Professional narrow-mindedness would be less of an issue except for a second dilemma. The prohibition of cameras assumes that a ban will keep coverage away from the "hallowed sanctuary" of the legal process, but that has not been the case. Exclusion has empowered irresponsible and sometimes openly antagonistic camera work just outside of courtroom doors. Left to its own devices, commercial television controls public opinion through images that seem authoritative through proximity. By converting still-life drawings of trials into live coverage of performers as they emerge from court, networks overwhelm the language of the law with the imagery of superficial side events. Shakespeare made the point four centuries ago, and he put it in the mouth of the smartest of Greeks. Ulysses speaks only the truth when he says, "Things in motion sooner catch the eye, / Than what stirs not."[25]

Existing tensions in legal doctrine are ill-equipped to cope with this dilemma even though aspects of it were glimpsed by the Supreme Court as early as 1941. As Justice Hugo Black wrote then in *Bridges v. California*, "Free speech and fair trials are two of the most cherished policies of our civilization, and it would be a trying task to choose between them." Freedom of the press remained Black's weathervane, but his fear that at some point an unwelcome choice might be required led him to voice the law's traditional distrust of the press and to add a warning. "Legal trials," he wrote, "are not like elections, to be won through the use of the meeting-hall, the radio, and the newspaper."[26]

The "trying task" glanced at in *Bridges v. California*, the dilemma of choosing between freedom of the press and the guaranteed right of a fair public trial, would come up again in 1966, this time with a more direct challenge to media directions. In *Sheppard v. Maxwell*, the Court reversed a conviction for murder on the basis of intrusive press coverage. It decided that "massive, pervasive, and prejudicial publicity attending petitioner's prosecution prevented the defendant from receiving a fair trial." The Court agreed that "a responsible press has always been regarded as the handmaiden of effective judicial administration," but its otherwise conventional support of freedom of the press contained a noteworthy hedge. Only a *responsible* press deserved the name. By implication, new pressures in coverage were carrying the press over an edge into *irresponsibility* and thus quite possibly beyond the protection of the First Amendment. Saturation coverage had become a significant worry. "From the cases coming here," the justices observed, "we note that unfair and prejudicial news comment on pending trials has become increasingly prevalent."[27]

The *Sheppard* Court finished with more warnings about unacceptable press behavior. "If publicity during the proceedings threatens the fairness of the trial, a new trial should be ordered," and it agreed that even this threat might not be enough of a safeguard. "Given the pervasiveness of modern communications and the difficulty of effacing prejudicial publicity from the minds of the jurors," the Court observed, "the trial courts must take strong measures to ensure that the balance is never weighed against the accused." Use of the word "never" seemed to suggest the same level of rigor in enforcing the Sixth Amendment that "strict scrutiny" tests gave the First Amendment right of freedom of the press. But these directives were more assertive in spirit than manageable in form. How was a lower court to judge the level of intrusiveness *not* to be granted a press entitled to its own freedoms as well as freedom of speech? The Court's cryptic answer came entirely from above: "Appellate tribunals have the duty to make an independent evaluation of the circumstances."[28]

The Court reserved for itself and other appellate courts a nearly unprecedented level of "independent" involvement in lower court rulings.

Too many constitutional values were apparently at stake to think otherwise, and this was particularly true where the Court's starkly declarative
First Amendment doctrines were relevant. If free expressions by individual citizens or a member of the press come into conflict with societal
interests, the Court had said it would apply a test of "strict scrutiny" to resist alternative interests. First Amendment rights trumped any restriction
in the absence of a compelling alternative interest, and even if an alternative interest became compelling, it could restrict freedom of the press
under strict scrutiny only when couched in the least restrictive manner
possible. A loaded balancing test had left a heavy burden of proof on *any*
restriction of a free press.[29]

In *Richmond Newspapers, Inc. v. Virginia* delivered by Chief Justice
Warren Burger in 1979, the Court pushed these assumptions. It welcomed
a famous comment by Jeremy Bentham as "a keystone" to its own thinking: "Without publicity, all other checks are insufficient: in comparison
of publicity, all other checks are of small account." A more concrete admission followed. "Instead of acquiring information about trials by firsthand observation or by word of mouth from those who attended," the
Court had come to realize, "people now acquire it chiefly through the
print and electronic media." Recognition of electronic dissemination as
a paramount source of information forced another step. "With the press,
cinema, and electronic media now supplying the representations or reality of the real life drama once available only in the courtroom," all media
could now rightly claim a special place in courtroom deliberations. "In a
sense," reasoned the Court, "this validates the media claim of functioning
as surrogates for the public."[30]

The surrogate status of the press made something else true in *Richmond Newspapers*. "While media representatives enjoy the same right of
access as the public," observed Chief Justice Burger, "they often are provided special seating and priority of entry so that they may report what
people in attendance have seen and heard." Media kept *all* of the people informed now that "attendance at court is no longer a widespread
pastime." Nor was that all. *Richmond* conflated freedom of speech and
freedom of the press, arguing that "these expressly guaranteed freedoms
share a common core purpose of assuring freedom of communication on
matters relating to the functioning of government." Freedom of speech
and freedom of the press formed "a nexus between openness, fairness,
and the perception of fairness." The people gained "the appearance of

justice," not just the fact of it, where "appearance" included a combination of "observation and experience" that conveyed "the means used to achieve justice." There was a visual emphasis in the Court's understanding. The chief justice spoke of a "fundamental, natural yearning *to see* justice done."[31]

Left unsaid in *Richmond* were the degree, the extension, and the larger implications of concepts like "seeing," "perception," and "appearance," but two years later, again through Chief Justice Burger, the Court decided that even cameras could be part of the publicity it saw as so important to a fair public trial. *Chandler v. Florida* argued that the receptivity of television had changed matters, although it did not say by how much. It grudgingly acknowledged that cameras did not *automatically* taint a trial or violate a defendant's rights.[32] Nor did the high-profile character of a given trial change matters. By settled law, people in the public eye could not be protected from media coverage even when unwillingly placed there. Courtrooms were public places, and the press was free to report and interpret whatever was said there no matter how far its reports deviated from legal fact. Two principles, somewhat in tension, controlled: the arduous search for truth in court had to be protected at all times, and the answer to falsehood as a general rule was "more speech, not enforced silence."[33]

Chandler opened a door without requiring anyone to go through it, and battles remain to be fought over whether the rights of print media create presumptive rights for image media. These uncertainties can best be pieced out in question form. What allows the media to embody the public interest in a primary or privileged sense? Do the media represent the public in court conditionally or unconditionally? What circumstances justify cameras in courtrooms? Or asked the other way, should cameras have a presumptive right to be present and require an active rebuttal to exclude them? What rights do video commentators have? Are they empowered under the same understanding as cameramen? When, if ever, should the right to *see* justice done extend beyond the right to *observe and then report* on it?

These questions reflect the current hiatus in legal interpretation. Media sources seeking camera coverage claim the declarative upside in judicial rhetoric as matters of right in response to the questions just raised, and they also point to improved, non-intrusive innovations in video projection and to the realities of perception in an image culture. The rhetoric of judicial interpretation has not reached anywhere near as far or as fast, and in consequence, debate about heightened courtroom coverage proceeds on separate levels, at cross purposes, and with different claims on expertise.

The law, at one level, can afford to be silent. Whatever media sources would like to claim about their rights, the ruling cases about cameras in courtrooms "have generally not been treated as raising significant First Amendment questions."[34] At another level, however, the law needs to respond to a changing situation. Questions and uncertainties about the implications of camera coverage persist, and they dominate public discourse when a high-profile case turns into a major news event.

Faced with this predicament and its own history, the Supreme Court has refused to make formal choices between First Amendment rights (freedom of the press) and Sixth Amendment rights (a fair public trial). On the edge of both, it has left the devil in the details of ad hoc interpretation, a policy of minutia that complicates doctrinal directions, leaving them to time, circumstance, and the judicial interpreter. In *Nebraska Press Assn. v. Stuart*, decided in 1976, the Court reversed a lower court decision that restrained the press from reporting a confession by a murder suspect. The case itself was easily dealt with; it went off on an unconstitutional prior restraint of press publication that could not overcome the "heavy burden" of First Amendment protections. But the Court went out of its way to qualify the scope of this decision, even though it didn't have to. It limited its holding sharply to the facts of the case, using the opportunity to point toward the problem on the horizon.

Nebraska Press gives us a court on the brink of discoveries partially withheld. "The authors of the Bill of Rights did not undertake to assign priorities as between First Amendment and Sixth Amendment rights, ranking the one as superior to the other," Chief Justice Burger observed, and neither would the Court; "it is not for us to rewrite the Constitution by undertaking what they declined to do." At the same time, the Court sympathized with the trial judge being reversed; he had justifiably concluded that "there would be intense and pervasive pretrial publicity concerning this case."[35]

Not for the first time, the justices worried about the growing challenge of saturation coverage while waffling in response. The Court saw "something in the nature of a fiduciary duty" on the part of the press to exercise its rights with restraint, while complaining it was "a duty widely acknowl-

edged but not always observed by editors and publishers." There was the
slightest glint of a sword in judicial hands. Despite the First Amendment,
the Court held that media *had* to "direct some effort to protect the rights
of an accused to a fair trial." It asked for a level of media restraint that it
was not seeing and did not say how it would insure that those greater
levels of restraint would come about.

All doctrinal language is to some extent subjective, but sequential resort to it should arrange and simplify matters for application in all courts.
The Court's "independent evaluation of the circumstances" test in *Sheppard v. Maxwell* instituted a case-by-case basis that gave appellate courts
confusing license to decide either way without clarifying philosophical
debate over First and Sixth Amendment issues. Following along, *Gentile
v. State Bar of Nevada* in 1991 added "an independent examination of the
whole record test" in a decision that upheld the First Amendment while
straining hard not to qualify the Sixth Amendment. The case involved a
defense attorney who held a press conference for his client in violation
of a Nevada Supreme Court rule that prohibited a lawyer from making
extrajudicial statements to the press.

In its recasting of the facts of pretrial publicity from the trial record,
Gentile reversed a lower court decision of guilt, finding that "vigorous
advocacy" in the absence of "any real or specific threat to the legal process," protected the rights of the defendant. Justice Anthony Kennedy,
speaking for a fragmented plurality, added a stray assertion to this test
of specificity. "And in some circumstances," he wrote, "press comment is
necessary to protect any real or specific threat to the legal process." But
which circumstances were to control future applications? The Court's
doctrine of "independent examination" avoided the problem by assigning such distinctions to future deliberations. Nonetheless, the scope—
some would say the prudence—of this evasion opened a different drawer
in Pandora's box. In *Gentile* the Court divided wildly on a relatively easy
case; it fought with itself over the license it claimed to possess in investi-
gating everything before it. [36]

The independent examination doctrine triggers concrete particulars
over strategic thinking. By empowering appellate courts to correct very
specific flaws, it delivers an oblique reaction to the massive technological
changes introduced by the media industry in recent decades. [37] The great
advantage of the doctrine comes in its ability to rectify without an act of

sweeping criticism. It allows a court to pick and choose useful particulars out of a voluminous record, and in keeping with *Nebraska Press*, it can hope thereby to sustain either First or Sixth Amendment rights without interfering the other way. Unfortunately, this policy also leaves the largest problems unresolved and opens the Supreme Court to seemingly contradictory counter-charges of activism and lack of direction.

The broadest claim for "the independent examination of the whole record" doctrine appeared in 1983. *Bose Corp. v. Consumers Union of United States, Inc.* turned on a timid application of bold assumptions. The majority opinion in this First Amendment case confined the doctrine of independent examination to "the evolutionary process of common-law adjudication" and established incremental limits "through the process of case-by-case adjudication." But the opinion refused to place any real curbs on what it acknowledged was "largely a judge-made rule of law," and it opened the scope of the doctrine to the widest applications. The *Bose* Court said that it felt obliged to enter into cases *wherever* it found a claim of denied rights under the Federal Constitution. Caught up in "the exigency of deciding concrete cases," the Court would exercise "independent judgment" even to elements of discretion customarily left to "the trier of fact." The Court could not be "bound by the conclusions of lower courts," and it would "regularly" assume its "special responsibility" to "re-examine the evidentiary basis on which those conclusions are founded."[38]

Constitutional experts have pointed to a variety of problems in the independent examination doctrine, and they have found particular fault with the expansive claims of *Bose v. Consumers Union.* In the words of one leading scholar, "the Court is proceeding on an ad hoc basis, failing to consider the systemic ramifications of its decisions." The justices have committed themselves to "law declaration" instead of "saying what the law is" with "serious consequences in a system of constitutional government." The independent examination doctrine "provides little guidance," overextends the Court, creates a "troublesome" rhetoric of obligation, kindles "the necessity for case-by-case adjudication," confuses questions of fact and law, raises "disquieting" assumptions about "distorted fact finding and law application" in lower courts, and leads an already divided Supreme Court to disagree "on the proper characterization of the question presented."[39]

Serious enough in any context, these problems grow large in the growing controversy over video broadcasting of trials. It seems likely, given
the weaknesses and confusions in the "independent examination of the
whole record" doctrine, that widespread public acceptance of postmodern telecommunications will eventually drive the wheel of change in the
absence of better legal formulations. The recognitions forced upon the
court in *Chandler v. Florida* will prevail, and those recognitions will become the relevant circumstance of the *Sheppard* Court's "independent
evaluation of the circumstances."[40]

Commercial television may continue to get its way, but in admitting
the problem, is there a solution to it? Thus far, in fact, there is not. A
standoff in basic values, freedom of the press against the right to a fair
public trial has privileged the predicament over answers to it.

As long as the competing principles in coverage of a high-profile trial
are equally valid, the struggle between them will not go away. Perhaps a
basic insight can supply the beginnings of a better response. If debates
over the competing rights of the media and the legal system turn on
where one stands on the First and Sixth Amendments—and that is the
way most current accounts describe the situation—the source of greatest difficulty is distinct from either. Generally welcome and unavoidable
technological advances have created the problem, and Jacques Ellul in
The Technological Bluff pinpoints the desired response when he argues
that the harmful effects of technical progress require more than "human
mastery over technique." Ellul asks for active engagement with the contingencies of change over passive participation in the momentums called
progress.[41]

Can the press continue to be properly free while the integrities of
courtroom procedures in a high-profile case are guarded against excessive publicity? Ellul's notion of "active engagement" implies common ground in the basic value that the First Amendment and the Sixth
Amendment share: namely, protection of the free use and reception of
words in public life. The analytical basis of interpretation given to courtroom events in earlier chapters can also help. The dynamic interactions
of courtroom and community, the continuum of publication around a
trial, the variables that produce a high-profile trial, the refractions of
language in such a case, and the capacity of such trials to be barometers
of thought in the culture at large belong to the same common ground.

WHAT MIGHT BE DONE?

Words imprison as much as they liberate, and in the instance of cameras in courtrooms, the law has been captured by its own language. Legal thought has confused the elements that it objects to, and primarily at fault has been the most basic element in all of legal reasoning, the use of analogy. "Analogical legal reasoning" provides "a critical locus of the law's normative claims." It is used all of the time, sometimes compulsively, "to apply the law as it is, however narrowly or broadly conceived, to the concrete facts of the case, in all their particularity."[42] The danger in this methodology, as just seen in "the independent examination of the whole record" doctrine, lies in the nature of choice: everything rises or falls on the quality of the particulars selected for comparison.

Although cameras show only what the holder of it decides to show, appreciation of that fact has been overwhelmed by a faulty analogy. Officialdom assumes that video images are the trouble to be met when the problem is better understood through the purveyor of those images. The live video image is what captivates, and the viewer of it remembers an ancient adage. When confronted with bad news, we have been taught to blame the message and not the messenger, but much turns on the seemingly helpless messenger in this situation and that recognition begets a new set of considerations.

The late Harold J. Rothwax, judge of the New York State Supreme Court and a canny observer of his times, illustrates the mistake so frequently made even as he saw the essential problem clearly. A legendary stickler for decorum in his no-nonsense approach to adventurism by attorneys who appeared before him, Judge Rothwax presided over the first high-profile trial to be televised from New York City, the murder trial of Joel Steinberg in 1989 with its related media frenzy. The experience taught him that cameras were basically "a part of the courtroom furniture." True enough, but which part of the furniture? "Ultimately I concluded there was no basis for distinguishing between a camera and a reporter," he thought. "If anything, a camera is less bothersome, it stands still, it doesn't move around, it doesn't make noise."[43] Accurate in immediate effect, this observation is imprecise in larger implication, and the gap has controlled legal debate about cameras in courtrooms.

No one questions that newspaper reporters are entitled to significant rights in observing a trial, and judicial decisions continue to confirm freedom of the press in this area. This is as it should be for the reasons outlined by the Supreme Court, but the entitlements gained through this ready analogy are not as apposite to broadcasting as impressions might indicate. Overlooked, though closer at hand, is a more precise comparison between observation and courtroom cameras, and it leads discussion in another direction. The better analogy is not of camera to newspaper reporter but of camera to courtroom recorder. Camera coverage can register legal proceedings with great exactitude. Correctly used, a camera conveys a record of what takes place in a courtroom as readily and more accurately than even a verbatim trial transcript can. If scrupulosity is the goal of transcription, cameras in courtrooms cannot be beat in rendering events that are geared to performative utterance.

One federal judge recently said as much when faced with the requirement that appellate courts would "review *de novo*" any departure in his district court from sentencing guidelines. Since "*de novo*" means fresh or first impression, Judge Jack Weinstein in the Eastern District of New York has asked that all sentencing hearings in his courtroom "be recorded by an appropriate video recording device" to insure fairness when an appellate court exercises "independent and plenary" review. He reasoned that reviewers of his decisions should "observe the actual people they are sentencing" because a "defendant's words, his facial expressions, and body language, the severity of any infirmity, the depth of his family's reliance, or the feebleness of his build cannot be accurately conveyed by a cold record."[44] By extension, the same "cold record" will prove deficient in any written representation of what a jury or judge actually saw in court. Weinstein rewards the visual. In such a serious matter as sentencing, a reviewer should reach beyond mere rules "to see" all of the facts in a judgment.

Of course, the utility of a video record is not the same thing as a decision to broadcast to the public, but interest in an enlarged viewing audience turns on the same reasoning as Judge Weinstein's decision to film sentences that may be reviewed. In both cases, full comprehension depends on "*seeing* justice done." The call for video broadcasting has increased because the possibility now exists in efficient and safer form. Miniaturized, unobtrusive, accurate video transmission supports the possibility of a general public having the *right to see* a trial in progress, and if so, there is no intrinsic reason to think of cameras as anything but the neutral vehicle of what *is seen*.

The analogy of camera to court recorder or transcriber applies directly. A courtroom camera can be distinguished from all active agents of interpretive power just as transcribers perform exclusively and separately as the vehicles of the record they produce. Under the National Court Reporters Association, the federal Court Reporter Act of 1944, and relevant state statutes, court transcribers have no rights of interpretation or extension, no right of official access to the press, no role to play beyond the timely and accurate production of a court record. Court transcribers work under the duty of confidentiality regarding all records, and they are not protected by judicial immunity if they stray from their official role. Violation of these standards can mean censure and decertification.[45]

The controls on the officials rendering a court record are exact. The National Court Reporters Association's "Code of Professional Ethics" orders court reporters to guard against the appearance as well as the fact of impropriety. Recorders must preserve the confidentiality and the security of all information entrusted to them. They are to refrain from "freelance reporting activities" that might interfere with official duties, and, even more broadly, they are to avoid any situation that gives "the appearance of a conflict of interest" in behavior beyond their official duties.[46]

Why shouldn't the same obligations devolve in spirit upon the holder of a camera in court? The right to show what is taking place in court does not include a right to shape what is taking place there or to replace the sound in court with the sound of a television reporter. Fairness may have to be perceived, but responsibility for it is lodged in the procedures of the court, *not* in the eye of the beholder; nor does it repose in the interpreter of the electronic eye who conveys the meaning of an image to an outside viewer.

The fundamental nature and context of *beholding* needs to be remembered here. Only the people have an absolute right to observe a trial in progress. To be sure, media representatives bring their own rights beyond citizenship to the same enterprise. They observe a trial *for* the people *as* the people's representatives in court, receiving priority seating and other privileges of access in consequence, but they do not *substitute* for the people's right to see, and they certainly have no right to control the people's act of perception.

Although media sources supply a conduit of information and a vital check on authority, the issue of camera coverage reaches beyond these explanations. No one suggests that media in the dissemination of information or even as a safeguard against arbitrary authority have the right to enter into the actual legal process. Nor does media participation necessarily mean control of the advanced technology that gives the people a platform of observation in a courtroom today. Nor, for that matter, is there any basis beyond the conventional assumptions of commercial providers for that platform to be tampered with by media commentary or visual manipulation for effect. The right of the people to see for themselves surely trumps media entitlement to represent the people when the two come into conflict.

Alarm bells over freedom of the press will begin to ring over the priorities just set forth, but an emphasis on accurate transcription and against misconception would seem to represent paramount values in any debate over the presentation of a courtroom event that enjoys the cloak of legal authority. What, then, might be done? More attention should be given to the nature rather than the fact of video coverage and to the level of integrity expected in the transmission of an event. A high-profile trial that either upsets, divides, or defines major aspects of a community should probably be televised. A people under a rule of law in a democratic republic have the right to know as accurately as possible what concerns them, and a properly televised trial promises the greatest accuracy.

Decisions whether or not to televise a trial should probably be left on first impression to the elected representatives of the people and not the courts to resolve. The deep suspicion of the media by all aspects of the legal profession is one consideration here, but there are more important ones. Legislative bodies, by definition, represent the people's needs and wishes, and they are in a more legitimate position to make a decision against a frivolous application based on mere curiosity or celebrityhood. Legislators, as the elected representatives of the people, decide where the public interest lies. Accordingly, either legislatures or the figures delegated by them should make an initial determination. A trial court would then be in a position to rebut that determination if Sixth Amendment rights were thought to be *clearly* in danger. Judicial discretion in this more limited regard would add legitimacy to the decision-making process in recognition that crime and its correction are local phenomena with primary interpretation required on the level of precinct, county, and district.

What should follow if a decision is reached to televise a trial? Such a broadcast should conform to the established format of a C-SPAN presentation: objective coverage from a set perspective, duplication of no more than the best seat of a courtroom observer, restriction to a certain distance of zoom lensing (a rough equivalent to the tighter focusing of an individual in court who is paying closer attention), absolute preservation of anonymity in audience and jury, no commentary except for placement of the procedural moment, subtitles to indicate the court agenda in progress. In all of these matters, accuracy and availability over active appreciation and viewer numbers should be the goal and standard of a broadcast.

A televised trial thus becomes the people's record rather than an orchestration by extraneous experts, and as the people's record, it justifies · a gag order applied to all official participants as they step beyond the courtroom. When everyone enjoys access to what has happened in court, external explanation by a trial participant is a pernicious influence and a step toward viewer voyeurism. No court officer can complain about a violation of free speech when a prior oath has circumscribed conduct as the price of participation.

The restrictions routinely placed on a courtroom transcriber apply here as well. All participants must avoid even the appearance of impropriety, a guideline that gives a trial court the leverage it will need to enforce its ruling. Anything said beyond the courtroom, with the exception of a judicial order, displays a level of self-interest on the part of a trial participant either in self-promotion or in an advantage sought in the case to be decided. Outside commentary by one involved always threatens the balances that govern inside. It should not be tolerated if video transmission is available to all.

The rights of print media would not change under such an arrangement; those of the video media would be qualified but only in the moment. Any other television network would have access to the official broadcast but not to live coverage. A lag period, perhaps only of hours, should be imposed with the stipulation that any rebroadcast must regularly identify through regular subscript and audio announcement the fact of secondary transmission by the rebroadcasting agent.

Finally, there should be no advertising connected to the broadcast of a trial. The patented insincerity of advertising, the cheerfully huckstering element that is the soul of its method, has no place near a courtroom dealing with people's misery. Justice is not for sale. Nothing that suggests the regular conventions of mere entertainment or the extraneous needs of a consumer should color the ongoing process of legal procedure. Interruptions to sell products during the dull or downtimes in a courtroom are similarly pernicious.

One of the clearest sources of legitimacy in a court proceeding resides in an observer's recognition of the patience and slowly developing understanding that come in the give-and-take, the challenge and response, the break for a ruling, that characterize litigation. As difficult as it may seem, a pause in court proceedings should be accompanied by either a pause in television delivery or a replay of what has gone before. Television audiences and video producers must learn to demystify the terrifying element of silence never allowed in a commercial broadcast. Silence, it should be remembered, is also a time for reflection.

The desirability of these several restraints should be evident. The people have a right to an unfiltered video experience of a trial if they have any right to see it at all. They are entitled to no more or less than they would receive in court. The danger of live commentary in immediate coverage is the platform of authority that commentators attain through their presence. Extraneous to the legal process itself, commentators gain a false legitimacy when they are the vocal organ of instantaneous transmission. Moreover, a frequent commentator on many trials gains unwarranted power as a TV personality. A trial is indeed about performative utterance. There should be no room for confusion in the authority of the speakers who perform in it as opposed to those who comment alongside.

There will be understandable protests against these recommendations. Who will want to televise such an event? Won't tight camera restriction render the event so visually boring that few will watch? What about restrictions on freedom of speech and freedom of the press to the video media who must wait before rebroadcasting an event their own way? Each of these questions raises issues. Against them are problems that predate the television age but that have mushroomed into chronic rather than episodic dangers in the communications explosion of the twenty-first century. There are risks in change but greater hazards in leaving these concerns to the happenstance of technological development.

The production required in televising a trial will not be the problem that many apprehend. Either documentarians (under the restrictions noted but perhaps with later license to create their own film from their coverage of the legal process) or the government itself will have the interest or the obligation to televise such a trial. Nineteenth-century transcribers of trials functioned in the first capacity while producing court records. Government broadcasting, as perhaps the better alternative, will be safe as long as the rigid rules of objective presentation apply to control the interests of authority. Ever-cheaper video production and the spread of video equipment through the legal system will soon make either possibility an option everywhere in the legal process. The cost in the transmission and the storage of a video record should also continue to drop. With a little imagination, many of the worrisome aspects of developing technologies can be turned to advantage through strategies to control their worth.

A C-SPAN gavel-to-gavel broadcast *will* be less visually interesting than Court TV, but the answers to this problem come much more easily. Trials are not designed to entertain. They seek only to be fair. Half of the current problems of cameras in courtrooms flow from the fact that legal procedure is a cool medium while television projection is instinctively hot in its search for the largest audience. Proper legal procedure, the hallmark of fairness, eschews drama for other values—order, prudence, routine, predictability, even-handedness, regularity, restriction, and relevance. Surprise, excitement, and speed thrive in commercial television; certainty, sober inquiry, and patience are the province of the courtroom. The working priorities of the law are all that anyone watching a trial in court or on television deserves to see. If no one watches a trial as presented, then decision makers have misgauged the case of communal need.

A community *will* watch a trial if it is concerned, and it is not a problem if viewers rely instead on subsequent commercial broadcasting in their desire for the stimulation of outside commentary and their preference for expert opinion. The availability of an official broadcast will remain a touchstone of public regard and a check on media excess. A commercial television station or other news source will be unlikely to contradict what anyone can see for themselves, and if it does, alternative press coverage will handle those inaccuracies in a spirit of competition. Other outlets will distinguish between willful and accidental error with the means to do so, the official video record, in front of them. We can even hope that an official video record that is closer to what is actually happening in court will temper at least some of the false enthusiasm currently infused into high-profile trials.

The rights of the video media present a graver problem. Under the

First Amendment, the parallels to print media have merit even if they are imperfect, and large elements of the citizenry now depend exclusively on television coverage. But custom and practice do not constitute legal entitlement. Thus far, the courts have not protected the right of television commentators as the voice of a trial. Nor should they. A voice-over in explanation of ongoing proceedings represents unprivileged speech outside of the norms of personal freedom and beyond the right of reportage. "The traditional Anglo-American distrust for secret trials" does not imply its opposite: a right to maximal publicity.[47]

The standards that safeguard a public trial have been simple access by the people to the courtroom itself and comparable access by the press, which enjoys added seating priority as the logical representative of people not there. Nothing in these standards guarantees a television observer of a trial a superior view or a better explanatory platform than a spectator in court receives. The television viewer and the physically present viewer should participate in the same immediacy of the moment of observation. They should be understood as the *same* public. The right to observe contains a right to inform others but only through knowledge gained in a prior act of observation. The perception of an unofficial physical observer has never justified speech *during* a proceeding. The presumption, in fact, has always been the reverse: absolute silence is the norm of an observer within courtroom decorums.

It follows that any decision to empower a television commentator to speak during trial proceedings would involve an extension of rights that courts have decided not to give as a constitutional right, even though they have occasionally allowed the voice-over in practice. The innately transgressive impulses of commercial television in this regard would seem to justify a continuing constitutional restriction.

There are stated reasons for leaving in place limitations on the further extension of media prerogatives when covering a live trial. *Sheppard v. Maxwell* and *Nebraska Press v. Stuart* both warned against the danger of "broadcasting enterprises" as "outside interferences," and both ordered courts to take strong action against the threat.[48] Television commentators belong to the category of "outside" even if they appear to be inside a courtroom through video access. Live commentary of proceedings represents more than a potential interference. The mere suggestion of insider status through a televised voice-over synchronized with legal proceedings verifies the legal need to guard against that inference by a viewing audience.

No legal regime can afford to be naive about the world around it, and the American system has responded thus far in negative or passive ways. The courts have exercised prudence in not formally expanding media rights into video transmission, but they have been lax in addressing the overall situation. They have failed to comprehend what media coverage can do to a trial in the postmodern era of telecommunications. The previous history of our legal system offers a cautionary tale in this regard. In crucial instances, documented in earlier chapters, the law has lost its way in the continuum of publication surrounding a trial, and the single most telling development in that negative history has been technological advance with concomitant media involvement.

Historically, more media involvement has not necessarily constituted infringement, but it invariably has meant greater influence. The power of the modern press has developed slowly at first but more recently with exponential speed, and the acceleration has caught everyone off guard. We have moved from printing techniques of limited, delayed coverage to instantaneous levels of image connection and responsiveness through computerization, global access, digitalization, and the electronic web.

The law must learn to design its own approach to the changing situation. It must meet the problems head-on instead of shunning major implications and leaving the details to outside purveyors with their own agendas. It must seize hold of available techniques and make them serve the public interest better than any vendor will. It must distinguish the people's right to know from the media's right to inform without interfering with the rights of either. At the very least, it must provide its own accurate record to as many people as possible to temper the current manipulations of saturation coverage in a high-profile trial.

When one thinks for even a moment about present circumstances, the passive decision to leave display of the legal process in a courtroom to commercial transmission represents a shocking development. Selective broadcasting of a high-profile trial to the largest paying cable market as entertainment runs against the values of restraint, balance, and thoroughness that obtain in a fair public trial. The license to advertise in proximity to televised courtroom rulings is also abhorrent to every legal decorum. Nothing about these trends is attractive or valuable. Parallel attempts to make independent commercial transmission more responsible while court officers remain fastidiously above the actual means of video production are as questionable as they are ineffective. Current thinking about the publicity around high-profile trials belongs to a policy of drift, and somewhere in the future, it will lead to a miscarriage of justice and perhaps to serious communal disruption.

One of the first great lawyers in the Anglo-American tradition, Francis Bacon, worried about passivity in the face of a changing world. From his perspective on the edge of modernity, he left this warning: "He that will not apply new remedies, must expect new evils; for time is the greatest innovator; and if time of course alter things to the worse, and wisdom and counsel shall not alter them to the better, what shall be the end?" The writer of these thoughts was steeped in the common law and the value it placed on the role of custom; still, he knew to add "a forward retention of custom is as turbulent a thing as an innovation; and they that reverence too much old times, are but a scorn to the new."[49]

At the forefront of dynamic change in Elizabethan England, Bacon was one of the first to sense the accelerating pace in modernity, and his recognition led to the realization that change had to be met and not just received to be deemed worthy of the term progress. His ranging mind would have labeled reflexive rejections of television by legal circles for what they are: a lack of imagination fueled by fear of the new.

JUSTICE SEEN

Disagreement represents the norm at trial, and "that is why legalism is so drawn to ideologies of agreement." Legal philosophy explains the ideological difficulty in reaching agreement this way: "Justice must be identified with insight into moral truth in the individual and with social harmony in collective life." Brought to the level of the trial, a decision in a courtroom must satisfy abstract social needs while making a personal determination; a general rule must be applied fairly to a specific instance.[50] Problems in this characteristic cast of the legal mind usually begin not with the rule but with the nature of its imposition. Movement from the general to the particular is both the adventure and the vulnerability in all of legal thought. The distance in between is where controversy thrives.

People accept rules but remain ambivalent about their application to an individual, whether in protecting one of their own or, alternatively, in condemning a monster in their midst. Too much or too little punishment is a frequent complaint. To be satisfied, an observer must believe that the decision reached has been in conformity to every consideration as well as established rules. Even if a judgment in court is perceived to be objective, it does not necessarily produce a dispassionate reaction.

For while everyone agrees that justice involves the equal application of rules, trials take place over what *really* happened, over what a *proportional* response should be, over *exceptions* to be made in a given situation. The constantly asked question in court—What is *fair?*—forces everything toward the particulars in play, and that is why the key to an accomplished litigator is mastery of detail.

The approach of the law can fail to satisfy communal expectations on these levels of particularity. Agreement over a court decision is therefore highly contingent. The people are never officially asked to verify what they think about a case, but even in that recognition, it must be remembered that a decision in court leaves an impression, and something generally believed in had better be conveyed through it. There must be a comfort level for a people taught to be skeptical of authority.

There have been many ways of talking about this communal need, most of them highly abstract. When justice is both served and accepted at trial, it is said to contain "a claim not only of the speaker's personal view but of an intuitive but grounded notion of justice that the speaker believes is shared by the community of moral individuals." Empirical studies end up in comparably vague conclusions: communal acceptance of law is "directly proportional to its moral credibility." Not the sanction, as such, but responses by the court that are both reasoned and reasonable are the keys to satisfying a community. Arguing more concretely but in the same vein, Learned Hand once observed that a judge "speaks with the mouth of others: the momentum of his utterances must be greater than any which his personal reputation and character can command . . . if it is to stand against the passionate resentments arising out of the interests he must frustrate."[51]

In one way or another, each of these formulations indicates that the words used in court must count in several different ways at once, but *how* they count turns on the study of language as much as the study of law and on the method that depicts ethical insight instead of just claiming it. Current fashion in legal thought measures the comprehension of language in terms of "transparency," but the making and receiving of words is a more central focus of literary analysis, and the better tool for interpretation from that realm, one long tested in the history of thought, turns on the concept of "sincerity."[52] Transparency is a mechanical term. It signifies the absence of intermediary obstruction and measures the effect rather than the means of clarity. Those who use the term fear misunderstanding and properly so, but there are many kinds of misunderstanding, and mere blockage only begins to explain the problem when the use of words is complicated by the manipulation of them.

Sincerity, from the Latin *sincerus*, means "genuine" or "whole," where "wholeness" emphasizes "completion" at all levels in an accurate transmission. It includes, among other qualities, "the absence of any apparent attempt on the part of the artist [or speaker] to work effects upon the reader which do not work for himself." Completion, in this sense, involves "the union of internal and external" components, an "accordance of our thoughts and feelings with reality" and the accurate expression of them.[53]

As a literary tool, "sincerity" is not without its detractors. The pursuit of it can obstruct creativity, imagination, and authenticity, but these objections are less relevant in a legal context.[54] A court of law creates its own authenticity by prolepsis, the answer foreclosed. A trial is a thing happening. What the court decides will be the law, and in declarations of that law, legal expression privileges accuracy and concordance over creativity and imagination.

The more serious complication in sincerity as a method of legal comprehension lies in its need to address an institutional and not merely a personal context. No one expects a hired lawyer to be forthcoming in representing a client. No other self-interested individual in court is understood to offer the complete truth. All courtroom participants are constrained in articulation by the specific role that each must play, and low cunning plays as much a role as candor in the adversarial process. Fortunately, however, the locus of legal sincerity belongs to another level of understanding altogether. It resides not in individual expression but in the fullness of the legal process itself, in the entire expression of a trial, in the understood modes of procedure that guide performance.

This welcome totality, this sum of sincerity, constitutes the level of wholeness currently endangered by the selective transmission of trials. Only the more exciting moments of courtroom performance are now offered to a continually shifting audience expecting entertainment and the distractions that television regularly offers. No one's future freedom or well-being should depend on such a standard.

My overriding claim in this book has been that the integrity of legal procedure—when followed, seen, and understood—offers the best hope of communal regard. The true meaning of "public" in public trial comes in the proper unfolding of the process through time. Justice, as it were, must be seen twice: intuited as a grounded notion in communal norms but then confirmed in knowing reaction to what has been said and done. The two together constitute the completion in legal sincerity. When a breach in the integrity of procedure is observed, objection and dissent follow, as well they should. Whatever the differences over argument at such a moment, the observed fact of presentation in court has been incorrect, and the failure, when objection is sustained, can be seen at a level that all can agree on.

The originators of procedural integrity in ancient Rome thought of their subject as sacred, and through their need to be exact, they established everywhere in Western law that a serious mistake meant that the whole thing had to be done over again. Nothing less would please the verities. Ever since that understanding, the first thing a law student learns about procedure is that it is no different from substance. The statement is true in the sense that procedure *is* the substance of the law. Procedure guarantees that accusation will be conducted fairly with every opportunity and aid provided for the accused to respond. Visibly rendered and experienced, procedure is the legitimating source of practice in the rule of law.

The "ideologies of agreement" in legalism all come down to this: the transformation from disagreement to acceptance, like most transformations, requires an act of belief. Professional explanations of the phenomenon tend to be highly philosophical and vague because that act of belief is almost impossible to describe, let alone measure. Belief takes place gradually in process over time. Courtroom observers are doubting Thomases when it comes to seeing the law at work. There is a slow, visceral quality to legal belief, and it comes through a response to the sequential integrities of procedure on display. Courts must render the path as well as the nature of their decisions. They must deliver "the cultural significance of sight" conjoined to "the cultural significance of sound."[55]

It is almost impossible to overemphasize the importance of sight and

sound together in this context. Speaking in 2006 of the difference between a transcription or report and actual observation in court, Daniel
Castleman, chief of investigations in the Manhattan District Attorney's
Office in New York, admitted, "There's a big difference between reading
it from a cold page and watching it." Much earlier, the historian Frederic
Maitland put the matter in even stronger language: "Justice must assume
a picturesque garb or she will not be seen."[56]

Seeing justice at work is indeed the best way to believe in its success,
and now, for the first time in history, an entire population has the opportunity to watch the wheels of justice turn when a courtroom event is
a source of trepidation. It can actually observe the routines of procedural integrity control disputed intricacies and provide the equanimity for
thought and reflection in the midst of conflict.

When a court speaks, as it must, with the mouth of others in mind, it
uses authoritative language, but it succeeds through its own pitch, tone,
expression, voice, and gesture as the symbolic sum of all other trials. It
registers, in the awareness and empathy of its voice, through the sincerity
of its purposes in all of their varied elements working against the passions
and resentments a case may have aroused. Reason dictates that all concerned, and especially the resentful, hear what is said in their name, as it is
said, in the way that it is said. Law, when it speaks in this vein, represents
public reason in a democratic republic. Law *is* the democratic republic in
this moment. An informed citizenry should not be denied the full effect
of its voices whether in prior conflict or the moment of decision.

Notes

PART ONE

1. Kenneth Burke, *The Philosophy of Literary Form*, 3rd ed. (1941; repr., Berkeley: University of California Press, 1973), 69.

2. *Walton v. Tryon*, 21 English Reports 262 (1753); repr., English Reports, vol. 21, Chancery, sec. 1 (Stevens & Son, London, 1902), 262–63. Hardwicke, lord chancellor of England at the time, paraphrases from Sir Edward Coke in *The First Part of the Institutes of the Laws of England*: "Certainty is the mother of quiet and repose, and uncertainty the cause of variance and contentions."

CHAPTER ONE

1. Unless otherwise indicated, the quotations and facts about the *Scopes* trial in this section are taken from Leslie H. Allen, ed., *Bryan and Darrow at Dayton: The Record and Documents of the "Bible-Evolution Trial"* (New York: Arthur Lee & Co., 1925), 1, 15–16, 70–72, 110–11, 148, 156–61; Ray Ginger, "To the Loser Belong the Spoils," in *Six Days or Forever? Tennessee v. John Thomas Scopes* (Boston: Beacon Press, 1958), 190–217; Lawrance M. Bernabo and Celeste Michelle Condit, "Two Stories of the Scopes Trial: Legal and Journalistic Articulations of the Legitimacy of Science and Religion," in *Popular Trials: Rhetoric, Mass Media, and the Law*, ed. Robert Hariman (Tuscaloosa: University of Alabama Press, 1990), 55–85; and Sam Roberts, "80 Years Ago, They Inherited the Wind," *New York Times*, July 26, 2005, F1.

2. The Darrow figure in the play wins a complete intellectual and moral victory over Bryan in the name of progress, literally reducing Bryan to a crying baby. See Jerome Lawrence and Robert E. Lee, *Inherit the Wind* (New York: Random House, 1955), as well as popular movie versions of the play.

3. The quotation is from a study of high school biology textbooks conducted by the National Research Council in 1990 and taken from Warren E. Leary, "Biology Teaching in U.S. Gets Stinging Criticism," *New York Times*, September 7, 1990, A20.

For the history of law surrounding the teaching of evolution, see Edward J. Larson, *Trial and Error: The American Controversy Over Creation and Evolution* (New York: Oxford University Press, 1985).

4. *John Thomas Scopes v. State of Tennessee*, 289 S.W. 363; "The End of the Scopes Case," *Literary Digest* 92 (February 5, 1927): 14–15.

5. Larson, *Trial and Error*, 168. See, as well, Cornelia Dean, "Opting Out in the Debate on Evolution," *New York Times*, June 21, 2005, F1, 6; Elisabeth Bumiller, "Bush Remarks Roil Debate Over Teaching of Evolution," *New York Times*, August 3, 2005, A14; and Laurie Goodstein, "Intelligent Design Might Be Meeting Its Maker," *New York Times*, December 4, 2005, sec. 4, pp. 1, 4.

6. Laurie Goodstein, "Issuing Rebuke, Judge Rejects Teaching of Intelligent Design," *New York Times*, December 21, 2005, 1, 34; Goodstein, "Schools Nationwide Study Impact of Evolution Ruling," *New York Times*, December 22, 2005, 20.

7. Louis Joughin and Edmund M. Morgan make this point vividly in *The Legacy of Sacco and Vanzetti* (1948; repr., Princeton, NJ: Princeton University Press, 1978), 196.

8. For the Dukakis proclamation and full chronicle of continuing debate over the guilt or innocence of Sacco and Vanzetti, which raged for decades, see William Young and David E. Kaiser, *Postmortem: New Evidence in the Case of Sacco and Vanzetti* (Amherst: University of Massachusetts Press, 1985), 1–9, 164. As the closest and most detailed modern interpreters of the case, Young and Kaiser conclude that "Sacco and Vanzetti, two innocent men, most probably were framed for a murder they did not commit." "The overwhelming probability is that . . . Sacco and Vanzetti were completely innocent of the South Braintree murders."

9. "The Accused's Right to a Public Trial," *Columbia Law Review* 49 (January 1949): 116–17.

10. Magali Sarfatti Larson, "The Production of Expertise and the Constitution of Expert Power," in *The Authority of Experts: Studies in History and Theory*, ed. Thomas L. Haskell (Bloomington: Indiana University Press, 1984), 51; in the same volume, Eliot Friedson, "Are Professions Necessary?," 10.

11. Louis Hartz, *The Liberal Tradition in America: An Interpretation of American Political Thought Since the Revolution* (New York: Harcourt, Brace & World, 1955), 10.

12. American Bar Association, Public Education Division, ed., *Law and the Courts: A Handbook of Courtroom Procedures with a Glossary of Terms* (Chicago: ABA Press, 1987), 12–13. Standard manuals on advocacy also stress the mechanics of point of view and "good storytelling." See, for example, Thomas A. Mauet, *Fundamentals of Trial Techniques*, 3rd ed. (Boston: Little, Brown, 1992), 43–44.

13. John 18:37–38. But see, as well, Bernard Williams, *Truth and Truthfulness: An Essay in Genealogy* (Princeton, NJ: Princeton University Press, 2002); and David Nyberg, *The Varnished Truth: Truth Telling and Deceiving in Ordinary Life* (Chicago: University of Chicago Press, 1993).

14. For storytelling in the law, including the quotation in the text, see W. Lance Bennett and Martha S. Feldman, "Storytelling in the Courtroom," *Reconstructing Reality in the Courtroom: Justice and Judgment in American Culture* (New Brunswick, NJ: Rutgers University Press, 1981), 3–18; and David Ray Papke, *Narrative and the Legal Discourse: A Reader in Storytelling and the Law* (Liverpool: Deborah Charles, 1991). For a practical demonstration of how notions of storytelling apply to courtroom narratives, see Karen Halttunen, " 'Domestic Differences': Competing Narratives of Womanhood in the Murder Trial of Lucretia Chapman," in *The Culture of Sentiment: Race, Gender and Sentimentality in Nineteenth-Century America*, ed. Shirley Samuels (Oxford: Oxford University Press, 1992), 39–57, 286–89.

15. The distinctions in these sentences, though not the legal applications, are from Walter Benjamin, "The Storyteller: Reflections on the Works of Nikolai Leskov," in *Illuminations*, trans. Harry Zohn (1968; repr., New York: Schocken Books, 1969), 100.

16. See Louis Mink, *Historical Understanding*, ed. Brian Fay, Eugene O. Golob, and Richard T. Vann (Ithaca, NY: Cornell University Press, 1987), 20–22, 47–48, 183–88, 196; and Peter Brooks, *Reading for the Plot: Design and Intention in Narrative* (New York: Knopf, 1984), 3–7, 37–38.

17. Mauet, *Fundamentals of Trial Techniques*, 43; Alex Berenson, "Jury Calls Merck Liable in Death of Man on Vioxx," *New York Times*, August 20, 2005, A1, B13; Berenson, "For Merck, the Vioxx Paper Trail Won't Go Away," *New York Times*, August 21, 2005, A1, 17; Berenson, "A Lawyer's Stock Rises with Victory over Merck," *New York Times*, August 22, 2005, C1, 3. The plaintiff won in what experts termed a relatively weak case.

18. See Alan M. Dershowitz, *The Best Defense* (New York: Random House, 1982), 392–96; and Shana Alexander, *Anyone's Daughter: The Times and Trials of Patty Hearst* (New York: Viking Press, 1979), 27, 47–48, 86, 271–72, 384–86, 458, 466–70, 484. President Jimmy Carter split the difference between the stereotypes of Patty Hearst by commuting her sentence after she had served twenty-three months of a seven-year term for bank robbery and the use of a firearm during the commission of a felony.

19. Helen Benedict, *Virgin or Vamp: How the Press Covers Sex Crimes* (New York: Oxford University Press, 1992). For how judges shape the facts to strengthen their opinions, see Richard A. Posner, *Cardozo: A Study in Reputation* (Chicago: University of Chicago Press, 1990).

20. For "reasonable doubt," "burden of proof," and "prima facie" and the law's defense of the accused in this paragraph and the next, see *Black's Law Dictionary*, 6th ed. (St. Paul, MN: West Publishing, 1990), 492, 1265, 196, 1189–90, 908, 1087.

21. Theophilus Parsons Jr., *Memoir of Theophilus Parsons, Chief Justice of the Supreme Judicial Court of Massachusetts; with Notices of Some of His Contemporaries* (Boston: Ticknor and Fields, 1859), 218–19, 156–57, 166, 206–8.

22. Archílochus of Paros (c. 680–640 B.C.) is quoted in Richmond Lattimore, trans., *Greek Lyrics*, 2nd ed. (Chicago: University of Chicago Press, 1960), 4; but see

also Isaiah Berlin, *The Hedgehog and the Fox: An Essay on Tolstoy's View of History* (New York: Simon & Schuster, 1953).

23. American Bar Association, *Law and the Courts*, 47–50.

24. Randy E. Barnett, "The Virtue of Redundancy in Legal Thought," *Cleveland State Law Review* 38 (Winter–Spring 1990): 153–68.

25. John Rawls, *A Theory of Justice* (Cambridge, MA: Harvard University Press, 1970), 48–49. For the translation into narrative terms, see Benjamin, *Illuminations*, 93, 86.

26. George William Hunter, *A Civic Biology* (New York: American Book Company, 1914), 196.

27. I paraphrase from E .P. Thompson, "The Rule of Law," in *Whigs and Hunters: The Origin of the Black Act* (New York: Random House, 1975), 258–69.

28. José Ortega y Gasset, *Concord and Liberty*, trans. Helene Weyl (New York: Norton, 1946), 29.

29. Robert Dardenne, "The Case of Clay Shaw (1967)," in *Illusive Shadows: Justice, Media, and Socially Significant American Trials*, ed. Lloyd Chiasson Jr. (Westport, CT: Praeger, 2003), 157.

30. William Blake, "A Divine Image" (1794), in *English Romantic Poets*, ed. David Perkins (New York: Harcourt, Brace & World, 1967), 65.

31. Baron de Montesquieu, "Of the Rack" (book 6, chap. 17), in *The Spirit of the Laws*, trans. Thomas Nugent (New York: Hafner Press, 1949), 92.

32. See William G. Shepherd, "Monkey Business in Tennessee," *Collier's Magazine* 76 (July 18, 1925): 8–9, 38–39; and John Porter Fort, "Behind the Scenes in Dayton," *Forum* 74 (August 1925): 259–65.

33. See Victor Turner, *The Ritual Process: Structure and Anti-Structure* (1969; repr., Ithaca, NY: Cornell University Press, 1977), 129, 92–96, 113, 132–33.

34. Kenneth Burke, *A Rhetoric of Motives* (Berkeley: University of California Press, 1969), 58.

35. In the disciplinary debates over the meaning of ritual, I accept Victor Turner's emphases but not his insistence upon a strict religious component. Sally Falk Moore, Barbara G. Myerhoff, and Clifford Geertz all use and accept Turner but extend his framework into secular dimensions. Moore and Myerhoff offer six useful formal properties for identifying secular ritual: (1) repetition; (2) acting; (3) special behavior or stylization; (4) order; (5) evocative presentational style or staging; and (6) the collective dimension. These elements dominate courtroom events. See Victor Turner, *From Ritual to Theatre: The Human Seriousness of Play* (New York: PAJ, 1982), 78–83; Sally Falk Moore and Barbara G. Myerhoff, eds., *Secular Ritual* (Amsterdam: Van Gorcum, 1977), 3–24; and Clifford Geertz, "Blurred Genres: The Refiguration of Social Thought," in *Local Knowledge: Further Essays in Interpretive Anthropology* (New York: Basic Books, 1983), 28.

36. Claude Lévi-Strauss, *The Savage Mind* (Chicago: University of Chicago Press, 1962), 32.

37. Polls in the summer of 1994 suggested that while 62 percent of whites believed O.J. Simpson to be guilty, only 38 percent of blacks agreed with them. Moreover, 74 percent of blacks living in Los Angeles were very sympathetic to Simpson, compared with only 38 percent of whites. Explained Dennis Schatzman of the *Los Angeles Sentinel*, a black-run newspaper, "A man who, in the minds of many, was either colorless or white has now been placed in the position of having to defend himself against a charge that he murdered a beautiful white woman and a white man. Everything is magnified, and black people, irrespective of the fact that he never set foot in South Central, can identify with him now." See Seth Mydans, "In Simpson Case, an Issue for Everyone," *New York Times*, July 22, 1994, A16; Ellis Cose, "Caught between Two Worlds: Why Simpson Couldn't Overcome the Barriers of Race," *Newsweek*, July 11, 1994, 28; and Lynda Richardson, "Where Thoughts of Simpson Linger," *New York Times*, July 6, 1994, A16.

38. The accusation of voyeurism was especially prominent in the murder trial of O.J. Simpson. "Plenty of folks, white and black, are secretly enjoying the spectacle of a successful black man's fall. . . . O.J. Simpson is simply one fallen black angel. We have plenty of others." Terry McMillan, *New York Times*, June 25, 1994, 23. See, as well, Frank Rich, "Addicted to O.J.," *New York Times*, June 23, 1994, A23; and Michiko Kakutani, "Why We Still Can't Stop Watching O.J. on TV," *New York Times*, July 3, 1994, E10. In Kakutani's words, "Behold a nation of voyeurs helpless in the grip of raw narrative appeal."

39. The national press gave prominent coverage to the murders before the discovery of the Clutter killers, Richard Hickock and Perry Smith. See *New York Times*, November 16, 1959. For accounts of the American "nightmare" and the Clutter family's horrifying plunge from out of the "American dream," see Conrad Knickerbocker, "One Night on a Kansas Farm," *New York Times Book Review*, January 16, 1966, 1, 37; "Horror Spawns a Masterpiece," *Life Magazine*, January 7, 1966, 58–74; and "Nightmare Revisited," *Life Magazine*, May 12, 1967, 99–104. The quotations in this paragraph and the next are from Truman Capote, *In Cold Blood: A True Account of a Multiple Murder and Its Consequences* (New York: Random House, 1965), 305, 248.

40. For the psychological transferences from oral exchange into print, see Don F. McKenzie, "The Sociology of a Text: Oral Culture, Literacy and Print in Early New Zealand," in *The Social History of Language*, ed. Peter Burke and Roy Porter (Cambridge: Cambridge University Press, 1987), 161–97.

41. See Turner, *From Ritual to Theatre*, 78–81; John T. Noonan Jr., *Persons and Masks of the Law: Cardozo, Holmes, Jefferson, and Wythe as Makers of the Masks* (New York: Farrar, Straus and Giroux, 1976), 14–28; and Moore and Myerhoff, *Secular Ritual*, 16–17. For law and ritual, see Victor Turner, *The Anthropology of Performance* (New York: PAJ, 1987), 93–94; and Sally Falk Moore, *Law as Process: An Anthropological Approach* (London: Routledge & Kegan Paul, 1978), 1–53.

42. See Victor Turner, "Variations on a Theme of Liminality," in *Secular Ritual*, ed. Moore and Myerhoff, 48–51, 16–17. See, as well, Walter Otto Weyrauch, "Law

as Mask—Legal Ritual and Relevance," *California Law Review* 66 (July 1978): 699–726.

43. "Cranks and Freaks Flock to Dayton," *New York Times*, July 11, 1925, 1–2; "Hostility Grows in Dayton Crowds; Champions Clash," "Dayton's Police Suppress Skeptics," *New York Times*, July 12, 1925, 1–2; "Dayton's One Pro-Evolution Pastor Quits as Threat Bars Dr. Potter from Pulpit," *New York Times*, July 13, 1925, 1, 5. "Bryan and Darrow Wage War of Words in Trial Interlude," *New York Times*, July 19, 1925, 1–2; "Dayton Fortified Against Last Shock of Darrow Attack," *New York Times*, July 20, 1925, 1–2; "Evolution Battle Rages Out of Court," *New York Times*, July 22, 1925, 1–2.

44. Joseph Wood Krutch, "Darrow vs. Bryan," *Nation* 121 (July 29, 1925): 137. The expression of a general presumption is from Krutch, who also quotes Mencken speaking directly to him at the trial.

45. For a sampling of the recognition of critical connections between law and literature, see Richard Weisberg, *The Failure of the Word: The Protagonist as Lawyer in Modern Fiction* (New Haven, CT: Yale University Press, 1984); Weisberg, *Poethics and Other Strategies of Law and Literature* (New York: Columbia University Press, 1992); James Boyd White, *Heracles' Bow: Essays on the Rhetoric and Poetics of the Law* (Madison: University of Wisconsin Press, 1985); White, *Justice as Translation: An Essay in Cultural and Legal Criticism* (Chicago: University of Chicago, 1990); Brook Thomas, *Cross-Examinations of Law and Literature: Cooper, Hawthorne, Stowe, and Melville* (New York: Cambridge University Press, 1987); Sanford Levinson and Steven Mailloux, eds., *Interpreting Law and Literature: A Hermeneutic Reader* (Evanston, IL: Northwestern University Press, 1988); Richard A. Posner, *Law and Literature: A Misunderstood Relation* (Cambridge, MA: Harvard University Press, 1988); Stanley Fish, *Doing What Comes Naturally: Change, Rhetoric, and the Practice of Theory in Literary and Legal Studies* (Durham, NC: Duke University Press, 1988); Papke, *Narrative and the Legal Discourse*; and Robert Cover, *Narrative, Violence, and the Law: The Essays of Robert Cover*, ed. Martha Minow, Michael Ryan, and Austin Sarat (Ann Arbor: University of Michigan Press, 1992). See, as well, a journal dedicated entirely to the subject, *Yale Journal of Law & the Humanities*.

46. Alastair Fowler, *Kinds of Literature: An Introduction to the Theory of Genres and Modes* (Cambridge, MA: Harvard University Press, 1982), 257ff.; Adena Rosmarin, *The Power of Genre* (Minneapolis: University of Minnesota Press, 1985), 39, 47, 44; Tzvetan Todorov, "Literary Genres," in *The Fantastic: A Structural Approach to Literary Genre*, trans. Richard Howard (Ithaca, NY: Cornell University Press, 1975), 3–23. The quotations in the text are from Rosmarin.

47. Jonathan Culler, *The Pursuit of Signs: Semiotics, Literature, Deconstruction* (London: Routledge and Kegan Paul, 1981), 103–4; Julia Kristeva, *Semiotiké* (Paris: Seuil, 1974), 388–89.

48. *New York Times*, September 28, 1994, A14.

49. See Robert A. Ferguson, "The Judicial Opinion as Literary Genre," *Yale Journal of Law & the Humanities* 2 (Winter 1990): 201–19. For the mechanics of authorita-

tive language, see M. M. Bakhtin, *The Dialogic Imagination: Four Essays*, ed. Michael Holquist, trans. Caryl Emerson and Michael Holquist (Austin: University of Texas Press, 1981), 253, 264–71, 280, 293, 342–44, 349–50; and George C. Christie, *Law, Norms and Authority* (London: Gerald Duckworth, 1982), 83–146.

50. For the relation between transgression and familiarity in genre theory, see Todorov, *The Fantastic*, 8. For genre theory in the "familiar patterns" of legal procedure, see Stephen C. Yeazell, "Convention, Fiction, and Law," *New Literary History* 13 (Autumn 1981): 92–94.

51. For the transformations between legal and nonlegal narratives, see Daniel A. Cohen, *Pillars of Salt, Monuments of Grace: New England Crime Literature and the Origins of American Popular Culture, 1674–1860* (Oxford: Oxford University Press, 1993); and Karen Halttunen, *Murder Most Foul: The Killer and the American Gothic Imagination* (Cambridge, MA: Harvard University Press, 1998).

52. Perry Miller, *The New England Mind: From Colony to Province* (1953; repr., Boston: Beacon Press, 1961), 189, 196, 207, 250; Paul Boyer and Stephen Nissenbaum, eds., *The Salem Witchcraft Papers: Verbatim Transcripts of the Legal Documents of the Salem Witchcraft Outbreak of 1692*, 3 vols. (New York: Da Capo Press, 1977).

CHAPTER TWO

1. Marvin W. Mindes and Alan C. Acock, "Trickster, Hero, Helper: A Report on the Lawyer Image," *American Bar Foundation Research Journal* 7, no. 1 (1982): 177–233.

2. Michael Pickering, *Stereotyping: The Politics of Representation* (New York: Palgrave, 2001), 25–28; Jacques-Philippe Leyens, Vincent Yzerbyt, and Georges Schadron, *Stereotypes and Social Cognition* (London: Sage, 1994), 11–18, 203–5; Gary Blasi, "Advocacy Against the Stereotype: Lessons from Cognitive Social Psychology," *UCLA Law Review* 49 (2002): 1241–50.

3. Michael Grossberg, *A Judgment for Solomon: The d'Hauteville Case and Legal Experience in Antebellum America* (Cambridge: Cambridge University Press, 1996), 238; Edward H. Levi, *An Introduction to Legal Reasoning* (Chicago: University of Chicago Press, 1949), 104.

4. Richard Taylor, "The American Judiciary as a Secular Priesthood," *Free Inquiry* 10 (Spring 1990): 37–43; Ronald Dworkin, *Law's Empire* (Cambridge, MA: Harvard University Press, 1986), 407. See, as well, Robert A. Ferguson, "Holmes and the Judicial Figure," *University of Chicago Law Review* 55 (Spring 1988): 506–47.

5. Richard Wightman Fox and James T. Kloppenberg, eds., *A Companion to American Thought* (Oxford: Blackwell, 1995), 361–62.

6. David Margolick, "At the Bar: The Lonely View from the Bench for the New Judge Who Must Undergo a Rite of Passage," *New York Times*, January 6, 1989, 20; Harold Faber, "100 Justices Finish Crash Course in Judging," *New York Times*, December 3, 1989, 22.

7. Laura Kalman, *Abe Fortas, a Biography* (New Haven, CT: Yale University Press,

1990), 311, 319–22, 358–78; Christine C. Biederman, "In the Center of Judicial Storm Is a Federal Judge in Texas," *New York Times*, November 5, 1995, 24.

8. In the trial of former beauty queen Bess Myerson in 1988 for bribery, New York Federal District Judge John F. Keenan was generally congratulated for imposing himself. See Arnold H. Lubasch, "Myerson Judge: A Limit on Theatrics," *New York Times*, November 25, 1988, 24. Washington Federal District Judge Gerhard A. Gesell was similarly praised for his "highly personalized imprint" during the trial of former White House assistant Oliver L. North on charges of perjury and obstruction in 1989. Gesell was "like God up there with his white hair. Sometimes you think he might be throwing thunderbolts." David Johnston, "Judge Leaving Personal Stamp on North Trial," *New York Times*, March 28, 1989, 1, 10.

9. Los Angeles County Superior Court Judge Joyce A. Karlin, a former federal prosecutor with a reputation for careful professionalism, experienced all of these forms of attack after she gave a lenient sentence in November 1991 to a fifty-year-old Korean grocer, a woman, who shot and killed a teenaged girl who had repeatedly attacked and knocked down the grocer. See Seth Mydans, "Los Angeles Votes on Lenient Verdict," *New York Times*, June 1, 1992, A13. Judge Lorin Duckman of Brooklyn Criminal Court in New York was removed from the bench for leniency in sentencing by the New York State Supreme Court. See Richard Perez-Peña, "Court Backs Ouster of a Judge Assailed for Lenient Rulings," *New York Times*, July 8, 1998, 1, B6; Jan Hoffman, "Federal Judge Overturns Murder Verdict, Fueling Feud on Judicial Power," *New York Times*, December 27, 1997, 1, A8. In 2005 Chicago Federal District Judge Joan Humphrey Lefkow had her husband and mother shot dead in her house after she received death threats over her decisions. See Jodi Wilgoren, "Judge Tries to Regain Balance in a Family Shaken by Killings," *New York Times*, March 10, 2005, A1, 22.

10. Neil A. Lewis, "Impeach Those Liberal Judges! Where Are They?" *New York Times*, May 18, 1997, E5. See, as well, the resignation of San Diego Federal District Judge J. Lawrence Irving over mandatory sentencing guidelines in "Criticizing Sentencing Rules, U.S. Judge Resigns," *New York Times*, September 30, 1990, 22.

11. Erwin S. Griswold, "Foreword: Of Time and Attitudes—Professor Hart and Judge Arnold," *Harvard Law Review* 74 (1960): 81–82.

12. Alexander Bickel, *The Least Dangerous Branch: The Supreme Court at the Bar of Politics* (New Haven, CT: Yale University Press, 1962), 16–28; John Hart Ely, *Democracy and Distrust: A Theory of Judicial Review* (Cambridge, MA: Harvard University Press, 1980), 4–5.

13. Michigan Circuit Court Judge Dennis Kolenda made this statement while considering a controversial verdict of manslaughter instead of outright murder. "Verdict Against Man Who Killed His Estranged Wife Is Condemned," *New York Times*, June 4, 1995, 13.

14. Felix Frankfurter, *Of Law and Men: Papers and Addresses of Felix Frankfurter*, ed. Philip Elman (Hamden, CT: Archon, 1956), 39.

15. Howell Raines, "Judge Frank Johnson Goes Home to the Hills," *New York Times*, February 26, 1999, A14.

16. Learned Hand, *The Bill of Rights: The Oliver Wendell Holmes Lectures, 1958* (Cambridge, MA: Harvard University Press, 1958), 71–72.

17. American Bar Association, Public Education Division, ed., *Law and the Courts: A Handbook of Courtroom Procedures with a Glossary of Legal Terms* (Chicago: ABA Press, 1987), 24. The characterization of the judicial figure in this paragraph and the next relies on this source and on Gerard E. Lynch, "Our Administrative System of Criminal Justice," *Fordham Law Review* 66 (May 1998): 2118–19. The ABA refers to the judicial figure as "impartial umpire." Professor now Federal District Judge Lynch carries the designation one step further when he describes "a relatively passive umpire." See, as well, Judge Marvin E. Frankel, "The Search for Truth: An Umpireal View," *University of Pennsylvania Law Review* 123 (May 1975): 1031–59.

18. "Frivolity Punished Here," *New York Times Magazine*, January 18, 1998, 8.

19. Lawrence Joseph, *Lawyerland: What Lawyers Talk about When They Talk about Law* (New York: Farrar, Straus and Giroux, 1997), 62–63, 78–79; Jan Hoffman, "Judge Hayden's Family Values," *New York Times Magazine*, October 15, 1995, 46–49, 74.

20. Sam Howe Verhovek, "Judge's Optimistic Signature on a Grim-Faced Death Row," *New York Times*, July 28, 1994, A10; Lis Wiehl, "Plea to Jurors by a Judge on Pistols Spurs Debate," *New York Times*, April 21, 1989, 21; William Glaberson, "Judge Censured for Remarks and He Agrees to Step Down," *New York Times*, October 4, 2003, B1.

21. Joseph, *Lawyerland*, 63–64.

22. This is a basic assumption of legal realism and critical legal studies. See William W. Fisher III, Morton J. Horwitz, and Thomas A Reed, eds., *American Legal Realism* (New York: Oxford University Press, 1993); and David Kairys, *The Politics of Law: A Progressive Critique* (New York: Pantheon, 1982).

23. Linda Greenhouse, "Justices Define Limits of Own Power," *New York Times*, November 22, 1991, A14; Greenhouse, "Justice Weights Desire v. Duty (Duty Prevails)," *New York Times*, August 25, 2005, A1, A16.

24. David J. Garrow, "Justice Souter: A Surprising Kind of Conservative," *New York Times Magazine*, September 25, 1994, 36–43; Don Van Natta Jr., "Judge Finds Wit Tested by Criticism," *New York Times*, February 7, 1996, B1–2. Judge Baer turns out to be fierce ("ruthlessly objective") *and* cuddly ("the judge's perpetual bemused smile").

25. The adage appears in many forms, but it always implies a coordination that might also be a conflict between justice and mercy. See *Black's Law Dictionary*, 6th ed. (St. Paul, MN: West Publishing, 1990), 840, 859, 862.

26. Judge Harold J. Rothwax, *Guilty: The Collapse of Criminal Justice* (New York: Random House, 1996), 33.

27. See Henry Ruth and Kevin R. Reitz, *The Challenge of Crime: Rethinking Our Response* (Cambridge, MA: Harvard University Press, 2003), 20–26, 77–91.

28. David Margolick, "Full Spectrum of Judicial Critics Assail Prison Sentencing Guides," *New York Times*, April 12, 1992, 1, 40. The same article shows that legislatures and the people support mandatory sentencing guidelines with enthusiasm. See, as well, Ian Urbina, "New York's Federal Judges Protest Sentencing Procedures," *New York Times*, December 8, 2003, B1, 4.

29. *United States v. Booker*, 543 U.S. 220 (2005); 125 S. Ct. 738 at 759. The emphasis is Breyer's.

30. "Mercy," *The Compact Oxford English Dictionary*, 2 vols. (Oxford: Oxford University Press, 1971), 1:1773; emphasis added; and *Black's Law Dictionary*, 1000.

31. Gerard E. Lynch, "Sentencing Eddie," *Northwestern University School of Law* 91 (Spring 2001): 565.

32. For the figures in this paragraph and the next, see N. Gary Holten and Lawson L. Lamar, *The Criminal Courts: Structures, Personnel, and Processes* (New York: McGraw-Hill, 1991), 93, 120. For the statistical figures in this paragraph, see Steven Duke, "Crime and Punishment," *New York Times Book Review*, March 31, 1996, 8; Ford Fessenden and David Rohde, "Dismissed by Prosecutors Before Reaching Court," *New York Times*, August 23, 1999, A15; Edwin H. Sutherland and Donald R. Cressey, *Principles of Criminology*, 7th ed. (Philadelphia: J. P. Lippincott, 1966), 441; Bruce Jackson, *Law and Disorder: Criminal Justice in America* (Urbana: University of Illinois Press, 1984), 79–80, Brian A. Reaves, "Felony Defendants in Large Urban Counties, 1998" (Washington, DC: U.S. Department of Justice, 2001), 24; and "Compendium of Federal Justice Statistics, 2000" (Washington, DC: U.S. Department of Justice, 2002), 53.

33. Albert W. Alschuler, "Courtroom Misconduct by Prosecutors and Trial Judges," *Texas Law Review* 50 (April 1972): 621–735, esp. 644–77. See, as well, Andrea Elliott, "Prosecutors Not Penalized, Lawyer Says," *New York Times*, December 17, 2003, B1, 4.

34. Paul B. Wice, *Chaos in the Courthouse: The Inner Workings of the Urban Criminal Courts* (New York: Praeger, 1988), 20. "Most of the judges within the criminal courts have prosecutorial inclinations (and in many instances, prosecutorial experience as well)." See, as well, Jackson, *Law and Disorder*, 139. ("To reach higher office you must have a box score on convictions.")

35. *Old Chief v. United States*, 519 U.S. 172 (1997), at 187–88.

36. Jerry L. Sumpter, "A Trial Lawyer's Greatest Tool: The Opening Statement," *Trial Lawyers Quarterly* 12 (Winter 1978): 34; Thomas A. Mauet, "Opening Statements," in *Fundamentals of Trial Techniques*, 3rd ed. (Boston: Little, Brown, 1992), 41; Kathryn Holmes Snedaker, "Storytelling in Opening Statements: Framing the Argumentation of the Trial," *American Journal of Trial Advocacy* 10 (1987): 102–3.

37. Robert Jackson, "The Federal Prosecutor," *Journal of the American Institute of Criminal Law and Criminology* 31 (May–June 1940): 3–6.

38. Abraham S. Blumberg, *Criminal Justice: Issues and Ironies*, 2nd ed. (New York: New Viewpoints, 1979), 132; Jackson, *Law and Disorder*, 110–11, 138–39.

39. Jackson, "The Federal Prosecutor," 3–6. Jackson paraphrases from one of the

rare court cases to require a new trial due to prosecutorial misconduct, *Berger v. United States*, 205 U.S. 78 (1935), at 88.

40. H. Richard Uviller, "The Virtuous Prosecutor in Quest of an Ethical Standard: Guidance from the ABA," *Michigan Law Review* 71 (May 1973): 1167–68; but see Alschuler, "Courtroom Misconduct by Prosecutors and Trial Judges," 629–33; Peter Krug, "Prosecutorial Discretion and Its Limits," *American Journal of Comparative Law* 50 (Fall 2002): 643–64; Krug, "Prosecutorial Discretion," *Georgetown Law Journal* 91 (May 2003): 187–200; and Tracey L. Meares, "Rewards for Good Behavior: Influencing Prosecutorial Discretion and Conduct with Financial Incentives," *Fordham Law Review* 64 (1995): 851–919.

41. Ruth and Reitz, *The Challenge of Crime*, 68–69, 288. "*A general expansion of the powers of the prosecution*" includes "authorizing preventive detention of defendants before trial, acknowledging that defendants who insist upon their right to a trial may be penalized with a heavier sentence than if they had pled guilty to the same charges, limiting the scope of the right to counsel on appeal and to other postconviction proceedings, laying down a relaxed definition of the minimal 'effectiveness' (skill and effort) required of defense lawyers, holding that prosecutors have no duty to present exculpatory evidence to grand juries, limiting the rights of state court defendants to challenge their convictions in federal court . . . and pronouncing that sentences may be calculated in part based on crimes of which defendants have not been convicted— including charges that have resulted in acquittals."

42. Hope Viner Samborn, "The Vanishing Trial," *ABA Journal: The Lawyer's Magazine* 88 (October 2002): 24–27. The statistic is taken from the Administrative Office of the U.S. Courts, and the judge quoted in the text is the Hon. Brock D. Hornby of the District of Maine.

43. When John Gotti, the head of the Gambino crime family, was acquitted of racketeering charges three times between the late 1980s and 1990, he became a celebrated figure while the government was chided for its mistakes. Edward W. Knappman, ed., *Great American Trials* (Detroit: Visible Ink Press, 1994), 816–20. See, as well, Henry Fielding, *The Life of Jonathan Wild the Great* (London, 1743), based on the life of a notorious thief of the day.

44. Sarah Kershaw, "In Plea Deal That Spares His Life, Man Admits Killing 48 Women," *New York Times*, November 6, 2003, A1, A30.

45. Lawrence M. Friedman, "Law, Lawyers, and Popular Culture," *Yale Law Journal* 98 (1989): 1592; David Johnston, "Justice Dept. Losses in High-Profile Trials Raising Questions of Fairness," *New York Times*, September 18, 1990, A18.

46. Adam Liptak, "U.S. Suits Multiply, but Fewer Ever Get to Trial, Study Says," *New York Times*, December 14, 2003, 1, 50.

47. Lord Acton, "Letter 74," January 1861, in *Lord Acton and His Circle*, ed. Abbot Gasquet (New York: Burt Franklin, 1968), 166.

48. Albert W. Alschuler, "The Defense Attorney's Role in Plea Bargaining," *Yale Law Journal* 84 (May 1975): 1279, 1205.

49. Blumberg, *Criminal Justice*, 244–45; Friedman, "Law, Lawyers, and Popular Culture," 1599.

50. Robert C. Post, "On the Popular Image of the Lawyer: Reflections in a Dark Glass," *California Law Review* 75 (1987): 379–89; Alschuler, "The Defense Attorney's Role in Plea Bargaining," 1202–3, 1241–48. Alschuler presents evidence that the quality of a defense often depends on the fee that a private defense attorney is able to collect, and he documents the prevalent lack of respect that a public defender receives from a client and sometimes from the court.

51. For the shameful implications in "snitching: its risks and its rewards," see Daniel C. Richman, "Cooperating Clients," *Ohio State Law Journal* 56 (1995): 77–88.

52. Christine Alice Corcos, "Prosecutors, Prejudices, and Justice: Observations on Presuming Innocence in Popular Culture and Law," *University of Toledo Law Review* 34 (Summer 2003): 793.

53. Frankel, "The Search for Truth," 1040; "Symposium: Responsibilities of the Criminal Defense Attorney," *Loyola of Los Angeles Law Review* 30 (November 1996): 1–138, 108. All eighteen contributors to this symposium complained of communal attitudes on defense attorneys.

54. The boast about guilty clients is the first of thirteen propositions that make up "The Rules of the Justice Game" promulgated by Alan M. Dershowitz, and Dershowitz also notes that "once I decide to take a case, I have only one agenda. I want to win." *The Best Defense* (New York: Random House, 1982), xiv–xxi, 20. The term "megalawyering" is from Dean E. Murphy, "Lawyers in the Limelight," *New York Times*, November 23, 2003, 20.

55. Walter Glaberson, "Courtroom Master of Saber Technique: Thomas Puccio Rattles It and Uses It in Representing Defendants," *New York Times*, December 29, 1996, 25, 30. See, as well, Peter Applebome, "Method or Madness? Lewinsky's Lawyer Baffles Washington Establishment," *New York Times*, March 24, 1998, A21.

56. In Clarence Darrow's classic formulation, "Even the civil lawyers know that poverty is the cause of crime, and that is why they don't practice criminal law. There is no money in it." Quoted in "Clarence Darrow Is Dead in Chicago," *New York Times*, March 14, 1938, 15.

57. Glaberson, "Courtroom Master of Saber Technique," 30.

58. Gordon Von Kessel, "Adversary Excesses in the American Criminal Trial," *Notre Dame Law Review* 67 (1992): 448–59. For the "star status" often conferred on leading defense counsel, see Stephen Gillers, "Great Expectations: Conceptions of Lawyers at the Angle of Entry," *Journal of Legal Education* 33 (1983): 666–67.

59. The quotations are from Jane Gross, "Brash Civilian Lawyer Battles Army in Court-Martial," *New York Times*, February 22, 1998, 12; and Howard Chua-Eoan and Elizabeth Gleick, "Making the Case," *Time* 146 (October 16, 1995): 55; but see, as well, Robert S. Bennett, "Press Advocacy and the High-Profile Client," and Barry Ivan Slotnick, "Defense Counsel as Advocate Outside the Courtroom," both in *Loyola of Los Angeles Law Review* 30 (November 1966): 13–20, 113–18; and Jan Hoffman, "May It

Please the Public: Lawyers Exploit Media Attention as a Defense Tactic," *New York Times*, April 22, 1994, B1.

60. I rely in this paragraph on the distinctions of Vivian Dicks, "Courtroom Rhetorical Strategies: Forensic and Deliberative Perspectives," *Quarterly Journal of Speech* 67 (1981): 178–92.

61. Dershowitz, *The Best Defense*, xiv, 404–5, 410–11.

62. F. Lee Bailey with Harvey Arenson, *The Defense Never Rests: The Art of Cross-Examination* (Ann Arbor: Graduate School of Administration, University of Michigan, 1971), 11–13. But see, as well, Clarence Darrow, *The Story of My Life* (New York: Charles Scribner's Sons, 1932), 2–7, 13–20, 32–37; Alan Dershowitz, "Growing Up Jewish in Boro Park," in *The Best Defense*, 7–13; Joe Jamail, *Lawyer: My Trials and Jubilations* (Austin, TX: Eakin Press, 2003), 18–34; Jeffrey Toobin, "Annals of Law: The Man with Timothy McVeigh," *New Yorker* 72 (September 30, 1996): 50–54; and Michael E. Tigar, "Acknowledgments," in *Examining Witnesses* (Chicago: American Bar Association, 1993), xvii.

63. "Is it proper to cross-examine for the purpose of discrediting the reliability or credibility of an adverse witness whom you know to be telling the truth?" asks Monroe H. Freedman, and his emphatic answer is "yes." Freedman, "Professional Responsibility of the Criminal Defense Lawyer: The Three Hardest Questions," *Michigan Law Review* 64 (June 1966): 1469, 1475. See, as well, Eleanor W. Myers and Edward D. Ohlbaum, "Discrediting the Truthful Witness: Demonstrating the Reality of Adversary Advocacy," *Fordham Law Review* 69 (2000–2001): 1055–82.

64. Soshana Feldman and Dori Laub, *Testimony: Crises of Witnessing in Literature, Psychoanalysis, and History* (London: Routledge, 1992), 3–5; John S. Applegate, "Witness Preparation," *Texas Law Review* 68 (December 1989): 341, 352.

65. Joseph Plescia, "The Oath-Formula," in *The Oath and Perjury in Ancient Greece* (Tallahassee: Florida State University Press, 1970), 1–14; Francis Bacon, *The Essays or Counsels, Civil and Moral* (1625) (Mount Vernon, NY: Peter Pauper Press, 1948), 12; David Mellinkoff, *The Language of the Law* (Boston: Little, Brown, 1963), 172–73, 383–84; John Henry Wigmore, "The Oath at Common Law," in *Evidence in Trials at Common Law*, 10 vols. (Boston: Little, Brown, 1976), 6:382–89; Kevin Tierney, *How to Be a Witness* (Dobbs Ferry, NY: Oceana Publications, 1971), 47–48. The quotation through Mellinkoff is from the California State Penal Code.

66. Daniel Webster, "The Salem Murder Trial, August 1830," in *The Papers of Daniel Webster: Speeches and Formal Writings, Volume 1, 1800–1833*, ed. Charles M. Wiltse (Hanover, NH: University Press of New England, 1986), 401.

67. I rely on Bernard Williams, *Truth and Truthfulness: An Essay in Genealogy* (Princeton, NJ: Princeton University Press, 2002), 11–15, 87–88, 126.

68. F. G. Bailey, "Do What You Will?" in *The Prevalence of Deceit* (Ithaca, NY: Cornell University Press, 1991), 128–29; Richard K. Sherwin, *When Law Goes Pop: The Vanishing Line between Law and Popular Culture* (Chicago: University of Chicago Press, 2000), 49.

69. Educator and philosopher David Nyberg describes "how deception might actually work to improve the moral character of our relationships with each other." Psychologist Kenneth Clark argues that acceptance of "moral duplicities . . . is an index of socialization and maturity," and novelist F. Scott Fitzgerald defines adulthood as the capacity to lie to a priest in confession. Nyberg, *The Varnished Truth: Truth Telling and Deceiving in Ordinary Life* (Chicago: University of Chicago Press, 1993), 195; Clark, "Moral Choices," *Miami Herald*, September 18, 1977, E6; Fitzgerald, "Absolution," in *The Short Stories of F. Scott Fitzgerald*, ed. Matthew J. Bruccoli (New York: Charles Scribner's Sons, 1989), 259.

70. Sutherland and Cressey, *Principles of Criminology*, 444. Nyberg, "Truth, Verdicts, and Justice," in *The Varnished Truth*, 176–91; Peter Meijes Tiersma, "The Language of Perjury: 'Literal Truth,' Ambiguity, and the False Statement Requirement," *Southern California Law Review* 63 (1989–90): 373–431; Tierney, "Keeping Witnesses Honest," in *How to Be a Witness*, 50–51; Tigar, *Examining Witnesses*, 82.

71. Michael P. Reynolds and Philip S. D. King, *The Expert Witness and His Evidence*, 2nd ed. (Oxford: Blackwell Scientific Publications, 1992), 175; Lewis W. Lake, *How to Win Lawsuits Before Juries* (New York: Prentice-Hall, 1954), 165; David Dressler, "Trial by Combat in American Courts," *Harper's Magazine* 222 (April 1961): 31–36.

72. Mauet, *Fundamentals of Trial Techniques*, 85–86.

73. Reynolds and King, *The Expert Witness and His Evidence*, 3.

74. Randall K. Hanson, "Witness Immunity Under Attack: Disarming 'Hired Guns,' " *Wake Forest Law Review* 31 (1996): 497–511; Tigar, *Examining Witnesses*, 245, 260. See, as well, James D. Griffin and William A. Yoder, "Using *Daubert* to Exclude Expert Opinions on Ultimate Issues," *For the Defense* 38 (June 1996): 20–25.

75. See Thomas L. Haskell, "Introduction," and Magali Sarfatti Larson, "The Production of Expertise and the Constitution of Expert Power," in *The Authority of Experts: Studies in History and Theory*, ed. Thomas L. Haskell (Bloomington: Indiana University Press, 1984), ix–xxxix, 28–80.

76. Reynolds and King, *The Expert Witness and His Evidence*, 3.

77. Tigar, *Examining Witnesses*, 212, 220, 229.

78. For the standard listing of jury strengths and weaknesses, see Harry Kalven Jr. and Hans Zeisel, *The American Jury* (Chicago: University of Chicago Press, 1966), 7–9.

79. William Blackstone, *Commentaries on the Laws of England*, 4 vols. (Oxford: Clarendon Press, 1765–69), 4:342–43; 3:349–85; Alexis de Tocqueville, *Democracy in America*, ed. Phillips Bradley, 2 vols. (1835; repr., New York: Vintage Classics, 1990), 1:284–85.

80. Roy Grutman and Bill Thomas, "The Myth of the Impartial Jury," in *Lawyers and Thieves* (New York: Simon & Schuster, 1990), 118–23; Rothwax, *Guilty*, 207.

81. Stephen J. Adler, *The Jury: Trial and Error in the American Courtroom* (New York: Random House, 1994), 46–50. Adler summarizes ABA findings in the quotations.

82. Jeffery Abramson, *We, the Jury: The Jury System and the Ideal of Democracy* (1994; repr., Cambridge, MA: Harvard University Press, 2000), 3–4; Robert A. Wenke, *The Art of Selecting a Jury* (Los Angeles: Parker and Son, 1979), 69.

83. Kalven and Zeisel, *The American Jury*, 4.

84. Adler, introduction to *The Jury*, xvi, 251n; Abramson, *We, the Jury*, 251. See, as well, Valerie B. Hans and Neil Vidmar, "From Trial by Ordeal to Trial by Jury," in *Judging the Jury* (New York: Plenum Press, 1986), 29–30.

85. James B. Thayer, "The Older Modes of Trial," *Harvard Law Review* 5 (May 1891): 45–70; Adler, *The Jury*, 245–46n; and Rita J. Simon, "Introduction and Brief History of the American Jury," in *The Jury: Its Role in American Society* (Lexington, MA: D.C. Heath, 1980), 3–9.

86. Abramson, *We, the Jury*, 8–9.

87. John Locke, *The Essay Concerning Human Understanding* (1690) (New York: Oxford University Press, 1979). See, as well, "John Locke," in *The Oxford Companion to English Literature*, ed. Margaret Drabble, 6th ed. (Oxford: Oxford University Press, 2000), 602–3; and Abramson, *We, the Jury*, 17–18.

88. Adler, *The Jury*, 58–59; Rothwax, *Guilty*, 200–203. But see also Grutman and Thomas, *Lawyers and Thieves*, 117–19 ("The legal system thrives on an uninformed populace"); Peter M. Tiersma, *Legal Language* (Chicago: University of Chicago Press, 1999), 196–98, 231–50 (on the failure in juror comprehension at trial); and Sherwin, *When Law Goes Pop*, 25 (on the shortened attention span of today's juror).

89. Kalven and Zeisel, *The American Jury*, 59, 494–97; Abramson, *We, the Jury*, 253–54; Norman J. Finkel, "Understanding Nullification," in *Commonsense Justice: Jurors' Notions of the Law* (Cambridge, MA: Harvard University Press, 1995), 23–40.

90. Kalven and Zeisel, *The American Jury*, 429.

91. Nancy J. King, "Nameless Justice: The Case for the Routine Use of Anonymous Juries in Criminal Trials," *Vanderbilt Law Review* 49 (1996): 123–59.

92. D. Brock Hornby, "How Jurors See Us," *Maine Bar Journal* 14 (July 1999): 174–80; Kalven and Zeisel, *The American Jury*, 499.

93. See *Apprendi v. New Jersey*, 530 U.S. 466; 120 S. Ct. 2348 (2000); and *Blakely v. Washington*, 124 S. Ct. 2531 (2004).

94. Liminality, a technical term taken from anthropology, signifies an in-between state in cultural formations, and observers of it want the suspension to end one way or another. Liminal personae are "threshold people" in a "necessarily ambiguous state" "neither here nor there." I rely on Victor Turner, "Liminality and Communitas," in *The Ritual Process: Structure and Anti-Structure* (Ithaca, NY: Cornell University Press, 1969), 95–97 and, more generally, 94–130. See, as well, Turner, "Liminal to Liminoid, in Play, Flow, and Ritual," in *From Ritual to Theatre: The Human Seriousness of Play* (New York: PAJ, 1982), 20–60.

95. See, in order, Charlie LeDuff, "Woman Sentenced in Daughter's Death," *New York Times*, August 1, 1996, B3; Sam Howe Verhovek, "Dallas Woman Is Sentenced to Death in Murder of Son," *New York Times*, February 5, 1997, A12; "Rochester Man Is

Convicted in the Serial Murders of 10 Women," *New York Times*, December 14, 1990, B1, 2; John T. McQuiston, "Rifkin at a Sentencing Apologizes for 17 Murders," *New York Times*, January 26, 1996, B6; Vivian S. Toy, "Brooklyn Man Is Guilty in Three Zodiac Killings," *New York Times*, June 25, 1998, B3; Richard W. Stevenson, "Keating Is Sentenced to 10 Years for Defrauding S. & L. Customers," *New York Times*, April 11, 1992, 1, 43; Rick Lyman, "For the [Winona] Ryder Trial, a Hollywood Script," *New York Times*, November 3, 2002, 9:1–8; Editorial, "Justice, Hollywood Style," *New York Times*, November 10, 2002, 4:12; Nick Madigan, "Actress Sentenced to Probation for Shoplifting," *New York Times*, December 7, 2002, A12; "Three Are Sentenced to 15 Years in Fatal Stop Sign Prank," *New York Times*, June 21, 1997, A7.

96. Morris Freilich, Douglas Raybeck, and Joel Savishinsky, "Introduction: The Anthropology of Deviance," in *Deviance: Anthropological Perspectives* (New York: Bergin & Garvey, 1991), 1–24.

97. Michel Foucault, "About the Concept of the 'Dangerous Individual' in 19th-Century Legal Psychiatry," *International Journal of Law and Psychiatry* 1 (1978): 1–3.

98. Paul Gewirtz, "Victims and Voyeurs: Two Narrative Problems at the Criminal Trial," in *Law's Stories: Narrative and Rhetoric in the Law*, ed. Peter Brooks and Paul Gewirtz (New Haven, CT: Yale University Press, 1996), 151.

99. See Wendy Lesser, "The Killer Inside of Us," in *Pictures at an Execution* (Cambridge, MA: Harvard University Press, 1993), 47–92.

100. William Glaberson, "Rethinking a Myth: 'Who Was That Masked Man?'" *New York Times*, January 18, 1998, Wk6; David Johnston, "Judge Sentences Confessed Bomber to Four Life Terms," *New York Times*, May 5, 1998, A1, 24; William Finnegan, "Defending the Unabomber," *New Yorker* 74 (March 16, 1998): 52–63.

101. Teachers accused of child abuse can expect professional ruin even if acquitted after what is now typically a high-profile case. See Robert Reinhold, "2 Acquitted of Child Molestation in Nation's Longest Criminal Trial," *New York Times*, January 19, 1990, A1, 18; and Reinhold, "Collapse of Child-Abuse Case: So Much Agony for So Little," *New York Times*, January 24, 1990, A1, 18.

102. For the distinction between "penalty" and "punishment," see Leo Katz, *Bad Acts and Guilty Minds: Conundrums of the Criminal Law* (Chicago: University of Chicago Press, 1987), 27–29.

103. Nigel Walker, "Stigmatizing," in *Punishment, Danger and Stigma: The Morality of Criminal Justice* (Oxford: Basil Blackwell, 1980), 142–63.

104. Erving Goffman, *Stigma: Notes on the Management of Spoiled Identity* (New York: Jason Aronson, 1974), vii, 21.

105. For "moral cruelty," see Judith N. Shklar, "Putting Cruelty First," in *Ordinary Vices* (Cambridge, MA: Harvard University Press, 1984), 37; and Shklar, *The Faces of Injustice* (New Haven, CT: Yale University Press, 1990), 36–37.

106. Norman Mailer, *The Executioner's Song* (Boston: Little, Brown, 1979), 91.

107. Goffman, *Stigma*, 5.

108. The acquittal of "the Iron Butterfly," Imelda Marcos, the widow of president of the Philippines Ferdinand Marcos, on charges of racketeering and embezzlement in 1990 brought a mixture of outrage and enjoyment in communal reactions with outrage reserved for the failed prosecution. See Adler, "Lawyer's Poker," in *The Jury*, 48–83.

109. A hemispheric menace as the dictator of Panama, General Manuel Antonio Noriega, becomes "the small man in a general's uniform" in Miami federal court when convicted of drug trafficking, racketeering, and conspiracy in 1992. See Knappman, *Great American Trials*, 798–801.

110. Ruth and Reitz, *The Challenge of Crime*, 12, 69 (emphasis in original). See, as well, Lynne N. Henderson, "The Wrongs of Victim's Rights," *Stanford Law Review* 37 (April 1985): 937–1021.

111. 42 U.S.C. #10606a and 10606b (1990) and 18 U.S.C.A. #3510 (1997). I am indebted in this paragraph and the next to the research of Jason F. Cole, "Voices Crying Out in the Wilderness, the Role of Victims in the American Trial: A Study of the Oklahoma City Bombing Trials" (seminar paper, Columbia Law School, December 9, 1998).

112. *Payne v. Tennessee*, 501 U.S. 808 (1991), at 826–27; *Booth v. Maryland*, 482 U.S. 496 (1987).

113. *Booth v. Maryland*, 482 U.S. 520; *Payne v. Tennessee*, 501 U.S. 834. For the acceptance of victim impact statements by the states, see Carrie Mulholland, "Sentencing Criminals: The Constitutionality of Victim Impact Statements," *Missouri Law Review* 60 (1995): 731, 742.

114. William Glaberson, "Court Backs Statements by Survivors," *New York Times*, June 29, 1996, L9; Tim Golden, "Jury Recommends Death for Killer of Polly Klaas," *New York Times*, August 6, 1996, A8.

115. Gewirtz, "Victims and Voyeurs," 149–51, 157.

116. Quoted from Michael J. Sandel, "The Hard Questions: Crying Justice," *New Republic*, July 7, 1997, 25.

117. Glaberson, "Court Backs Statements by Survivors," L9; Brent Staples, "When Grieving 'Victims' Can Sway the Courts: Americans Join the Culture of Revenge," *New York Times*, September 22, 1997, A26. (The writer's brother was murdered while begging for his life.)

118. Staples, "When Grieving 'Victims' Can Sway the Courts," A26.

119. John T. McQuiston, "Victims of Rail Shootings Join to Urge Life Sentence," *New York Times*, March 22, 1995, B12; Eleanor Randolph, "Ferguson Ordered to Prison for Life," *Washington Post*, March 23, 1995, A4.

120. Sandy Banisky, "Survivors to Get Their Day in Court," *Baltimore Sun*, June 4, 1997, A1, 9; Laurence H. Tribe, "Op-Ed: McVeigh's Victims Had a Right to Speak," *New York Times*, June 9, 1997, A25.

121. Andrew Karmen, *Crime Victims: An Introduction to Victimology*, 3rd ed. (New

York: Wadsworth, 1996), 192ff. See, as well, Esther Chinkanda, "Victimization of Women: Some Cultural Features," in *Victimization: Nature and Trends*, ed. W. J. Schurink, Ina Snyman, and W. F. Krugel (Pretoria: HSRC, 1992), 227–331.

122. "Pain and suffering," in *Black's Law Dictionary*, 1109. For a parallel argument on which I rely, see Joseph A. Amato, "Pain and Suffering," in *Victims and Values: A History and a Theory of Suffering* (New York: Greenwood Press, 1990), 14–17.

123. Quoted in Kevin Sack, "Tell It to the Jury: The Killer Is Not a Demon," *New York Times*, June 15, 1997, E3.

124. Leslie A. Fiedler, *An End to Innocence: Essays on Culture and Politics* (1948; repr., Boston: Beacon Press, 1955), 21.

125. Robert Hughes, *Culture of Complaint: The Fraying of America* (New York: Oxford University Press, 1993), 4, 8–9.

126. William Shakespeare, *Hamlet, Prince of Denmark*, I.v.25, 85–86; III.iii.72–78.

127. Homer, *The Iliad*, trans. Richmond Lattimore (Chicago: University of Chicago, 1951), 388; book 18, lines 500–505.

128. For the meaning of "aura," see Walter Benjamin, "The Work of Art in the Age of Mechanical Reproduction," in *Illuminations*, trans. Harry Zohn (1968; repr., New York: Schocken Books, 1969), 221–24.

129. Keir Elam, *The Semiotics of Theatre and Drama* (1980; repr., London: Routledge, 1988), 8. For parallels between law and drama, see Milner S. Ball, "The Play's the Thing: An Unscientific Reflection on Courts Under the Rubric of Theater," *Stanford Law Review* 28 (November 1975): 81–115; and Ball, "All the Law's a Stage," *Cardozo Studies in Law and Literature* 11 (Winter 1999): 215–21.

130. Roland Barthes, *Camera Lucida: Reflections on Photography*, trans. Richard Howard (New York: Hill and Wang, 1981), 76.

131. Harold Clurman, *On Directing* (1972; repr., New York: Simon & Schuster, 1997), 35, 57, 100–101, 111–15, 123.

132. For elaborate attention given to every aspect of courtroom space, see Space and Facilities Committee of the Judicial Conference of the United States, *U.S. Courts Design Guide*, 3rd ed. (Washington, DC: Administrative Office of the U.S. Courts, 1991).

133. These examples are from Stanley L. Brodsky et al., "Attorney Invasion of Witness Space," *Law and Psychology Review* 23 (Spring 1999): 49–63; and Leonard Matheo and Lisa L. DeCaro, "11 Ways to Improve Courtroom Performance," *Brief* 38 (Fall 2001): 58–66.

134. Edward T. Hall, *The Hidden Dimension* (1966; repr., New York: Anchor Books, 1990), 117–24.

135. Jeffrey S. Wolfe, "Toward a Unified Theory of Courtroom Design Criteria: The Effect of Courtroom Design on Adversarial Interaction," *American Journal of Trial Advocacy* 18, no. 3 (1995): 608–9. See, as well, Wolfe, "The Hidden Parameter: Spatial Dynamics and Alternative Dispute Resolution," *Ohio State Journal on Dispute Resolution* 12, no. 3 (1997): 685–738; and Wolfe, "The Effect of Location in the Court-

room on Jury Perception of Lawyer Performance," *Pepperdine Law Review* 21 (1994): 731–76.

136. Peter W. Murphy, " 'There's No Business Like . . . ?': Some Thoughts on the Ethics of Acting in the Courtroom," *South Texas Law Review* 44 (Winter 2002): 117; Donald B. Fiedler, "Acting Effectively in Court: Using Dramatic Techniques," *Champion* 25 (July 2001): 23; Katherine E. Finkelstein, "Relieved, Combs's Lawyer Basks in Victory," *New York Times*, March 19, 2003, B3; Dominick Dunne, "All O.J., All the Time," in *Justice: Crimes, Trials, and Punishments* (New York: Crown, 2001), 151.

137. Richard Severo, "Melvin Belli Dies at 88; Flamboyant Lawyer Relished His Role as King of Torts," *New York Times*, July 11, 1996, B13; Jamail, *Lawyer*, 54; Kate Zernike, "The Wifely Art of Standing By," *New York Times*, October 19, 2003, A1, 7.

138. David Margolick, "With Tale of Racism and Error, Simpson Lawyers Seek Acquittal," *New York Times*, September 29, 2005, A1, A22; "Race Cards and Rebuttals," *New York Times*, September 30, 1995, 18; Chua-Eoan and Gleick, "Making the Case," 57, 54. (Cochran is quoted in *Time*.)

CHAPTER THREE

1. For an account that sees this issue as "the real treason," see Gordon S. Wood, "The Real Treason of Aaron Burr," *Proceedings of the American Philosophical Society* 143 (June 1999): 280–93.

2. Joanne B. Freeman, "Dueling as Politics: Reinterpreting the Burr-Hamilton Duel," *William and Mary Quarterly*, 3rd ser., 53 (April 1996): 289–318. The involved rituals around a challenge usually led to an accommodation. Hamilton, for example, had been involved in ten previous affairs of honor without engaging in combat.

3. One witness of Burr's frequent boast—a witness who then called it murder— was Jeremy Bentham in 1808. See Milton Lomask, *Aaron Burr*, 2 vols. (New York: Farrar, Straus and Giroux, 1979–82), 2:309. I rely on this standard biography when there are conflicts about the life and surrounding events.

4. John Adams to Thomas Jefferson, November 15, 1813, in *The Complete Correspondence Between Thomas Jefferson and Abigail and John Adams*, ed. Lester J. Cappon, 2 vols. (Chapel Hill: University of North Carolina Press, 1959), 2:399.

5. Aaron Burr to Sally Burr Reeve, January 17, 1774, in Lomask, preface to *Aaron Burr*, 1:xix.

6. Seymour Martin Lipset, *The First New Nation: The United States in Historical and Comparative Perspective* (New York: Basic Books, 1963).

7. Edmund Stedman, "Aaron Burr's Wooing" (1887), in *The Poems of Edmund Clarence Stedman* (Boston: Houghton Mifflin, 1908), 389–90.

8. For the shifts in Aaron Burr's reputation and depiction of them, see Charles J. Nolan Jr., *Aaron Burr and the American Literary Imagination* (Westport, CT: Greenwood Press, 1980).

9. Gore Vidal, *Burr: A Novel* (New York: Random House, 1973); Roger G. Kennedy,

Burr, Hamilton, and Jefferson: A Study in Character (Oxford: Oxford University Press, 2000), 87–110, 353, 377. The quotations in the text are from Kennedy. See, as well, Thomas Fleming, *Duel: Alexander Hamilton, Aaron Burr, and the Future of America* (New York: Basic Books, 1999).

10. Lomask, *Aaron Burr*, 2:235–36, 275. See, as well, Herbert S. Parmet and Marie B. Hecht, *Aaron Burr: Portrait of an Ambitious Man* (New York: Macmillan, 1967), 299–300; Nolan, *Aaron Burr and the American Literary Imagination*, 35–36; and, most recently, Buckner F. Melton Jr., *Aaron Burr: Conspiracy to Treason* (New York: John Wiley & Sons, 2002), 210–13.

11. Robert A. Ferguson, "The Configuration of Law and Letters," in *Law and Letters in American Culture* (Cambridge, MA: Harvard University Press, 1985), 1–83.

12. For the controlling importance of Wickham's argument, the quotation cited (from Littleton W. Tazewell, a respected lawyer but also a member of the grand jury responsible for the indictment of Burr), and Luther Martin's eloquence, see Lomask, *Aaron Burr*, 2:270–72, 245–46, 277–79. The trial transcript reveals Wickham's dominance as well. Case reporter David Robertson placed Wickham's decisive argument at the end of volume 1 of his *Reports*; much of the advocacy in volume 2 revolves around Wickham's argument.

13. Art. 3, sec. 3, part 1, of the U.S. Constitution reads, "Treason against the United States shall consist only in levying War against them, or in adhering to their Enemies, giving them Aid and Comfort. No Person shall be convicted of Treason unless on the Testimony of two Witnesses to the same overt Act, or on Confession in open Court."

14. David Robertson, *Reports of the Trials of Colonel Aaron Burr, Late Vice President of the United States, for Treason and for a Misdemeanor . . . in the Circuit Court of the United States Held at the City of Richmond, in the District of Virginia, in the Summer Term of the Year 1807*, 2 vols. (Philadelphia: Hopkins and Earle, 1808), 2:96–97. Blennerhassett is Blannerhassett throughout the transcript. All further references to Robertson's *Reports* will be to this edition in parenthetical citations in the text.

15. Samuel Johnson, "Rambler 2," in *Essays from the Rambler, Adventurer, and Idler*, ed. W. J. Bate (New Haven, CT: Yale University Press, 1968), 4.

16. John Milton, *Paradise Lost*, book 1, lines 254–55.

17. Samuel Johnson, *The Vanity of Human Wishes*, lines 27–28, 263–64, in *The Works of Samuel Johnson*, ed. E. L. McAdam Jr. and George Milne, 12 vols. (New Haven, CT: Yale University Press, 1964), 6:90–109. Samuel Johnson was "by far the most widely available author, English or American, in the American book trade" and maintained "an astonishing dominance of the American periodical press throughout the late eighteenth and early nineteenth centuries," exceeding reference to even George Washington and Benjamin Franklin in the periodical press by 1810. See James Basker, "Samuel Johnson and the American Common Reader," in *The Age of Johnson: A Scholarly Annual*, ed. Paul J. Korshin (New York: AMS Press, 1994), 6–13.

18. William Shakespeare, *Hamlet, Prince of Denmark*, I.ii.129–59.

19. "Deciders perceive whole stories" and "the way you tell it makes all the dif-

ference." Michael E. Tigar, "The Theory of the Case," in *Examining Witnesses* (Chicago: American Bar Association, 1993), 4–16. See, as well, Anthony G. Amsterdam and Jerome Bruner, "On Narrative," in *Minding the Law* (Cambridge, MA: Harvard University Press, 2000), 110–42.

20. William Blackstone, *Commentaries on the Laws of England*, 4 vols. (Oxford: Clarendon Press, 1765–69), 4:74–75. See, as well, Karen Halttunen, "The Murderer as Common Sinner," in *Murder Most Foul: The Killer and the American Gothic Imagination* (Cambridge, MA: Harvard University Press, 1998), 7–32.

21. John Adams to Benjamin Rush, September 1, 1807, and Benjamin Rush to John Adams, July 9, 1807, in *The Spur of Fame: Dialogues of John Adams and Benjamin Rush, 1805–1813*, ed. John A. Schultz and Douglass Adair (San Marino, CA: Huntington Library, 1966), 98–99.

22. Robert Middlekauff, "The Ritualization of the American Revolution," in *The Development of an American Culture*, ed. Stanley Coben and Lorman Ratner (Englewood Cliffs, NJ: Prentice-Hall, 1970), 31–44; Robert N. Bellah, "Civil Religion in America," *Daedalus* 96 (Winter 1967): 1–21. The quotation is from Middlekauff, "Ritualization," 41.

23. Alexander Hamilton, "The Federalist No. 72," in *The Federalist: A Commentary on the Constitution of the United States*, ed. Edward Mead Earle (New York: Modern Library, 1937), 470; John Adams to Benjamin Rush, August 23, 1805, in *The Spur of Fame*, ed. Schultz and Adair, 34; and Schultz and Adair, "The Love of Fame, the Ruling Passion of the Noblest Minds," in *The Spur of Fame*, 1–18.

24. "Thomas Jefferson: Memorandum of a Conversation with Burr," in *Political Correspondence and Public Papers of Aaron Burr*, ed. Mary-Jo Kline and Joanne Wood Ryan, 2 vols. (Princeton, NJ: Princeton University Press, 1983), 2:962–63. All further quotations in the next two paragraphs are from this source.

25. Thomas Jefferson to Dr. Joseph Priestley, January 29, 1804, in *Thomas Jefferson: Writings*, ed. Merrill D. Peterson (New York: Library of America, 1984), 1142.

26. Thomas Jefferson to General James Wilkinson, September 20, 1807, in *The Writings of Thomas Jefferson*, ed. Albert Ellery Bergh, 20 vols. (Washington, DC: Thomas Jefferson Memorial Association, 1907), 11:375.

27. Andrew Delbanco, *The Death of Satan: How Americans Have Lost the Sense of Evil* (New York: Farrar, Straus and Giroux, 1995), 44, 234.

28. Joyce Appleby, *Inheriting the Revolution: The First Generation of Americans* (Cambridge, MA: Harvard University Press, 2000), 1–55.

29. John R. Adams, *Edward Everett Hale* (Boston: Twayne, 1977), 27, 111; "Edward Everett Hale, 1822–1909," *Nation* 83 (June 17, 1909): 604–5.

30. Edward Everett Hale, "The Man without A Country," *Atlantic Monthly* 12 (December 1863): 665–79. All further references to the story are to this original version and will be noted parenthetically by page number in the text. (Hale made minor adjustments in later versions of the story to increase its narrative claims to authenticity as history.)

31. Edward Everett Hale, "Author's Note to Edition of 1897," in *The Man without a Country and Other Stories* (Boston: Little, Brown, 1899), 4, 11–13.

32. Ibid., 3. For scholarly confirmation of this point, see Carl Van Doren, introduction to *The Man without a Country* (New York: Marchbanks Press, 1936), ix.

33. Hale, "Author's Note to Edition of 1897," 16–19. Hale's compulsive desire to authenticate his story is shown in his minor corrections of historical fact in later editions. I am indebted for the full extent of Hale's compulsive authentications in later editions to John Seckinger, " 'The Man without a Country': Its Moment of Production, Moment of Representation, Reception History, and Adaptations" (course essay submitted in the graduate program of the Department of English and Comparative Literature, University of California at Irvine). See, as well, Adams, *Edward Everett Hale*, 30.

34. Mark, 5:1–15.

35. For readers' reactions, see Jean Holloway, *Edward Everett Hale, a Biography* (Austin: University of Texas Press, 1956), 139ff.

36. David Richard Kasserman, "Public Justice," in *Fall River Outrage: Life, Murder, and Justice in Early Industrial New England* (Philadelphia: University of Pennsylvania Press, 1986), 213–45.

37. Lomask, *Aaron Burr*, 2:232–35, 251, 199. For the direct source of Jefferson's comment and other public statements regarding Burr's guilt, see *American State Papers: Miscellaneous* (Washington, DC: Government Printing Office, 1835), 1:472; see, as well, James Richardson, ed., *A Compilation of Messages and Papers of the Presidents, 1789–1897*, 10 vols. (Washington, DC: Government Printing Office, 1896–99), 1:406, 412–17.

38. Implied and direct threats of impeachment against Marshall appear in Robertson's *Report* at 2:193, 200, 205, 238; and Raymond E. Fitch, ed., *Breaking with Burr: Harman Blennerhassett's Journal, 1807* (Athens: Ohio University Press, 1988), 61. See, as well, Lomask, *Aaron Burr*, 2:276–77; and Samuel H. Smith and Thomas Lloyd, eds., *The Trial of Samuel Chase, an Associate Justice of the Supreme Court of the United States, Impeached by the House of Representatives, for High Crimes and Misdemeanors, before the Senate of the United States*, 2 vols. (Washington, DC: Samuel H. Smith, 1805), 1:8ff.

39. *Ex parte Bollman*, 4 Cranch 75, 115, 125–27 (1807).

40. G. Edward White, *The American Judicial Tradition: Profiles of Leading American Judges* (New York: Oxford University Press, 1976), 11–15; Albert J. Beveridge, *The Life of John Marshall*, 3 vols. (Boston: Houghton Mifflin, 1919), 3:504.

41. *The Private Journal of Aaron Burr, During His Residence of Four Years in Europe; with Selections from His Correspondence*, ed. Matthew L. Davis, 2 vols. (New York: Harper and Brothers, 1838), 1:382.

42. Ibid., 1:228, 411; 2:53.

43. Ibid., 1:435, 428, 413, 441; 2:32–33, 82, 108.

44. Ibid., 1:431, 124, 412, 434, 127, 228, 333, 300; 2:27, 72, 80, 95.

45. Ibid., 1:72–73, 114; 2:10.

46. Ibid., 1:94, 227; 2:10.

47. Ibid., 2:128.

48. For the symbolism and cultural importance of the Panthéon, see Priscilla Parkhurst Ferguson, *Literary France: The Making of a Culture* (Berkeley: University of California Press, 1987), 1–7.

49. Quoted in James Parton, *The Life and Times of Aaron Burr* (New York: Mason Brothers, 1858), 670.

50. Lomask, *Aaron Burr*, 2:405–6.

CHAPTER FOUR

1. Ralph Waldo Emerson to Sarah Swain Forbes, October 26, 1859, in *The Letters of Ralph Waldo Emerson*, ed. Ralph L. Rusk, 6 vols. (New York: Columbia University Press, 1939), 5:179–80.

2. *The Oxford Companion to American Literature*, 4th ed. (New York: Oxford University Press, 1965), 724; Henry James, *The Art of the Novel: Critical Prefaces* (1907; repr., New York: Charles Scribner's Sons, 1937), 33–34.

3. David Potter, *The Impending Crisis, 1848–1861* (New York: Harper & Row, 1976), 358. See, as well, Frederick Douglass, "John Brown," in *A John Brown Reader*, ed. Louis Ruchames (New York: Abelard-Schuman, 1959), 322.

4. John Brown to Judge Daniel R. Tilden, November 28, 1859, and John Brown to his family, November 30, 1859, quoted in *John Brown*, ed. Richard Warch and Jonathan Fanton (Englewood Cliffs, NJ: Prentice-Hall, 1973), 98, 100.

5. "A Conversation with Brown: Harper's Ferry, October 19, 1859," in *The Life, Trial and Execution of Captain John Brown, known as "Old Brown of Ossawatomie," with a full account of the attempted Insurrection at Harper's Ferry*, ed. Robert M. De Witt (1859; repr., New York: Da Capo Press, 1969), 45. I prefer this source as the first relatively complete and widely circulated record of all of the events in the Brown saga and because it had great impact at the time.

6. For the failure of the raid, see Warch and Fanton, *John Brown*, 59; and Stephen B. Oates, *To Purge This Land with Blood: A Biography of John Brown*, 2nd ed. (Amherst: University of Massachusetts Press, 1984), 294–302. For a minority view, see Karen Whitman, "Re-evaluating John Brown's Raid at Harpers Ferry," *West Virginia History* 34, no. 1 (1974): 46–84.

7. In stressing Hawthorne's understanding of the romance, I enter scholarly controversies about the definition of the romance and about the possibly exaggerated role assigned to Hawthorne in supplying those definitions. I justify it here in terms of Hawthorne's influence on the other intellectual figures that I examine in regard to John Brown. Hawthorne alludes to these figures—Theodore Parker, Richard Henry Dana Jr., William Ellery Channing, Ralph Waldo Emerson, Henry Thoreau, and Henry Wadsworth Longfellow—in the widely read prefaces in which he gives his

version of the romance, and all of them were familiar and comfortable with his definition. I try to restrict my own definition of the romance to those characteristics
accepted today by all parties as generally prominent in the 1850s. See George Dekker,
"Once More: Hawthorne and the Genealogy of American Romance," *ESQ: A Journal of the American Renaissance* 35, no. 1 (1989): 69–83; and John McWilliams, "The
Rationale for 'The American Romance,'" *Boundary 2* 17 (Spring 1990): 71–82. For
the best argument questioning the clarity of the term in the 1850s and Hawthorne's
influence on it, see Nina Baym, "Concepts of the Romance in Hawthorne's America," *Nineteenth-Century Fiction* 38 (March 1984): 426–43. For a partial counter, see
J. Lasley Dameron, "Hawthorne and the Popular Concept of the Prose Romance,"
English Studies 68 (April 1987): 154–59.

8. Quoted in James R. Mellow, *Nathaniel Hawthorne in His Times* (Boston:
Houghton Mifflin, 1980), 551–52. See also Nathaniel Hawthorne to H. Woodman,
June 26 1862, in *The Letters, 1857–1864*, vol. 18 of *The Centenary Edition of the Works of
Nathaniel Hawthorne*, ed. Thomas Woolson et al. (Columbus: Ohio State University
Press, 1987), 463–64.

9. Nathaniel Hawthorne to James T. Fields, November 3, 1850, in *The Letters, 1843–
1853*, vol. 16 of *Centenary Edition*, 371.

10. Louis Filler, *The Crusade Against Slavery, 1830–1860* (New York: Harper & Row,
1960), 241; Potter, *Impending Crisis*, 357–62.

11. John Brown to Mary Ann Day Brown, November 10, 1859, quoted in Oswald Garrison Villard, *John Brown, 1800–1859: A Biography Fifty Years After* (Boston:
Houghton Mifflin, 1910), 540.

12. During the six-day trial, Brown was represented by six lawyers in all, none of
whom are formal defense counsel for more than half of the proceedings. Charles J.
Faulkner and Lawson Botts, of the Virginia bar, were assigned by the court to represent Brown, but Brown rejected each in turn at strategic moments. When Faulkner
resigned at the end of the first day of proceedings, the court added Thomas C. Green,
another member of the Virginia bar. George H. Hoyt of Massachusetts, Henry Griswold of Ohio, and Samuel Chilton of Washington, D.C., arrived on the third and
fourth days of the trial to take up the defense with Green and Botts resigning on the
arrival of "foreign counsel." Brown followed the advice of his lawyers only when it was
convenient for his own purposes and did what no lawyer welcomes—he insisted on
speaking for himself. See De Witt, *The Life, Trial and Execution*, 55, 58, 61, 72, 77–78.

13. The quotations are from "The Last Days of John Brown" and "A Plea for Cap-
tain John Brown." Both speeches relied heavily on newspaper coverage. See Wendell
Glick, ed., *Henry D. Thoreau: Reform Papers* (Princeton, NJ: Princeton University
Press, 1973), 145, 125.

14. August 8 and August 25, *The Records of the Federal Convention of 1787*, ed. Max
Farrand, rev. ed., 4 vols. (New Haven, CT: Yale University Press, 1966), 2:220–23, 415–
19. See, as well, Gary B. Nash, "The Failure of Abolitionism," in *Race and Revolution*
(Madison, WI: Madison House, 1990), 25–55. James Madison was one of the first to

call the institution of slavery "a peculiar one" in the republic of laws in "The Federalist No. 54," in *New York Packet*, Tuesday, February 12, 1788.

15. For estimations that only one of every twenty Northern voters was an abolitionist in the 1840s and early 1850s and the history of "gag rules," see David Herbert Donald, *Liberty and Union* (Boston: Little, Brown, 1978), 16–20; and Glyndon G. Van Deusen, *The Jacksonian Era, 1828–1848* (New York: Harper & Brothers, 1959), 108, 133–35.

16. For the negative aspects of Brown's life, see Filler, *Crusade Against Slavery*, 239–43; and Warch and Fanton, *John Brown*, 1–12. Oswald Garrison Villard's assessment of Brown's clear responsibility for "the Pottawatomie Massacre" on the night of May 23–24, 1856, is now generally accepted. See Villard, *John Brown*, 170–88.

17. For Brown's business failures and lawsuits between 1837 and 1854, see Oates, *To Purge This Land*, 37, 45–49, 76–77.

18. For Brown's contempt for politics and politicians, see ibid., 20–21.

19. John Brown to Harry Stearns, July 15, 1857, in *The Life and Letters of John Brown*, ed. Franklin B. Sanborn (Boston: Roberts Brothers, 1891), 12–17. All references to the Brown "autobiography" in the text are from this source.

20. Potter, *Impending Crisis*, 356.

21. Ralph Waldo Emerson, "July 12–14, 1842," in *Emerson in His Journals*, ed. Joel Porte (Cambridge, MA: Harvard University Press, 1982), 287. Proclus (410?–485 A.D.) was a Neoplatonic Greek philosopher who emphasized that thoughts, not things, comprise reality.

22. For Brown's tendency to lie and his ineptitude in business, see Oates, *To Purge This Land*, 10, 45, 56–57, 76–77, 187, 203–4.

23. Ibid., 20, 53.

24. For an analysis of the American self in these terms, see Larzer Ziff, *Writing in the New Nation: Prose, Print, and Politics in the Early United States* (New Haven, CT: Yale University Press, 1991), xi, 77, 114.

25. Fred Somkin, *Unquiet Eagle: Memory and Desire in the Idea of American Freedom, 1815–1860* (Ithaca, NY: Cornell University Press, 1967).

26. See George Dekker, *The American Historical Romance* (Cambridge: Cambridge University Press, 1987); and Gillian Brown, *Domestic Individualism: Imagining Self in Nineteenth-Century America* (Berkeley: University of California Press, 1990).

27. See Peter Brooks, *The Melodramatic Imagination: Balzac, Henry James, Melodrama, and the Mode of Excess* (New Haven, CT: Yale University Press, 1976), 1–23, 198–206; Richard Chase, *The American Novel and Its Tradition* (1957; repr., Baltimore: Johns Hopkins University Press, 1980), 1; and Michael Taylor, "Reluctant Romancers: Self-Consciousness and Derogation in Prose Romance," *English Studies in Canada* 17 (March 1991): 89–105.

28. These quotations and paraphrases are from Hawthorne's prefaces to his romances. *The Blithedale Romance*, vol. 3 of *The Centenary Edition*, 2; and *The Scarlet*

Letter, vol. 1 of *The Centenary Edition*, 33–36. Subsequent references refer to these editions.

29. Hawthorne, *The House of the Seven Gables*, 2.

30. "A Conversation with Brown," in De Witt, *The Life, Trial and Execution*, 49.

31. Hawthorne, *The House of the Seven Gables*, 8; John Brown quoted in Oates, *To Purge This Land*, 351. See, as well, the Epistle of Paul the Apostle to the Hebrews, 9:12–25.

32. Abraham Lincoln, "Second Inaugural Address, March 4, 1865," in *The Collected Works of Abraham Lincoln*, ed. Roy P. Basler, 9 vols. (New Brunswick, NJ: Rutgers University Press, 1953–55), 8:333.

33. For these qualities of the romance, see Dekker, "Once More," 78–79; Evan Carton, *The Rhetoric of American Romance: Dialectic and Identity in Emerson, Dickinson, Poe, and Hawthorne* (Baltimore: Johns Hopkins University Press, 1985); McWilliams, "The Rationale for 'The American Romance,'" 72–73; Michael Davitt Bell, *The Development of American Romance: The Sacrifice of Relation* (Chicago: University of Chicago Press, 1980); Frederick Newberry, "A New Perspective on the American Romance: A Review Essay," *Poe Studies* 14 (December 1981): 33–39; and E. Miller Budick, "The World as Specter: Hawthorne's Historical Art," *PMLA* 101 (March 1986): 225ff.

34. For the prominence of the grotesque in the American romance and in Hawthorne in particular, see Robert S. Levine, *Conspiracy and Romance: Studies in Brockden Brown, Cooper, Hawthorne, and Melville* (Cambridge: Cambridge University Press, 1989).

35. See Oates, *To Purge This Land*, 294–99, 356. See also Cecil D. Eby, ed., "The Last Hours of the John Brown Raid: The Narrative of David H. Strother," *Virginia Magazine of History and Biography* 73 (April 1965): 169–77. The quotation about Watson Brown's body is from Truman Nelson, "John Brown Revisited," *Nation* 135 (August 31, 1957): 86–88.

36. The first quotation in this sentence is from Thoreau, "A Plea for Captain John Brown," 190. The second is from Colonel J. T. L. Preston of the Virginia Military Institute, observing Brown's execution: "So perish all such enemies of Virginia! All such enemies of the Union! All such foes of the human race!" in Oates, *To Purge This Land*, 352.

37. The quotations here and in the next four paragraphs of Thoreau's critique of Brown are all from "The Last Days of John Brown," 192–98.

38. Thoreau's unworthy readers are Hawthorne's uncomprehending companions in the Custom-House. See *The Scarlet Letter*, 3–4, 20–25, 38–40, 44.

39. Michael Meyer, "Thoreau's Rescue of John Brown from History," in *Studies in the American Renaissance 1980*, ed. Joel Myerson (Charlottesville: University of Virginia Press, 1980), 301–16, Donald Pease, *Visionary Compacts: American Renaissance Writings in Cultural Context* (Madison: University of Wisconsin Press, 1986).

40. Although many commentators note the power of Brown's words at trial, most ignore the context and give the trial itself cursory treatment. The compilation of materials on Brown by Richard Warch and Jonathan Fanton gives less than 5 of 178 pages to the trial. Stephen Oates's definitive biography of Brown describes the trial in just 4 pages. See Warch and Fanton, *John Brown*, 79, 81–84; and Oates, *To Purge This Land*, 324–27.

41. See, in particular, Kenneth L. Smith, "Edmund Ruffin and the Raid on Harpers Ferry," *Virginia Cavalcade* 22, no. 2 (1972): 28–37; Craig Simpson, "John Brown and Governor Wise: A New Perspective on Harpers Ferry," *Biography* 1 (Fall 1978): 15–38; Isaiah A. Woodward, "Document: John Brown's Raid at Harpers Ferry and Governor Henry Alexander Wise's Letter to President James Buchanan Concerning the Invasion," *West Virginia History* 42 (1981): 307–13; and Donald Brooks Kelley, "Harper's Ferry: Prelude to Crisis in Mississippi," *Journal of Mississippi History* 27 (November 1965): 351–72.

42. De Witt, *The Life, Trial and Execution*, 50. All further references to this account of the trial are noted parenthetically in the text.

43. "The Virginia Judiciary," *New York Times*, October 24, 1859.

44. Hawthorne, "The Custom-House," in *The Scarlet Letter*, 35–36.

45. References to the devil in John Brown were frequent in Southern commentary. See, for example, Edward White, "Eyewitness at Harpers Ferry," *American Heritage* 26, no. 2 (1975): 57.

46. Smith, "Edmund Ruffin," 33, 37.

47. Ibid., 36.

48. Quoted in Simpson, "John Brown and Governor Wise," 17.

49. Emerson and Thoreau both used Governor Wise's acknowledgment of Brown's courage to portray Brown's inherent superiority. See John J. McDonald, "Emerson and John Brown," *New England Quarterly* 44, no. 3 (1971): 385; Thoreau "A Plea for Captain John Brown," 175–76. Brown's attorneys repeatedly referred to their client's integrity through his courage. See De Witt, *The Life, Trial and Execution*, 67, 89.

50. De Witt, *The Life, Trial and Execution*, 100–101.

51. John Brown to his family, November 30, 1859, quoted in Warch and Fanton, *John Brown*, 100.

52. Quoted in Oates, *To Purge This Land*, 319. See, as well, Theodore Parker to Francis Jackson, November 24, 1859, in Ruchames, *A John Brown Reader*, 265–66.

53. Biblical references are frequent and precise in Brown's prison letters. See Brown to "E.B.," November 1, 1859 ("You know that Christ once armed Peter. So also in my case I think he put a sword into my hand"); Brown to his family, October 30, 1859 ("I am in charge of a jailer like the one who took charge of Paul and Silas"); Brown to Reverend James W. McFarland, November 23, 1859 ("I think I feel as happy as Paul did when he lay in prison"); Brown to Reverend Dr. Heman Humphrey, November

25, 1859 ("If the cause in which I engaged in any possible degree approximated to be 'infinitely better' than the one which Saul of Tarsus undertook, I have no reason to be ashamed") ("I did not tell Delilah"); Brown to his family, November 8, 1859 ("Remember, my dear wife and children all, that Jesus of Nazareth suffered a most excruciating death on the cross as a felon, under the most aggravated circumstances"); Brown to Reverend H. L. Vaill, November 15, 1859 ("I, at least, am on the 'brink of Jordan.' See Bunyan's 'Pilgrim' "). All quoted in Warch and Fanton, *John Brown*, 90, 90, 96, 98, 92, 94.

54. Brown to Reverend James W. McFarland, November 23, 1859, in ibid., 96. Emerson's comment that Brown "will make the gallows glorious, like a cross," appeared in a Boston lecture entitled "Courage" on November 7, 1859, quoted in McDonald, "Emerson and John Brown," 386–87. Emerson removed the comment from the published version of the final essay, and McDonald traces the tangled history of treatment of the passage.

55. Peter Brooks analyzes the "literary aesthetic of excess" of the period in *The Melodramatic Imagination*, 200–202. See, as well, Perry Miller, "From Edwards to Emerson," in *The Errand into the Wilderness* (1956; repr., New York: Harper & Row, 1964), 184–203; Ralph Waldo Emerson, "Nature" (1836), in *The Complete Essays and Other Writings of Ralph Waldo Emerson*, ed. Brooks Atkinson (New York: Random House, 1940), 15.

56. The need to find purity in Brown obsessed Northerners. See, for examples, Louisa May Alcott's "With a Rose That Bloomed on the Day of John Brown's Martyrdom," and John Greenleaf Whittier's "Brown of Osawatomie," in Ruchames, *A John Brown Reader*, 271, 295.

57. De Witt, *The Life, Trial and Execution*, 79–81.

58. See ibid., 58, 62–63, 78–79.

59. Andrew Hunter, the special prosecutor of Governor Henry A. Wise, was a relative of the militiaman from Charlestown, Henry Hunter, who admitted on the witness stand that he had murdered a defenseless captured raider. Hunter was also related to one of the town victims at Harpers Ferry, the mayor of the town, Fontaine Beckham. See ibid., 74–76; and Oates, *To Purge This Land*, 296–97, 309, 325.

60. Oates, *To Purge This Land*, 309.

61. The charge of insanity challenged Brown's whole stance of self-sacrifice, and he worried enough about it to mount a public relations campaign against from prison. See Brown to Reverend Dr. Heman Humphrey, November 25, 1859, and Brown to Judge Daniel R. Tilden, November 28, 1859, in Warch and Fanton, *John Brown*, 97, 99.

62. See Oates, *To Purge This Land*, 293–94.

63. Ralph Waldo Emerson, "Eloquence," in *The Complete Works of Ralph Waldo Emerson*, 12 vols. (Boston: Houghton Mifflin, 1903–4), 8:125.

64. Journal entry for October 6, 1834, in Porte, *Emerson in His Journals*, 128.

65. All quotations from Brown's presentencing speech in these four paragraphs are from De Witt, *The Life, Trial and Execution*, 94–95.

66. For evidence that Brown meant to start an insurrection at Harpers Ferry, see Potter, *Impending Crisis*, 365–68. As Brown told Frederick Douglass, in trying to recruit him, "When I strike, the bees will swarm, and I shall want you to help hive them." Quoted in Oates, *To Purge This Land*, 283.

67. This passage is the heart or middle of Brown's brief speech, sentences eight through fifteen of the twenty-six that he offered to the court.

68. Entry from May–July 1851, in Porte, *Emerson in His Journals*, 426.

69. Matt. 7:12.

70. Brown to Reverend James W. McFarland, November 23, 1859, in Warch and Fanton, *John Brown*, 96. "These ministers who profess to be Christian, and hold slaves or advocate slavery," wrote Brown, "I cannot abide them. My knees will not bend in prayer with them, while their hands are stained with the blood of souls." For these reasons, Brown refused a state-sanctioned minister at his execution. See Brown to Mrs. George L. Stearns, November 29, 1859, in ibid., 99.

71. Hans-Robert Jauss, "Literary History as a Challenge to Literary Theory," *New Literary History* 2 (1970): 7–19; Susan R. Suleiman, "Introduction: Varieties of Audience-Oriented Criticism," in *The Reader in the Text: Essays on Audience and Interpretation*, ed. Susan R. Suleiman and Inge Crosman (Princeton, NJ: Princeton University Press, 1980), 35–40.

72. Hayden White, "The Historical Text as Literary Artifact," in *Tropics of Discourse: Essays in Cultural Criticism* (1978; repr., Baltimore: Johns Hopkins University Press, 1990), 88.

73. Ralph Waldo Emerson, "John Brown," in *The Complete Works*, 11:279.

74. Boyd B. Stutler, "John Brown's Body," *Civil War History* 4 (September 1958): 251–60.

75. Roland Barthes, *Image, Music, Text*, trans. Stephen Heath (New York: Farrar, Straus and Giroux, 1977), 79.

76. Wolfgang Iser, "Interaction between Text and Reader," in Suleiman and Crosman, *The Reader in the Text*, 113–18.

CHAPTER FIVE

1. Relevant figures and percentages are taken from "Death Row USA," NAACP Legal Defense Fund Report for 2004–2005, also at http://www.deathpenaltyinfo.org/womenstats.htm; *Bureau of Justice Statistics, 2000–2003*; and Victor L. Streib, *Death Penalty for Female Offenders, January 1, 1973, through December 31, 2004*, at http://www/law.onu.edu/faculty/streib/documents/FemDeathDec2004.pdf. Consult these sources for further updates, but see, as well, Elizabeth Rapaport, "Staying Alive: Executive Clemency, Equal Protection, and the Politics of Gender in Women's Capital Cases," *Buffalo Criminal Law Review* 4 (2000–2001): 967–1007; and Rapaport, "Equality of the Damned: The Execution of Women on the Cusp of the 21st Century," *Ohio Northern University Law Review* 26, no. 3 (2000): 581–600. Rapaport, giving numbers

as well as percentages, reports that more than six hundred men but only four women were executed between 1976 and 2000. See, as well, Victor L. Streib, "Death Penalty for Female Offenders," *Cincinnati Law Review* 58, no. 3 (1990): 845–81.

2. Accounts differ on the timing of Payne's words but not their content. See Dorothy Meserve Kunhardt and Philip B. Kunhardt Jr., *Twenty Days: A Narrative in Text and Pictures of the Assassination of Abraham Lincoln and the Twenty Days and Nights that Followed—The Nation in Mourning, the Long Trip Home to Springfield* (New York: Harper and Row, 1965), 210; John A. Gray, "The Fate of the Lincoln Conspirators: The Account of the Hanging, Given by Lieutenant-Colonel Christian Rath, the Executioner," *McClure's Magazine* 82 (October 1911): 635–36; and Guy W. Moore, *The Case of Mrs. Surratt: Her Controversial Trial and Execution for the Conspiracy in the Lincoln Assassination* (Norman: University of Oklahoma Press, 1954), 58–60. For a partial counterquestioning of Payne's claim, see Roy Z. Chamlee Jr., *Lincoln's Assassins: A Complete Account of Their Capture, Trial, and Punishment* (Jefferson, NC: McFarland, 1990), 462.

3. Benn Pitman [recorder to the commission], "Frontispiece," in *The Assassination of President Lincoln and the Trial of the Conspirators* (New York: Moore, Wilstach & Baldwin, 1865).

4. Ibid., 18.

5. James O. Clephant [official reporter], *Official Report of the Trial of Mary Harris, indicted for the Murder of Adoniram J. Burroughs, before the Supreme Court of the District of Columbia, (Sitting as a Criminal Court)* (Washington, DC: W. H. & O. H. Morrison, 1865).

6. See, for example, Philip K. Hastings, "Level of Information and Opinion Content," *Political Science Quarterly* 69 (June 1954): 235–40; and Gary Blasi, "Advocacy Against the Stereotype: Lessons from Cognitive Social Psychology," *UCLA Law Review* 49 (June 2002): 1243, 1247–50, 1278.

7. Moore, *The Case of Mrs. Surratt*, 108. The Rev. J. G. Butler of St. Paul's Church reports these words of Andrew Johnson in explanation of his denial just hours after the execution.

8. Pitman, *Trial of the Conspirators*, 22–44; Moore, *The Case of Mrs. Surratt*, 86–89. The government would also seize Ford's Theatre when Ford tried to reopen it on July 11, 1865.

9. Pitman, *Trial of the Conspirators*, 280, 292; *Harper's Weekly*, July 22, 1865, 457.

10. Abraham Lincoln, " 'A House Divided': Speech at Springfield, Illinois, June 16, 1858," in *The Collected Works of Abraham Lincoln*, ed. Roy P. Basler, 9 vols. (New Brunswick, NJ: Rutgers University Press, 1953), 2:461.

11. The most widely known rendition of this theme came in a novel by a Union Civil War veteran published in 1867, which describes a Southern belle who chooses a dissipated Southern colonel as her husband but leaves him when she learns of more disgraceful behavior. Learning from her mistake after her husband conveniently dies in battle, she marries again, this time to the suitor she first ignored, a proper New

England abolitionist. See John W. DeForest, *Miss Ravenel's Conversion from Secession to Loyalty* (New York: Penguin Books, 2000).

12. Paul H. Giddens, "Benn Pitman on the Trial of Lincoln's Assassins," *Tyler's Quarterly Magazine* 22 (July 1940): 19. (Pitman, the trial recorder, quotes the tribunal directly here.). For the quotations of Andrew Johnson, see Moore, *The Case of Mrs. Surratt*, 115, and Chamlee, *Lincoln's Assassins*, 444.

13. Blasi, "Advocacy Against the Stereotype," 1241–81.

14. Pitman, *Trial of the Conspirators*, 18. All further references to the transcript in this section will be to this official edition and by page number in the text. A heavy veil was allowed Mrs. Surratt instead of the hood worn by the other conspirators.

15. See Thomas Reed Turner, *Beware the People Weeping: Public Opinion and the Assassination of Abraham Lincoln* (Baton Rouge: Louisiana State University Press, 1982), 138–54, 251–52.

16. For a fuller account of the government's suppression of Booth's diary, see Philip Van Doren Stern, "Introduction to the Facsimile Edition" in Benn Pitman, *The Assassination of President Lincoln and the Trial of the Conspirators* (New York: Funk & Wagnalls, 1954), xiv–xv.

17. Pitman's complete statement, recorded on December 11, 1910, in Cincinnati, Ohio, is given in Giddens, "Benn Pitman on the Trial of Lincoln's Assassins," 20–21. Giddens gives a thorough account of each of Pitman's statements on the trial.

18. The nature and power of Booth's reputation and his influence over others, especially women, is described at length by John Ford, the owner of the theater in which Booth often acted and where Lincoln was shot. See John T. Ford, "Behind the Curtain of a Conspiracy," *North American Review* 148 (April 1998): 488, 490–91. Although it was carefully overlooked at trial, Booth was the fiancé of Lucy ("Bessie") Hale, daughter of John P. Hale, the U.S. senator from New Hampshire. He was free to move in the most exalted circles of Washington society, including attendance at Lincoln's Second Inauguration. See Kunhardt and Kunhardt, *Twenty Days*, 34–35.

19. See Thomas Reed Turner, "Voices from the Pulpit," in *Beware the People Weeping*, 77–99.

20. For the classic analysis of separate spheres with women confined to the domestic sphere, see Nancy F. Cott, *The Bonds of Womanhood: "Woman's Sphere" in New England, 1780–1835* (New Haven, CT: Yale University Press, 1977), 197–205.

21. Pitman, as the official stenographer, felt that he had "the best opportunity of forming a correct judgment of the guilt or innocence of Mrs. Mary Surratt." He concluded it was "probable" she knew something of earlier plans to abduct Lincoln but not of the plan to kill him. See Giddens, "Benn Pitman on the Trial of the Lincoln Assassins," 6–7.

22. Tom Taylor, *Our American Cousin: The Play That Changed History*, ed. Welford Dunaway Taylor, modern reading edition (Washington, DC: Beacham, 1990), 82–83 (III.ii). Further references to lines in *Our American Cousin* are from this edition and will be given by act and scene in the text.

23. The actor who spoke these words as Asa Trenchard on April 14, Harry Hawk, confirmed that the assassination took place at this moment, and he elaborates on the raucous and prolonged nature of audience reactions to that line in the play. Quoted in Albert Furtwangler, *Assassin on Stage: Brutus, Hamlet, and the Death of Lincoln* (Urbana: University of Illinois Press, 1991), 101.

24. Winton Tolles, *Tom Taylor and the Victorian Drama* (New York: AMS Press, 1966), 173–80. *Our American Cousin* was produced in New York as late as 1915.

25. For overlapping examples all from *Harper's New Monthly Magazine*, see Elizabeth D. B. Stoddard, "Childless," *Harper's* 30 (May 1865): 696; Frances Pratt, "Almost Divorced," *Harper's* 30 (December 1864): 64–68; Katherine F. Williams, "Contrast," *Harper's* 31 (June 1865): 63–67; John W. DeForest, "Tom Mallory's Revenge," *Harper's* 31 (September 1865): 443–53; Katherine F. Williams, "Mr. Raspton's Resurrection," *Harper's* 30 (March 1865): 453–58; "The Old Letter," *Harper's* 30 (May 1865): 799; Jane Thorneypine, "Miss Milligan's Sermon," *Harper's* 30 (April 1865): 593–601.

26. Julia T. Snow, "Wanted—an Education," *Harper's New Monthly Magazine* 30 (February 1865): 361–65.

27. All articles in this paragraph are from *Godey's Lady's Book and Magazine*. See, in order, "Cupid *Versus* Kerosene," *Godey's* 70 (June 1865): 513–22; Marian Douglas, "Minus a Bonnet," *Godey's* 70 (May 1865): 433–40; "The Family Circle," *Godey's* 71 (July 1865): 67; "The Wife to Her Husband," *Godey's* 71 (December 1865): 524.

28. "Editor's Table," *Godey's* 71 (December 1865): 536–37; "Editor's Table," *Godey's* 70 (March 1865): 278–79; "Editor's Table," *Godey's* 71 (August 1865): 173.

29. Clephant, *Official Report of the Trial of Mary Harris*, 6, 181. Further references to the trial will be to this source by page number in the text.

30. See Mary Carpenter, *The Duty of Society to the Criminal Classes* (Montreal: Daniel Rose, 1873), 9; and Frances Florenz Planisheck, "Women Prisoners," in *Behind Prison Walls* (Boston: Meador, 1933), 71–74.

31. For other examples beyond those given earlier, see C. P. Cranch, "The Sparcotes," *Harper's New Monthly Magazine* 30 (February 1865): 301–7; and Florence Farleigh, "On the Beach," *Godey's* 70 (June 1865): 512.

32. For women in government positions during the Civil War, see Cindy Sondik Aron, *Ladies and Gentlemen of the Civil Service: Middle-Class Workers in Victorian America* (New York: Oxford University Press, 1987).

33. For the numbers in this paragraph, see Kunhardt and Kunhardt, *Twenty Days*, 127, 140, 205; and "The End of the Conspirators," *Harper's Weekly* 9 (July 22, 1865): 454.

34. "The Week," *Nation* 1 (July 13, 1865): 33.

35. "The South as It Is," *Nation* 1 (September 28, 1865): 395. See, as well, *Nation* 1 (July 27, 1865): 109; and *Nation* 1 (September, 14, 1865): 335.

36. See, in order, "The South as It Is," *Nation* 1 (August 31, 1865): 270; and "The South as It Is," *Nation* 1 (October 15, 1865): 458.

37. "The Temper of the South," *Nation* 1 (October 26, 1865): 523.

38. "A Word with Sensible Southerners," *Nation* 1 (December 21, 1865): 774.

39. "Jeff Tries to Escape in Women's Clothes," *New York Daily Tribune*, May 15, 1865, 1; "Who Is President of the Confederacy," *New York Times*, May 17, 1865, 4.

40. "Who Is President of the Confederacy," *New York Times*, 4; "Capture of Jefferson Davis, at Irwinville, Ga., at Daybreak," *Frank Leslie's Illustrated Newspaper* 20 (June 3, 1865): 161; "Ain't You Going to *Recognize* Me!" *Harper's Weekly* 9 (June 3, 1865): 352.

41. Turner, "Implication of Southern Leaders in the Assassination," in *Beware the People Weeping*, 127–28 and, more generally, 125–37.

42. Quoted in "Mrs. Surratt," *New York Daily Tribune*, July 14, 1865, 7.

43. *Chicago Tribune*, July 7, 1865, 1.

44. M. Helen Palmes Moss, "Lincoln and Wilkes Booth as Seen on the Day of the Assassination," *Century Magazine* 77 (April 1909): 953.

45. Julia Adelaide Sheppard to her father, April 16, 1865, in "Lincoln's Assassination Told by an Eye-Witness," *Century Magazine* 77 (April 1909): 917–18.

46. For the details and quotations from events in this paragraph and the next, I depend on Jean H. Baker, *Mary Todd Lincoln, a Biography* (New York: Norton, 1987), 239–51, 277.

47. For Mrs. Lincoln's own comment and the explanation of her refusal of Springfield's site of burial, see the autobiography of her White House attendant. Elizabeth Keckley, *Behind the Scenes: Thirty Years a Slave and Four Years in the White House* (New York: Arno Press and the New York Times, 1968), 199–200. See, as well, the *Columbus Sun*, October 4, 1867.

48. Seaton Munroe, "Recollections of Lincoln's Assassination," *North American Review* 162 (April 1896): 425.

49. John Creahan, *The Life of Laura Keene: Actress, Artist, Manager and Scholar* (Philadelphia: Rodgers Publishing, 1897), 24, 25, 99.

50. *New York World*, May 3, 1865; *New York Tribune*, May 6, 1865; *Boston Journal*, May 9, 1865; *New York Times*, May 12, 1865.

51. *New York Daily Tribune*, July 18, 1865.

52. *New York Times*, April 19, 1865, 1.

53. *New York Daily Tribune*, May 13, 1865, 1; *New York Daily Tribune*, May 12, 1865, 5.

54. *New York Times*, May 15, 1865, 1; *New York Daily Tribune*, May 15, 1865, 1, 6; *New York Daily Tribune*, May 11, 1865, 1.

55. "End of the Assassins," *New York Times*, July 8, 1865, 1.

56. Most reporters assumed Mrs. Surratt was chained at the time. See *New York Times*, May 15, 1865, 1; and *New York Daily Tribune*, May 15, 1865, 1. For the claim of having heard "chains clank," see Jane G. Swisshelm, "Was Mrs. Surratt Manacled?" *New York Daily Tribune*, September 16, 1873, 8. For the ongoing debate, see A. Oakley Hall, "The Surratt Cause Célèbre," *Green Bag* 8 (May 1896): 197.

57. Gray, "The Fate of the Lincoln Conspirators," 626, 634–36; Kunhardt and Kun-

hardt, *Twenty Days*, 176–82, 210–15. All major newspapers carried either photographs or drawings of the execution.

58. Quoted in Moore, *The Case of Mrs. Surratt*, 23. See, as well, Kunhardt and Kunhardt, *Twenty Days*, 209.

59. Allen Thorndike Rice, "The Trial of Mary Surratt," *North American Review* 131 (September 1880): 239.

60. *Washington Daily Morning Chronicle*, July 8, 1865.

61. *Ex parte Milligan*, 4 Wallace 2 (1866). Mrs. Surratt had applied for and been denied a change of venue to a court of civil jurisdiction in 1865 as a civilian outside of military lines.

62. Moore, *The Case of Mrs. Surratt*, 75–90.

63. Rice, "The Trial of Mary Surratt," 223–40; "New Facts about Mrs. Surratt," *North American Review* 147 (July 1888): 84, 90, 83–94; "The Assassins of Lincoln," *North American Review* 147 (September 1888): 314–19.

64. ."The Assassins of Lincoln," *North American Review*, 316, 319.

65. Hall, "The Surratt Cause Célèbre," 195; Rice, "The Trial of Mary Surratt," 224.

66. "License of Speech and Assassination," *New York Times*, April 21, 1865, 4.

67. Pitman, *Trial of the Conspirators*, 22, 127–37, 352.

68. Ibid., 363.

69. Ibid., 363–80.

70. "The Rebellion," *New York Times*, April 17, 1865, 4; "The Assassination and the Rebellion," *New York Times*. April 20, 1865, 4.

71. "The Assassination Plot," *Harper's Weekly* 9 (May 20, 1865): 307; "Assassination," *Atlantic Monthly* 16 (July 1865): 86.

72. "The Week," *Nation* 1 (November 23, 1865): 643 (emphasis added).

73. "The Week," *Nation* 1 (December 28, 1865), 801.

74. "Is Anybody to Be Punished?" *Nation* 28 (September 28, 1865): 389.

75. Stephen G. Christianson, "Henry Wirz Trial: 1865," in *Great American Trials: From Salem Witchcraft to Rodney King*, ed. Edward W. Knappman (Detroit: Visible Ink Press, 1994), 146–49.

76. "Assassination," *Atlantic Monthly*, 87.

77. "The Week," *Nation* 1 (July 13, 1865): 34.

78. Ibid.

79. "The Last Act of the Tragedy," *Frank Leslie's Illustrated Newspaper* 20 (July 22, 1865): 274. See, as well, William Shakespeare, *Macbeth*, 5.1.38.

80. "The Muddle and the Way Out," *Nation* 1 (September 1865): 359.

81. Michael Billig, "Imagining 'Us' as the National Community," in *Banal Nationalism* (London: Sage, 1995), 70–73.

82. Pitman, *Trial of the Conspirators*, 352, 363, 402. (I paraphrase from the prosecution where I do not directly quote its words in these first two sentences.)

83. Billig, "Waved and Unwaved Flags," in *Banal Nationalism*, 41–42.

84. Pitman, *Trial of the Conspirators*, 299.

CHAPTER SIX

1. This quotation and the facts and quotations concerning the Haymarket affair in this section, unless otherwise noted, are from the definitive modern history of the subject, Paul Avrich, *The Haymarket Tragedy* (Princeton, NJ: Princeton University Press, 1984), xi–xii, 11–12, 208–39, 375–78, 393.

2. For point of view as a critical tool, see Henry James, "Preface to *The Portrait of a Lady*" (1908), in *The Art of Fiction* (New York: Charles Scribner's Sons, 1962), 46ff.; J. M. Lotman, "Point of View in a Text," *New Literary History* 6 (Winter 1975): 339; and Percy Lubbock, *The Craft of Fiction* (1921; repr., New York: Charles Scribner's Sons, 1955), 251–64.

3. For the quotes in this paragraph and the next, see Carl Sandburg, "School Days," in *Always the Young Strangers* (New York: Harcourt, Brace, 1952), 132–35.

4. For the quotations in this paragraph and the next, see "Voice of the Press," *Chicago Tribune*, May 7, 1886, 4. For similar newspaper accounts, see Avrich, *The Haymarket Tragedy*, 217–18.

5. "The Movement Not So General as Has Been Expected" and "Labor Troubles Leaving Their Impress on the Market," *Chicago Tribune*, May 2, 1886, 11, 28; "The Catholic Church and the Knights [of Labor]," *Chicago Tribune*, May 3, 1886, 2; "The Season of Strikes," *Chicago Tribune*, May 2, 1886, 27; "The Railroads Don't Know What the Strikers Will Do" and "The Great Cry of Labor," *Chicago Tribune*, May 3, 1886, 1; "A Wild Mob's Work," *Chicago Tribune*, May 4, 1886, 1, 4; "Storm of Strikes," *Chicago Tribune*, May 2, 1886, 9.

6. "The Riot Comes to a Point," *Chicago Tribune*, May 5, 1886, 4.

7. "The Un-Americanized Element" and "Stamp Out the Anarchists," *Chicago Tribune*, May 7, 1886, 3.

8. "A Hellish Deed," *Chicago Tribune*, May 5, 1886, 1.

9. "Anarchy's Red Hand," *New York Times*, May 5, 1886, 1.

10. Avrich, *The Haymarket Tragedy*, 218. See, generally, John Higham, "Crisis in the Eighties," in *Strangers in the Land: Patterns of American Nativism, 1860–1925* (New Brunswick, NJ: Rutgers University Press, 1994), 35–67.

11. George C. Ingham, "Argument for the Prosecution in *The People vs. Spies, et al.*," in *The Haymarket Affair and the Trial of the Chicago Anarchists 1886: Original Manuscripts, Letters, Articles, and Printed Materials of the Anarchists and of the State Prosecutor, Julius S. Grinnell (Grinnell's Own Collection)*, ed. John S. Kebabian (New York: H. P. Kraus, 1970), 39.

12. Quoted in *Public Opinion* 3 (1887): 49 (emphasis added); and Higham, *Strangers in the Land*, 55.

13. See Higham, *Strangers in the Land*, 46–50.

14. Edward Everett, "Discovery of America" and "Editorial," *Nation* 35 (July 12, 1883): 22; quoted in Edith Abbott, ed., *Historical Aspects of the Immigration Problem* (Chicago: University of Chicago Press, 1926), 785–86, 858.

15. Richard Hofstader, *The Paranoid Style in American Politics* (1952; repr., Cambridge, MA: Harvard University Press, 1996), 5–40.

16. Orm Overland, *Immigrant Minds, American Identities: Making the United States Home, 1870–1930* (Urbana: University of Illinois Press, 2000), 16, 26–46, 175; Higham, *Strangers in the Land,* 32–34.

17. Avrich, *The Haymarket Tragedy,* 262–68; Samuel P. McConnell, "The Chicago Bomb Case: Personal Recollections of an American Tragedy," *Harper's Monthly Magazine,* May 1934, 732–34.

18. Joseph E. Gary, "The Chicago Anarchists of 1886: The Crime, the Trial, and the Punishment," *Century Magazine* 45 (April 1893): 803–37.

19. McConnell, "The Chicago Bomb Case," 734.

20. For Judge Gary's conduct and rulings taken from the trial transcript, see "Brief and Argument for Plaintiffs in Error," in *August Spies et al., v. The People of the State of Illinois* (Chicago: Barnard and Gunthorp, 1887), 381–408.

21. Quoted in Avrich, *The Haymarket Tragedy,* 289.

22. "Brief and Argument for Plaintiffs in Error," 408–15. Quotations of the prosecutor in this paragraph are taken from the record on appeal.

23. For the difficulty of overturning a trial judge in even egregious cases, see Louis Joughin and Edmund M. Morgan, "The Prejudice of the Trial Judge," in *The Legacy of Sacco and Vanzetti* (1948; repr., Princeton, NJ: Princeton University Press, 1978), 142–48; and Dan T. Carter, "A Cold, Hard Vengeance," in *Scottsboro: A Tragedy of the American South,* rev. ed. (Baton Rouge: Louisiana State University Press, 1979), 274–329.

24. *Spies and others v. People,* 122 Illinois 1; 12 N.E. 865 (1887), quoted at 258 [990] and quoted in Avrich, *The Haymarket Tragedy,* 334.

25. *Spies and others v. People,* 157 [941], 228–38 [975–81].

26. McConnell, "The Chicago Bomb Case," 734.

27. *Spies and others v. People,* 244–47 [984], 255–66 [988–93], 261–66 [991–93].

28. *Spies v. Illinois,* 123 U.S. 131; 8 S. Ct. 22. Quoted at 131, 179–80, 181, 182 (emphases added).

29. Raymond Toole Stott, "Frank Harris's Last Interview," *Everyman,* December 10, 1931, 665. See, as well, Robert Brainard Pearsall, *Frank Harris* (New York: Twayne, 1970), 64.

30. Frank Harris, *The Bomb* (Chicago: University of Chicago Press, 1963), 163, 313, 109, 152–53, 250–51, 310, 262, 268, 100–101, 300, 204, 179, 92, 320. All further references to the novel will be to the Chicago edition and noted parenthetically by page number in the text. Harris made Rudolph Schnaubelt his fictional bomb thrower after a real historical figure often accused of throwing the bomb. Schnaubelt was the one person named in the prosecution's indictment to elude capture and, thereby, to avoid trial. His absence made it convenient to charge him with the crime, although scholarship has shown that he was almost certainly *not* the bomb thrower. See Avrich, *The Haymarket Tragedy,* 235–39, 437–35.

31. Frank Harris, "Afterword to 'The Bomb' Written in 1920," in *The Bomb*, 323–24; quoted in Philippa Pullar, *Frank Harris* (London: Hamish Hamilton, 1975), 247.

32. Robert Herrick, "America: The False Messiah," in *Behold America!*, ed. Samuel D. Schmalhausen (New York: Farrar & Rinehart, 1930), 55–56 and, more generally, 53–66. For Herrick's obsession over writing the great American novel, see Herrick, "The Background of the American Novel," *Yale Review* 3 (January 1914): 213–33. These writings come after *The Memoirs of an American Citizen*, but they summarize the writer's philosophy from first to last.

33. See Louis J. Budd, *Robert Herrick* (New York: Twayne, 1971), 123–24.

34. Robert Herrick, *The Memoirs of an American Citizen* (Cambridge, MA: Harvard University Press, 1963), 70–75. All further parenthetical references to the novel in the text are to this edition.

35. Paul Harvey, ed., "Herbert Spencer," in *The Oxford Companion to English Literature*, 3rd ed. (Oxford: Oxford University Press, 1948), 742.

36. Herrick, "The Background of the American Novel," 222–27, 233.

37. Ibid., 233.

38. W. D. Howells, "The Novels of Robert Herrick," *North American Review* 189 (June 1909): 812, 815–17; Howells, "Editor's Study," *Harper's Magazine* 74 (May 1887): 987.

39. WDH to Burt G. Wilder, August 26, 1889, in *W. D. Howells: Selected Letters, Volume 3: 1882–1891*, ed. Robert C. Leitz III et al. (Boston: Twayne, 1986), 258. For an evaluation of realism in these terms, see Walter Benn Michaels, "*Sister Carrie*'s Popular Economy," *Critical Inquiry* 7 (Winter 1980): 378.

40. For Howells's despair over the Haymarket affair, see Kenneth S. Lynn, *William Dean Howells: An American Life* (New York: Harcourt, Brace, Jovanovich, 1971), 282–303. For criticism of him, see Timothy L. Parrish, "Haymarket and *Hazard*: The Lonely Politics of William Dean Howells," *Journal of American Culture* 17, no. 4 (1994):, 23–32. For Howells's own comments in this paragraph and the next, see WDH to John G. Whittier, November 1, 1887; WDH to Roger A. Pryor, September 25, 1887; WDH to Anne H. Frechette, November 18, 1887; WDH to William M. Salter, November 20, 1887; WDH to William C. Howells, November 13, 1887; and WDH to William M. Salter, December 25, 1887, all in *Howells: Selected Letters III*, 198, 197, 206, 208, 212.

41. William Dean Howells, "Bibliographical," in *A Hazard of New Fortunes* (New York: Modern Library, 2002), 4. (Howells wrote this short retrospective preface in July 1909.)

42. For how the genteel tradition harmed Howells's reputation, see Jerry Herron, "Howells on My Mind: Reflections on the Dean's Sesquicentennial," *New England Quarterly* 61 (June 1988): 183–200.

43. For a complete list of the parallels to the Haymarket trial in the novel, see Lynn Marie Messina, "Freedom or Anarchy, the Capital-Labor Struggle in William Dean Howells' *A Hazard of New Fortunes*," *CEA Critic* 58 (Fall 1995): 60–65.

44. See Edwin H. Cady, *Young Howells and John Brown: Episodes in a Radical Education* (Columbus: Ohio State University Press, 1985). WDH to the Editor of the *[New York] Tribune*, November 12, 1887, in *Howells: Selected Letters III*, 201. (Howells never sent this letter but kept it as a declaration of his views, which already had been expressed in an earlier letter to the *Tribune*.)

45. WDH to the editor of the *[New York] Tribune*, November 12, 1887, in *Howells: Selected Letters III*, 201.

46. For the quotations in this paragraph and the next, see WDH to Samuel L. Clemens, December 29, 1889, in ibid., 266. See, as well, Lynn, *William Dean Howells*, 294–97; and Arthur Boardman, "Social Point of View in the Novels of William Dean Howells," *American Literature* 39 (March 1967): 42–59.

47. WDH to William C. Howells, February 2, 1890, in *Howells: Selected Letters III*, 271.

48. WDH to Henry James, October 10, 1888, in ibid., 231.

49. See Richard Foster, "The Contemporaneity of Howells," *New England Quarterly* 32 (March 1959): 54–78.

50. William Dean Howells, *A Hazard of New Fortunes* (New York: Modern Library, 2002), 25, 15. (All further references to the novel in the text are to this edition, which accords with the standard Indiana University Press edition from 1976.)

51. WDH to William C. Howells, December 23, 1888, in *Howells: Selected Letters III*, 241.

52. See, for example, Charles Harmon, "*A Hazard of New Fortunes* and the Reproduction of Liberalism," *Studies in American Fiction* 25 (Autumn 1997): 183–95.

53. WDH to Edward E. Hale, October 28, 1888, in *Howells: Selected Letters III*, 233.

54. For the parallels in expression of grief, see *Howells: Selected Letters III*, 247–55.

55. For Howells's condescension regarding his daughter's artistic talents, see WDH to Auriella H. Howells, January 5, 1890, in ibid., 269–70.

56. Alexander Pope and Jonathan Swift are the greatest satirists in the English language because, whatever their cynicism, they hold a vision of a better world. See, for example, John Paul Russo, "Homer and the Heroic Ideal," in *Alexander Pope: Tradition and Identity* (Cambridge, MA: Harvard University Press, 1972), 83–132; and Edward W. Rosenheim, *Swift and the Satirist's Art* (Chicago: University of Chicago Press, 1963). See, more generally, Alvin B. Kernan, *The Plot of Satire* (New Haven, CT: Yale University Press, 1965).

57. Samuel Taylor Coleridge, "Chapter XVII," *Biographia Literaria* (1817), in *Criticism: The Major Texts*, ed. Walter Jackson Bate (New York: Harcourt, Brace, and World, 1952), 379–81. See, as well, Amy Kaplan, " 'The Knowledge of the Line': Realism and the City in Howells's *A Hazard of New Fortunes*," *PMLA* 101 (January 1986): 76.

58. WDH to Hamlin Garland, January 15, 1888, in *Howells: Selected Letters III*, 215.

59. William Dean Howells, "Editor's Study," *Harper's New Monthly Magazine*, September 1886, 641.

60. Ibid.

61. WDH to Francis F. Browne, November 4, 1887, in *Howells: Selected Letters III*, 200; Avrich, *The Haymarket Tragedy*, 301.

62. WDH to George W. Curtis, August 18, 1887, and WDH to Hamlin Garland, January 15, 1888, in *Howells: Selected Letters III*, 193–94, 215. See, as well, Clara and Rudolf Kirk, "William Dean Howells, George William Curtis, and the 'Haymarket Affair,'" *American Literature* 40 (January 1969): 487–98; and Dyer D. Lum, "Preface" and "Captain Black's Address," in *A Concise History of the Great Trial of the Chicago Anarchists in 1886* (Chicago: Socialist Publishing, 1887), 6, 187.

63. The quotations in this paragraph and the next are from John Peter Altgeld, "Executive Pardon Issued at Springfield, June 26, 1893," in *The Mind and Spirit of John Peter Altgeld: Selected Writings and Addresses*, ed. Henry M. Christman (Urbana: University of Illinois Press, 1960), 85, 95, 102–4.

64. Vachel Lindsay, "The Eagle That Is Forgotten," in *The Mind and Spirit of John Peter Altgeld*, ed. Christman, 14; and William O. Douglas, *Being an American* (New York: John Day, 1940), 3. For a novel glorifying Altgeld, see James Marshall, *Ordeal by Glory* (New York: Robert M. McBridge, 1927).

65. Quoted in Ray Ginger, "The Pardon," in *Altgeld's America: The Lincoln Ideal versus Changing Realities* (Chicago: Quadrangle Books, 1965), 77, 87.

66. The passage from the *Washington Post* and other condemnations of Altgeld can be found in Ginger, *Altgeld's America*, 85–86. The other quotations in the text are from "They Call Altgeld an Alien," *New York Times*, June 29, 1893, 1; "Pardon for the Anarchists," *New York Times*, June 27, 1893, 1; and "Altgeld and the Anarchists," *New York Times*, June 28, 1893, 4. For a summary of newspaper condemnations across the country, see "Pardon of the Chicago Anarchists," *New York Daily Tribune*, June 28, 1893, 7.

67. For these quotations and other attacks on Altgeld in the presidential and gubernatorial campaign of 1896 in this paragraph and the next, see Harry Barnard, *Eagle Forgotten: The Life of John Peter Altgeld* (New York: Bobbs-Merrill, 1938), 383–93.

CHAPTER SEVEN

1. Judge Irving R. Kaufman, "Sentences," in *Transcript of Record: Supreme Court of the United States, October Term, 1951: No. 111, Julius Rosenberg and Ethel Rosenberg, Petitioners vs. The United States of America*, 2 vols., 2:1614–15. (All further references to the transcripts of both the original trial and the appeals will be to this source unless otherwise identified and will be noted as *Transcript of Record*.)

2. J. Edgar Hoover, "The Crime of the Century," *Reader's Digest*, May 1951, 167.

3. *New York Times*, June 20, 1953.

4. William J. Broad, "The Impossible Task for America's Spies," *New York Times*, May 11, 2003, sec. 4, pp. 1, 14; Michael Dobbs, "Julius Rosenberg, Spy: But His KGB Handler Says His Role in Stealing Atom Bomb Was Minor," *Washington Post*, March 24, 1997, National Weekly Edition, 6–7. See, as well, information on Rosenberg from

the Russian Venona papers of the 1940s, which American intelligence had decoded by the time of the *Rosenberg* trial, in Nigel West, *Venona: The Greatest Secret of the Cold War* (London: HarperCollins, 1999), 157–70.

5. This unpleasant middle reality is the conclusion of Ronald Radosh and Joyce Milton, *The Rosenberg File: A Search for the Truth* (New York: Random House, 1983), 4, 432–54.

6. Michael E. Parrish, "Cold War Justice: The Supreme Court and the Rosenbergs," *American Historical Review* 82 (October 1977): 805–6, 840–41.

7. *Transcript of Record*, 2:1513; 1:182.

8. See ibid., 1:446–48, 689–90; 2:1521. See, as well, Virginia Carmichael, "Embedded Story," in *Framing History: The Rosenberg Story and the Cold War* (Minneapolis: University of Minnesota Press, 1993), 49–121; and Marjorie Garber, "Jell-O," in *Secret Agents: The Rosenberg Case, McCarthyism and Fifties America*, ed. Marjorie Garber and Rebecca Walkowitz (New York: Routledge, 1995), 11–22.

9. *Transcript of Record*, 2:1520; Parrish, "Cold War Justice," 812n23.

10. *Transcript of Record*, 1:479–80, 500–502; 2:903–15. See, as well, Radosh and Milton, *The Rosenberg File*, 186–92.

11. For only the most recent of many claims that the defense's decision to keep the Greenglass drawings from public view was an inexplicable blunder, see Joseph H. Sharlitt, *Fatal Error: The Miscarriage of Justice That Sealed the Rosenbergs' Fate* (New York: Charles Scribner's Sons, 1989), 15–16.

12. Daniel Patrick Moynihan, "A Culture of Secrecy," in *Secrecy: The American Experience* (New Haven, CT: Yale University Press, 1998), 154.

13. Moynihan, *Secrecy*, 163; *Transcript of Record*, 2:1159–64, 1345–56.

14. The claim of two cases comes first from Leslie A. Fiedler, "Afterthoughts on the Rosenbergs," in *An End to Innocence: Essays on Culture and Politics* (1948; repr., Boston: Beacon Press, 1955), 25–26.

15. Paul Ricoeur, *Time and Narrative*, trans. Kathleen McLaughlin and David Pellauer, 2 vols. (Chicago: University of Chicago Press, 1984), 1:49, 31; Tzvetan Todorov, "The Grammar of Narrative," in *The Poetics of Prose*, trans. Richard Howard (Ithaca, NY: Cornell University Press, 1977), 111.

16. *Transcript of Record*, 2:1614–16.

17. Ibid.

18. Ibid., 2:1616.

19. Ibid., 1:179.

20. Ibid., 1:179, 186, 1512 (emphases added). See, as well, Sharlitt, *Fatal Error*, 11–18.

21. *Transcript of Record*, 1:180. (Emphases added to show the ingredients of narrative.)

22. Ibid., 2:1521.

23. Ibid., 1:184; 2:1512.

24. Ibid., 1:178–79.

25. Ibid., 2:1512.

26. The quotations and paraphrasing about the law of conspiracy in this paragraph and the next two come from Joseph F. McSorley, *A Portable Guide to Federal Conspiracy Law: Tactics and Strategies for Criminal and Civil Cases*, 2nd ed. (Chicago: ABA Book Publishing, 2003), 12–13, 21, 28, 30, 35, 227. See, as well, *United States v. Burgos*, 94 F.3d 849, 858 (4th Cir. 1996); *United States v. Recio* 123 U.S. 819 (2003); and *United States v. Wiener*, 3 F.3d 17, 21 (1st Cir. 1993).

27. *Transcript of Record*, 1:182–83; 2:1519 (emphasis added).

28. Recent scholarship is fairly unanimous on this point. "Anyone reading the transcript of the trial and the other information available to the government, such as the study of the Joint Committee on Atomic Energy, reaches the conclusion that the government (in this case, the Department of Justice and the U.S. attorney Saypol and his staff) knew very well that in David Greenglass and his sister and brother-in-law they had small potatoes before them. It is clear that the prosecution communicated with Atomic Energy Commission personnel, and had been informed that the real traitor was in jail in England more than three thousand miles away, months before the Rosenberg trial began." Sharlitt, *Fatal Error*, 252. See, as well, Radosh and Milton, "The Scientific Evidence," in *The Rosenberg File*, 432–49.

29. Ricoeur, *Time and Narrative*, 1:36–38; Terry Eagleton, *Literary Theory: An Introduction* (Minneapolis: University of Minnesota Press, 1983), 105–6.

30. D. A. Miller, preface to *Narrative and Its Discontents: Problems of Closure in the Traditional Novel* (Princeton, NJ: Princeton University Press, 1981), ix.

31. Wolfgang Iser, "Indeterminacy and the Reader's Response in Prose Fiction," in *Aspects of Narrative: Selected Papers from the English Institute*, ed. J. Hillis Miller (New York: Columbia University Press, 1971), 12–17, 41–45. I am indebted to conversations with Kenji Yoshino, of the Yale Law School, for a discussion of this aspect of narrative theory.

32. *Transcript of Record*, 1:182; 2:1515, 1532, 1535.

33. Ibid., 2:1512.

34. Ibid., 1:178, 182–83; 2:1512, 1535.

35. Ibid., 1:182.

36. Ibid., 2:1512–13, 1535.

37. The original indictment named Morton Sobell, the Rosenbergs, Anatoli A. Yakovlev, and David Greenglass. A severance was granted for Yakovlev and Greenglass, who pleaded guilty. Sobell would receive the maximum prison sentence of thirty years in jail. Ibid., 1:2; 2:1620.

38. Ibid., 2:1517–18.

39. Ibid., 1:178, 182–83; 2:1518–19.

40. Ibid., 2:1519, 1508.

41. Ibid., 1:177, 180, 182; 2:1519, 1535.

42. Alexander Feklisov, Rosenberg's presumed KGB contact, would later assert that Rosenberg thought of himself as "a 'hero' who helped the Soviet Union in its hour of need in World War II." See Dobbs, "Julius Rosenberg, Spy," 6–7. All imputed

acts of atomic espionage that came out at trial occurred before the end of the war. See Sharlitt, *Fatal Error*, 16.

43. *Transcript of Record*, 1:177.

44. Commission on Protecting and Reducing Government Secrecy, *Secrecy: Report of the Commission on Protecting and Reducing Government Secrecy* (Washington, DC: Government Printing Office, 1997), appendix A, p. 37; Moynihan, *Secrecy*, 154; Allen Weinstein and Alexander Vassiliev, *The Haunted Wood: Soviet Espionage in America— the Stalin Era* (New York: Random House, 1999), 340–41; Ellen Schrecker, " 'They are Everywhere': The Communist Image," in *Many Are the Crimes: McCarthyism in America* (Boston: Little, Brown, 1998), 119–53.

45. I paraphrase from Wolfgang Iser, "The Reading Process: A Phenomenological Approach," in *The Implied Reader: Patterns of Communication in Prose Fiction from Bunyan to Beckett* (Baltimore: Johns Hopkins University Press, 1974), 279–80.

46. *Transcript of Record*, 1:180–84.

47. Ibid., 1:188.

48. Ibid., 1:182–84; 2:1515, 1519, 1535, 1581–82, 1613–15.

49. For the media's lack of interest in the Rosenberg defense and tendency to report only the prosecution's narrative, see Carmichael, *Framing History*, 60–66.

50. *Transcript of Record*, 2:1614.

51. The full story is told in Parrish, "Cold War Justice," 805–42. For Felix Frankfurter's comments, see ibid., 808, 823, 841; and Sharlitt, *Fatal Error*, 56n. For Frankfurter's objection to "strangling technicalities," see *Fisher v. United States*, 328 U.S. 463 (1946), 476–77, 489.

52. Sharlitt, *Fatal Error*, 7, 256; Radosh and Milton, *The Rosenberg File*, 453–54; Stephen J. Whitfield, *The Culture of the Cold War* (Baltimore: Johns Hopkins University Press, 1991), 31–33; Weinstein and Vassiliev, *The Haunted Wood*, 339–44.

53. Quoted in Adam Liptak, "Truth, Fiction and the Rosenbergs," *New York Times*, January 21, 2006, B13.

54. E. L. Doctorow, *The Book of Daniel* (New York: Random House, 1971), 101.

55. Ibid., 177. For Doctorow's recognition and interest in being named after Edgar Allan Poe, see E. L. Doctorow, "Childhood of a Writer," in *Reporting the Universe* (Cambridge, MA: Harvard University Press, 2003), 9. For the many connections between Doctorow's characters and the brother and sister in "The Fall of the House of Usher," see Samuel B. Girgus, "In His Own Voice: E. L. Doctorow's *The Book of Daniel*," in *A Democracy of Perception: A Symposium with and on E. L. Doctorow*, ed. Herwig Friedl and Dieter Schulz (Essen: Verlag Die Blaue Eule, 1988), 82.

56. Doctorow's indebtedness to Hawthorne is noted in Paul Levine, "*A Multiplicity of Witness*: E. L. Doctorow at Heidelberg," in *A Democracy of Perception*, ed. Friedl and Schulz, 195.

57. Quoted in Liptak, "Truth, Fiction and the Rosenbergs," B13.

58. Doctorow is quoted in Arthur Bell, "Not the Rosenbergs' Story," *Village Voice*, September 6, 1983, 42. For the quotation about Hawthorne, see Herman Melville to

Nathaniel Hawthorne, April [?] 16, 1851, in Herman Melville, *Correspondence*, ed. Lynn Horth (Evanston, IL: Northwestern University Press and Newberry Library, 1993), 186. For Doctorow's comments on the themes of literary protest and injustice, see "Texts That Are Sacred, Texts That Are Not," and "Deism," in Doctorow, *Reporting the Universe*, 52, 71.

59. Richard Trenner, ed., *E. L. Doctorow: Essays and Conversations* (Princeton, NJ: Ontario Review Press, 1983), 61; Levine, "E. L. Doctorow at Heidelberg," 191.

60. The speaker of these lines is Binx Bolling in Walker Percy, *The Moviegoer* (1961; repr., New York: Avon Books, 1980), 83.

61. Richard King, "Between Simultaneity and Sequence," in *A Democracy of Perception*, ed. Friedl and Schulz, 52. Commentators contrast the critical success of *The Book of Daniel* with the commercial success of the more popular *Ragtime*. See, for example, Robert Forrey, "Doctorow's *The Book of Daniel*: All in the Family," *Studies in American Jewish Literature* 2 (1982): 167–73; and Cushing Strout, "Historicizing Fiction and Fictionalizing History: The Case of E. L. Doctorow," *Prospects: An Annual Journal of American Cultural Studies* 5 (1980): 423–37.

62. E. L. Doctorow, "False Documents," *American Review* 26 (1977): 231. For Doctorow's struggle with narrative in *The Book of Daniel*, see Geoffrey Galt Harpham, "E. L. Doctorow and the Technology of Narrative," *PMLA* 100 (January 1985): 84.

63. *Transcript of Record*, 1:178–79.

64. Doctorow, *Reporting the Universe*, 36–37, 53; Levine, "E. L. Doctorow at Heidelberg," 183.

65. Doctorow, *The Book of Daniel*, 126–28, 242–45. The scene of Rochelle's arrest ends with the biblical reference "DIDN'T MY LORD DELIVER DANIEL?"

66. McSorley, *A Portable Guide to Federal Conspiracy Law*, 78.

67. Fyodor Dostoyevsky, *The Brothers Karamazov*, trans. David Magarshack, 2 vols. (Harmondsworth, UK: Penguin, 1958), 1:379–80.

68. Quoted in Liptak, "Truth, Fiction and the Rosenbergs," B13.

69. *Ex parte Bollman*, 4 Cranch 75 (1807).

70. See Robert A. Ferguson, *The American Enlightenment, 1750–1820* (Cambridge, MA: Harvard University Press, 1994), 81–84.

71. "The Cask of Amontillado" is regarded as Poe's finest tale of horror. See *The Collected Works of Edgar Allan Poe*, ed. Thomas Ollive Mabbott, 3 vols. (Cambridge, MA: Harvard University Press, 1978), 3:1252–66.

72. See Michelle M. Tokarczyk, "From the Lion's Den: Survivors in E. L. Doctorow's *The Book of Daniel*," *Critique: Studies in Modern Fiction* 29 (Fall 1987): 3–15.

73. Susan E. Lorsch, "Doctorow's *The Book of Daniel* as *Kunstlerroman*: The Politics of Art," *Papers on Language and Literature* 18 (Winter 1982): 386; Winifred Farrant Bevilacqua, "Narrating History: E. L. Doctorow's *The Book of Daniel*," *Revue Française d'Études Américaines* 12 (February 1987): 62.

74. Doctorow, "The Little Bang," in *Reporting the Universe*, 75.

75. Daniel is hurt but Susan Isaacson is destroyed by the lost importance of her

parents. Doctorow, *The Book of Daniel*, 77–82, 150–53. See, as well, Paul Levine, "The Conspiracy of History: E. L. Doctorow's *The Book of Daniel*," *Dutch Quarterly Review of Anglo-American Letters* 11 (1981): 90–94.

76. Judith N. Shklar, "The Ambiguities of Betrayal," in *Ordinary Vices* (Cambridge, MA: Harvard University Press, 1984), 138–39.

77. Doctorow, "Texts That Are Sacred, Texts That Are Not," 51; Levine, "E. L. Doctorow at Heidelberg," 189.

78. Doctorow, "False Documents," 227.

79. Parrish, "Cold War Justice," 807.

80. Judith N. Shklar, "Giving Injustice Its Due," in *The Faces of Injustice* (New Haven, CT: Yale University Press, 1990), 15–19.

81. Cicero, *De officiis* (bk. 1, chaps. 7, 9), in *Cicero*, trans. Walter Miller, 28 vols. (Cambridge, MA: Harvard University Press, 1985), 21:21–25, 29–31.

82. Shklar, *The Faces of Injustice*, 40–41.

83. E. L. Doctorow, *Ragtime* (1975; repr., Harmondsworth, UK: Penguin, 1996), 71.

84. Cicero, *De officiis*, 25 (bk. 1, chap. 7).

CHAPTER EIGHT

1. For the most famous diatribe against television, quoted here, see Neil Postman, *Amusing Ourselves to Death: Public Discourse in the Age of Show Business* (New York: Penguin, 1986), 3–16, 24, 83–99. For positive assessments in this paragraph and the next, see John Hartley, "Democratainment," in *The Television Studies Reader*, ed. Robert C. Allen and Annette Hill (London: Routledge, 2004), 524–32; John Fiske and John Hartley, *Reading Television* (London: Methuen, 1988), 15–18; and John Fiske, *Television Culture* (London: Routledge, 1989), 65, 309–26.

2. For the characteristics assigned to television in this section, see Raymond Williams, *Television: Technology and Cultural Form* (1974; repr., Hanover, NH: Wesleyan University Press, 1992), 39–40, 67; Ronald Primeau, *The Rhetoric of Television* (New York: Longman, 1979), 38–41, 50, 95; Joshua Meyrowitz, *No Sense of Place: The Impact of Electronic Media on Social Behavior* (New York: Oxford University Press, 1985), 308–25; Fiske, *Television Culture*, 21, 90–91, 192, 317–25; Fiske and Hartley, *Reading Television*, 123; Paul Thaler, *The Watchful Eye: American Justice in the Age of the Television Trial* (Westport, CT: Praeger, 1994), 3–7; Kevin G. Barnhurst and Catherine A. Steele, "Image-Bite News: The Visual Coverage of Elections on U.S. Television, 1968–1992," *Harvard International Journal of Press/Politics* 2 (February 1997): 40–41; and Stuart Ewen, *PR!: A Social History of Spin* (New York: Basic Books, 1996), 373–414.

3. John Corner, *Critical Ideas in Television Studies* (Oxford: Clarendon, 1999), 108 and, generally, 108–19.

4. Thaler, *The Watchful Eye*, 7; David L. Altheide, "TV News and the Social Construction of Justice," in *Justice and the Media: Issues and Research*, ed. Ray Surette (Springfield, IL: Charles C. Thomas, 1984), 299–301. For Justice Scalia's comment,

delivered on NBC's *Today,* see "National Briefing," *New York Times,* October 11, 2005, A19.

5. For the contingencies in media development, see Paul Starr, *The Creation of the Media: Political Origins of Modern Communications* (New York: Basic Books, 2004).

6. Louis D. Brandeis, *Other People's Money and How the Bankers Use It* (Washington, DC: National Home Library Foundation, 1933), 62.

7. For the dangers of cameras in a courtroom discussed in this paragraph and the. next, see Christo Lassiter, "TV or Not TV—That Is the Question," *Journal of Criminal Law and Criminology* 86, no. 3 (1996): 928–1095.

8. For a standard analysis of celebrity status at trial, see Susan J. Drucker and Janice Platt Hunold, "The Claus von Bulow Retrial," in *Popular Trials: Rhetoric, Mass Media, and the Law,* ed. Robert Hariman (Tuscaloosa: University of Alabama Press, 1990), 133–47. See, as well, John Langer, "Television's 'Personality System,'" *Media, Culture, and Society* 4 (1981): 351–65.

9. David A. Harris, "The Appearance of Justice: Court TV, Conventional Television, and Public Understanding of the Criminal Justice System," *Arizona Law Review* 35 (1993): 785–827, particularly 807–15.

10. Jeffrey Abramson, introduction to *Postmortem: The O.J. Simpson Case,* ed. Jeffrey Abramson (New York: Basic Books, 1996), 26–27; Janice Schuetz, "Introduction: Telelitigation and Its Challenges to Trial Discourse," in *The O.J. Simpson Trials: Rhetoric, Media, and the Law,* ed. Janice Schuetz and Lin L. Lilley (Carbondale: Southern Illinois University Press, 1999), 4–5; Vincent Bugliosi, *Outrage: The Five Reasons Why O.J. Simpson Got Away with Murder* (New York: Norton, 1996), 79–82. Media covering the trial also included nineteen full television stations, eight radio stations, and twenty-three newspapers and magazines.

11. For the *Simpson* trial in this paragraph and the next, see Paul Thaler, *The Spectacle: Media and the Making of the O.J. Simpson Story* (Westport, CT: Praeger, 1997), 119–41, 165–72, 263, 280–84, 303; Jeffrey Toobin, *The Run of His Life: The People v. O.J. Simpson* (New York: Random House, 1996), 109, 198, 285, 406–11, 420–38; and Abramson, *Postmortem,* 93, 131, 151, 196–98.

12. Quoted in Abramson, *Postmortem,* 151; see, as well, 195–98.

13. Stanley Crouch, "The Good News," in *Postmortem,* ed. Abramson, 228–35.

14. See Roger Sherman, *The O.J. Simpson Trial: Beyond Black and White* (Learning Channel, 1996); and, generally, Toni Morrison and Claudia Brodksy Lacour, eds., *Birth of a Nation'hood: Gaze, Script and Spectacle in the O.J. Simpson Case* (New York: Pantheon, 1997). See, as well, Harold Garfinkel, "Conditions of Successful Degradation Ceremonies," *American Journal of Sociology* 61 (March 1956): 420–24.

15. Steven Brill, "Courtroom Cameras," *Notre Dame Law Review* 72 (1996–97): 1184. Brill is the founder of the television channel Court TV.

16. Sandra F. Chance, "Considering Cameras in the Courtroom," *Journal of Broadcasting & Electronic Media* 39 (Fall 1995): 555. See, as well, "O.J. Case, Despite Excesses, Shows Camera's Value," *USA Today,* July 10, 1995, 10A; "Verdicts in West Palm Beach,"

New York Times, December 13, 1991, A38; "Mistrial Is Declared for One Brother Accused of Killing His Parents," *New York Times*, January 14, 1994, A26 (with accounts of the televised "tearful and compelling testimony" of both brothers); "The Jury Tells Judge It Is Deadlocked in Murder Trial of Brothers," *New York Times*, January 11, 1994, A15.

17. Richard V. Ericson, "How Journalists Visualize Fact," *ANNALS, AAPSS* (November 1998): 83, 89. Ericson argues that the immediacy in visual components of television "gives it greater believability than newspapers and radio news." See also Steven Chaffee and Stacey Frank, "How Americans Get Political Information: Print Versus Broadcast News," *ANNALS, AAPSS* (July 1996): 48–58.

18. Lassiter, "TV or Not TV," 929–34.

19. See Glenn S. Koppel, "A Tale of Two Counties: Divergent Responses in Los Angeles and Orange County Superior Courts to the Ban on Electronic Recording in *California Court Reporters Ass'n v. Judicial Council*," *San Diego Law Review* 37 (Winter 2000): 47–100.

20. Ralph E. Roberts Jr., "An Empirical and Normative Analysis of the Impact of Televised Courtroom Proceedings," *SMU Law Review* 51 (1998): 621–66.

21. Unless otherwise indicated, the facts and quotations on the *Gilmore* trial and execution in this paragraph and the next come from "Death Wish," *Newsweek* 88 (November 29, 1976): 1, 26–35; Jon Nordheimer, "Death Wish Is Discerned in Poetry and Killings by Doomed Convict," *New York Times*, November 15, 1976, 24; "Death and Confusion at the Court," *Time* 108 (December 13, 1976): 85–87; and Norman Mailer, *The Executioner's Song* (Boston: Little, Brown, 1979), 32, 406, 413–14, 443–44, 798, 982–86.

22. *Furman v. Georgia*, 408 U.S. 238 (1972); *Gregg v. Georgia*, 428 U.S. 153 (1976).

23. For the quotations in this paragraph and the next, see Mailer, *Executioner's Song*, 492, 673, 890; "A Sudden Rush for Blood," *Time* 108 (November 22, 1976): 56; "Death Wish," *Newsweek*, 26; and "Playboy Interview: Gary Gilmore," *Playboy*, April 1977, 72.

24. For the quotations in this paragraph and the next, see "Gilmore's Execution" and "Gilmore Gets His Wish," *Newsweek* 88 (January 24, 1977): 35, and (January 31, 1977): 31–32; "Death Watch in Salt Lake City" and "After Gilmore Who's Next to Die?" *Time*, January 24, 1977, 51–52, and January 31, 1977, 48–49; Mailer, *Executioner's Song*, 483, 652, 809–15, 831, 846, 831, 895, 936–54, 978.

25. Fyodor Dostoyevsky, *The Idiot*, trans. David Magarshack (Harmondsworth, UK: Penguin, 1955), 86–87 (part 1, chap. 5). See, as well, William Barrett, *Irrational Man: A Study in Existential Philosophy* (London: Mercury, 1958), 124. Dostoyevsky wrote from personal experience: he was nearly executed himself when led to the scaffold before being reprieved at the last moment.

26. "Wallowing in Misery," *New York Times*, December 6, 1988, 26.

27. My analysis of the *Steinberg* trial depends heavily on information gathered in still the best single case analysis of a televised trial in Paul Thaler, "Part Two:

The Steinberg Trial: A Case Study," in *The Watchful Eye*, 99–203. Thaler, however, is openly skeptical of cameras in courtrooms. Television "has infiltrated" or "invaded" the courtroom in a "Faustian Bargain"; see xix–xxiii, 7, 107, 111, 116, 133, 153–68, 189–92. See also Patricia Volk, "The Steinberg Trial: Scenes from a Tragedy," *New York Times Magazine*, January 15, 1989, 22–25.

28. Floyd Abrams, "Watching Steinberg," *New York Times*, January 4, 1989, 19. Abrams, at the time, was a member of the committee appointed by Sol Wachtler, then chief judge of the New York Court of Appeals, to review courtroom television in the state.

29. Thaler, *The Watchful Eye*, 201.

30. Ibid., 103; Campbell Robertson, "Joel Steinberg's First Free Day Is a Frenzy," *New York Times*, July 1, 2004, B1, B6. Steinberg had served two-thirds of his maximum sentence of twenty-five years and, therefore, was entitled to release under New York State law.

31. Pierre Bourdieu, *On Television*, trans. Priscilla Parkhurst Ferguson (New York: New Press, 1998), 51.

32. Found guilty of murder and, hence, subject to death penalty consideration on November 12, 2004, for the deaths of his wife and unborn child, Scott Peterson received exclusive front-page coverage by the *New York Post* and the *Daily News* on the following day, November 13, 2004. The *Post* gave the guilty verdict all of its attention on pages 1–5 with the following headlines, "Frey Him" (a pun upon "fry him" in an allusion to the girlfriend who testified against Peterson, Amber Frey); "Killer Hubby: A Just Verdict Finally Wipes That Silly Smirk Off Lousy Creep's Face"; "Women Weren't Fooled by Slimeball's Pretty-Boy Looks." The *New York Daily News* gave all of its own coverage on pages 1–4 with similar headlines: "He's Toast"; " 'He's a Sicko. He Needs to Fry.' " Ignored in both papers on these leading pages were the chaotic funeral of Palestinian leader Yasir Arafat, heavy fighting with American casualties in Iraq, widespread violence with massive migrations on the Ivory Coast, the capture of terrorists in the Netherlands, and the resignation of a cabinet minister in the United States. Even the *New York Times* made the guilty verdict front-page news and its most prominent national story. See "Guilty Verdict Is Reached in Peterson Murder Case" and "Jury Finds Scott Peterson Guilty of Wife's Murder," *New York Times*, November 13, 2004, A1, A10.

33. *People v. Menendez*, No. BA 068880 (Super. Ct. for the County of Los Angeles, Cal.); *State of Virginia v. Bobbitt*, Case #–viz. cr-33821 (in Circuit Court of Prince William County, Judge Herman A. Whisenant, Jr., presiding); *State v. Smith*, Nos. 94-GS-44–906 (Union County, S.C. Ct. Gen. Sess.); *Commonwealth v. Woodward*, 7 Mass. L. Rptr. 449 (Mass. Super. Ct., Nov. 10, 1997) (No. Crim. 97–0433); *People v. Peterson*, No. 1056770 (Super. Ct. for the county of Stanislaus, Cal.) [venue transferred to San Mateo, County]. Only the first *Menendez* trial and the *Bobbitt* and *Woodward* trials were televised.

34. *United States v. Noriega*, No. 88–79-CR (S.D. Fla.); Larry Rohter, "After 7

Months and a Final Skirmish, the Noriega Case Goes to the Jury," *New York Times*, April 5, 1992, L29; Larry Rohter, "U.S. Jury Convicts Noriega of Drug-Trafficking Role as the Leader of Panama," *New York Times*, April 10, 1992, A1, A24; David Johnston, "No Victory for Panama," *New York Times*, April 11, 1992, 1, 12; Nancy McKenzie Dupont, "The Case of Manuel Noriega (1991–1992)," in *Illusive Shadows: Justice, Media, and Socially Significant American Trials*, ed. Lloyd Chiasson Jr. (Westport, CT: Praeger, 2003), 161–82. (Dupont documents the sharp drop in media interest.)

35. *People v. Warmus*, No. 1538–90 (County Ct. for Westchester, N.Y.) (citation for both the trial and retrial after a hung jury in the first trial); Edward W. Knappman, ed., "Carolyn Warmus Trials: 1991 & 1992," in *Great American Trials: From Salem Witchcraft to Rodney King* (Detroit: Visible Ink Press, 1994), 790–93. See, as well, "Death Imitates Art as Police Charge Teacher Carolyn Warmus with a 'Fatal Attraction' Killing," *People*, February 26, 1990, 81. For a general account, see Michael Gallagher, *Lovers of Deceit: Carolyn Warmus and the "Fatal Attraction" Murder* (New York: Doubleday, 1993). Between 1990 and 1993, "fatal attraction" was a theme in 336 of the 706 articles devoted to the *Warmus* case ("All News Plus Wires," *Westlaw*).

36. Press fascination over the *Stewart* case far outstripped coverage in the same year given to Mark A. Belnick, Tyco International's former general counsel, on charges that he stole millions of dollars from the company; or of L. Dennis Kozlowski and Mark H. Swartz, the chief executive officer and chief financial officer of Tyco, on charges of stealing $170 million from their company; or of Kenneth Lay, chief executive officer of Enron, accused of insider trading that netted a $90 million profit and false representations that would destroy the retirement pensions of 4,200 employees; or of Bernard Ebbers, convicted of $11 billion in fraud as the chief executive of WorldCom. See Patrick McGeehan, "Masters of the Universe, Leashed (for Now)," *New York Times*, July 18, 2004, wk 3; and Ken Belson, "Ex-Chief of WorldCom Is Found Guilty in $11 Billion Fraud, *New York Times*, March 16, 2005, A1, C8.

37. David Kaczynski, the younger brother of Ted Kaczynski, went to the FBI in 1996 after reading the Unabomber's newspaper manifesto and told them that his brother could be the man they were looking for, and his information led directly to the arrest. See William Glaberson, "Kaczynski Avoids a Death Sentence with Guilty Plea," *New York Times*, January 23, 1998, A1, A18, A23; and Glaberson, "In Book, Unabomber Pleads His Case: A Message for the World—and for a Brother," *New York Times*, March 1, 1999, A12.

38. See, for example, Rick Bragg, "McVeigh Dies for Oklahoma City Blast: No Final Words Before He Is Executed," and Pam Belluck, "Calm at Execution Site and Silence of McVeigh Prove Unsettling for Some," *New York Times*, June 12, 2001, A1, A26, A27.

39. James Dao, "Defense Rests in Sniper Case After Less than 3 Hours," *New York Times*, November 13, 2003, A18; Dao, "Penalty Phase of Sniper Trial Nears End," *New York Times*, November 21, 2003, A22; Adam Liptak, "Sniper Defendant Working on His Boyish Appearance," *New York Times*, November 15, 2003, A10.

40. Joseph Fried, "Sheik and 9 Followers Guilty of a Conspiracy of Terrorism," *New York Times*, October 2, 1995, A1, B5; Benjamin Weiser, " 'Mastermind' and Driver Found Guilty in 1993 Plot to Blow Up Trade Center," *New York Times*, November 13, 1997, A1, B5; Benjamin Weiser, "A Jury Torn and Fearful in 2001 Terrorism Trial," *New York Times*, January 5, 2003, 1, 28.

41. For the facts and quotations about the *Bobbitt* trial in this paragraph and the next four paragraphs, see "Husband Tells Court of Sexual Mutilation by Wife," *New York Times*, November 10, 1993, A28; Stephen Labaton, "Husband Acquitted of Assault in Mutilation Case," *New York Times*, November 11, 1993; "Husband Tells of Mutilation as Wife's Trial Starts," *New York Times*, January 11, 1994, A19; David Margolick, "Witnesses Say Mutilated Man Often Hit Wife," *New York Times*, January 12, 1994, A10; Margolick, "Wife Tells Jury of Love Story, Then 'Torture,' " *New York Times*, January 13, 1994, A7; "The Ballad of John and Lorena," *New York Times*, January 13, 1994, A20; Margolick, "Witness Says Lorena Bobbitt Earlier Threatened to Maim Husband," *New York Times*, January 20, 1994, A12; Margolick, "Lorena Bobbitt Acquitted in Mutilation of Husband," *New York Times*, January 22, 1994, 1, 7; "A Million Mrs. Bobbitts," *New York Times*, January 28, 1994, A22.

42. "The Ballad of John and Lorena," *New York Times*, A20; "A Million Mrs. Bobbitts," *New York Times*, A22.

43. See, for example, Stephanie Coontz, *The Way We Never Were: American Families and the Nostalgia Trap* (New York: Basic Books, 1992); and Ann Hulbert, *Raising America: Experts, Parents, and a Century of Advice about Children* (New York: Knopf, 2003).

44. For the facts and quotations in this paragraph and the next five paragraphs, see Carey Goldberg, "A Murder Trial about More than a Nanny," *New York Times*, October 24, 1997, A8; "A Child in Charge of Children," *Daily Telegraph*, October 29, 1997, 17; Goldberg, "Protesters Back Au Pair in 2 Towns Far Apart," *New York Times*, November 4, 1997, A25; Goldberg, "Her Lawyers Ask Freedom for Au Pair," *New York Times*, November 5, 1997, A10; Goldberg, "Trial of Au Pair Reveals Unease in U.S. Society," *New York Times*, November 10, 1997, A14; Goldberg, "In a Startling Turnabout, Judge Sets Au Pair Free," *New York Times*, November 11, 1997, A1, A22; "Justice Restored," *New York Times*, November 11, 1997, A26; Goldberg, "Pediatric Experts Express Doubt on Au Pair's Defense," *New York Times*, November 12, 1997, A14; Orla Healy, "Mommy Guiltiest? In the Nanny Case, Deborah Eappen and All Working Mothers Stand Accused," *New York Daily News*, November 13, 1997, 55; "Au Pair's Agency Is Ending Payments," *New York Times*, January 20, 1998, A22; Goldberg, "Massachusetts High Court Backs Freeing Au Pair in Baby's Death," *New York Times*, June 17, 1998, A1, A24; Sarah Lyall, "Au Pair Tells BBC She Was U.S. Scapegoat," *New York Times*, June 24, 1998, A25. I am also indebted to collected information from two student essays: Michelle Greenberg Kobrin, "Deborah Eppen: The Universal Other" (1998), and Gregory Klingsporn, "Can Justice Be Televised? The Louise Woodward Murder Trial and Television in American Courtrooms" (1998).

45. Coontz, *The Way We Never Were*, 18–19, 266–67.

46. Michael Ignatieff, "What You See is What You Feel: Our Imagination Is Corrupted by the Unreal Images of Real-Time Television," *[London] Financial Times*, January 21, 1998, 3.

47. Peter Clarke and Eric Fredin, "Newspapers, Television, and Political Reasoning," *Public Opinion Quarterly* 42 (Summer 1978): 144–45.

48. In a typical example of proactive response patterns, the popular television trial show *Law & Order* recently allowed its viewers to vote online to decide whether to save or kill one of its leading characters. See David Carr and Michael Joseph Gross, "She's a Killer, and Her Life Is in Your Hands," *New York Times*, October 16, 2004, B7, B12.

49. Mark Jurkowitz, "The Woodward Ruling: The Day After/News Analysis," *Boston Globe*, November 12, 1997, A1.

50. Lauren Berlant, quoted in Rick Perlstein, "If Journalists Listened to Media Scholars," *University of Chicago Magazine* 96 (August 2004): 37.

51. Goldberg, "Protesters Back Au Pair," A25.

52. Jack Rosenthal, "What Belongs on the Front Page of the New York Times," *New York Times*, August 22, 2004, wk 2.

53. Barnhurst and Steele, "Image-Bite' News," 40, 55, and, more generally, 40–58. For an example of "faster flow," the average presidential campaign sound bite on network news was 43 seconds in 1968 and 8.2 seconds in 1996. See Steven Hill, *Fixing Elections: The Failure of America's Winner-Take-All Politics* (New York: Routledge, 2002), 189–90.

54. Hartley, "Democratainment," 524–33; Louis Banks, "The Rise of the Newsocracy," *Atlantic Monthly* 249 (January 1981): 56–57. For more on "an increase in news being structured along entertainment lines," see Steven A. Esposito, "Source Utilization in Legal Journalism: Network TV News Coverage of the Timothy McVeigh Oklahoma City Bombing Trial," *Communications and the Law* 20 (June 1998): 15–33.

55. Jack Hitt, "American Kabuki: The Ritual of Scandal," *New York Times*, July 18, 2004, wk 1, 3.

56. Quoted in ibid. The expert on scandal quoted is Suzanne R. Garment, *Scandal: The Culture of Mistrust in American Politics* (New York: Random House, 1991).

57. See Peter Brooks, *The Melodramatic Imagination: Balzac, Henry James, Melodrama, and the Mode of Excess* (New Haven, CT: Yale University Press, 1976), 4, 11, 202.

58. Stephen Gillers, "Upholding the Law as Pretrial Publicity Goes Global," *New York Times*, April 27, 2003, 14wk.

59. I quote and paraphrase in this paragraph and the next from Jim Rutenberg, "Presumed Innocence? Not on Capable TV News," *New York Times*, April 26, 2003, A16. See, as well, Maria Elizabeth Grabe, "Narratives of Guilt: Television News Mag-

azine Coverage of the O.J. Simpson Criminal Trial," *Howard Journal of Communications* 11 (2000): 35–48.

60. I quote and paraphrase here and in the next paragraph from Jack Rosenthal, "What to Do When News Grows Old Before Its Time," *New York Times*, August 8, 2004, wk 2.

61. Gerald F. Uelmen, "The Five Hardest Lessons from the O.J. Trial," *Issues in Ethics* 7 (Winter 1996): 2–3. (Uelmen was co-counsel for the defense in the trial of Simpson.)

62. John Fiske, "Admissible Postmodernity: Some Remarks on Rodney King, O.J. Simpson, and Contemporary Culture," *University of San Francisco Law Review* 30, no. 4 (1996): 928.

63. Bourdieu, *On Television*, 2.

64. Fiske, "Admissible Postmodernity," 10.

65. See Michael Kent Curtis, "Democratic Ideals and Media Realities: A Puzzling Free Press Paradox," *Social Philosophy and Policy Foundation* (2004): 409.

66. All of the quotations in this paragraph are from Uelmen, "The Five Hardest Lessons from the O.J. Trial," 2–3.

67. Adam Liptak, "Privacy Rights, Fair Trials, Celebrities and the Press," *New York Times*, July 23, 2004, A20.

68. I quote and paraphrase from Liptak, "Privacy Rights, Fair Trials," and from Kirk Johnson, "The Bryant Trial: Anatomy of a Case That Fell Apart," *New York Times*, September 3, 2004, A14. The crucial Supreme Court case that refuses to restrict the press on the publication of news, even on issues of national security or on a criminal defendant's fair-trial rights, is *New York Times Co., v. United States*, 403 U.S. 713 (1971), better known as the Pentagon Papers case.

69. Jurkowitz, "The Woodward Ruling," A1, 3.

70. Peter Golding, "Telling Stories: Sociology, Journalism, and the Informed Citizen," *European Journal of Communications* 9 (1994): 461; Curtis, "Democratic Ideals and Media Realities," 386.

71. Thomas Jefferson to Edward Carrington, January 16, 1787, and "Second Inaugural Address" (March 4, 1805), in *Thomas Jefferson: Writings*, ed. Merrill D. Peterson (New York: Library of America, 1984), 880, 522 (emphasis added). For Jefferson's frequent extolling of freedom of the press as the benchmark in liberty, see as well 71, 244, 495, 1146–47.

CHAPTER 9

1. Genesis, chaps. 18, 27–34.

2. For the quotation, the emphasis on decentered identity, and "the crucial association" of "mass consumption and information processing" as controlling characteristics of postmodernism, see Peter Hansen, "Postmodernism," in *A Companion to*

American Thought, ed. Richard Wightman Fox and James T. Kloppenberg (Oxford: Blackwell Publishers, 1995), 534–35. See, as well, John Paul Russo, *The Future without a Past: The Humanities in a Technological Society* (Columbia: University of Missouri Press, 2005), 23–28.

3. For the technological developments in this section, see Roy Armes, *On Video* (New York: Routledge, 1988), 39–46, 60, 74–77, 82–84; Albert Abramson, "The Invention of Television," in *Television: An International History,* ed. Anthony Smith (Oxford: Oxford University Press, 1995), 25–29, 33; and Abramson, *The History of Television, 1942 to 2000* (Jefferson, NC: McFarland, 2003), 60–76, 118–22, 176, 186–205.

4. Daniel J. Boorstin, *Image: A Guide to Pseudo-Events in America,* rev. ed. (New York: Atheneum, 1978).

5. "Media and Technology in 2004: As 2 Powerful Industries Converge, Change Will Abound," *New York Times,* December 29, 2003, C1; Mark Lander, "Sony Is Selling Convergence, but Will Europe Buy It?" *New York Times,* September 8, 2003, C1.

6. Steven M. Barkin, *American Television News: The Media Marketplace and the Public Interest* (Armonk, NY: M. E. Sharpe, 2003), 111ff. See, as well, Wireless/getvcast.com and http://www.forbes.com.business/2006/01/23/google-economics-trends-cx_0124mckinsey.html.

7. Kevin G. Barnhurst and Catherine A. Steele, "Image-Bite News: The Visual Coverage of Elections on U.S. Television, 1968–1992," *Harvard International Journal of Press/Politics* 2 (February 1997): 40–43.

8. Quoted in Marlys Harris, "Making Crime Pay: Steven Brill's Court TV Shows America the Law, Torts and All," *People,* April 20, 1992, 93.

9. See the mission statement of C-SPAN at www.c-span.org/about/company/index.asp.

10. "Soap opera," *Webster's Third New International Dictionary* (Springfield, MA: Merriam-Webster, 1993), 2160.

11. Ruth Rosen, "Soap Operas: Search for Yesterday," in *Watching Television: A Pantheon Guide to Popular Culture,* ed. Todd Gitlin (New York: Pantheon, 1986), 44–45, 50–51, 55–56.

12. The information and quotations in this paragraph and the next, unless otherwise indicated, are from Ronald L. Goldfarb, "The Crucible: Court TV," in *TV or Not TV: Television, Justice, and the Courts* (New York: New York University Press, 1998), 124–53.

13. Quoted from Steven Brill, "Courtroom Cameras," *Notre Dame Law Review* 72 (1996–97): 1181; and Alice Steinbach, "Steven Brill Plans to Bring the O.J. Simpson Trial to the Small Screen," *Baltimore Sun,* September 25, 1994, 1J.

14. Paul Thaler, *The Spectacle: Media and the Making of the O.J. Simpson Story* (Westport, CT: Praeger, 1997), 106.

15. Both of these criticisms are raised and commented on in Paul Thaler, *The Watchful Eye: American Justice in the Age of the Television Trial* (Westport, CT: Praeger, 1994), 70–71.

16. Susan Drucker, "Cameras in the Court Revisited," *New York State Bar Journal*, July–August 1992, 47–48.

17. Brill, "Courtroom Cameras," 1183, 1186.

18. G. W. F. Hegel, *The Phenomenology of Mind*, trans. A. V. Miller (Oxford: Clarendon Press, 1977), 103 (A.3; final paragraph).

19. For how video journalists are controlled by market forces, media consolidations, ratings, collusion, and homogenization, see Pierre Bourdieu, *On Television*, trans. Priscilla Parkhurst Ferguson (New York: New Press, 1998), 23, 36–39, 48, 69.

20. Russo, *The Future without a Past*, 3–9.

21. *State v. Hauptmann*, 115 N.J. L. 412 (1935); American Bar Association, Canons of Judicial Ethics, Canon 35 (1937). See, as well, current ABA Code of Judicial Conduct Canon 3(A)(7)(b), *American Bar Association Reports* 62 (1937): 1134–35; and Gregory K. McCall, "Cameras in the Criminal Courtroom: A Sixth Amendment Analysis," *Columbia Law Review* 85 (1985): 1546–71.

22. *Estes v. Texas*, 381 U.S. 532, 535, 538–39, 552, 565, 580–86 (1965).

23. "Note: Television Coverage of Trials: Constitutional Protection Against Absolute Denial of Access in the Absence of a Compelling Interest," *Villanova Law Review* 30 (1985): 1267–1308; *Chandler v. Florida*, 449 U.S. 560 (1981) (permitting electronic media coverage and still photography of judicial proceedings subject to the control of the presiding judge); Charles R. Nesson and Andrew D. Koblenz, "The Image of Justice: *Chandler v. Florida*," *Harvard Civil Rights and Civil Liberties Law Review* 16 (1981): 406–13. Today, Canon 28 of the Canons of Judicial Ethics allows "the televising of court proceedings under properly supervised and controlled condition" as long as the trial judge permits it, but few do.

24. For existing studies and their inconclusiveness, see Goldfarb, "A Thing Observed, a Thing Changed: What Is the Impact of Television on Trials?" in *TV or Not TV*, 96–123. See, as well, the divided recommendations of the New York State Committee to Review Audio-Visual Coverage of Court Proceedings, published as *An Open Courtroom: Cameras in New York Courts* (New York: Fordham University Press, 1997).

25. William Shakespeare, *Troilus and Cressida*, III.iii.183–84.

26. *Bridges v. California*, 313 U.S. 260, 271 (1941).

27. *Sheppard v. Maxwell, Warden*, 384 U.S. 333, 334, 350, 362–363 (1966).

28. Ibid., 362–63.

29. On strict scrutiny doctrine, I rely on Matthew D. Bunker, "Scrutinizing Scrutiny," in *Justice and the Media: Reconciling Fair Trials and a Free Press* (Mahwah, NJ: Lawrence Erlbaum Associates, 1997), 1–14.

30. *Richmond Newspapers, Inc. v. Virginia*, 448 U.S. 555, 569, 572–73 (1979). *Richmond* carried the Court's reliance on the Bentham quotation well beyond its own previous use of it in *In re Oliver*, 333 U.S. 257 at 270–71 (1948), which indicated more conservatively that "one need not wholly agree with a statement made on the subject by Jeremy Bentham."

31. *Richmond Newspapers, Inc. v. Virginia*, 448 U.S. 572–73, 552–55, 563–77, 580 (1979). See, as well, "Legal History: Origins of the Public Trial," *Indiana Law Review* 35 (1960): 251–58.

32. *Chandler v. Florida*, 449 U.S. 560, 581–82 (1981).

33. *Whitney v. California*, 274 U.S. 377 (1927), reiterated in *Brown v. Hartlage*, 456 U.S. 61 (1982). See, as well, *New York Times Co. v. Sullivan*, 376 U.S. 254 (1964).

34. Bunker, "Scrutinizing Scrutiny," 4. More recently, see *New York v. Santiago*, 712 N.Y.S. 2d 244 (2000), citing *Globe Newspaper Co. v. Superior Court*, 457 U.S. 596 (1982), and *Richmond Newspapers, Inc. v. Virginia*, 448 U.S. 596 (1979), as proof that "although the United States Supreme Court has interpreted the 1st Amendment to guarantee the press and the public a right of *access* to criminal trials, the Court has not reached the question of whether such access encompasses the right to broadcast from the courtroom."

35. For the quotations in this paragraph and the next, see *Nebraska Press Assn. v. Stuart*, 427 U.S. 539, 558, 560–63, 570 (1976). See also Bunker, *Justice and the Media*, 68.

36. *Gentile v. State Bar of Nevada*, 501 U.S. 1030, 1032, 1038, 1057–58 (1991). The record of division between the justices of the Court speaks for itself: "KENNEDY, J. announced the judgment of the court and delivered the opinion of the Court with respect to Parts III and VI, in which MARSHALL, BLACKMUN, STEVENS, and O'CONNOR, JJ., joined, and an opinion with respect to Parts I, II, IV, and V, in which MARSHALL, BLACKMUN, and STEVENS, JJ., joined. REHNQUIST, CJ., delivered the opinion of the Court with respect to parts I and II, in which WHITE, O'CONNOR, SCALIA, and SOUTER, JJ., joined, and a dissenting opinion with respect to Part III, in which WHITE, SCALIA, and SOUTER, JJ., joined. . . . O'CONNOR, J., filed a concurring opinion."

37. "The independent examination of the whole record" doctrine originates in civil rights cases, where a more intense and open federal examination of the facts in state decisions "corrected" presumed bias in local officials. See, in particular, *Edwards v. South Carolina*, 372 U.S. 229, 235–36 (1962), and for developments toward it, *Blackburn v. Alabama*, 361 U.S. 199, 205 (1959). *New York Times Co. v. Sullivan*, 376 U.S. 254, 285–86 (1964) carried "independent examination" doctrine into cases involving freedom of the press even though the presumed danger of bias did not apply in the same way.

38. *Bose Corp. v. Consumers Union of United States, Inc.* 466 U.S. 485, 501–5, 509–11, 514 (1983); *Time, Inc. v. Pape* 401 U.S. 279 (1971) (emphasis added in the quotation).

39. For criticisms of the "independent examination" doctrine and the quotations in this paragraph, see Henry P. Monaghan, "Constitutional Fact Review," *Columbia Law Review* 85 (March 1985): 232, 243–46, 267, 276.

40. *Sheppard v. Maxwell*, 384 U.S. 333, 362 (1966).

41. Jacques Ellul, *The Technological Bluff*, trans. Geoffrey W. Bromiley (Grand Rapids, MI: William B. Eerdmans, 1990), 54–60, 149–59, 401–5.

42. Lloyd L. Weinreb, *Legal Reason: The Use of Analogy in Legal Argument* (Cam-

bridge: Cambridge University Press, 2005), 14–15, 103. See, more generally, 65–102, on "Analogical Legal Reasoning."

43. Quoted in Thaler, *The Watchful Eye*, 111. See, as well, Harold J. Rothwax, *Guilty: The Collapse of Criminal Justice* (New York: Random House, 1996).

44. *In re Sentencing*, 219 F.R.D. 262–64 (E.D.N.Y. 2004). See, as well, Jack B. Weinstein and Diane L. Zimmerman, "Let the People Observe Their Courts," *Judicature* 61 (October 1977): 156–65.

45. See *Court Reporter Act of 1944*, 28 U.S.C. §§ 751–53; see, as well, *ABA Model Rules of Professional Conduct*, Rule 3.6 (2003); and *Antoine v. Byers & Anderson, Inc.* 508 U.S. 429, 432–38 (1993), in which the Supreme Court holds that court reporters are not entitled to immunity as part of the judicial function because their obligation to provide a verbatim record of what transpires in court affords them "no discretion in the carrying out of this duty."

46. National Court Reporters Association, "Rules 2, 3, 4, 5, 6," in "Code of Professional Ethics," available at http://www.ncraonline.org/infonews/ethics/index.shtiml (2004).

47. *In re Oliver*, 333 U.S. 257, 268 (1948).

48. *Sheppard v. Maxwell*, 384 U.S. 333, 363 (1966); *Nebraska Press Assn. v. Stuart*, 427 U.S. 539, 560 (1976).

49. Francis Bacon, "Of Innovations," in *The Essays or Counsels, Civil and Moral* (1625) (Mount Vernon, NY: Peter Pauper Press, 1948), 96–97.

50. Judith N. Shklar, *Legalism* (Cambridge, MA: Harvard University Press, 1964), 109–14. "Resolving of a particular case in accordance with a general rule that would thus satisfy the demands of justice and at the same time be suited to the sentiments of the rightful and the ethical" begins in Roman law, and its precepts have been adopted as the primary cast of legal thought everywhere in the Western world. See John Maxcy Zane, "The Roman Creation of Modern Law," in *The Story of Law*, 2nd ed. (1927; repr., Indianapolis: Liberty Fund, 1998), 162–64.

51. Paul Robinson and John M. Darley, "Why Community Views Should Matter," in *Justice, Liability, and Blame: Community Views and the Criminal Law* (Boulder, CO: Westview, 1995), 1, 5–7; Learned Hand, "Mr. Justice Cardozo," in *The Spirit of Liberty*, 3rd ed. (Chicago: University of Chicago Press, 1960), 130.

52. For the history of "sincerity" as a critical term, one that connects its use to current problems in technology and one that I rely on in this section, see John Paul Russo, "Belief and Sincerity," in *The Future without a Past*, 120–48.

53. The quotations are from the leading critic of the concept of sincerity, I. A. Richards, *Principles of Literary Criticism* (1924; repr., London: Routledge, 2001), 253, and *Practical Criticism: A Study of Literary Judgment* (1929; repr., New York: Harcourt, Brace & World, 1956), 270 and, more generally, 263–74.

54. For detractors who nonetheless find the concept useful, see Lionel Trilling, *Sincerity and Authenticity* (Cambridge, MA: Harvard University Press, 1971); and Henri Peyre, *Literature and Sincerity* (New Haven, CT: Yale University Press, 1963).

55. Bernard J. Hibbits, " 'Coming to Our Senses': Communication and Legal Expression in Performance Cultures," *Emory Law Journal* 41 (Fall 1992): 873–960.

56. Quoted in Anemona Hartocollis, "In Summation, Power to Win Jury's Favor," *New York Times*, January 23, 2006, B4; Frederic Maitland, "Outlines of English Legal History, 560–1600," in *The Collected Papers of Frederic Maitland*, ed. H. A. L. Fisher, 3 vols. (Cambridge: Cambridge University Press, 1911), 2:417–47, available at http://oll.libertyfund.org/Texts/LFBooks/Maitland0161/CollectedPapers/Vol2/HTMLs/0242–02_Pt05_Essays5.html.

Index